The Divine Dance of The Universe

The Divine Dance of The Universe

Cosmic Consciousness Freedom from Body and Mind The Evolutionary Journey to Authentic Spirituality

MICHAEL R MUNDY

First edition published 2022 by Michael R Mundy

Copyright © 2022 Michael R Mundy

The moral right of the author has been asserted.

All rights reserved.

No part of this book may be reproduced, stored, or transmitted by any means—whether auditory, graphic, mechanical, or electronic—without written permission of both publisher and author, except in the case of brief excerpts used in critical articles and reviews. Unauthorized reproduction of any part of this work is illegal and is punishable by law.

Because of the dynamic nature of the internet, any web addresses or links contained in this book may have changed since publication and may no longer be valid.

The views expressed in this work are solely those of the author and do not necessarily reflect the views of the publisher, and the publisher hereby disclaims any responsibility for them.

 A catalogue record for this book is available from the National Library of Australia

978-0-9876228-3-9 Ebook
ISBN: 978-0-9876228-2-2 (paperback)
Interior and Cover Layout: Pickawoowoo Publishing Group
Print and Distribution: Lightning Source | Ingram (USA/UK/EUROPE/AUS)

"For my daughter Julianna and my son Jason Robert."

"Most people, in a kind of optical delusion of consciousness, embrace their life experience as being something individual and totally separate from the rest of the functioning universe. The primary task of humanity is to free itself from this self-imposed psychological prison, and through expressions of compassion and kindness find the reality of Oneness with the formless source of all life and with all formed life itself".

This is the only true pathway to close the gap that separates humanity's consciousness from Universal Consciousness. This is the truth that brings the psychological freedom and peace for body and mind that both Jesus and the Buddha spoke of. This is the true pathway that sets us free".

Contents

The Divine Dance of The Universe xiii

Preface xxi

Introduction xxxv

Chapter 1 The Axial Age The Birth, the Reign, and the Death of Authentic Life Changing Religion. 1

Chapter 2 The Divine Purpose for Humanity. The Cosmological Mystery of Our Existence The Three Stages. 49

Chapter 3 The Transcendent Nature and Unlimited Potential of Humanity. 61

Chapter 4 The Many Names and Different Interpretations of God 109

Chapter 5 The Cosmological and Ecological Connectedness of The Universe. 121

Chapter 6 Universal Consciousness The Creative Cosmic Loom Weaving the Fabric of The Universe. 147

Chapter 7 Awareness The Operational Platform of Consciousness. 165

Chapter 8 The Evolutionary Journey of Consciousness. 199

Chapter 9 This Unconscious Universe Why Humanity Thinks and Behaves as it Does 229

Chapter 10 Christianity and Jesus Islam and Muhammad The Three Reasons Jesus Appeared on Earth. 295

Chapter 11 Divine Principle The Vibrational Pulse Sustaining and Supporting the Fabric of The Universe. 321

Chapter 12 Becoming Imitators of Christ..................................363
Chapter 13 The Shift The Death of Institutionalised
            Religion and The Resurrection of Authentic
            Life Changing Spirituality. 393
Conclusion 427
Daily Spiritual Practices 437
7 Daily Habits to Cultivate 443
A Prayer of Gratitude and Intent..447
Simple Tips to Rise Above Ego Mind Identification................451
The Daily Mantra...453
The Moola Mantra...457

MICHAEL ROBERT MUNDY

(Taran Nam Singh)

Spiritual Philosopher and Author

<u>Taran Nam Singh</u>

The courageous Lion

who carries others across the perilous oceans

of the material world to spiritual awareness

through

remembering God's Name

THE DIVINE DANCE OF THE UNIVERSE

> "O'day arise, shine your light, the atoms are dancing. Thanks to Him the universe is dancing, overcome with ecstasy, free from body and mind. I'll whisper in your ear where their dance is leading them. All the atoms in the air and in the desert are dancing, puzzled and drunken to the ray of light, they seem insane.
> All these atoms are not so different than we are, happy or miserable, perplexed, and bewildered, we are all beings in the ray of light from the beloved. Nothing can be said".
> The Poem of Atoms by Rumi

The title for this book, "The Divine Dance of The Universe", Cosmic Consciousness Freedom from Body and Mind, came in a reflective moment after I read the above poem, when I realised that in many ways, life, or our life experience as we commonly call it, is meant to be like the dance of the atoms as creatively expressed by Rumi in his poem. A life lived with an ongoing awareness of our complete interconnectedness with both God, humanity, the universe, and all it contains. Meant to flow with fluidity, co-operation, co-dependence and with grace, as a beautiful ballet performance would flow, regardless of circumstance, and regardless of the influence of untoward factors.

That I am sure is what the Divine Creator of this universe would want for all of us.

But life is not like that, not due to any fault on the part of the Creator, because it is we not God who create our present reality. You know some of the most gifted ballet dancers in the world just keep on performing, even when in pain, just out of dedication and a deep desire to not for the slightest moment allow the concept of failure to enter, and to not let themselves or their audience down.

Unfortunately in this modern day, for many people, focused purely on their own existence, the old self-survivalist nature kicks in, and life becomes more like a progressive barn dance, rather than a ballet dance, isolationist in form and inclination, having only superficial and mostly impersonal contact with those who pass by our way, full of twists and turns and a lack of real psychological, physical, and emotional connectedness with others involved in the dance.

The true Dance of Life is meant to provide a connection with others or an enhancement of an existing vibrational connection, not foster or fuel an ongoing disconnection. From a spiritual perspective physical dance provides both a physical and a spiritual connection with others. When our spirits align, and we experience movement together, it provides the bliss we seek in the spirit of fellowship.

The magical feeling of connecting to others in a higher dimension through the art of dance is what heightens the spiritual experience in physical dance activity. In the dance the boundaries between body and soul are effaced. The body moves itself spiritually, the spirit bodily, in line with Divine Principle that states, "and the two shall be as one". Life can be like that if we are prepared to contribute to making it so.

Rumi was a 13th century Persian poet considered by many to be a Sufi saint. Sufism is a mystical branch of the Islamic religion. The history of Islamic Mysticism is largely a history of individual mystical experience similar in some ways to Christian Monasticism and

Christian Gnosticism. Even though Rumi is recognized as an Islamic poet, his work has a transcendent appeal that has enabled it to be embraced by various cultures around the world, regardless of their religious or spiritual faith.

The ecstatic poems of Jalal ad-Din Muhammad Rumi, born 813 years ago have sold millions of copies in recent years, making him the most popular poet globally, with many of Rumi's poems, because of their mystical nature, embodying the theme of creative love and the inbuilt desire of the human soul to re-join or be connected to the Spirit of the Divine.

His was a firm belief that this is the goal of every living thing whether human or animal, whether consciously or sub-consciously, to transition from form into the formless, from the visible into the invisible, as the Soul returns to the source from whence it came. Not only is the above poem by Rumi exquisitely beautiful in its content from a literary perspective, but as you dwell on some of the phrases you can see a combined scientific and spiritual significance to them in an almost prophetic way.

It was Albert Einstein the renowned scientist who said, "the most beautiful and profound emotion we can experience is the sensation of the mystical, it is the power behind all true scientific discovery". Einstein was speaking of the connection between his scientific achievements and the world of spirit, between the visible and the invisible, the connective influence of all things in the functioning universe we live in, and the power to tap into it through a creative intuitive thought process, or as he expressed it, through the sensation of the mystical.

Einstein is most widely known for having in 1905 proved mathematically the existence of atoms, which thus helped revolutionize all the sciences through the use of statistics and probability. Yet we see Rumi so many centuries earlier speaking of atoms not only existing but dancing together in one accord.

Although the concept of the atom itself wasn't physically discovered until the 19th century, some early Greek and Indian philosophers had an idea of the existence of atoms, which they saw as invisible particles being the smallest unit of matter. But it was still Einstein who, in 1905, mathematically spoke of atoms dancing, proving without doubt the existence of atoms and in doing so he helped to revolutionize all the sciences. This poem of Rumi's captures the idea that all living things, even the smallest pieces of matter are participating in a universal dance in the Light of the Divine, or you could call it a unification dance in the Spotlight of the Divine.

Today, largely due to the work of scientists such as Einstein, it is known that sub-atomic particles rotate around a nucleus, planets rotate around the stars, and stars circle around galaxies, all participating in the magnificent light filled dance of the universe and all connected in an unseen but irrevocable way; all from the very small to the extremely large participating in an interconnected orbital dance, a form of cosmic dance with no clear beginning or end.

Rumi goes on to say in his poem, "we are all beings in the ray of Light from the beloved". In a scientific sense light is necessary for life, for without the light of the sun none of us would be here. In literature light has a variety of meanings, it could be the light of the sun, but could also be the light of knowledge, of illumination, or of the Divine Presence itself. He then says, "all these atoms are not so different than we are", meaning that all of life is made up of the same particles, the same hydrogen and helium of the stars that formed this galaxy billions of years ago. All of life is connected, interwoven, and continuously interrelating.

Dr. Martin Luther King Jr., the great civil rights leader in America, spoke passionately about the desire of the hidden intelligence of the universe to see humanity become aware of the cosmic nature of its own existence and the interconnectedness of all beings in Universal Consciousness, but to do it without all the effort attached to achieving that realisation. He once said, "all of life is interrelated, we are all caught up in an inescapable network of mutuality, tied into a single garment of destiny".

But even though Rumi was a Muslim Mystic, it is not just in Islamic Mysticism that this belief is held. We see also in Christian Mysticism the promulgation of this non-dualistic concept of the universe, and the religion of Buddhism teaches that there is an invisible web of interconnectedness in all things, between human and human, between nature and nature, and between humanity and nature. It teaches that all beings and phenomena exist only because of their relationship and connectedness with all other beings and phenomena, that we are all living, breathing, co-dependent beings.

There is also in the religion of Hinduism a power filled mantra called Ek Ong Kar, which means, "the creator and the creation are one, we are all of one Spirit", and in the New Testament in the Book of John Jesus says, "I and the Father are one".

The three largest religions in the world and the most well-known spokespeople for these religions, the Buddha, Jesus, and Muhammad, all speaking of the invisible web of connectedness between an invisible Infinite Intelligence, the Creative Spirit, and all things that have been created.

You see even a mother, after she gives birth, after she creates a child, never loses touch with that distinctive connection, psychologically and genetically, that was formed with the child in the womb. The ancient prophets spoke of this mystical connection that we all have with Divine Intelligence as seen in the writings of the Prophet Jeremiah where he quotes God saying, "before I even formed you in the womb, I knew you".

When I use the term "mystics" I am not referring only to some cloistered group tucked away in a monastery in the hills, whilst they are included, I am also referring to spiritual seekers of both Eastern and Western orientation desiring, and subsequently daring, to delve past the literalism of the institutionalised nature of their inherited or chosen religious belief system, into the realm of the heart. Some seekers know and go on to experience the realisation of this desire, yet many others, whilst feeling the pull, sometimes, usually due to fear of the unknown, continually resist it. Yes, Rumi was classed as a Muslim Mystic, but the truth is that at heart we are all mystics, searching for true reality, and the peace that passes all understanding that Jesus spoke of that comes with it.

A mystic is not someone who ignores the Holy Book that their own chosen or inherited religion is aligned with, but someone who seeks to learn the esoteric teachings hidden in their Holy Book from a place of love, stillness, and silence. Most of the utterances of Christian Mystics are inspired by the teachings of the New Testament and of Jesus, and most of the utterances of Muslim Mystics are inspired by the teachings of the Qur'an and the Prophet Muhammad, and most of the utterances of Hindu Mystics are inspired by the teachings in the Upanishads.

Whether we perceive this mystical Divine Creative Intelligence to exist in our culture, in a particular religion, in a particularly brand of that religion, or in some other form of human tradition or human spiritual practice or discipline, or whether we just catch glimpses of it in a Holy Book, or in co-incidences that become realised in our daily life, or simply sense it during a visit to a church at Christmastime, we all unconsciously are drawn to seek out and be united with that which is beyond the limitations of our finite minds and our fragile, fast paced and sometimes chaotic and seemingly insane existence; which is why some people regularly visit astrological sites on the web for a reading or diligently look for guidance in their daily or weekly horoscopes. They want to get in touch with the source of truth beyond the visible world.

But perhaps one of the most significant lines in Rumi's Poem of The Atoms is where he says the following:

The Divine Dance of The Universe

> *"Thanks to Him the universe is dancing, overcome with ecstasy, free from body and mind".*

Thanks to who? Thanks to the Divine Creative and Infinite Intelligence, the God of the Universe, Rumi says the whole universe is free from **"body and mind"** and in a state of ecstasy, intimating that if we are not, we should be. Unfortunately, due to a corrupted thinking process, much of humanity is not living in a state of joy and ecstasy, free from concern about the body and the mind, but rather in a state of despondency and despair, and in a state, not only in some instances of physical lack but psychological lack also, psychological lack being a lack of true Wisdom.

The only way to truly move past the level of body and mind both of which operate from a low level of spiritual energy, is to move our thought-based life into a higher realm of energy, which can only come from the source energy of Universal Consciousness or Infinite Intelligence, the creative Spirit of God, the thought energy of the God Mind, and the mother or birthplace of true Wisdom. That is the only source energy that has ascendancy and thus power over rational thought energy. To be free from mental machinations and bodily suffering is indeed to be in a state of ecstasy.

This is the mystery hidden in the teachings of Jesus revealed when He said, "you shall know the truth and the truth shall set you free". (The Book of John). He was not talking about setting one free from sin and its consequences of going to hell as is often taught. He was talking about being set free from the Soul-destroying influences of the "rational thought process" and replacing that thought process with a new thought process, Divine Wisdom that operates from a higher vibrational level than human intelligence. The Hindu religion describes it as a state of ecstasy or pure bliss. We are no longer being tormented in any way by the life disrupting attacks on our body or in our mind.

A state of ecstasy is a mental state of great happiness, joyful excitement, and blissful peace, underpinned by a conviction that this is what I have been searching for, this is where I was meant to be, and this is where I want to stay. There are millions of people in this world who are continuously tortured by their minds, some in a minor way, many in a major way. This is the voice in their head that creates doubt, fear, uncertainty, and suffering. Many are aware that this is what is happening to them, but don't know how to find freedom from it and in finding that freedom begin living a life of ecstasy, a calm but emotionally euphoric life, a life of psychological and physical freedom.

Life is a spiritual dance with the Divine, and our unseen partner has steps to teach us if we will allow ourselves to be led by the Master. My hope is that the contents in this book The Divine Dance of The Universe will be a catalyst providing a roadmap for you to discover the true nature of your existence and with that lead you to the freedom of body and mind that is your Divine birthright. The next time and the next time and the next time you feel restless in heart and mind, remind yourself, it is the universe asking, "shall we dance".

PREFACE

Over these last few decades as I have explored the behavioural patterns of successive generations as they attempted to successfully navigate life, there is one thing I have particularly observed that is obvious in all of them. It is that in some way or another, at some time or another, all generations have come to three similar conclusions; number one, that something is wrong, something is broken; number two, that their particular generation had reached a turning point in history; and number three, that the problems of the day were insurmountable and that it would take a miracle to overcome the difficulties stifling the ongoing progress, peace and stability in society, and return humanity to a unified, peace filled progressive existence.

Most generations have resigned themselves into believing that this is as good as it gets. Most generations at some time or another have reluctantly come to believe that inner personal peace and outer societal peace would perhaps not be possible in their lifetime. Beyond the negative thought patterns that underpin these frustrating life situations that bring with them for many an unwelcome measure of despair and disillusionment, lies a deeper spiritual crisis that most people fail to recognize simply because of a lack of wisdom and spiritual insight. And so instead, in their futile search for answers, they begin looking for something or someone to blame for the present state of their personal world or the state of society in general.

They begin to justify in thought and reinforce in conversation their opinion about the ongoing societal malaise, that it is just a regrettable by-product of the ignorant and ideologically driven leadership of those who have been placed in positions of power above them. Or, if their problem is personal, that it is simply the result of the attitudinal and behavioural shortcomings of the people in their current relationships. Society's problems are all the politician's fault, my personal problems are all my partner's fault or for many they are my parents' fault. And so, a small degree of psychological comfort is found in playing the blame game.

Very few people look to their own individual contribution or lack of it for the current situation before them, but rather point the finger of blame at others.

And so, the blame game commences its public debut using ego driven argument, via all manner of digital technology and conversational communicative methods that are available to get the proponent's point across; methods such as Twitter and Facebook in particular. And in certain circumstances as much physical might that can be mustered through protest marches and even violence against their fellow citizens to emphasis what they believe is the reason for their current predicament. It becomes all about the use of verbal and physical hostility towards others as the primary mechanism to get their opinion across, an opinion which they believe is the only one that is right, and the only one that truly matters. Thus the ego mind is fulfilling its mission.

Physical and verbal emotion filled aggression becomes the manipulative tool used against another individual or the rest of society to convince others that I am not the problem, everybody else is the problem. That I am being wrongfully deprived of my own deserved peace, pleasure, and success by the actions and behaviour of others. Why is this so? Why do people choose this path, the blame game? Why do people choose hostile behaviour over hospitable behaviour? Why do people choose enmity and acrimony over agreeance and alliance? Why do people choose conflict over communicative consensus? Why do people fuel the flame rather than look for a common ground or course of action to put the fire out? It is simply the result of spiritual depletion which brings about wrongful perception and subsequent wrong thought processes and behaviours.

When we are physically deprived of food our body tires, so too when our Soul or mind is deprived of spiritual food, we become psychically depleted. Ancient spiritual philosophers and teachers knew this and so wrote, "if anyone lacks wisdom, then ask for it". They were indicating that as we need to refuel our bodies to sustain and energise them, so too, we need to refuel our Soul to sustain and energise it. When people run out of spiritual fuel an attitudinal disposition of self-interest comes into play, a self-survivalist attitude. An attitude that says, "I must save me no matter what it takes and to hell with everybody else".

This then gives them the immediate psychological and emotional self-gratification and release they are looking for. That's why some people are violent with their partners and lash out physically during a difference of opinion. They are spiritually depleted which brings out a psycho-spiritual laziness, an "I don't want to think about it" attitude. It's too hard to figure this out so I'll use violence instead to get my point across immediately.

The ego mind will always channel resentment and a feeling of deprivation, a feeling of being personally wronged, into a physical or emotional reaction rather than seek an intuitive answer, rather than seek wisdom on how to best handle a situation. The ego mind will never cave to the spiritual mind, they are opposing energetic forces continually in combative mode.

So, for most people it's easier to react emotionally rather than to respond by looking intuitively into why things are as they are, for to do so opens a person to the possibility that in fact maybe they need to correct their interpretation of events, or even that they are part of the problem, that their own behaviour has contributed to the situation. When we look inside ourselves rather than outside of ourselves for answers, to see if we are either consciously or unconsciously contributing to or reinforcing a problematic situation through wrong thinking and subsequent wrong behaviour, we begin to create the circumstances that bring about inner change which is the true effective catalyst for outer change.

The Old Testament's King David we read in the Book of Psalms carried out the process this way. He simply prayed, "search me God and know my heart and show me if there be any wicked way in me". Or as the Contemporary English Version of the Psalms put it, "look deep into my heart God, and find out everything I am thinking and why". Wrong behaviour in the individual will never be corrected until right thinking comes into play. You see:

"Thought contains vibrational energy, energy to create after its own kind. Thought sets intention, and intention is the birthplace for future behaviour".

Human physical and emotional behaviour will not change unless our human perceptive abilities change, until how we look at things and the manner in which we interpret them changes. And if there is one thing that the ego mind does not want it is inner change, particularly if it comes as a result of a person's drawing down of Godly Wisdom, even unconsciously.

Why is that? Because true inner change leading to realistic outer change requires firstly an abdication of self-interest, which is anathema to the ego mind, because it necessitates one stepping back from the "it's all about me personality pattern", into the "it is all about us" pattern. A universality of purpose. It involves one embracing the universality of humanity rather than purely the hubris of the individual. Self-analysation, looking within, leads to self-realisation, which brings about change.

Fix the inner person and the outer circumstances heal themselves or at the minimum don't affect us as much personally. Societal outer peace will only be fully realised when individual inner peace is achieved. This is a **Divine Principle,** a law of the universe. That's why Jesus was called the Prince of Peace not the prince of protestation. In speaking of the coming of Jesus the Old Testament Prophet Isaiah around 700 BCE said, "for unto us a child is born, to us a son is given, and the government (spiritual government of humankind) will be on his shoulders. And he will be called Wonderful Counsellor, Mighty God, Everlasting Father, **Prince of Peace.**

The well-known spiritual teacher Jiddhu Krishnamurti, when once asked what gives you happiness and peace replied, "I simply just don't mind what happens". He continually surrendered to and embraced peace rather than surrendering to circumstance. When we are resisting what takes place, we prolong our confusion, we prolong our pain, and we prolong our suffering. It is only when we submit or surrender our habitual way of thinking and responding to the wisdom of Divine Principle or the Laws of the Spirit, God's way of thinking, that we are truly liberated from the enslavement of our egoic thought patterns.

To surrender does not mean to give up or give in but rather to choose a different path, the Divine path. Whilst many people are slow learners it still must eventually become obvious to all, even the seemingly most psychologically dumb of the dumb, that the other path does not bring about long-term results.

The current Neo-Nazi and White Supremacist groups and radical Islamic extremists with their failed but still ongoing Jihadist movement are good examples of this, and if they continue on that path all participants in the delusion will eventually go to their graves never having known the truth. I mean seriously, how low does the level of basic human intelligence have to fall, very low I would think, to bring a person to believe that the failed attempts of a madman in the form of Hitler might work if we give them a second go.

Sadly however, we live in a world where in many situations our desire and subsequent wretched ability to mutilate either psychologically or physically our fellow citizens, to raise our supposed right way of thinking above their purported wrong way of thinking, has not lost its intensity in each successive generation. Sadly, a propensity to look within our inner self for answers exists in only a small amount of people. The rest just look without for the answers, who or what can be blamed for this situation I am in or the situation we are in, which then manifests in an unholy attitude towards those components of society who they see as impeding their own personal progress and peace filled existence.

Throughout the known history of civilization this way of thinking and doing has not lessened regardless of the brilliant scientific progress made, because brilliant achievements in the intellectual or scientific arena have unfortunately significantly outpaced brilliant progress in the spiritual and psychological arena, resulting in a shortfall of Godly Wisdom, and subsequently a decline in right and righteous thought processes. Much of society in this modern day has morphed into a subtle state of psychological stupidity, where shoot your mouth off first and ask questions or seek truth filled answers later has become a common practice. One only needs to look at the insane comments on Twitter to see this kind of attitude in play.

What our modern world has suffered from most of all is a lack of understanding of the workings of the mind and its relationship with the Soul, that place of inner stillness, the temple within, where the Christ Mind dwells. The rational mind does not have the spiritual or you could call it cosmic energy necessary to give this understanding to the individual. It is an energy that must come from another higher level within the human psyche. Spiritual work has to do with spiritual energy rather than solely with what we call thought and the intellectual argument that surfaces from rational thought.

This book is not meant to strengthen one's intellectual experience, rather to help strengthen one's intuitive capability, to help take you the reader a step forward in your internal understanding of both the workings of the mind, and its relationship to the workings of the Soul. To enable greater understanding of the cosmic connectedness of the human mind and the God mind.

To the extent that the world confines its religious or spiritual experience to pomp and ceremony and ritualistic behaviour, and confines its religious or spiritual education to spasmodic episodes of intellectual and emotional stimulation at church on Sundays, it will continue to limit its people's spiritual transition and growth and further open all to the prey of academicism, dogmatism, ideological obsession or fanaticism and the resultant violence that can follow these paths, as people with ruthless determination set about trying to convince others that their way is the only right way.

The explosion of the first atomic bomb over Hiroshima in August 1945 that saw the immediate death of some 80,000 innocent people, and the suffering, pain, and subsequent death of hundreds of thousands later from the effects of radiation, was heralded by many as the result of a wonderful intellectual and scientific discovery, that being the splitting of the atom. But in truth the bombing of Hiroshima and Nagasaki in the name of peace, merely brought to the fore the nihilistic self-destructive capability that the intelligence of humankind alone was capable of engendering hidden under the cloak of a wonderful scientific and intellectual achievement.

Increased knowledge and intelligence, technological genius in the individual has continued to outpace and stifle the psychological and spiritual development of the Soul. Sadly, we have seen that for many the pace of development of the Soul, or "inner person", has not kept pace with the speed of development of the "outer person", the physical and intellectual capability of humanity.

The mind alone, the mind that is not nourished with Godly Wisdom through the silence of the fertile void of pure Being, as such is incapable of guiding human life successfully. The ordinary, isolated intellect, no matter how brilliant or inspired, has not the cosmic vibrational energy necessary to command our thoughts, words, impulses, memories, and experiences in a way that conforms to truth and goodness.

This in sum is the tragedy of our modern era, of our increased level of knowledge in the modern world. All that science has brought us, the phenomenal, wondrous discoveries it has brought us about life, matter, and the universe, will eventually bring us nothing but destruction, because we have forgotten that the mind alone cannot direct itself or the whole of ourselves. It does not have the energy for this. It is an energy that must come from another higher level of consciousness that is within the human psyche. A level of consciousness, that of Cosmic Consciousness, which is experienced in silence and stillness, not in mindless argument, debate, and ideological obsession.

What our modern world has suffered from most of all is runaway ideology, whether it be political, academic, or religious, the dysfunctional attachment in thought to someone else's corrupt and dysfunctional thinking. However, the good thing is that I believe this is starting to change through the emergence of a new generation of spiritual teachers, who bring with them not a new religion, not a new ideology, not a new belief system, but simply a new way of "being, "and with that a new way of thinking, behaving, and living.

Some people do intuitively recognize this lack of spiritual energy and attempt to deal with it in some specific but many times spiritually superficial way, in that they join a church, or they join a yoga or meditation class, or they begin following a specific spiritual teacher on Facebook, or when the Divine Principle of compassion touches their thoughts, do attempt a small amount of charity work that will not take up too much of their time.

But sadly, sometimes even those with an ear to hear in terms of their own personal spiritual lack, in a relatively short time of trying, cease their search for understanding and truth, and their religious or spiritual practical experience becomes merely one of hiding behind the cloak of a religious or spiritually aligned ritual once a week, such as going to church, or a yoga session, or a meditation class, or helping out at Meals on Wheels. But when contrary to what was promised the experience does not provide the perfect panacea for personal peace and prosperity as promised by those teachers of the group, and as such when the newness and potential effectiveness of the experience wanes, so does the self-discipline required to continue to attend the practice wane.

Others catch a momentary glimpse of the reality of what I am talking about, find a religion or spiritual discipline, settle into it, but eventually discover traditional religious practice hypocritical and superficial, so rather than just settling into religion's ritualised approach they give up and turn to art, music, dance, sport, or drugs. They turn to anything that may perhaps give them the transcendent experience they long for in their earnest desire to transcend from what they see as a hopeless present into a hope filled hereafter, a somewhere over the rainbow destination they have dreamt of.

According to many theologians, religion was and is supposed to be the prescription for what ails humanity, but in some instances, it has become a pariah merely reflecting the selfish attitudes of many ideologically driven individuals.

Unless we see spiritual evolution occur to keep pace and eventually outpace our technological revolution, we are doomed to perpetuate the same atrocities against our fellow human beings as witnessed in the Holocaust, the bombings of Hiroshima and Nagasaki and in the attack on the World Trade Centre in New York. A purely rational pathway of self-education will not suffice, for we must remind ourselves that great universities and schools of education existed in the same vicinity as the concentration camps of Europe and the World Trade Centre in New York. These events like so many others around the world have borne witness to what can happen when the sacred inviolability of a human being and their God given peace filled inheritance is violated in favour of the selfish desire of another.

But it is not just in the human arena that this is happening, we see it also occurring in nature and the environment, with certain species of animals moving closer to extinction, some in fact already having been, in these last few years, officially designated to be extinct. We risk environmental disaster because we fail to recognize the Spirit in all things, we no longer see the earth and all it contains as holy, but rather see it as a separated "resource" for our own personal and corporate economic gain.

For many there is little regard for the preciousness of the universe we live in nor for the health and well-being of those who inhabit this universe with us. The only "meaning" the world holds for some is its potential for self-gain or what can be extracted from it for self-survival and success.

In 1946 a former inmate of a Nazi concentration camp, Viktor Frankl, wrote a book titled Man's Search for Meaning. A survey completed by the Library of Congress included his book in their list as one of the top ten most influential books of all time. In his book according to Viktor after a period spent observing those around him, he concluded that it was not the present moment experience that decided his future, but that it was the way that a prisoner imagined the future to be that affected his present longevity. He concluded that a person's psychological reaction to their dire circumstances was not solely the result of the conditions in their life, but rather their way of perceiving them and that they were controllable and could be purposefully directed to a better outcome, but here's the proviso, "if the prisoner chose to do so".

Outcomes can be controlled by our will and our willingness to allow Divine Principle to be the guiding compass in all we do. Outcomes don't have to be just an inevitable consequence of circumstance.

You see human beings are all "meaning seekers" and individuals can very easily fall into despair if they cannot find significance or value in their lives, or alternately turn to others perhaps through joining a protest movement to try and find that value rather than look within themselves and witness it intuitively revealed. As the renowned psychoanalyst Carl Jung said, "your vision will only become clear when you look into your own heart. Who looks outside dreams, who looks inside will awaken".

Circumstance does not necessarily have to control the outcome of our lives, there is a way past circumstance to serenity. Circumstance was not allowed to control the life of Viktor Frankl nor the likes of Nelson Mandela who spent 27years of his life in prison and went on to become President of South Africa, and thousands of others throughout the history of humanity who chose to see beyond circumstance and tap into the unlimited potential lying dormant within the Soul of humankind. And so, it need not do so for you. But it requires one to choose to take a different pathway from the one they have spent most of their lifetime on up until now, a pathway with Divine support, and it is that choice which will make all the difference to their future circumstances.

The Prophet Jeremiah in the Old Testament in prophesising the Voice of God said, "I have set before you the way of life (living according to Divine Principle) and the way of death (living according to egoic thought patterns), choose life". Put very succinctly by the poet Robert Frost, "two roads diverged in a wood, and I took the one less travelled by and that has made all the difference". The two roads that have been put before humanity are the Law of Sin and Death which is the law of an unregenerated or unrenewed state of mind, an ego-controlled mind, and the Law of the Spirit, which is the Law of the Christ Mind within.

I would encourage all with love to choose wisely. The Gospel of Thomas says, "whoever finds the interpretation of these sayings", referring to spiritual insight into the Wisdom teachings of Jesus, "will not experience death", meaning spiritual death.

People hover between life and death, being aware of both but not fully experiencing either. People hover between the Light of The

Spirit and the darkness of ignorance in a state of double mindedness. They are not sure of who they are, a physical being or a spiritual being, not sure whether they came from the spiritual realm or the physical realm, and a house divided cannot stand.

My task in writing this book was not to drag the world kicking and screaming into a new awareness, my job was to simply do my work, sacredly, secretly, and silently, and those with eyes to see, and ears to hear will become cosmically conscious and respond. Cosmic Awareness is the greatest agent for irreversible psychological and thus circumstantial change. My hope is that the words in this book may become signposts helping point you in the direction of who you truly are. Be blessed in your endeavours.

> "What our modern world is suffering from most of all is runaway ideology, whether it be political, academic, philosophical, or religious, the dysfunctional attachment in thought to someone else's corrupt and dysfunctional thinking. What the world needs is not a new ideology, not a new belief system, not a new movement, not a new religion, not a new political party, but to simply transcend to a new way of perceiving, thinking, and behaving, and with that a new way of "being".

INTRODUCTION

We live in a world where millions of people from all different races and religious backgrounds openly profess to believe in the existence of a force beyond themselves, an Infinite Intelligence, a supernatural spiritual force, but at the same time continue to deny or ignore and certainly fail to apprehend the life changing power of its presence in their own personal lives.

It is an undisputable fact that many people believe, some even in a most dedicated way, in the existence of this higher force commonly referred to as God, who is there to watch over us and take care of us, but at the same time live lives of seeming powerlessness, purposelessness, and quiet desperation, being psychologically and physically buffeted like a small ship on a storm driven sea, spasmodically tossed backwards and forwards by all the adversities that seem to cross their path.

For many people life has become an ongoing never-ending journey of ducking and weaving their way through what seems to be a sometimes temporary and at other times endless maze of difficulties. It is a self-evident truth that in society today many "religious people" hold to an outward appearance of religion but demonstrate in their everyday coping skills what appears to be a visible repudiation of its true reality, its authenticity.

The Apostle Paul, similarly, in his day saw evidence of this as we witness in his teaching in the Book of Timothy, when as he sat in stillness and in a state of contemplative reflection alone in his prison cell, knowing the end of his earthly life was imminent, he wrote of people holding a form of godliness but in their thoughts, attitudes, and actions denying the true power of it, denying the authentic life-changing power of it.

My primary intent in writing this book was twofold. Firstly to give you the reader a deeper understanding of the cosmology of this universe, and how Infinite Intelligence, the God of the Universe fits into this cosmology in its relationship with a living, breathing, functioning humanity. And secondly to give you the reader greater understanding of the Divine Principles or Laws set in place by this Intelligence in the beginning, metaphysical laws that influence the functioning of the universe and all it contains for the better, enabling all human beings to thus begin living a purposeful and peace of mind existence that is their Divine birthright.

This detail does exist in all the holy books of the major religions of the world, some obvious, some being hidden in a mystery, and although mostly not taught, it is detail that is meant to, when acted upon, create a bridge of commonality, a universality of the faith and with that a new universal way of thinking and behaving and existing in society. Detail that creates a commonality of purpose, a commonality of psychological perception, our way of viewing life, a commonality of intent, what we prioritise in life, and a commonality in subsequent behaviour, our way of communicating and relating to other individuals in society.

These were all commonalities that were either lost or severely compromised when faith in God and a true belief in the life-changing power of God became institutionalised, and when the purpose filled power inherent in Divine behavioural principles such as love, compassion, kindness, and mercy, were set aside in favour of a purposeless legalistic framework of dogma and doctrine, pomp, ceremony, and ritual. It was a time when "doing became hoping" hidden under the blanket of a faith-based approach, and when "being was set aside in favour of obedience to church law" rather than the appropriation of Divine Law.

Introduction

It was a time when the laws of the institutions took precedence over the Laws of the Spirit, when many believers became hearers of the Word only, instead of doers of the Word, deceiving themselves; believing at the same time that their priest or pastor's silence or indifference was a sign of acquiescence, and that this was okay so long as they attended mass or church each week and always gave a proportion of their income to the church. Thus turning the religious relationship of many with Infinite Intelligence into merely a weekly transactional experience rather than an authentic daily spiritual experience.

I am fully aware that many myths and misconceptions have been perpetuated about the pathway to the Divine Life that have seen various groups emerge and subsequently partition themselves off from one another as they took hold of one man's misperceptions or deliberate deceptions and turned them into a religion or a specific religious denomination or just simply a secular spiritual type of tool.

Hence in this book I will also show Holy Book examples of existing parallels between the Divine truths believed by all the major religions of the world, but not necessarily taught, parallels in Divine Law principles that have remained to still co-exist as trickles of truth hidden midst the hardened rocks of institutionalised religion's mostly theological interpretation of ancient scriptures over the centuries. These hidden truths I believe are the inter-faith and inter-society bridge builders, Divine Principle the Laws of the Spirit, that will create a oneness of thought and behaviour and thus propagate ongoing peace on earth and expressions of goodwill to all of humankind.

Opposing these truths we have the governing principles of institutionalised religion. The institutionalised dogma, doctrine, discipline, and creed of the "religious world" has only cemented in the minds of some adherents age old historical deceptions, and for many societies only created continuous disunity, despair, psychical and for some, physical death. The only true way that the world can come to a unity or universality of the faith that the Apostle Paul spoke of, is through

Divine Principle in practice, not through dogmatic doctrinal disputations. We all then begin functioning from the same spiritual page.

> *"What is arising in the world now is not a new belief system, not a new religion, not a new spiritual ideology, or mythology, not a new secular tool for self-improvement, but a new way of being and doing. We are fast coming to an end of ideologies and biased and bigoted belief systems that have gotten us nowhere".*

It is not my intention to put down or intentionally invalidate anyone else's spiritual path or approach, for in the final analysis all the words in this book are just that, words, providing a window for some and an open door and opportunity to grow further spiritually for others. Spiritual teachers of all ages would put it this way. "We can unlock the cage, and we can open the door, but in the end, it is only the individual who can step on through it and find their way home."

However, there is one starting premise we need to have. We need to accept that there is an egotistical component of our lower nature that exists to obstruct and hinder our spiritual evolution, and that it is a powerful influencer on the direction our everyday spiritual life takes. In using the term ego or ego self or ego mind I am not using it in the way that most of us would at some time in our life have heard the word ego being used, as in 'he's got a big ego', meaning he has an overinflated sense of his own importance. From a spiritual perspective whilst it does include the personality pattern of an inflated attitude of self-importance, or self-pride, in its spiritual context it holds a much deeper meaning.

The ego's outworking or communication process manifests as that little voice in our head that quietly opposes every new spiritual truth that comes across our mind, in many cases because of an inbuilt fear that by embracing new truth we are going against our existing institutionalised religious way of interpreting the things of God. It appears as that little voice in our head that says things such as "no, that can't be right" or "can't be, that's not what I was taught by my church," or "that's not what my church believes," or phrases similar.

We must believe that the egoic aspect of our mind is real, that it is alive and confrontational, and that it continually seeks to control our every attempt to raise our level of consciousness. This is a spiritual warfare we are involved in, a cosmic warfare in the heavenlies being played out on earth. Now to some that may sound a little spooky, but it's true, and it is a truth that we must accept if we are determined to progress in our spiritual life. The ancient Chinese general Sun Tzu said:

> "Know thy enemy and know yourself; in a hundred battles, you will never be defeated. When you are ignorant of the enemy but know yourself, your chances of winning or losing are equal. If ignorant both of your enemy and of yourself, you are sure to be defeated in every battle".

The ego is a type of psychological stalker, stalking our mind, always attempting to hinder and attack right or righteous thought processes. It vehemently opposes Divine Principle in every way it can. Call it an entity, call it Lucifer, call it the deceiver, call it the devil, call it Satan, call it an energetic life force or a negative vibration, call it an illusion creator, call it what you will it matters not, but recognize and accept that it is there, that it is real, and that its sole aim is to create some type of disruption in your thinking or disunity in your interaction with others.

The ego mind desires above all else to maintain the unconscious sense of alienation from Divine Intelligence and psychological separation from the rest of humanity, that all human beings are born with and journey through life with; its mission being to keep you from progressing in your evolutionary journey through consciousness and thus reaching the finishing line of that journey. To keep you ignorant of Divine Truth is a major weapon in its armoury.

We may call the ego what we want but must understand that as Infinite Intelligence is the guiding Light of our ongoing potentially enlightened reality, so this invisible entity we refer to as the ego is in fact the guiding darkness of our existing unenlightened and false reality, and darkness always causes disorientation in thought and subsequent actions, which is its sole intention. The ego has a purpose in you just as Divine Intelligence has a purpose in you. That's the warfare. It's a war of two minds, the God Mind, and the ego mind.

The ego mind is the faulty compass that deliberately and in a cunning manner gives our ship of life a false reading, corrupting our perceptive abilities, our way of thinking, sending our ship in the wrong direction straight onto the rocks. Divine Intelligence, the voice of the Mind of God within us is our lighthouse, warning us through intuition or you could call it intuitive enlightenment of the wiles of the ego compass and giving our ship of life the means of safe passage forward. Which is why when our intuitive mind, call it conscience if you like speaks to us, we must act on the words of its still small voice within. Be aware of the ego's existence but be not afraid of its persistence.

One of the primary weapons the ego uses is doubt. Doubt is a spiritually energetic force, and it is the enemy of truth. Doubt brings about distrust, which causes division, which promotes or leads to some form of retreat from an objective or connected relationship, whether that be spiritual or physical.

Doubt induced distrust working with fear can become, if embraced, responsible for a lack of progress in any aspect of our lives where we allow it to encroach. It is equally at home working in the spiritual dynamic, in our relationship with Divinity, as it is in the personal dynamic, in our relationship with a human being. Doubt is the primary energetic fuel that conspiracy theorists use to weaponize their agenda.

In the early stages of this book, in Chapter 1 to be exact, I will go into some detail on a time in world history when society saw things differently than it does today and reacted to the times differently than the way in which societies today react to their circumstances. It was a time that is simply described in literature as The Axial Age, a phrase coined by the German philosopher Karl Jaspers. Chapter 1 contains subject matter to enable one to come to an understanding of how, at a certain stage of history, authentic, life changing religion did in fact exist.

It was an era when a specific type of spiritual guidance was given by the spiritual teachers of the day, which demonstrated through its application and subsequent results that a power exists beyond the realm of the conscious mind to change attitudes and behaviours, thus influencing for good both the spiritual trajectory of a person's level of being or consciousness and with that influencing for the better both individual and societal behaviour.

It was a totally different situation from what we witness in the world today, where institutionalised religion holds little sway in its power to influence many individuals or societies for the better, rather in some instances influencing them to behave worse. Modern religious teaching has been so intellectualised, theologised, and diluted that it registers very low on the credibility scale in terms of its power to change individual lives and societal behaviour.

The Axial Age was a period in history when religious practice was not powerless but powerful in changing societies. It was a pivotal moment in the spiritual development of humanity occurring between the years of 900 BCE to 200 BCE which saw some of the world's great spiritual traditions come into being to nourish humanity. Monotheism in Israel, (the doctrine or belief that there is only one God), Hinduism and Buddhism in India, Mysticism in India, Confucianism and Daoism in China, and philosophical rationalism in Greece.

It also witnessed the rise of spiritual and philosophical prophets and sages such as the Buddha, Socrates, Confucius, Jeremiah, and the mystics of the Upanishads, Mencius, and Euripides. It was an age when true spirituality was not just a system of beliefs and accompanying ritualistic practices, but rather a time of spiritual pioneering, of exploring an entirely new kind of "human experience". What mattered most to these sages was, **"not what you believed, not what religion you followed, but rather how you behaved".**

Rabbinic Judaism, Christianity and Islam were all latter-day flowerings of the Axial Age, albeit in many ways not as focused on engendering in a practical way a life changing experience as were the teachings of the Axial Age. That period, the Axial Age, was the most influential, formative and spiritually ground-breaking period of intellectual, psychological, philosophical, and religious change in recorded history and I detail some of what occurred during this time in Chapter 1.

We are all Divine storehouses with the Wisdom of God hidden within our inner being waiting to be tapped into, waiting, and earnestly desiring to fulfil its purpose to come to the conscious surface of our humanity. My desire is that the words in this book will help you to accomplish that purpose. We human beings are temples of the Divine with hidden treasures, unlimited potential within us, waiting and wanting to be discovered.

But this discovery cannot occur without our active participation which first involves our being instructed in the Wisdom and Knowledge of the Kingdom. What did Jesus really mean when he spoke of his desire to give his followers the Keys of The Kingdom. This book will reveal that to the reader.

Awakening to the true reality of who we are is not just a one-time event and that's it. It is a transitionary event and consequently has a gradual unfolding as a flower's petals unfold in the light of the sun, but more quickly with greater exposure to the sun; an unfolding that we need to gain understanding of to successfully navigate forward in our spiritual evolution.

Introduction

In the following chapters as we embark on our journey of discovery into living a life in accordance with Divine Principle, you will find that I utilize references to confirm the universal truths I am sharing with you. There may be philosophical references, there may be psychoanalytic references, there may be spiritual references of a variety of religions and faiths, and there may be scientific references.

Why scientific and psychoanalytic references? What I would argue is that all genuine scientific and psychological investigation is a necessary part of the journey to authentic religion and that this distinction between the religious and the secular, between science and spirituality, between psychology and religion, has been for the most part purely artificial, contrived by some leaders in those fields who are more concerned with ego driven exclusivity, rather than genuine inclusivity and connectedness.

But not all scientific leaders and not all psychologists. Which is why throughout this book, primarily at the beginning of each chapter, I give examples of certain scientists, psychologists, and cosmically conscious creative people, in times past, who had a deep understanding and conviction of the involvement of an Infinite Intelligence in the ongoing evolution of the universe and in their own discoveries, one such scientist being the man regarded as the greatest physicist ever, Albert Einstein. For scientific successes are in many ways a visible demonstration of the expansion of the human consciousness creatively at work.

In using them I am reinforcing the fact that over the centuries many different people of many different beliefs and backgrounds, but all with a common yearning to know more about the spiritual and the metaphysical side of life, have in many ways, all separately reached the same conclusions about life and how it all works, albeit they expressed it differently in their writings and research because of their chosen profession. The teaching then becomes what I refer to as universal truth.

My hope is that by understanding and subsequently applying the truths in this book the reader will move into a pattern of successfully navigating those psychological and physical impediments and barriers that hold many people hostage, stifling their ability to create an ongoing continuous joyous and peace filled experience in life that is their Divine birthright. Impediments that have also thrown into chaos the progression of their evolutionary journey through consciousness back to the source from which their Soul first emerged.

In terms of the spiritual references and as a demonstration of the universality of the truths I am sharing, I use the Qur'an (Koran) of the Islamic faith, the Upanishads (Vedanta) the foundational text in the theological discourse of Hindu tradition, some of which overlap with the earliest Buddhist tradition. With regard to any spiritual principles coming out of Buddhism, rather than use the Tripitaka, which is the earliest recognized canonical list of sacred books officially accepted as genuine teaching of Theravada Buddhism, I instead use the teachings of the Buddha known as "dharma", that centre on the virtues of wisdom, kindness, patience, generosity and compassion, as these teachings are more commonly attuned to the understanding of most people.

With regards to the Christian faith, I use the Bible, its westernised interpretation being easily recognized and understood, but also in particular I use The Gospel of Thomas whose existence I would think is unknown to most people including many church attending Christians. The Gospel of Thomas is a Gnostic text focused on the teachings of Jesus, that was archeologically discovered along with other hidden Gospels at Nag Hammadi in Egypt in 1945, the account of which I describe in detail in my previous book Everything's Gonna Be Alright-The Holy Spirit Knows What She's Doin'.

This book, The Divine Dance of The Universe, the Evolutionary Journey to Authentic Spirituality, was written to help you the reader arrive at a greater understanding of Infinite Intelligence and its creative presence in your life, and its role as the creative implementer of Divine Principle, God's Laws that are designed to metaphysically influence and guide humanity's successful functioning in the evolutionary journey of the universe. The degree of willingness in which you choose to incorporate them into your daily life will determine how soon you begin to see psychological and subsequent behavioural change in your life, subtle change at first and then increasingly sophisticated.

We are all living at a time in the evolution of humanity when an enlightened state of being and an enlightened way of becoming should no longer be regarded as an alternate state or even a spiritual luxury, rather more a spiritual necessity. We are living at a time I think it is correct to say when much of humanity is hell bent on self-destruction, psychologically and for some societies even physically.

One only has to look at the mental health statistics and the destruction occuring through physical and ethnic wars around the globe to see this. Hence with wars, rumours of wars, and societal unrest ever present, there is an even greater urgency for us all to rise to higher levels of Cosmic Consciousness. We must never forget that this Divine Force or Infinite Intelligence that we refer to simply as God, is a God of order and peace, not a God of hate fuelled fear, chaos, cruelty, and confusion.

Whilst an occasional time of reflection is important in your reading of this book more important is the making of a conscious decision to implement those things that speak to you, to put certain things into a regular routine habit. The Qur'an describes the acquisition of knowledge without the internalisation of it through Wisdom, meaning putting it into practice in your life, as being likened to a donkey carrying its own personal library of books on its back, a statement which is self-explanatory I would think.

In summary I have written this book in the hope that its content will encourage you the reader to push on past an intellectual institutionalised understanding of God and religion and stir you into undertaking an experiential journey with Infinite Intelligence, a life lived according to Divine Principle. A journey enabling your earthly walk to be as a heavenly walk bearing witness to everyone you meet of the availability of the prize of a truly resurrected life, an enlightened state of being, a heaven on earth experience, a state of ecstasy, right here right now in the present moment. A journey that will enable you to be transported from a present life of self-absorbed personhood into a future life of purposeful presence.

I have presented the overall contents of this book as a mixture, each chapter containing historical truth, spiritual truth, psychological truth, philosophical truth, scientific truth, and my own personal revelatory truth. I am trusting that blended together they will give you greater insight into the mysteries of God, and the ancient wisdom of the sages of ages, the wisdom of the masters who have gone before, masters in both Eastern and Western religion who have understood these Divine Principles and lived their lives in accordance with them.

Be blessed in knowing that regardless of the chaos and confusion that you witness increasingly around you, and the accompanying discouragement and disillusionment that may come with it, there is no reason to be concerned for God's Spirit of Grace is sufficient.

So be not dismayed or fearful in any way, rather rejoice and be comforted in the knowledge that once you begin participating in the Divine Dance of The Universe, from the first moment you partner up with Divine Principle, the creative influencer and initiator of the metaphysically manifesting might of Infinite Intelligence, that you are in the place you were meant to be and have commenced your true journey through consciousness back to your true home.

The spiritual pointers spread throughout the pages of this book are just that, they are pointers, signposts directing you on a road that you may not have travelled on before, but a road that will take you on a journey to the true Divine Purpose for humanity's evolutionary

Introduction

existence. Signposts that when used to direct your life experience through earnest desire and an attitude of fixed intention and attention, will lead you to the One that institutionalised religion may have lost sight of, but the One who has never lost sight of us. As the Islamist Mystic Rumi said:

> "We are all pure hearts open to the Light of the Divine and will be filled with the elixir of Truth, free from the untoward chaotic influences of body and mind".

I trust that this will be your experience as you read this book. Everyone's path to spiritual awakening is different, linked intrinsically to one's own life circumstances it is naturally different; but there are common features also which I am trusting this book will help explain and put into context for you. Finally, may I say this. You need not to believe the truths in this book, you need not accept them, and you need not even welcome them, and some readers with hereditary fixed religious mindsets may actively resist them. None of this will matter or decrease their might.

May I also say that as most people are caught up in the world of perception, they are also caught up in a dream from which they cannot escape without help. Infinite Intelligence is that help, and Infinite Intelligence is the only one that can enable us to escape from the dreamworld by teaching us how to reverse our thinking and unlearn our mistakes, thus opening our eyes to true reality.

The world of human perceptual experience comprises a world of time and change, and new beginnings and new endings, however it is based on interpretation not on truth filled fact. It is based on self-interpretation, not on God (Infinite Intelligence) interpretation or Godly Wisdom. It is a world of birth and death, and a transitory experience rooted and grounded in the belief in scarcity, in loss, in suffering and in separation, and finally in death. It is unstable in its functioning and unreliable in its intent, always using as its barometer the current level of intellectual learning you have attained and the measure of both good and bad experience you have had thus far in your life.

The words in this book in themselves won't change your past experience but will if reflected on and acted on release the power of Infinite Intelligence to metaphysically neutralise their power to haunt you in the present. Infinite Intelligence can negate their power and Infinite Intelligence can take the words of this book and working with a measure of your own earnest desire and set intent, turn them into a catalyst for your own Divine personal perceptual experience of God who is Infinite Intelligence. The creative Mind of God can take any truth that you embrace willingly and turn it into circumstantial reality. Be blessed in your endeavours.

❝ *"There are it is true many differences between the various religions. True authentic spirituality is meant to focus on the commonalities, not the differences; the unifying nature of this then serving as an instrument by which all of humankind, regardless of our religious preference, can come to understand the universality and interconnectedness of our existence, the true reality of life itself, that we are all living functioning beings within the totality of the whole of Being".*

The Axial Age
The Birth, the Reign, and the Death of Authentic Life Changing Religion

ONE

> "Compassion and kindness fertilise the soil of authentic religion. Without these two elements the weeds of self-interest, self-servitude, and apathy, will quickly grow, choking off the flowering of the fruit of the Spirit that true religion was designed to produce in abundance".

Karl Theodor Jaspers (23rd February 1883 to 26th February 1969) was a German-Swiss psychiatrist and philosopher who had a strong influence on modern theology, psychiatry and philosophy. After completing his training in his chosen profession of psychiatry, he turned his attention towards philosophical inquiry. Philosophical inquiry, when used in reading, writing, and communicating, is a tool to help us better understand ourselves, our peers, and our world. It is basically the process of being curious and asking focused questions about the best way to live a rich and fulfilling life.

Born in a farming community in Oldenburg, a city in Lower Saxony in Germany, since his father was a jurist, which was the name given to a specialist legal scholar, in his educational and career ambitions Karl's first inclination was to study law, which he did, but eventually switched to studying medicine. After earning his medical doctorate, he began work at a psychiatric hospital, but in his time there he became increasingly dissatisfied with the way the medical community approached mental illness. So having given himself the challenge of changing this, he went on to secure a post as a psychology teacher at the University of Heidelberg.

In 1921 at the age of 38 years Karl changed direction in a way that saw him move from a sole focus on psychology, towards philosophy, working and writing in Germany using the themes he had developed in his psychiatric work. After the rise of Nazism and its seizure of power in 1933 he was forced to retire from teaching and was unable to have any of his writings and findings published. Since Jasper's wife was Jewish, he was also under the constant threat of, along with his wife, being sent to a concentration camp, which forced him to keep a low profile. When his hometown of Oldenburg was finally liberated by American troops in 1945, he found himself free to continue his work and his writing.

Most commentators merely associate his later work with the philosophy of existentialism, a philosophical theory which determines that each individual person is a free agent determining their own development through acts of self-will, but in fact his work involved much more than this. Being aware that the topic of individual freedom permeated much of his writing, in 1932 he introduced a new theme to his work, which pointed out that as a human being begins to question their reality, they begin to confront borders that an empirical or scientific method simply cannot transcend, meaning cannot give answers, and that the only choice an individual has in a situation such as that is to give up on their search for true reality, or alternately take a leap of faith into the transcendent nature of humankind, using that as a means of finally discovering an authentic existence.

We have all heard I am sure the expression "transcendental meditation", and most have probably never questioned what the word "transcendental" in that phrase actually means. Transcendence to Jaspers was a journey into that which exists beyond the world of time and space and place, a journey of true freedom, as against the controlled freedom of the human experience alone, which having experienced life in Nazi Germany he was well versed in. In this new theme to his work, whilst he showed an interest in Eastern philosophies particularly Buddhism, he was particularly attracted to Mystic traditions and their practices during the Axial Age and beyond.

As mentioned in the Introduction of this book, The Axial Age, a name coined by Jaspers himself, was a pivotal moment in the spiritual development of humanity occurring between the years of 900 BCE to 200 BCE, trickling down to the Common Era or CE, which saw some of the world's great spiritual traditions come into being to nourish and serve humanity. (CE is the secular equivalent of what was originally A.D. from the Latin, anno Domini, meaning "the year of our Lord"). Traditions such as Monotheism in the Middle East, (the doctrine or belief that there is only one God), Hinduism and Buddhism in India, Confucianism and Daoism in China, and philosophical rationalism in Greece.

These were the traditions which witnessed the emergence of timeless teachers, prophets, mystics, and philosophers such as the Buddha, Confucius, the author of the Dao De Jing in China, the great Hebrew prophets such as Jeremiah, Hosea, and Amos and the mystics of the Upanishads in India, along with the great fifth century philosophers such as Socrates, Plato, and Aristotle; all timeless teachers and all espousing an entirely new type of human experience. Note that the spiritual traditions such as Rabbinic Judaism, Christianity and Islam were all latter-day flowerings of that Axial Age.

During this time, we saw the birth of what is known as Axial Consciousness, which is a sense of individual identity as distinct from tribal identity. The Axial Age was a pivotal time in human history when human beings began to reflect for the first time about individual existence and the meaning of life and death. If there was one noticeable thing that all those movements involved in the Axial Age had in common, it was this. All of them had an acute awareness and concern for the ongoing suffering they witnessed, not only the suffering present in their own respective societies, but suffering holistically, suffering of the mind, body, and spirit. Suffering that was an ongoing condition of a spiritually, politically, and economically evolving yet unstable world.

That period, the Axial Age, was the most formative, influential, and spiritually ground-breaking period of intellectual, psychological, philosophical, spiritual, and religious change in recorded history. It was also a time in which most of the main religious and spiritual traditions in Eurasian (Europe and Asia) societies emerged, many of which are still impacting on society today in a more global sense, when by contrast, the Egyptian, Greek, and Mesopotamian religions that emerged at the same time have had no obvious impact on today's religious and spiritual life.

Most of these philosophers, mystics, sages, and poets had not one skerrick of interest in doctrine or creed or a person's religious affiliation. Sages like the Buddha were totally indifferent to a person's theological beliefs and religious brand. Some of them would when questioned steadfastly refuse to enter into any conversation about theological beliefs, saying it was distracting, unhelpful, and spiritually destructive. Why would they do this? Because discussions of this nature, many birthed out of ego driven hereditary religious bias, would inevitably lead to differences of opinion which subsequently would lead to dissent and potential conflict, in some cases even physical, which was not only unedifying but also spiritually and societally disconnecting.

You see when serious conflicts of opinion appear, and cause fear, strife, and terror to run rampant in society, it not only affects some people, but it also affects in some way most people. Strife and turmoil infect people's thoughts, their dreams, their relationships, their desires, their ambitions, and their behaviours. Not one element of their physical life is left untouched and for many not one element of their psychological life as well.

The Axial Sages knew this, and so devised and taught principles rooted in the deeper, less conscious levels of the self, the Soul, the inner person, that which is without form. The fact that they all came up with such similar solutions regardless of their spiritual brand, whether they were Buddhist, Confucianist, Indian Mystic or Judaist (Jewish) Mystic, demonstrated that they indeed had discovered something transcending human rational thought, and intellectualism, the way most human beings internalise the visible, the way they perceive or interpret their circumstances and experiences.

They all came to the conclusion that if people made a disciplined effort to re-educate themselves and realign their thinking with God's, or Brahman's or The Great Ultimate's (Tao in Confucianism) way of thinking, or whatever name they had for God, if people changed their way of thinking and perceiving to the God Mind way of thinking and perceiving, and then subsequently alchemised (transmuted or converted) that "re-educated or realigned thought process" into specific behavioural change, in other words if they started doing things differently, doing things according to Divine Law, God's way of thinking, they would most assuredly experience a positive enhancement to their humanity.

For instance, when the world thinks and says, "do unto others as they do unto you", or "react towards other as they react to you", Divine Principle or Divine Law or the God Mind in assessing the situation at hand would say, "no, do unto others as you would have them do unto you". In other words, responding rightly according to Divine Law, not reacting wrongly from the ego mind's point of view or from a habitual and pre-determined viewpoint. You see what most people don't understand is that Divine Principle or Divine Law is built into the cosmological and metaphysical fabric and functioning of this universe.

The Axial Sages taught that to live in accord with cosmological and metaphysical law is the only way to ensure life's positive benefits flow, primarily happiness and peace. And the Divine Principle, God's cosmological and metaphysical law that is relevant to the "do unto others" scenario is the **Law of Reciprocity**. The Law of Reciprocity is a cosmic law that the sages and mystics taught exactly as Jesus and Muhammad who came later taught, that when someone curses you, you don't curse them back, but rather bless them back. When someone wrongs you, you don't look for revenge, rather you forgive them. When the Law of Reciprocity comes into play, or you could call it The Law of Reciprocal Response, and someone expresses kindness to you, then you will be automatically driven to return kindness to them or someone else.

You see Divine Law has a multiplying effect. The Axial Sages taught that if we show mercy rather than demanding retribution, mercy will be given back to us by the universe. They taught that if you want peace, you must first extend the hand of peace. What does all this mean? It simply means that you choose to not react from your offended ego mind's point of view, rather live life responding from God's point of view, God's rule of law.

The Divine Law of Reciprocity in social psychology is a social norm of responding to a positive action with another positive action. Social psychologists would say that reciprocity as a social construct means that in response to friendly actions given to them, people are frequently much nicer and much more co-operative in their response. Reciprocity makes it possible to build continuing relationships and co-operation. But these laws cover the negative aspects of life as well seeing elements emanating from a different energetic realm of the cosmos responding reciprocally to a particular negative behaviour.

For instance, in response to hostile actions, this law can initiate a much nastier and even more brutal response. Which then commences an ongoing cycle of hostile action and subsequent hostile reaction and response. Which is why world wars last so long. They last until one party extends the hand of peace and the other party sensing a bad end for themselves because they are losing then reciprocate.

In personal relationships we see this in instances of one person "holding a grudge" against another. Which basically is an ongoing fixed attitude and behaviour that prolongs ill will against another person. In continuous cyclical motion, that's how long running family feuds continue, that's how wars between nations commence and continue. All it takes is an individual's or a collective's offended ego to assume control of the response and ongoing conflict is released by the darker energies of the universe to create distress and suffering and a psychological and practical disconnection at varying levels of intensity. Even for those innocent bystanders caught up as collateral damage in the ongoing events.

Jesus was a perfect example of one who lived in accordance with Divine Law. But not only did He set the example through His own behaviour, much of His teaching had a specific Divine Law underpinning it even though at times it was hidden in "the mystery of a parable". Jesus taught the Law of Reciprocity, even if only sometimes in parables and then lived according to that law to show others by His life example "the way" of the same. To cement it into their psychological and behavioural being.

He taught the Law and lived the Law. That is why many times throughout the Bible we see him referenced as "teacher" and witness Him commencing a lot of what He taught with the simple words, "It is written." Similarly in the teachings of the Axial Sages a re-education into right or righteous thought processes, came at the same time as the redirection of society into right and righteous behavioural patterns and responses. The Axial Sages didn't take the approach of the institutionalised church that teaches the Wisdom of Jesus and then just as an afterthought hopes someone might listen and do something. But if not, never mind as long as the sermon is praised by the parishioner as they depart the building and shake the hand of the priest or pastor.

In the Axial Age this re-education of their thought processes and practical application of the Divine principle eventually brought about a long-term psychological change in their personality patterns, the hereditary or self-developed and more often than not ego driven thought patterns that they had been taking direction from and responding to all their lives. The teachings of the sages and mystics were designed to eradicate the egoic response, behaviour stemming from an offended ego, and to give society a dose of "ekstasis".

Ekstasis is a Greek word meaning "to be or stand outside of one's self". It is where our word "ecstasy" comes from, a word commonly used in the Hindu religion also. It is a stepping out from one's habitual, self-absorbed consciousness, the self, enabling a person to apprehend the reality of the God Consciousness and enabling a God orchestrated and God supported and ongoingly God sustained change and more enlightened life experience.

When Jesus described Himself as "the Way", when He said, "I Am, the Way, the Truth, and the Life", He was not saying that He Jesus was the Way, He was saying, I Am is the Way. He was saying God's Way is the Way or you could say God's Pathway is the only true way. And of course, God's pathway for humanity is Divine Principle. What does "I Am" mean? "I Am" is the metaphysical consciousness of the Divine, it is the way God described himself in the Old Testament. It is Universal Consciousness, the God Mind. Jesus was saying that this is the pathway to truth and life. The God Mind is the way.

You see both the sages of the Axial Age and Jesus who came later, did not give instruction in the way of traditional institutionalised religion, which teaches that first you must discover your belief in God, then follow this up with adherence to church law and then God will change you into the person you desire to be. That type of traditional institutionalised religious teaching all centres on obedience to the ecclesiastical authorities, not on in the first instance obedience to Divine Law. Which is why if you are a movie buff you would probably have seen movies depicting gangsters murdering people and then in the next instant going to Mass or befriending a priest. Or as seen with Muslim extremists, murdering people and then giving obeisance to Allah five times a day the same day the murder is committed.

What does that mean in practical terms in daily life? It may mean some people will get more concerned about missing Mass than about sorting out a dispute with their neighbour. It may mean some people will be more concerned about giving money to the church rather than helping a homeless person. It may mean some people prefer to hold grudges rather than to forgive an offence against them. With Jesus it was the exact reverse.

Jesus taught that first you must believe Him, and then follow is His way of living, how He approached life and his behavioural responses in all situations, which was of course a response according to the "way" of Divine Law or Divine Principle. As just mentioned, this is why you see in the New Testament that so many times Jesus prefaced what He was about to teach with the Words, "It is written". The core principle underpinning all of the teachings of Jesus was the Divine Principle or Law of Reciprocity. As you think and behave so it shall be done unto you. As you forgive so shall you be forgiven. Or as we forgive another's trespasses against us so to the same measure will God forgive our trespasses. He taught that in the Lord's Prayer. And it goes on. If you curse you will be cursed. Draw near to God and God will draw near to you. Give and it will be given unto you.

I recall when I was a Pentecostal Pastor, during church services we sang a chorus "move Holy Spirit, move in my life, move Holy Spirit to make me like Christ". That's the institutionalised church way of thinking. They focus on the Divine doing all the work, without any focus in the first instance on us as an act of our will initiating the changed attitude and behaviour we desire. With regards to psychological or circumstantial change, the Holy Spirit or Infinite Intelligence or the Ruh al-Qudus as it is known in Islam, can only sustain and support that which we initiate in the first instance in our own attitudes and behaviours in life.

The other way is a lazy type of spiritual life journey. We say, "yeah well I asked God to stop me from being angry and it didn't work, I still get angry". No, and it never will. That's why there is so much unanswered prayer, people adopting a one sided "gimmee gimmee God attitude". Our spiritual and thus our circumstantial life journey is meant to be all about reciprocity.

With regards to anger what must happen in the first instance is that with sincerity, we verbally and physically stop doing angry things, just stop it, it's called self-control, and the Creative Spirit will eventually remove angry responses totally from your life. I once had an instance when confronting a man about the way he continually yelled at his wife during a disagreement say to me, "I can't help it, it's just in my nature." No it wasn't. That was simply an excuse for him to take no personal responsibility for his "chosen behaviour". He was right in a way though. It was in his lower nature that his choice had come from. He was reacting out of selfishness emanating from the darker hidden side of his nature, his lower self, that he had habitually embraced every time it suited his ego.

Sure, if in the heat of the emotional moment you occasionally "lose it", you react angrily without thinking, then apologize immediately after and ask for forgiveness for your outburst. This then brings the energetic vibrational force of forgiveness into the picture which dissipates energetically and immediately the bad vibe of the moment. Forgiveness has a higher vibrational energetic wave frequency than anger, so in a way you could say forgiveness smothers anger and puts a pillow over potential ongoing ill will, deadening its ongoing effect and, in an instant, restores the relationship to what it was prior to the outburst. That's the power of Divine Principle in action.

If you are aware of an existing anger problem choose to change in the first instance, don't just wait for God to miraculously reach out to change you. Then you will transcend that behavioural pattern, whether it is hereditary, you know the "aw anger runs in our family", or the "it's in my nature", self-justification for doing it, or whether it is self-developed through adopting anger as a habitual damaged ego response, which in most cases it is. The practical outworking of choosing to change is the "turn the other cheek" Divine Principle that Jesus spoke of. Why or how is anger self-developed? Through an offended ego that is frustrated with not getting its own way. Anger is a self-interested and selfish emotional response.

Evidence of its removal may not be totally obvious in the first instance if it has become habitual, if it has become an instinctive response, because the ego mind is persistent, and will attempt to catch you unawares, but change will happen if you sincerely desire it. Then as you sense change coming take time to reflect in a ruthlessly honest way on what causes you to get angry, is it just selfishness or is there a deeper root cause. You may find that it goes deeper than the immediate situation. Perhaps you were bullied at school and were unable to fight back, the emotional impact of that event lying dormant in your sub-consciousness, or your little corner of the collective unconscious waiting to emerge and express itself at the right moment. The ego is fully aware of what pushes your buttons. It's a warfare of two minds.

The sages taught that first you must practice disciplined empathy and compassion towards your fellow citizen, and practice Divine Principle in your daily interactions with your fellow human being, and that by doing this you will transcend human thought and move into the "Divine way of thought", which meant you became a "doer" of Divine Wisdom rather than a "hearer" only, deceiving yourself.

You moved into psychological or mental alignment with Divine Presence, which was you could say a radical change to how the society of the day lived their lives. Because for aeons society had relied on hostile responses and on all other manner of lawless behaviour, in the name of law enforcement, believing that it was the only way to achieve stability in the societal environment. The societies of that day believed that might was right.

The sages and mystics had discovered that if we in a methodical and disciplined way cultivate an entirely different mind-set, that if we respond to every situation looking at it from Divinity's point of view rather than reacting to it from the egoic mind's point of view, we progressively experience an alternate state of consciousness and grow in grace and holiness from a spiritual aspect, and in peace and harmony from a societal aspect. The consistency in which all the sages and mystics, regardless of their theological brand, returned to **"the golden rule"**, the do unto others and it shall be done unto you rule, which is the Law of Reciprocity, demonstrated something important about the structure of our nature and certainly was a key process in society's transitionary journey to higher levels of consciousness.

Most of the Axial philosophers had no interest in doctrine or creed. A person's theological beliefs were a matter of total indifference to a sage like the Buddha. All the teaching of Axial Age traditions pushed forward the concept of psychological and spiritual transcendence and embraced the concept that one should never entertain or accept any religious teaching centred on faith alone, rather that it was essential to test that teaching against your own personal experience.

This teaching was very similar to those Gnostics of early post-Christ Christianity who I discussed in detail in my previously published book, Everything's Gonna Be Alright, the Holy Spirit Knows What She's Doin'. Simply said what mattered most in the Axial Age was not what you believed, but rather "how you behaved".

Whilst some sages and mystics still valued some sort of ritual in their lives, they gave it a new ethical significance and put morality at the heart of the spiritual life. It is interesting that in more modern times of individual personal or alternately societal crisis, many men and women turn back to the sayings of Confucius and the teachings of the Buddha and of Jesus for guidance. In its original conception in reference to the religions of their time, the Axial Age served its intent to initiate the beginning of a new modern era, an era of Socrates, and of Confucius, and of the Buddha, and the teaching of the sages became very important in the lives of those early inhabitants.

Why? Because those same inhabitants were on the spot witnesses to the remarkable peace filled societal cohesion and new positive way of living and doing that came about through their embracing and acting upon these teachings. They believed why? Because seeing was believing. Because they had witnessed and involved themselves in their implementation and experienced their results. There have been many scientific, spiritual, and philosophical enquiries over the centuries by independent people trying to ascertain, or you could say gain some sort of commonality in their interpretation of those times.

For example, was it the commonality of purpose that brought about society's radical change in behaviour and subsequent cohesion and unity, or was it some Divine force that activated these results due to the catalytic effect of a uniform thought process in society? The sages believed this to be true. They saw it as a realisation and materialisation of the work of the Divine Principle that reads, "if two or more agree on earth concerning anything that they will ask, it will be done." But regardless of whether scholars have agreed or disagreed with what caused the change in society's way of behaving, the one thing they could all agree on was that the Axial Age was one of, if not the most genuinely transformative times intellectually, psychologically, philosophically, socially, and spiritually in recorded history.

That cannot be argued, and the reason for that is evident in the fact that since that time, wherever religion or spirituality has traversed on this earth, the thinkers and sages of that time have continued to inspire ongoing generations and continually weathered the emerging storms in society giving a measure of comfort to those who turn to their teachings. Most psychoanalysts, philosophers, and historians, whilst having agreed on the transformative aspect of that time, have also reached consensus that that time in history was more than any other era one of widespread inner reflection, as opposed to continual outer reflection. It was a time when "societies began in earnest focusing on the inner Soul of the human being rather than only the outer circumstances".

Yes, reflection was a key element of those times, but please don't make the spiritual journey difficult by worrying about whether you are reflecting right, the yoke of Jesus is meant to be easy and light and bring rest to the soul. There is no right or wrong way. Choose your place and time. King David of the Old Testament spent time walking in the peace filled surrounds of nature. He took time out from his physical circumstances and strolled besides the still waters. To reflect means simply to think about something in a peace filled way to gain greater insight about the matter and gain greater wisdom in how to deal with it.

We are told in the ancient Proverbs to "above all else get wisdom and understanding". In speaking about reflection Iman Ali, the cousin and son-in-law of the Prophet Muhammad, the spiritual leader and founder of the Muslim religion said the following:

> *"Your sickness is coming from within you, but you do not perceive it, and your remedy is within you, but you do not sense it. You presume you are a small entity, but within you is unfolded the entire universe. What you seek is within you if only you reflect".*

You see in the centuries prior to this Axial Age transition, the life focus of society was purely one of survival. Survival midst wars, survival midst famines, survival midst droughts, survival midst epidemics, survival midst plagues and persecution, survival midst alienation, and during those survival marathons, the compensating and for some comforting thing that kept many going was that much of their religious practice was intrinsically linked to cultural mythology. But their mythology gave them a measure of comfort only, not a change of environment. Similarly, as most religious institutions do in this day.

Most religious institutions in this modern day, try as they may, bring only a measure of comfort to society and not radical behavioural change and with that positive circumstantial change. The religious wars between the Catholics and Protestants over many years is a good example of this, of the lack of behavioural change that a powerless institutionalised religion is capable of engendering or in the case of the Irish wars, two powerless religious institutions, Catholicism and Protestantism.

Regarding hereditary mythological religious influences, prior to the Axial Age spirituality was a religion of Gods and Goddesses, of Divine Beings and Devilish Deities. Religious activity was built on a platform of what was in many ways make-believe, all about the mythos of a culture, culturally driven tales about the origin and purpose of humanity, rather than the Logos, the principles of Divine Reason and creative order. The renowned psychoanalyst Carl Jung in his life's work was very interested in the way societies and different cultures for hundreds of centuries have used archetypes in myths, attaching a specific archetype to a mythological story to enable a culture or tradition to be easily passed down, almost in storybook mode, from generation to generation.

We see this often in certain Eastern Religions but not as much in Western Religion. However, some over superstitious elements of Christianity are still very reluctant to entertain the possibility that some stories in the Bible may in fact be of a mythological nature to teach some moral or spiritual lesson; stories such as Noah and the ark, or the story of Jonah and the whale in the Old Testament. George Walton Lucas Jr., the Filmmaker, Philanthropist and creator of the Star Wars and Indiana Jones franchises once rightly said, "I've concluded that mythology is really a form of archaeological psychology. Mythology gives you a sense of what a society believes, and what they fear."

In relation to spirituality, myths, with their archetypal lead characters, are stories of an imaginative type that are eternal and mysterious, and that seem to fulfil in various cultures a need to find a deeper meaning and understanding of life as we know it. Many spiritual myths give clues as to the spiritual potential of human life and are sometimes used as an excuse for what does or doesn't happen in one's spiritual life, and this was certainly the case in the pre-Axial Age times. In many ways you could say that myths are stories that link together the outer with the inner, the experience of life on the physical plane with the human mind's need for an explanation of the spiritual or inner life of a person.

In pre-Axial societies historical influences such as myths that would see them through tumultuous times were easier to grasp than to try and achieve answers through internal reflection and contemplation. Why was this? Because they were able to be understood at the level of Simple Awareness which fitted into their hectic lifestyle rather than taking time out to reflect through Cosmic or Intuitive Awareness.

The Axial Age however saw the birth of the opposite. Internal reflection became preferential over mythological belief. If one took a line in the sand approach to looking at the pre-Axial Age as against the Axial Age itself, you could recognize that society in the Axial Age took a far more reflective attitude to their habits and behaviours than those in the pre-Axial Age. Reflection being more serious contemplative type thought about something, rather than merely looking at the visible circumstances. From a spiritual perspective the pre-Axial society had a "let's focus on local circumstance" approach to life, rather than a universal approach to the concept of spiritual awareness and cosmic societal connection. They followed the religious rituals, practices and beliefs demonstrating the supposed power of mythical deities that had been carried down from many generations before them.

These were myths and stories about how they came to be and reinforced their reliance on Gods and Goddesses. These stories then became the staple spiritual diet they fed to each child they brought into the world. The stories were not regarded as true or false, mythical, or not, rather that consideration didn't matter. You could say they just blindly accepted that the stories were true and certainly the answer to any inner questioning they might have about the meaning of life.

Their lives did not involve any inward reflection on what was truth and reality and what wasn't. So, the status quo of religious ritual and ceremony involving their chosen deities just automatically continued, regardless of how dire their circumstance might become as they were continually immersed in the toxic life destroying culture of warring tribes. The problem with that was that without inner reflection there can be no outer change. And so, the wars continued, starvation continued, man's inhumanity to fellow man continued; alienation continued, deportations continued, massacres continued, the destruction of cities continued, all clothed in the cloak of political, social, and economic upheaval.

But during the Axial Age the importance of continuing with this long -accepted institutionalised and culturized way of thinking and behaving was set aside, and through radical reflection on the lack of long-term benefits of this type of spiritual path, that historically hereditary inherited path of mythology and ritual, the conclusion was reached that human behaviour could not be changed according to mythological, historical, or institutionalised belief systems.

A realisation occurred in societies, brought about by the teachings of the sages and mystics of that time, that outward behaviour stemmed from an internal condition, and that to radically change behaviour everyone needed to focus individually on their own internal condition, the condition of their Soul, and not on their previous historical conditioned way of doing things. It was all about cognitive change not purely about a yearning for circumstantial change or a measure of comfort through myth.

It was all about in the first instance a change in the way of thinking and the way in which a human being internalises or perceives outside circumstance. You could say that it was a change from mythic culture to consciousness culture. The Axial Age was a time of moral and ethical alchemy, a process of inner transformation that led to outer circumstantial transformation. Ethical behaviour became the priority. You see:

> "Outward behaviour stems from an internal condition. To radically change outward behaviour, everyone in society must first focus on their internal condition, the condition of their Soul. A transformed life is firstly about cognitive change, which gives one the motivation for behavioural change, and from this circumstantial change will automatically flow".

The Axial Age you could say specifically redefined the spiritual life because it was not based on historically engendered unproductive cognitive change alone, or on increased intellectual capacity, but on "cognitive change that would lead to behavioural change". Cognitive change, a change in one's way of perceiving and thinking, that would lead to a change in their way of doing and behaving. It was argued by the Axial Sages that real change in a human being and in society itself, real transformation in the behavioural pattern of a society was intrinsically linked to self-discipline and selflessness.

And the writings of these sages and mystics of that time are still read today. Why? Because people are subconsciously attracted to what they were teaching. That attraction then similarly flowed through to the latter flowerings of that age, through the likes of Jesus and Muhammad and other prophets that came later such as Rumi the mystical Islamist. As I mentioned in the beginning of this book, the ecstatic poems of Jalal ad-Din Muhammad Rumi have sold millions of copies in recent years, making him the most popular poet globally. Rumi's poetic verse does not attract people to a new way of life that is geographically different or financially or economically different, but rather psychologically different, a new way of thinking.

Which includes a fresh emphasis on the morality and self-discipline that is necessary to not only engender psychological change, a new way of thinking about life, but with that a new way of "doing life", a new way of behaving and interacting with our fellow human beings. This then enables the creative Law of Reciprocity to spring into action and initiate circumstantial change for the better. Jesus put it very succinctly when He said as we read in the New Testament:

"Seek ye first the Kingdom of God, and all these things shall added unto you".

What was He referring to when He said seek the Kingdom of God first? He was speaking of reflecting in the first instance on Divine Law or Divine Principle, reflecting on what God says about life or your situation. He was not telling us to "hunger after heaven" or to go to church more often, as much of institutionalised Christianity has taught. He was telling us to hunger after a Kingdom Life, a new way of living, a life lived in accord with the Laws of the Spirit of God, which are the same Divine Principles that Jesus taught, such as the Law of Reciprocity that I spoke of earlier in this chapter. And what are the "all these things" that Jesus was referring to in that verse. Not purely riches and material wealth in the first instance although that can be a part of it, but primarily happiness and peace for "peace is the Divine Watchman over our lives". As the Prophet Isaiah said:

"You will be kept in perfect peace if your mind is stayed or fixed on God".

When Jesus said, "all these things", He was referring to both psychological and circumstantial change. He was talking about us stepping out of the psychological transitional roadblock, the negative thinking environment that is in some way unsettling us, into a positive environment that brings with it enough of a measure of circumstantial change to allow presence or the peace of God to begin flooding our being.

Enough to enable our level of consciousness to resume its evolutionary journey once again at a much faster pace towards a higher level because it is vibrationally energised through the presence of peace. And morality, ethical behaviour, and self-discipline were the key components of this lifestyle that Jesus and the sages of the Axial Age taught. It was about the unity of moral purpose and not the individuality of immoral purpose. It was all about inner Divine Presence and not outer self-preservation.

To put it simply the sages of those ages brought about through their "radical" teaching, psychological change, which then in its wake witnessed long term cultural change. By encouraging through their teaching attitudinal and behavioural changes in the areas of empathy, compassion, kindness, charity, respect, mercy, love, forgiveness, aligned with a condemnation of greed filled intent and conspicuous consumption, as all these changed individual behaviours began to emerge, we witnessed more broadly from a social and societal point of view a much more cohesive society and much positive economic and intellectual change. Which took society from the lower level of psychological functioning, that of Collective Unconsciousness as Carl Jung described it, to the higher state of Collective Consciousness, which precedes the achievement of Universal or Cosmic Consciousness.

Spiritual movements of most generations, purely to keep their institutions alive and financially viable, often make concessions about the kind of life they ask their followers to lead, and many in this modern day in some way compromise their expectations of their parishioners and in doing so end up splitting the believers into two camps you could say, two broad classes. Christianity has a term "committed Christian" which automatically creates the space for uncommitted Christians whatever they are, although I am aware that some Christian churches use that term for those members who do not participate in extracurricular church activity or tithe a proportion of their income.

The term committed Christian has been commonly used by the church to describe someone who is actively involved in church activities. The church gives the title of an uncommitted Christian to anyone who is not fully immersed in church activity, which of course is a load of rubbish. No one knows another's heart fully save God. In the Axial Age there were the individuals who were deeply involved in practice and behaviour to a spiritual life, including people such as the sages and priests, but for some the aesthetic constraints of such a religious life were self- relaxed in favour of what you could call a less restrictive lifestyle.

But it was not as conspicuous or intense as we witness in this modern day where we have religious people who purport to a visible form of religion, but still their guiding focus in life is the world of the material. We have seen that evidenced with the spread over these last few decades of offshoots of Pentecostalism in the form of certain megachurches, whose underlying goal is to build a spiritual powerbase to increase their level of political influence and a financial powerbase to increase their personal wealth in the process.

The "post" Axial latter-day flowering saw sages such as Jesus and Muhammad speak out about these excesses, calling out those people who honoured God with their words and ritualistic modes of practice and the mouthing of pious platitudes, but their hearts, their way of thinking and behaving were totally opposite from their public religious persona. Not so during the Axial Age. The focus of the majority of those who responded to the teachings of the sages was one of perceptual change, their way of seeing or thinking about things, resulting in procedural change, their way of doing and behaving. Public and personal behaviour changed, which was an immediate noticeable by-product of that changed way of perceiving and thinking.

What was particularly obvious during this time, was that humankind became conscious of being part of the whole of humanity, or you could say a cosmic awareness emerged, and societies became conscious of the importance of living an ethical life based on that realisation, a life actively demonstrating integrity towards all human beings and respect for all human beings. During the Axial Age visible changed personality patterns emerged demonstrating newfound expressions of kindness, love, empathy, courage, and solidarity of purpose and from a cosmic point of view higher levels of consciousness. There was a psychological transcendence from a state of Universal Unconsciousness to a state of Collective Consciousness.

But it was not for all, particularly for those tribes who felt that self-interest was meant to be at the front of the pack not the back and who subsequently hung on to the belief that life was primarily all about self-survival, which of course had been the only experience that generations had had up until this time.

In today's modern religious society, it is by and large not totally different. Many "religious people" tinker around the edges of a true spiritual experience, whilst living in a world at times quite often embroiled in physical and psychological chaos and confusion. In times of social crisis and war do we see the "highest" religious leaders in the world give true emphatic spiritual and moral guidance and instruction to their followers and hold them to account? No, often we merely witness a quick press release or speech calling for peace from a bunker or a balcony somewhere out of harm's way. What is needed to fix this is simply a transcendence of thought processes by all, including the world leaders of religion.

From the "person in the pew" to the "priest or preacher in the pulpit", from the pastor to the Pope, all religious leaders need to "transcend or go beyond" the way in which they have traditionally responded. All levels of religious life need to respond righteously and rightly. The word transcendence, in a literal sense, means to go beyond. Transcendental refers to things that lie beyond the practical experience of ordinary people and cannot be discovered or understood by ordinary reasoning or simple awareness, far beyond the range of usual perception. During the period of the Axial Age, we saw a transcendence in the psychological makeup of the human being, in the human being's way of thinking. about the world and navigating the world.

Their initial goal in transcending was to achieve a higher level of conscious awareness of not just their own Divine nature but the Divine nature of all of humanity, and with that a new way of existing as a human being.

"The Axial Age was a time of going beyond what the people always thought, had always been taught, or told by those who had gone before. A time of going beyond or transcending the world's historic social individualization and religion's impersonal ritualisation, that had evolved over previous centuries and of going forward embracing instead the cosmic interrelatedness of all humanity".

Prior to the Axial Age most of society was caught in a cultural and religious time warp. Everything they thought and every behaviour they exhibited was harnessed to their historical and hereditary cultural beliefs, which included their mythological beliefs that I spoke of. The Axial Age brought with it a new social paradigm, a shift in thinking about how life should work, causing much of society to step away from community containment into a more cosmological approach to life. They started to think about the whole world and how it worked rather than just their own personal little corner of the world.

We saw the rise of a second order of thinking a new way of thinking. The Axial Age was in fact a time of transfer, a transfer of perception, all things visible and audible were mentally interpreted differently, seeing Divine Principle being brought into the picture. A "how would God handle this" type of thinking, or a "what would God do in this situation", new thought process emerged.

The Axial Age, a spiritual revolution you could call it as against a physical revolution, made an indelible impression on the why and the how of the way human beings related, not only to other human beings, but also to themselves and the world around them. All those who participated, regardless of what religious banner they lived under, became acutely conscious of the suffering that seemed to be an inescapable part of the human condition, and all hungered for what they saw was the need for a more spiritually and physically active and constructive type of religion, a religion that put Divine Principle and Godly interest ahead of self-interest. One that was not so engrossed in or so heavily dependent on external reason and external rituals to justify its existence.

There was a deep concern about ethical and moral behaviour, which was seen as not just being a matter of giving up conventional rights and adopting a new way of worshipping, but rather it all centred on first and foremost, focusing on a new way of behaving, and letting the religious ritualistic component of life work itself out. There was a concern about giving each other a hope for the future rather than simply through their behaviour reinforcing an ongoing despair about the present. The Old Testament Prophet Jeremiah put it this way in quoting a message he received from Infinite Intelligence intuitively in a reflective moment:

> 'For I know the plans I have for you, declares the Lord, plans to prosper you and not to harm you, plans to give you a hope and a future".

All the sages, mystics, prophets and philosophers, people like the Buddha, Confucius, Hosea, Jerimiah, or Amos, absolutely recoiled from the violence of their time and first and foremost taught the ethics of compassion and morality. Much of society just ceased performing the conventional rites of their religious brand, and spiritual practices in terms of ritualistic behaviour came secondary to the importance of how they treated their fellow creatures, always mindful as to whether it was in a respectful manner or was it disrespectfully. In some quarters many people even adopted a hostile attitude to the ingrained institutionalised ancient myths that had in many ways controlled the spiritual development of their own society and their practical relationships with other societies up until that time.

But it was not for all, some of the most sophisticated religious systems found that it was impossible to function spiritually without their institutionalised mythology and so they continued in their new Axial Age spiritual lives but still with a leaning towards mythology, albeit more subtle.

The more reflective of the communities however slowly came to realise that they no longer shared the same nature as these mythical creatures. In fact, as we moved further forward in the centuries following this, right up until the 19th century we saw a change in attitude where some religions started to think that institutionalised religion itself alienated people from the rest of humanity.

The 19th century well known German philosopher and socialist revolutionary Karl Marx whilst being a staunch advocate for communism, which has its own inherent corruptible and divisive principles, perhaps rightly believed that religion was a symptom of a sick society. You could say that in some ways the sages of the Axial Age were of similar thought, believing that the mythological driven religion of their time sustained a sick society and prevented it from moving forward morally and ethically with social coherence. The Axial Age for many became a time of questioning old religious traditions and the subsequent behaviour that emanated from holding on to these practices.

But it was not all confined to what we commonly refer to as Eastern Religion. This time of what you could call religious and spiritual transition, apart from occurring in the Arab nations also began to surface in the kingdoms of Israel and Judah. The prophets of Israel and Judah, having analysed the events in the Middle East, began challenging a lot of the notions of the Divine that they had religiously and psychologically inherited. Some of the prophets were beginning to be critical of ritual and wanted a more ethically and morally based religion.

So we see around 780 BCE, a prophet named Amos from the Kingdom of Judah suddenly overcome by what he believed was the Divine influence of Infinite Intelligence calling him to address this situation. It was written that whilst he didn't see himself as a prophet as he was shepherding his flock the Divine spoke to him. He experienced the Divine Spirit as a disruptive energising force that snatched him away from everything that was familiar to him.

You see, prior to this, the Hebrew prophets were not of a mystical nature. They didn't have any mystical aspect to their religion. They did not experience the Buddhist Enlightenment within. So, for this shepherd come prophet Amos, it was a totally different experience. He felt possessed by a power that seemed to come from outside of him but impacted inside of him, and it seemed to disrupt his normal way of thinking. His old way of thinking and of interpreting life events that had guided him all of life thus far was removed, insomuch that he began to see the futility of Israel's beloved religious rituals. He was tired of their sacrifice; he was tired of listening to the peoples chanting and devout strumming of harps.

He wanted instead to see justice, integrity, compassion, and humility as a central aspect of their faith, rather than what he saw as the false pride most Israelites had in what they saw as their unique relationship with the Divine compared to other religions. Which was very similar to how in this modern day the leaders of the Catholic Church see Catholicism for the Vatican believes that Catholicism is the only true religion. And in doing so in one foul swoop Amos delivered a severe blow to Israel's over-inflated sense of religious self-esteem, to Israel's religious ego.

He took on the nationalistic religious ego of Israel which bred self-interested behaviour and injustices towards others, and in its place, he promoted ethical behaviour. He was in fact encouraging the Israelites in *kenosis* that I mentioned previously, the process of emptying themselves.

Like the prophet Hosea, Amos demanded a greater spiritual awareness. He demanded that the Israelite people should no longer take their religion for granted and perform it in such a rote, ritualistic manner. He demanded that people become more conscious of what they were doing and how they were behaving. He was trying to make the people look beneath the veneer of ancient myths and ancient stories and emulate the empathy and compassion of God.

Both the prophets Amos and Hosea introduced what was to become an important new dimension in religion in Israel. They both believed and insisted that without good ethical behaviour ritual alone was worthless and that religion and religious ritual should not be used to inflate societal and church pride. They encouraged the abandonment of these negative aspects of human nature, an abandonment of the egotistical component of the human being and replacing it with a more mystical or cosmic approach.

Amos and Hosea were both basically encouraging the Israelites to examine their inner lives, to reflect and analyse their feelings towards others and the behaviours that came out of embracing these feelings, and to develop a deeper authentic spiritual vision based on inner reflection and contemplative introspection. Whilst many theologians have branded these two prophets as prophets of doom and destruction, the Talmud, the primary source of Jewish religious law claims that Hosea was the greatest prophet of his generation, and whilst the

Qur'an of the Islamic faith mentions only some prophets by name, many Muslim scholars such as Ibn Ishaq speak of Hosea as one of the true Hebrew prophets of Israel.

To define authentic religion or authentic spirituality in its deepest meaning you could say that:

> *"Meaningful and authentic religion or spirituality must at its highest point of achievement lead ultimately to a person's realization of the oneness of a person's inner nature or inner self with that which is the innermost aspect of the universe, the Cosmic Creative Spirit of Universal Consciousness".*

I call it the Cosmic Creative Spirit because to refer to it simply as God merely puts a theological umbrella over it, and in some ways, it almost seems to humanise God. The cosmic nature of God and the cosmic oneness between Divinity and humanity is the true meaning of religion as taught and understood by those of the hierarchy of mystical sages and initiates both in Eastern religions and in some Western Religions throughout the ages, those people who had already received and understood experientially the full knowledge pertaining to their Divine Nature and the spiritual power that comes with it. So, the sages' teachings were not just mere philosophical concepts or intellectualised doctrines and dogmas of the faith. They were teachings based on lived experience.

Regardless of whether it was the early Gnostic Christian, the Buddhist, the Hindu, the Jewish or the Muslim Mystic (the Sufi), all the original mystical pioneers of these faiths were birthed into their spiritual journeys with the intent and determination to discover the real self which is inherently and intrinsically immortal. The hidden self, which, though sometimes hidden in the mystery of His parables, was present in the life and teachings of Jesus, regardless of how much the church has obscured it and dumbed it down through a literal interpretation of the scriptures.

The teachings of the Axial sages were not of a religious nature but more so focused on firstly helping people discover their belief in a higher nature or power, then having discovered it, helping them to authentically live out in their own life the character qualities of that power, a compassionate and ethical based life in accord with the nature of that Divine power.

> *"In its essence you could say that the Axial Age was a journey into Divine Truth, as opposed to mere theological truth. It was a spiritual journey out of hereditary ritualised religious behaviour, into practical consistent moral and ethical behaviour, with the qualities of tolerance and compassion towards the rest of humanity at the forefront of that journey".*

The teaching of the sages centred on the fact that when you embrace a disciplined empathy and a sympathetic and compassionate approach to the rest of humankind, you transcend the ego driven psychological barriers of self interest in the mind. Barriers that have been present in humanity for aeons due to the self-defensive, self-survivalist nature of humanity that emerged with the psychological fall from oneness with the Divine that occurred in early creation. A fall which is documented in mythical type stories such as Adam, Eve, and the serpent in the Garden of Eden in the Old Testament and in other spiritual writings such as the Pistis Sophia, a Gnostic text discovered in 1773, believed to have been written around the 3rd or 4th century A.D.

Ever since human beings living in caves, emerged from the fortress like environment of their physical existence, or ever since humanity emerged out of the psychologically fortified existence of their Garden of Eden lifestyle, that self-protecting nature of humanity, the survival of the fittest and fastest, the me first attitude, has continually risen when human beings are threatened by animal predators or what they interpret as hostile human behaviour.

However, the sages taught that if we through transcendence discard that hereditary mindset and methodically cultivate a whole new way of thinking, that whole new way of thinking would cause us to experience a whole new state of consciousness and with that a whole new way of behaving towards the rest of humanity.

This was what the Apostle Paul was referring to when speaking to the Roman people he said, "be transformed by the renewing of your Mind". Renewing it to what? To right and righteous thought processes. And how is that transcendence evidenced in a practical sense in daily life without necessitating one's running off to a Buddhist monastery? It really is so simple.

In a practical sense it means that every time we find ourselves in the position of potential verbal or physical conflict and are tempted to say something hostile to or about a fellow human being, or do something hostile to a fellow human being, we consider how would we feel if that was being done to us. We understand and accept that this is not the God way of thinking and behaving, the "do unto others as you would have them do unto you" way, and in that moment make a conscious choice to refrain from participating in our ego's hostile inclination. Seemingly hard at first yes, for some, but change will happen as habitual personality patterns are broken.

That simple step initiates a moment of transcendence, we cross over into a state of ectasis which is not some kind of exotic transcendental trance. It is by choice, a stepping out from old personality patterns of behaviour, whether they be of a mythical, hereditary or the common well practiced self-developed kind, and instead embrace ethical and moral practices in our response to life events, particularly if they are of a combative nature. It is a process which when embraced will see a new sense of relief and joy enter our life. We start to really feel good about ourselves.

The Axial Sages of those ages trashed self-interest, trashed selfishness, placing any hint of their potential arising in subservience to ethical behaviour, putting love, compassion, and kindness at the top of their character quality intentions. For them, this was what authentic religion was supposed to be, a life continuously lived according to the Golden Rule, a life that would cause them not to transcend to some defined place such as heaven, rather to a new defined state of being in the present moment, a state of ecstasy. They were not saying that all theology should be scrapped. They were basically saying that conventional religious theology and some of the associated beliefs about God and how God works were ultimately wrong.

Christianity, for example, placed great store in doctrinal orthodoxy and so many Christian leaders even in this modern day could not imagine their religion without its institutional and conventional beliefs. Which is not a problem if a dogma addresses profound spiritual truth. But the true test of the truth and resultant effectiveness of any of those dogmas is whether they bring out the character quality of compassion and tolerance or conversely the character qualities of indifference and belligerence. Belligerence and intolerance are prideful and unkind behaviours expressed in word or deed towards another human being. They are behaviours that the religion of Buddhism politely refers to as being "unskilful and unhelpful".

The Apostle Paul in the post-Axial early years of Christianity, in speaking to the Philippian people told them not to lay down the law about God and their beliefs, not to lay down the law about the incarnation, but urged them rather to practise kenosis, a self-emptying, a denial of self-interested behaviour in the first instance and that then they would discover spiritual truth. You see chasing after the tail of why something is happening and always focusing on who's to blame and at the same time wanting to exact justice by our own means, whether that be verbal or physical, prolongs the hurt or chaos in our own lives, we become ourselves trapped in our retributive mindset, leaving us continually engaged in the never-ending cycle of reactive response.

Reactive responding is judgementally responding and when Jesus said, "judge not less you be judged", He said that for a reason. Why? Because all the thoughts that we send out into the universe and the words that proceed from our mouth judgemental or otherwise, are energetic forces that are subject to the **Divine Law of Reciprocity** that I previously spoke of. What is that? It is a Divine Law or Divine Principle of cause and effect. Social psychologists describe its operation this way.

When someone does something to you either in speech or deed you will have a deep-rooted psychological urge to do something similar in return. Someone does something nice for you, you will have a deep-rooted psychological urge to do something nice for them in return. How many people have at some stage received an unexpected Christmas gift from someone attending their home and been extremely bothered that they did not have a gift to give that person in return? Bothered to a point where some will even scurry to find something in the house to regift to that person. Perhaps some gift never used such as what is the most common one, bath salts given to them from the previous Christmas.

However, the Law of Reciprocity equally applies if someone does something nasty to you. Someone hits you, the first thing you want to do is hit them back. Someone is angry at you; you get angry back at them. King David in the Old Testament understood this which is why he prayed:

"Let the words of my mouth (every word I speak) and the meditation of my heart (every thought I think), be acceptable in your sight Oh Lord".

So, does that mean that if we surrender to peace or seek peace rather than conflict or fight back, we are surrendering to the dysfunction and evil around us and regarding as acceptable the wrong behaviour of others? No of course not.

"To surrender to peace is to embrace the present moment and all it contains, without immediate demonstrative judgement in thought or deed of that thing or person who is disturbing us".

The key point in that phrase above is, "without immediate demonstrative judgement in thought or deed". This was the message of those early mystics and is the message that Jesus of the Christian faith, Muhammad of the Islamic faith, Gautama Buddha of the Buddhist faith, Confucius of Confucianism, all espoused, and the same message that many others spiritual masters over the centuries all attempted to portray and thus convey by their own life example.

Confucius, who did not even see himself as a religious leader rather a philosopher, emphasized personal and governmental morality, correctness of social relationships, justice, kindness, sincerity, and integrity. Confucianism was in its day part of China's social fabric, its way of life; to Confucians this behaviour was their religion. Communist ideology, China's current secular religion you could call it, is the enemy of Confucianism because it is designed in its practical application to control both the thought process and behavioural instincts of the individual completely. It disrupts the internal peace of most even if they are too fearful of retribution to admit it does.

Jesus preached "blessed are the peacemakers," because it is a Divine Principle with psychologically transformative qualities. He did not teach blessed are those who judge and react in a hostile manner to those who disagree with their opinion, or religion, or political or philosophical persuasion. A peacemaker is someone who reconciles people with each other, not one who riles people against each other. Jesus was called the **"Prince" of Peace**. Why?

Because He went further than simply by example reconciling people with each other, He took on the job of reconciling humanity with God, of psychologically reconciling and reconnecting the individual and Collective Mind of Humanity with the Mind of God. Not in the first instance reconciling a particular religious institution with a different one of differing beliefs, because Jesus knew if He could initiate the reconciliation of humanity's mind with God's Mind then religious reconciliation would just automatically flow from this.

He was the prototype of the Atonement process, the implementation of God's plan for the psychological redemption of all of humanity, demonstrating practical examples in his own life for us to follow as we choose to participate in that Atonement process. Practical examples such as sowing kindness, showing compassion, showing respect, showing courtesy; demonstrating a capacity to accept all manner of sinner and saint, prepared at the same time to admonish and encourage in a peace filled manner all to turn away from their hostile behavior, away from their antagonistic attitude towards other members of society, and embrace the oneness of the universe.

The practical life of Jesus was about rejecting all hostility towards others, and at the same time recognizing all human beings' equality in God's sight and potential for redemption, regardless of their ego driven hostile behavior.

Similarly, in the religion of Islam one of God's names according to the Qur'an is As-Salaam, which means peace. Moreover, the Qur'an states that the Prophet Muhammad was sent to the world as a gift of mercy to mankind, not a gift of murderous intent as promulgated by Islamic extremists. According to true Islam, peace is the rule and war is only an exception. The word *Islam* means "to surrender, to submit," and comes from the triliteral root *sin-lam-mim*, which can also mean "well-being, completion, freedom and peace." Linguistically then, the word *Islam* can be said to mean, "to surrender in peace."

Muhammad's religion was called Islam because it means "surrender". The core of Muhammad's teaching centred on an individual's existential surrender of their lives, which included their way of thinking and behaving to God's way of thinking and behaving. Not the Old Testament way of thinking and behaving in a retributive or vengeful way, as Islamic extremists espouse, but a new way of thinking and behaving. A way of compassionate surrender. It was all about a psychological surrender in the first instance, a surrender of mind, which would then initiate with Divine support a behavioural surrender.

Whilst the teaching of the Axial Age sages, mystics and prophets that came before him were slightly different in that they advocated a joint surrender of both thought and behaviour simultaneously, they knew that overall success was contingent on the surrender of thought, otherwise the new change in behaviour would not last. The prophets of Judea in the Axial Age, Amos, Hosea, and Jeremiah that I spoke of earlier, told the people that when they were threatened, firstly to scrutinise their own conduct. I would say, whenever we feel threatened by someone, psychologically or emotionally through their words and opinions, as well as perhaps physically, then before reacting, examine our own thoughts and opinions and see if there be any wicked, ungodly prejudices buried beneath them.

The Indian doctrine of Karma insists that all our deeds have long lasting consequences, and the Buddha insisted that the blaming of others without examining how our own failings might have contributed to a disastrous situation was in fact unskilful, unrealistic, and irreligious. The key to realistic examination of ourselves however must not be just a cursory mental glance at our own shortcomings. It must involve solitude, silence, and quiet reflection. To use a modern expression, "take some time out to chill" and in an emotionally detached way, to think about the situation.

What appears to be most important in the attitudes of many of the vocal elements in today's modern society is an earnest desire "to be right rather than to be truly righteous". With Divine Principles, which are really the threads that has been impregnated by Infinite Intelligence into the spiritual fabric known as this universe", this is not so. The most important thing to Divinity in designing them to sustain and support the ongoing functionality of the universe was "the sacredness and sanctity of life", all of life.

What is necessary in this modern day of ideological, political, and religious extremism is not more hostility and belligerence rather more self-denial, less self-interest, more compassion, less prejudiced judgement, and more empathy. Religion by itself certainly no longer cuts it. Religion without remorse is useless. Ideology no longer cuts it. Movements born out of ingrained bias no longer cut it. Some modern-day spiritual teachers of mystic orientation have seen this and have begun to teach it. We often still hear people use that age old term, "an eye for an eye".

However, Jesus in his time said that that maxim is no longer valid and never has been in God's thinking. In this modern age then, what should our response be to the verbal and physical hostility and violence of our times? Well, if you asked the Axial Sages and Prophets, they would probably give us this sage advice:

"All individuals must examine their own hearts (thoughts) to see if there be any wicked way or wicked intent in them. All must regularly undertake times of inner self-reflection on their inner reasoning, rather than merely outer reflection on their existing circumstances."

They would probably also say:

"People must first begin to examine their own behaviour, deal with the speck in their own eye, which is psychologically blinding them, before even considering attempting to remove the speck from another's eye".

Jesus put it this way as we see in the Book of Matthew, "you hypocrite, play actor, pretender, first remove the log out of your own eye, and then you will see clearly whether or how to take the speck out of your brother's eye." (Amplified Version). He was talking about having a good look at ourselves, and then changing our level of perception to one of a Divine level, a level emanating from our Divine nature rather than the carnal level it is now functioning at, the level of our lower nature.

How do we change our own psychological perception? We begin by deliberately perceiving and thus thinking differently in the first instance. We see things from God's point of view. We observe the situation at hand and then ask ourselves the question, "how would Jesus' handle this?"

This then changes the metaphysical vibration of the equation. It is first the mind, and then the motion. But here is the thing. It also works in reverse. As you specifically choose to behave differently your discernment or understanding of spiritual things will grow.

Eckhart Tolle the teacher said in his book The Power of Now:

"Humanity is now faced with a stark choice: evolve or die. If the structures of the human mind remain unchanged, we will always end up recreating the same world, the same evils, the same dysfunction."

Similarly, as occurred during the Axial Age, I believe similarly it will occur in the days ahead, that at a given time the world will come to see the futility of its current way of thinking and behaving. I would contend that the teachings of the Axial Age sages and of the latter-day spiritual teachers such as Jesus and Muhammad, point a way to the progressive achievement of Cosmic Consciousness for all, and that those teachings and those of like-minded masters are the only way of achieving lasting societal change, a way of freedom from the ideological and politically driven mess that society finds itself immersed in right now in this modern day.

If we continue to entertain or radically embrace the belief that certain individuals or groups in society are in essence evil, and that this necessitates a hostile response by ourselves, it will continue to isolate us one from another, cause distrust amongst each other and make the realization of our mutual cosmic connectedness unreachable, which in turn impacts greatly on the progressive achievement of cosmic unity that so many spiritual leaders have taught as the goal of the universe. The achievement of Cosmic Consciousness by all depends on our acceptance of the sacredness of all, and our embracing of the Divine principles of forgiveness, kindness, and compassion towards all.

Therefore, religious extremists who continually perpetrate violence against other faiths will never achieve Cosmic Consciousness, because Cosmic Consciousness involves acceptance and respect for all life in the universe regardless of a human being's religious preference, and an understanding of the sacredness and oneness of all life.

You see, contrary to what many people would believe, Muhammad, the spiritual founder of the Islamic faith accepted Jesus not only as the greatest of the prophets, but as standing on a spiritual level distinctly higher than that of Adam, Noah, and Moses. Muhammad, being aware of the tendency of some towards extremism said, "and we sent Noah and Abraham and placed in their seed prophecy and the Book; and some of them are guided, though many of them are workers of abomination".

Then he said, "we followed up their footsteps with our apostles and we followed them up with Jesus the son of Mary and we gave Him the gospel and we placed in the hearts of those who followed Him kindness and compassion". (Part 2 of the Qur'an. Translated from the Arabic by E.H. Palmer).

Muhammad regarded Jesus with veneration, and even went as far to call Him the "Spirit" and the "Word" and the "Messiah". All anti-Muslim advocates particularly those of Christian orientation need to reflect on this. The Islamic religion is not the problem. The problem lies with those ideologically and self-interested ego driven individuals who have hi-jacked the religion and the true teachings of Muhammad and turned them into an ideologically driven cause. Similarly with Christian White Supremacists, Christianity is not the problem. The biased and bigoted ego driven beliefs of the founders of the White Supremacist movement are the problem.

> "The Qur'an teaches, that whatever good reaches us is from Allah (God), but whatever of evil befalls us is from ourselves, or in another place puts it, whatever of misfortune befalls us, it is because of what our hands have earned. Meaning it comes about automatically in response to our own behaviour".

God does not punish us; we punish ourselves through our own behaviour. It is the Law of Reciprocity coming into play. If civil law doesn't have the mechanism in place to find you and punish you according to civil law, you eventually will be punished because Divine Law indicates you will return your own behaviour on yourself, that eventually your behaviour will come back and bite you. The Bible refers to that particular Divine law as one of the "Laws of the Spirit". Buddhism calls it the Law of Karma. Karma is an ancient Sanskrit word. In Buddhism Karma is the law of cause and effect at play whereby each individual creates his own destiny by his thoughts, words, and deeds.

According to the theory of Karma, you have a cupboard filled with Karma: personal Karmas, and cultural Karmas. Karma is that which involves the entire human race, and stems from both Hindu and Buddhist belief systems and is closely aligned in theory to the findings by the Carl Jung the psychoanalyst, who referred to this "cupboard of Karma" as the Collective Unconsciousness of humanity.

For the Buddhist and Hindu it is the process of Divine Principle, the Divine Laws that govern the universe in action, or simply said the realisation of the Golden Rule. It is the law of cause and effect or the social psychologist's Principle of Reciprocity in action. Spiritual masters of all faiths have long believed that physical and psychological behaviour influence metaphysical behaviour leading to specific consequences.

Holy Books such as the Bible and the Qur'an teach that neither the physical of the universe, nor the spiritual of the universe, nor the metaphysical of the universe can be separated. We are all functioning as one whole. You see:

> "Physics cannot be separated from metaphysics. To everything there is both an inner and an outer dimension. Metaphysical causes, plus physical causes, lead to consequences. Moral causes, plus physical causes, lead to consequences. Meta-physics plus physics leads to consequences".

It is a reminder that whilst society has made tremendous advances in science, scientists must come to understand that in the quest for increased scientific knowledge, there is a force beyond physics which governs and controls the physical consequences they are attempting to change; this force is controlled by what we call Infinite Intelligence, the Universal Mind of the cosmos.

On the microscopic level there is the mind of the individual, the mechanism for our own personal and individualised way of perceiving and thinking, but on the macroscopic level there is the God Consciousness, the God Mind of the universe, the God way of perceiving and thinking. The renowned scientist, Albert Einstein in speaking of this said, "I have a rapturous amazement at the harmony of natural law, which reveals an intelligence of such superiority that, compared with it, all the systematic thinking and actions of human beings are but an utterly insignificant reflection".

In this time of world political, social, and material uncertainty, as all generations in history at some time or other have realised, we can only conclude that our current way of doing things, of responding to life events, is just not cutting it. The Axial Sages developed and taught a compassionate and caring approach to their respective societies whilst the world around them was suffering in the most violent of circumstances. These sages were not meditating in monasteries or praying earnestly in great cathedrals but were living in frightful circumstances midst warring tribes and unmitigated violence and yet they found the answer.

They were not dreamers, they were not hopers merely hoping for change and relying only on regular ritualistic religion to relay their concerns to God, they were practical passionate priests of the day who sought and implemented spiritual and practical ways to bring about a new way of living in societal peace and prosperity.

Some were even involved in political structures, but always put the people before the personal and political, not just in word but also in deed. They saw that compassion and concern for everybody was the best policy and the only effective way to achieve lasting success. Displacing the old self-interest way and replacing it with an "other's first" way demands not an impressive time-consuming approach, but rather an all-consuming alternate attitudinal approach. A change of our attitude first, which precedes a change of action.

The Chinese Confucians of the Axial Age recognized the importance of making a deliberate choice to develop a new way or a new attitude to life which was designed to create what they called a "Junzi", a new psychologically developed human being, one with humane and ethical conduct at the forefront of their lives and a moral exemplar, including in all human relationships. They discovered that as they began not treating others carelessly or perfunctorily or selfishly, they transformed themselves and brought out a new level of holiness in themselves and the object of their attention.

This was the method of all the great sages of history including Jesus and Muhammad and the Buddha. Do unto others as you would have them do unto you. The sages demanded that every individual take responsibility for their own behaviour, that they become in the first instance self-conscious of their own behaviour, rather than simply always continually conscious and mostly critical of everyone else's behaviour.

In this modern day as society moves ahead in leaps and bounds digitally, militarily, politically, and economically, we must now once again develop not only a God Consciousness but also a global consciousness, for in their metaphysical essence both are intrinsically linked. Whether we appreciate it or not, the fact of the matter is that in this global society that exists, which the recent pandemic has borne witness to, if we develop and cultivate the reflective insights similar to those of the Axial Age, we too can play our part in what might go down in history as the most spiritually, socially, and technologically revolutionary period of humankind's evolutionary journey ever.

The Axial Sages of their time identified that empathy and sympathy and compassion cannot be confined to one individual or to one nationality, but that they had to cultivate what Buddhism calls an "immeasurable outlook", that extends to the ends of the earth without excluding anyone from its vision, and to adopt a new practically expressed respect for all of creation which, in this modern day is right now probably the most indispensable item necessary for a peace filled and prosperous global co-existence. If we want to change the course of our personal world or society, we must first see an inner dimensional change occur, to align our inner dimension, that which we cannot physically see, the world of spirit, with the outer dimension, that which we can see, the world of form.

We must embrace the interrelatedness of all sentient beings with each other and with the metaphysical. We must align our thinking and subsequent behaving with Divine Principle, the cosmic thread that created, sustains and continues to weave the moral fabric of this universe. If our inner dimension or thought life is misaligned with the spiritual dimension, there can be no hope for positive outcomes.

If we want to change our outer circumstances, we must first change our inner self and align that with Divine Law the outer dimension. This is how the ancient sages of the Axial Age saw it, and so responded accordingly. They transcended their rational thought process, the normal way of looking at and interpreting the events of the present moment, which of course at times took courage, but they knew they truly had Infinite Intelligence on their side. And if God is for us, who can be against us.

They cultivated the habit of not judging the present moment if it was impacting adversely on their own lives, and then taught others this new pathway of thinking and behaving that focused on responding to life according to Divine Law rather than reacting against life out of their own sense of lack. And then they set about adjusting their behavioural patterns towards each other until it simply became a new way of living. They had transcended firstly their thought process, which then was the catalyst for transcending their way of behaving and doing. This then automatically brought into play the creative powers of the universe to enable them to transcend their current socio-economic circumstances, as well as their existing level of intellectual knowledge, which resulted in an "evolution without extreme effort" in society.

The people of this Axial Age, through the seeds of truth planted in the teachings of the mystics and sages, had discovered the overall Divine purpose for humanity, and in that discovery, immersed in the peace of mind it brought with it, each and everyone's individual purpose in life was released to come forth to the surface of their lives and blossom.

First came the spiritual revelation of the Divine purpose for humanity, then came the psychological transformation, then came by choice, a pro-active demonstration of transformed behaviour, resulting in the physical restoration of all good things, the active participation of the Spirit of Grace and with that Divine blessing. It's about spiritual revelation, leading to psychological transformation, which initiates a pro-active purposeful determination to embrace behavioural change. This is how it works, it's as simple as this:

> *"Seek first through reflection, spiritual revelation, (Wisdom), from the Kingdom of God within you, which will lead to a psychological transformation, (a change of mind) and a pro-active purposeful determination to think and subsequently behave differently. Resulting in the restoration of all things psychological and physical through the active participation of Infinite Intelligence, the Spirit of Grace in one's life".*

Jesus simply put it this way, "but first and most importantly seek, aim at, strive after, His Kingdom and His righteousness, His way of doing and being right, the attitude and character of God, and all these things will be given to you also." (Matthew 6:33 Amplified Version).

> "Life is primarily a transitionary spiritual journey linked to a transitionary psychological and physical journey. It is not meant to be just a stop, start, and sometimes-stationary hectic physical journey only, a mentally draining journey of chance, containing elements of success and failure.
>
> We must come to understand and appropriate the metaphysical aspect of our eternal existence and not just the particularity or peculiarity of our temporary existence. We must come to understand the cosmic nature of life and not just the carnal nature of it. We must deliberately seek out the Divine Purpose in all our life circumstances, and not just stagnate in their seemingly purposeless appearance."

The Divine Purpose for Humanity
The Cosmological Mystery of Our Existence
The Three Stages

TWO

> "It is the ultimate purpose of Divinity for humanity to continuously evolve, physically, psychologically, and spiritually, for change is evidence of growth. If rather than embrace change and welcome it, we fear change, we will stifle growth, and thus stall the evolutionary cosmic journey of humanity".

Paul the Apostle, originally Saul of Tarsus, Tarsus in Cilicia, now in Turkey, is believed to have been born around 4 BCE and to have died around CE 62-64 in Rome Italy. Paul was one of the leaders of the first generation of Christians, and often considered by many religious historians to be the most influential leader after Jesus in the early evolution of Christianity. Not only was he a well-known and much loved and respected figure within the Christian community, but, because of his outspokenness and what was seen by some as his sometimes-radical way of interpreting the things of God and subsequent teaching, he also had many enemies and detractors in the religious fraternal, and in his day was not given as much respect by them as were other Apostles such as Peter and James.

However, his surviving writings have had an enormous influence on Christianity in the centuries following and to this present day. When the Apostle Paul recounted his conversion from being a persecutor of Christians to a devout Christian himself, he described his conversion process on the road to Damascus in this way. "I was caught up into paradise to the third heaven, whether in the body or out of the body I do not know, but I was caught up into Paradise and heard things that are not to be told that no mortal is permitted to repeat", speaking of the mysteries of God that had been revealed to him.

There are many instances in relation to mystery recorded in the Bible, in fact you could say the Bible is littered with both obvious and subtle references to mystery, especially throughout the New Testament, as we see in the life of Jesus where many times He spoke in parables because those who He was addressing were not ready, not spiritually mature enough, not intuitively receptive enough to receive or even understand the profound teachings He had come to deliver. Mystery surfaces even in Old Testament books such as the Books of Daniel, Amos, Job, Psalms, Proverbs, and others, which reveal that our life experience can in many instances be an ongoing confrontation with mystery, and it is the mystery that makes life entrancing and fascinating.

I believe however that God, whilst delighting in mystery, does accommodate our hunger for a revelation of truth about that which is hidden in a mystery, for none of us like secrets being kept from us, and as we read in one of the Wisdom books in the Old Testament, the Book of Proverbs, "it is the glory of God to conceal a thing: but the glory of kings to search it out." The Apostle Paul spoke of the mystery of life itself when in addressing the people of the City of Ephesus, saying that the mysteries of God were revealed to him by revelation, revelation simply being Divine Knowledge and Divine Truth given to one in intuitive reflective thought by God's Spirit.

Physicists will tell us that hidden away in every physical manifestation in the universe around us is mystery, and Quantum theory upon which much of modern physics is based, theory which has unleashed the whole realm of nuclear fission, has at its heart, say the physicists, a principle of indeterminism, a hidden principle. It states that we can never scientifically discover fully the truth about anything and that there is an element of hidden information about every subject we go into. But in sciences' evolutionary journey that never prevents most scientists from searching for deeper answers.

In terms of the evolution of our spiritual journey, God says when speaking about that which appears to be hidden in a mystery, whether in the Bible or just in the spiritual life generally, God through Jesus said, "seek and ye shall find, knock and the door shall be opened unto you, for everyone who seeks shall find."

You will see me at various times in this book use the expression, "the mystery of God's Cosmic plan for the universe," and very likely may at some stage ask yourself well what is that? What is this mysterious plan that God has set in place for the universe? It is very important for us to understand what it is because the Atonement process, that which brings us back into fellowship with the Light of God, prototyped by Jesus, through his life, crucifixion, and resurrection, was a key component of that mystery. So, in understanding the mystery we begin to fully understand what this whole crucifixion of Jesus and resurrection event that many people celebrate at Easter time each year was all about.

God's Cosmic plan for the universe, the primary essential teaching of the ancient masters since the beginning of time, the same teaching which for the most part was systematically removed from the original text in the construction of the Bible or if not totally removed then the parts remaining were selectively and carefully overwritten to hide their true meaning, was all about **"three mysteries."** Three mysteries that are the major cornerstones of God's Cosmic plan. Jesus refers to these mysteries in part when He said to His disciples as we read in the Book of Luke, "unto you it is given to know the mysteries of the Kingdom of God, but to others it is given only in parables."

There are three mysteries that form the basis of God's Cosmic Plan for the redemption of the universe, and I share them with you here. Mystery number one is **"the cosmology of an Outgoing"**, mystery number two is **"the cosmology of an Evolution"**, and mystery number three is **"the cosmology of a proposed Involution or Return"**. Cosmologies refer to the origin and development of the universe.

The **first mystery** contains information relating to the **Outgoing**. It speaks of how the universe was created by the Outgoing of God into manifested form, the Outgoing of God's creative life stream into the void that existed, which saw the creation of this universe, as we now know it, including the parts we have seen or are aware of, and the parts we have not seen and are not aware of.

That life stream or energetic force or essence that created the universe is referred to in the book of Genesis as "the Word." It says, "In the beginning was the Word, and the Word was with God, and the Word was God." It's not talking about the Bible, which is sometimes described by the church as the Word of God, because the Bible did not exist in the beginning. The Word that Genesis refers to is the spoken creative life stream of God, an essence, a creative energetic life force.

The **second mystery** contains information relating to the **Evolution** or journey of the universe. The main thrust of it centres on the psychological separation that came about after that manifested universe, that Outgoing that came from God, stepped out from being under the psychological umbrella of Light and repositioned itself under the psychological umbrella of Darkness. The only slight reference to this mystery that survived in the Catholic construction of the Bible is what we see in the Garden of Eden story, which has no cosmic overtones and only takes the form of a sort of mythical or archetypal explanation on how sin came into the world.

That story is historically referenced by most churches only as "the Fall," and that's all that many Christians know about it; that the story of Adam and Eve in the Garden of Eden is all about the fall of humankind out of a life of grace and into a life of sin. It is much more than that.

That second mystery, the Evolution of humanity, yes it does involve a type of fall, but it involves a fall from a psychologically connected state, a state of one mindedness between the Mind of God and the Mind of Humanity that God had created. A fall into a state of psychological separation, and with regards to true Wisdom, which is a chief character quality of the Mind of God, a fall into psychological poverty, that saw the birth of an ongoing self-survivalist attitude to life come into play. The fall involved a separation of the human mind from the God Mind, or you could say a separation of the human thinking and perceptual process from the God thinking and perceptual process, and the resultant imbalanced thought processes and subsequent unbalanced behaviours that came out of it.

That second cosmological mystery then details the commencement of humanity's journey out of that fallen state back to God, its source, and the process on how it would happen, namely through the appearance and activity of Him who would lead humanity out of it, the man Jesus, God in flesh. Why God in flesh? Because the carnal or physically visible lifestyle was now after "the fall" the only state of being that humankind understood. It had lost all contact with the invisible or spirit side of its existence. It had lost its intuitive cosmic connection with God, and so God in the flesh in the form of Jesus, had to come to meet humanity at humanity's level of existence or being, and restore the connection.

But it had to be done in a way they could understand, a human way, which was through Simple Awareness, using the sensory perceptions, of seeing, hearing, and touching. That in seeing they might understand.

The **third mystery** pertaining to God's Cosmic plan for the universe references the **Involution** of everything, the return to God of all that was manifested in the first mystery, and all that evolved over time in the second mystery, back to that from which it originally came out of, the Word, the creative source or life stream of God. The Involution can be likened in a physical sense to the return of the uterus to normal size after childbirth. The Apostle Paul spoke of it albeit in a mystery in his Letter to the Romans where he said, "I consider our present sufferings," meaning this evolutionary life on earth, "insignificant compared to the glory that will soon be revealed to us," referring to the final stage of the third mystery, the Involution or Return of all our Souls to the bosom of God.

He then went on further to say, "we know that the whole creation has been groaning as in the pains of childbirth," referring to the ongoing evolution of humanity and the suffering it endures, during the second mystery, "as we wait eagerly for our adoption to sonship, the redemption of our bodies." The redemption of our bodies that Paul spoke of is that third mystery, the Involution or Return; it's the return of our Soul to the universal source from which it originally came in the beginning, the same source whose breath gave it life and whose essence has sustained it in its evolution. Christianity has dumbed that down to the simple teaching that "when we die if we have been a good Christian we will go to heaven". It is much more than that.

There are numerous stories in the Bible about this separation and redemption principle at work usually centred on the alienation of a singular human or a group of humans from God and the redemptive process that restores them to their original state. We see it in the story of Adam and Eve, we see it in the story of Moses and the Israelites, and in the story of Joseph, and we see it in the story of the prodigal son in the New Testament. The spiritual mystery hidden in these stories having been dumbed down theologically and interpreted merely as the suffering of one individual or a nation.

Now it is necessary to understand the following. The early church fathers of the Catholic Church have either through poor theological interpretation, or through deliberate scriptural manipulation, changed the true meaning of the Outgoing, the Evolution, and the Return to basically mean we are born, (the Outgoing), we live according to Catholic beliefs, (the Evolution), and if we do this, then when we physically die, we will journey to heaven, (the Return). The Catholic Church, and to a slightly lesser extent certain branches of the Islamic religion, have taken Divine purpose, the proposed psychological and metaphysical journey of humanity through the realms of consciousness back to its source, and turned it into a physical journey into heaven, a physical place, or paradise as Islamists call heaven.

All conditional on the individual's adherence to church law or religious jurisprudence rather than Divine Law. And that was the point at which life-changing authentic religion was institutionalised and lost.

Concerning these three mysteries, what is self-evidently true in this ancient wisdom of a variety of different faiths, is that when the universe has completed its Evolution, mystery number two, which is the stage in which the universe is progressing through right now, then, all of humankind who have traversed their conscious existence aligned with Infinite Intelligence, will ultimately return to their source, and regain their oneness with God, their oneness with Universal Consciousness, their oneness with the life stream of God, the Word, from which they originally came out of.

That is when as the Bible expresses it those who are living will be caught up in the clouds and the dead "in Christ" shall rise. That will be at a time of God's choosing and will initiate the end of this world, as we know it. What comes next after the end of this world? Whilst no one knows for certain, the Apostle John, a man of mystic disposition who more than any other Apostle understood the three mysteries of God gave us what might be an indication as we see written in the Book of Revelation, "then I saw a new heaven and a new earth, for the first earth had passed away."

However in terms of humanity's evolutionary journey through consciousness as spoken of by spiritual masters of all religious persuasions over time, what all this simply means is that every individual, during this time of Evolution that we are in now, must recover from this state of psychological alienation from God or separation from Source that occurred in "the fall' and remerge as a new creation manifesting in their life the attributes of the Divine nature, the Fruit of the Spirit as they are described in the New Testament.

What are the Fruit of the Spirit? You could simply say they are the character qualities evidenced in the life of Jesus, given to the universe at the beginning of its created existence, which was the Outgoing, lost in the separation, in its ongoing Evolution, but able to be regained through living a life in line with **Divine Principle** or Divine Law.

The longer this takes in terms of chronological time, then the longer the cycle of birth and death will continue in the world for all those who have not yet reached an individual readiness to cross over. Who have not reached the highest level of consciousness in their earthly walk, through perhaps not having made the necessary karmic restitution if it is required, or who have not embraced the Atonement, who have not completed their evolutionary journey of consciousness.

Jesus himself had reached that point of readiness to cross over hence His not so final physical death evidenced in His resurrection. He had conquered death. The Book of Corinthians tells us that the last enemy to be conquered as the final act of our psychological evolutionary journey is death.

Jesus had completed the first two stages or passed through the first two mysteries and as such He was resurrected and returned to the Father, the source from whence He came, completing the third mystery, the Involution, the return to his source. In doing so He left His earthly life journey, what He did and what He said, as a lived witness and example for us to follow, that we too might be imitators of Christ. He lived His life, everything He said and did, and every attitude He embraced, in accordance with **Divine Principle**, the "it is written" principle, and then he received the prize, a cosmological reunification with the creative source and sustaining power of his earthly existence, known in spiritual writings as the Word.

> *"Life is meant to be centred on a psychological transformation of the self, that initiates a subsequent evolutionary transition in consciousness. Much of humanity has got it all backwards, focusing, primarily in an ego driven and me-centric way, on transforming their personal self-interests, their temporal visible present circumstances, giving nary a glance at the invisible, eternal, and psychological nature of their existence".*

The Transcendent Nature and Unlimited Potential of Humanity

THREE

> "Success, like happiness, cannot be pursued; it must ensue, and it only does so as the unintended side-effect of one's personal dedication to a cause greater than oneself, or as the by-product of one's surrender to a person other than oneself".
>
> Viktor Frankl

Viktor Emil Frankl, was born 26th March 1905 and passed 2nd September 1997 aged 92 years. He was an Austrian neurologist, psychiatrist, philosopher, and author of some 39 books and numerous scientific psychology papers, more commonly remembered as the author of Man's Search for Meaning, a best-selling literary work. Frankl was the founder of what is known as logotherapy, a school of psychotherapy which deals primarily with the concept that the search for meaning and purpose in life, is the central motivational force in all human beings. Logotherapy comes out of existential and humanistic psychology theories.

He was also a Holocaust survivor, the name given to people who survived the Holocaust, the word Holocaust commonly used to describe the persecution and attempted annihilation of the Jewish people by Nazi Germany and its allies before and during World War 2 in Europe and North Africa. What was Nazi Germany? The term Nazi was the name given to all those German people who were members of Germany's National Socialist Workers Party, which in real terms was the German Communist Party, membership which eventually became highly necessary if one wanted to avoid being killed.

A term that was also used for this reborn German Communist Party was the Third Reich, a name which Adolf Hitler chose to use in January 1933, as he saw himself and his party as the presumed successor of the medieval and early modern Holy Roman Empire of 800 to 1806 (the First Reich) and the German Empire of 1871 to 1918 (the Second Reich). Hitler seeing himself similarly as did Charlemagne, or Charles the Great as he was called, the medieval emperor who ruled much of Western Europe from 768 to 814. Charles the Great with regards to his personal opinion of himself, described himself as, "the most serene, crowned by God, great and pacific emperor, governing the empire given him".

It was a term that was later discarded because it was too clumsy for Charlemagne to say. Hitler simplified it also by adopting for himself the title Fuhrer, meaning "absolute authority". Such was the egoic demon driven psychopathic madness of the man.

The Holocaust was the genocide of some six million Jews, around two-thirds of Europe's Jewish population, carried out ruthlessly and with unwavering determination by Nazi Germany using various means including pogroms, which are orchestrated violent riots aimed at the massacre of ethnic groups, as well as mass shootings, and physical extermination through abusive labour in concentration camps; which basically involved working a person to such a point of exhaustion that they subsequently died.

Those who, through sheer human willpower refused to die in this manner, were summarily executed on masse using gas chambers. In his book Man's Search for Meaning, Frankl tells how he survived the Holocaust by taking a psychological approach and finding personal meaning in every moment of the experience, which gave him the will to live and press on.

Frankl's interest in psychology surfaced while he was in junior high school. So compelling was it, that he began taking night classes on applied psychology, and further to this, even as a teenager, he began contacting in writing those involved in psychiatric science, people such as Sigmund Freud.

After his graduation from high school in 1923, he went on to enrol in the University of Vienna where he studied medicine. But due to his leaning towards psychology, as part of his studies he specialised in the subjects of neurology and psychiatry, with a very keen interest in the topic of depression and its capacity to drive some extremely depressed people to commit suicide. Whilst still in school as his interest in this subject deepened, he felt led to organise youth counselling centres to address what was at the time, the high number of teen suicides occurring amongst his fellow classmates, who either suicided or were having suicidal thoughts particularly during the period when the end of the year report cards came out.

It was purely voluntary on his part, done as an act of service to his fellow students, with no thought or desire for any kind of financial recompense for his involvement. He used his study and lesson breaks to go out and actively recruit others for this act of voluntary service, and he also elicited the help of outside trained psychologists to help in consultation and counselling sessions. His efforts paid dividends, for in the school year of 1931, for the first time not one student committed suicide.

After obtaining his medical degree he gained work experience at the Steinhof Psychiatric Hospital in Vienna, which was opened in 1907 but was renamed after renovations in 2001 as the Otto Wagner Hospital, where his major focus was in treating suicidal women who were being admitted there. Around 1937, approximately one year before the German troops with the aid of Austrian Nazis, marched into Austria in 1938 to take control and annex the German speaking nation for the Third Reich, perhaps intuitively knowing what was to follow, Frankl resigned from his position at the Steinhof Hospital and went on to begin his own private practice. He was right in his anticipation of what was to come under the German Nazi occupation.

In 1938 an extensive network of facilities was established by the German Nazi authorities for the documentation, observation, evaluation and subsequent selection and isolation of all children and adolescents whose lineal parentage, social behaviour, school assessments, employer information (if applicable), and or disabilities, did not comply with the standards set by Nazi ideology.

By 1942, 72 percent of newborns in Vienna were documented within their first year of life. As well as this, every person, adult, or child, who contacted or met with a health institution of any kind, was systematically recorded into a hereditary data base. It was not a safe time to even visit your local general practitioner for a health check-up. Since part of the Steinhof Hospital, where Frankl had previously worked, contained a children's clinic, between 1940 and 1945 those children and adolescents who did not pass the "Nazi ideology assessment criteria", were admitted and became unwitting subjects of medical experiments and victims of nutritional and psychological abuse.

Subsequently the Nazi Child Euthanasia Policy was implemented, whereby any child or adolescent who failed the test was killed if not by experientially induced disease, starvation, or deliberate exposure to the elements, then alternately by lethal injection or through gas poisoning. Their brains were then preserved in jars and housed in the hospital.

The German Nazi party had a phrase they used to describe these human beings, *Lebensunwertes Leben* which meant, "a life unworthy of life". This was a designation given to any class of individuals who the Nazis felt had no right to live because they did not fit in with Nazi ideology. They were thus targeted to be euthanised by the state. This inhumane concept was a key component of the Nazi Party's ideological plan and eventually helped lead to the establishment of concentration camps and the reality of the Holocaust itself.

It was similar, but more immediate in outcome than another Nazi policy called *Untermensch*, a word used as a Nazi term for non-Aryan "inferior people" often referred to as the masses from the East, which included all Jews, Slavs, and all Black People. Hence after the Nazis annexation of Austria in 1938 Frankl found himself extremely limited in his capacity to treat patients, the reason being that he was Jewish.

In 1940 he joined the Rothschild Hospital, which at that time was the only hospital left in Vienna that was still admitting Jewish people, taking on the position as head of the Neurology Department, where he focused on helping numerous patients avoid this Nazi euthanasia programme. In terms of the adult population, the Nazi programme specifically targeted mentally disabled people, which did include however perfectly healthy Jewish people, the Nazis having branded all Jewish people as mentally disabled so that they could be exterminated according to Nazi ideology.

This apart from his own Jewish heritage made Frankl a prime target for the Nazi agenda and in 1942, not more than 12 months after marrying, both Frankl and his wife, as well as the rest of his birth family were sent to the Theresienstadt concentration camp, where his father not long after died from starvation and pneumonia.

In 1944, Frankl and the surviving members of his family were taken to the Auschwitz concentration camp, where his mother and brother were gassed. His wife, Tilly Grosser, later died of typhus in Bergen-Belsen concentration camp. Following the American and Allied Forces liberation of Nazi occupied Europe and the war's ending, Frankl became head of the neurology department of the Vienna Polyclinic Hospital and established a private practice in his home.

If there was one significant aspect of his work that stood out more than others, it was his dogged determination that previous psychotherapeutic approaches, that he saw as being so dehumanising to the patient, needed to be done away with. He advocated that in their place, as a matter of urgency, a policy of compassionate re-humanization rather than dehumanisation needed to be officially adopted in all psychotherapeutic services.

Then on September 2nd, 1997, Viktor Frankl, a man who had opportunity to have his theories regarding the way to find purpose and meaning in life, the way to transcend the adverse circumstances of not only our individual existence, but also the psychological and physical malaise of our societal existence, tested in the crucible of Nazi concentration camps, and having discovered his own purpose during this time, died peacefully at the age of 92 years.

During his post-concentration camp life, in his work as a neurologist and psychologist, Frankl founded what he called the field of Logotherapy, which was later dubbed the "Third Viennese School of Psychology", following Sigmund Freud and Alfred Adler, the Austrian originators of the first two schools. The concept of Logotherapy was developed in and through Frankl's personal experience in the Theresienstadt Nazi concentration camp.

His years spent there deeply affected his understanding of reality and non-reality and the true meaning of life, including what it is that causes some human beings to fall by the wayside in their journey through life, unable to cope, and for many so seriously unable to cope psychologically that they choose not to go on with life physically, and yet with others caught up in similar circumstances, to in some seemingly supernaturally empowered way, find the will to press on. To press through mentally and physically and come out even stronger on the other side.

What is it that enables certain people to cope, to quietly embrace what are seemingly impossible circumstances, psychologically or mentally accept them, and then use the motivation appropriated to propel them successfully through to a positive outcome? Logotherapy literally means "therapy through meaning". The name coming out of Frankl's conviction that even amidst suffering a human being has the potential to use that suffering as a means of transcending to good outcomes.

Logotherapy is a school of psychological thought and a philosophy based on the idea that all human beings are subconsciously strongly motivated to live purposefully, and meaningfully, and that meaning in life is not birthed in existing circumstances but comes through responding authentically and humanely as a matter of habit, to not just life's challenges, but also to the world around us in general terms.

You could say that Frankl's school of Logotherapy was based on the idea that the universe evolves, circumstances evolve, situations arise, some good, some not so good, joy arises, grief arises, sadness arises, chaos arises, peace arises, positivity arises, and negativity arises, and how we respond in all situations is pre-determined by the attitude and habits of response that we have pre-embraced through our life preceding the circumstances that are causing us difficulty in the present moment. Whether or not we have psychologically programmed and through disciplined consistency, built purpose filled intent as a regular habit into our lives, or whether we have not.

We must remain acutely aware that problems will always arise for all individuals in the universe as humanity progressively evolves through the various stages of consciousness that I spoke of in the previous chapter. Why? Because at times life is in fact a spiritual warfare for the soul of humanity, and during this war some will get washed away mentally and emotionally by the human or principality and power induced circumstances they are encountering; and yet others, such is the platform of psychological programming and disciplined habit that has been established in their life thus far, will "transcend their existing situation" and use those winds and waves of adversity that are buffeting their ship of life to propel their safe passage to future freedom and peace.

We read in the Bible, the Apostle Paul in addressing the citizens living in an uncertain existence at the time said, "we wrestle not just with flesh and blood (with human beings and circumstances), but against principalities and powers and the forces of darkness in the universe". Paul was saying that this is both a spiritual and a physical world we live in, it is both carnally and cosmically influenced, and that whilst sometimes people are the cause of our problem many times the powers of darkness in their efforts to stall your evolutionary journey into a higher level of conscious existence are the instigators of our problem, manifesting their workings through a willing participant.

He was saying don't blame the "participant", hold them accountable yes, but in the first instance blame the principality or power that is in an ego influencing way encouraging that person to behave as they are behaving. Suffering is not necessary for us to spiritually evolve, but at times it will happen, and when it does, we need to be vigilant and prepared for when it does. You see:

"Life is basically an existential psychological and physical vacuum looking for something or someone to suck into it, to fill that void of mental and physical isolation and separateness from its source".

Looking for something or someone that will bring practical peace, positive purpose, and enduring clarity of thought, rather than just continuous psychological, physical, and emotional discomfort, unrest, and confusion. But if we have given our life nothing to suck into that void except unrest and confusion and lack of wisdom, through wrong thinking processes, then life will continue to manifest unrest and confusion and lack of wisdom as difficulties occur; for in the outworking of Universal Law, "like produces like". Lack of preparedness equates to lack of any kind of resourceful, right, righteous, wise and timely response.

That existential vacuum will manifest primarily as a state of boredom, and so your life in a practical or physical sense will search out something, anything, to relieve that boredom. From a psychological point of view your life will take whatever it is "given in the moment" or, and this is a big or, whatever the mind is programmed to believe as reality or truth, and life will run with that. Alternately it will reject whatever is being given it in the moment, in that it will knock it out of the park, and substitute in its place that which is more real to it than this illusionary disruptive influence or circumstance that is trying to enter its space of consciousness. What is more real to it? It is that which you have pre-programmed your mind with, which is more real to you than the interloper which is trying to hijack your thoughts.

And it all comes back to the state of habitual preparedness that one has psychologically banked up until this time; what beliefs and attitudes and habits one has continually embraced and consistently lived as an act of spiritual and psychological preparedness for any warfare that may come their way at a future time. Life will respond, sometimes with little effort on our part, according to our psychological state of preparedness, "our state of mind". It will be simply automatic.

A life void of an attitude of prioritising and embracing Infinite Intelligence (Divine Wisdom) in all situations, a prioritised state sometimes referred to as a state of Buddha Mindedness or a Spirit Led Life, will embrace purely the Simple Awareness way of interpreting and responding to the circumstances it is confronted with. (I explain in more detail what Simple Awareness is in Chapter 7). Life will embrace the same tired, fruitless old way of perceiving and behaving that it always has, but, if that life has remained psychologically vigilant, having already tilled and fertilised the "soil of the mind" so to speak, if your life has developed the art of a Cosmic Conscious existence, the right road to be travelled will automatically be chosen, the habitual Simple Awareness thought pattern will be transcended, and Cosmic Conscious thought, the mother of Wisdom, Infinite Intelligence will appear and take charge.

The Apostle Paul of the Christian faith said in speaking of the forces of darkness that influence our way of thinking and thus behaving, "be aware, be vigilant, your adversary the devil prowls around like a lion seeking someone to devour". To be aware and vigilant in simple terms means to "be prepared".

And in terms of cultivating this habitual preparedness the Prophet Muhammad of the Islamic faith taught it this way. "The more we are committed to abiding by God's laws, the greater our container for *Iman* becomes, (Iman being our mental conviction of our oneness with Divinity), for without *Iman*, then *Islam* (our religion) is like a body without a soul, it is lifeless and inflexible". Sadly, we see so much of this evidenced in institutionalised religion in this modern day, its container of *Iman* is empty.

Outer preparedness through ongoing adherence to Divine Law and an inner sense of oneness with Divinity are like threads joining to create an unbreakable braid. Our religion then, whether it be of the Eastern or Western kind becomes a life of *Ihsan* as it is termed in the Islamic religion, "one of spiritual excellence and perfection producing circumstantial excellence". We have transcended the psychological separateness from Divinity that we have existed in thus far, and both the inner and the outer dimensions of our life become as one positive and purposeful state of being. And Ishan has a primary dimension, which is:

"Being consistently present, by being God conscious in all our present states of mind and God conscious in all our physical circumstances".

It is basically what Christianity would describe, but few Christians practice consistently, as a life lived in the Spirit, or Mindful Christianity as it is sometimes described in the modern day, which includes having "no fear or worry thoughts or anxiousness for tomorrow" as Jesus in the New Testament expresses it.

What we must understand is that when we are no longer able to physically change a situation, we are challenged to change ourselves, or change the approach we are taking, changing the approach of interpreting the situation from the lens of Simple Awareness to a metaphysical one, a state of Cosmic Awareness, one of looking at the situation through the lens of God. That is the only alternate pathway out of it, there is in fact no other option. If our state of preparedness thus far is unable to change a situation, perhaps it would be wise to upgrade our state of preparedness. You see:

"There is a space or gap between circumstantial stimulus and our response, and in that infinitely invisible microscopic present moment it is in our power to choose our response rather than have other forces choose it for us".

The type of response we make will be in accord with our mental and spiritual state of preparedness, and in our response lies our potential for some sort of growth of our consciousness which will enhance our lives. If our state of preparedness has been voided of Divine Wisdom, relying continually on Simple Awareness alone to deal with adverse circumstances, our level of consciousness will decrease, but if our life in a thinking and behavioural sense has had an ongoing underlying platform of Godly Wisdom sustaining it, and we choose Godly Wisdom in that moment, our state of consciousness will be enhanced, and we will evolve to a higher level of conscious awareness or presence, and with that a higher level of sustained circumstantial success.

Life is all about filling the psychological and practical vacuum in our existence with things eternal not things temporal, and if this is happening then life will automatically bring forth circumstances and results in accord with all things eternal, in accord with Divine Principle or Universal Divine Law.

The Divine Law of Reciprocity or the Law of Reciprocal Response says, "like produces like". If our life preparedness has primarily been about everything temporal or carnal, and our eternal or cosmic existence has been neglected, then life will, to relieve this ongoing subconscious sense of boredom, bring about a continuous cycle of replacing those things that are temporal as they rust and decay, with more temporal things, and it will continue this way, new material things, new experiences, new relationships, an endless cycle of rust and decay and replacement, and then we physically die having never reached a state of consciousness higher than that of Simple Awareness, and the legacy we leave behind for humanity is simply one which too shall eventually rust and decay.

Between circumstantial stimulus and our response there is a silent space, and in that space lies Wisdom or Infinite Intelligence, the power to choose a right response. Our response must come out of the Wisdom of Infinite Intelligence because in our response lies our growth and freedom, our transcendence to a higher state of consciousness, a higher level of being.

The Buddha describes that silent space in the following way, which interestingly aligns with a common saying most people have used at some time in their lives. In discussing say with an agitated friend, a critical decision, that they must make in relation to a difficult situation, the friend might say, "look, just take a deep breath and have a think about it". In describing the act of meditation, with regards to that silent space or gap between deep breaths the Buddha said:

> *"Whilst sitting silently, just watching your breath, there is an inhalation, then a gap (a silent space) and then an exhalation; then an inhalation, a gap, and then an exhalation. That gap is the most mysterious phenomenon inside you. When the breath comes in and stops and there is no movement, (inner and outer stillness), that is the point where one can meet God", Infinite Intelligence the mother of all Wisdom".*

The Old Testament Book of Ezekiel also speaks of this gap in thinking that enables Divine Wisdom to express itself. The Prophet Ezekiel through the Spirit said, "the people of the land have practised extortion and committed robbery. They have oppressed the poor and needy and have exploited the foreign resident without justice. I searched for a man among them to repair the wall and "stand in the gap before me" on behalf of the land, so that I should not destroy it. But I found no one". That gap is the one the Buddha was speaking of. It's a state of "no mind". It's the pause between breaths in meditation. It's that time of stillness of body and all thought.

In the Shaivite tradition of the Hindu religion, the Creative aspect of Infinite Intelligence that one can meet with in a pause in the thinking process is referred to as Shiva, the Supreme Lord who creates, protects, and transforms the universe. Lord Shiva who is also regarded as the patron god of meditation, yoga, and the creative arts, put it this way in speaking of that gap between exaltation and inhalation:

"As long as you are breathing, I reside in you: the moment you stop breathing you reside in me".

You see physical things human and non-human eventually decay, rust away, dissipate, disappear, or dissolve, because they are visible and thus time bound, they transcend backwards, back into a non-created state, they dissolve into dust, into nothingness; whilst the things of the mind and spirit (the soul) are continuous and sustained because they are timeless, which means they remain long after our physical body has ceased functioning. As our bodies are sustained and grow through correct nourishment and care, so too do the things of the Soul, whilst we are physically alive, which enables them to transcend us forward and to grow in Grace.

But, and once again this is a big but, only if they, the things of the Soul (those of the mind and spirit), are fed the right food. If fed, deliberately or unintentionally the wrong food (bad thoughts, habits, and behaviours), they remain at a stationary level of awareness and thus stifle our growth in consciousness. But here's the difference between the body and the things of the Soul. When the body dies it disappears into nothingness, but the Soul continues in a state of somethingness. The essence of the Soul never, whether we are physically alive or physically dead, disappears completely.

When we are alive and breathing the things of the mind, whilst appearing to be gone away are all simply locked away in our memory safety deposit box until the ego decides it is time to make a withdrawal to use them either to disturb our peace (bad memories) or to give us a counterfeit substitute for true peace (good memories).

Alternately they just stay hidden, and if they are what is termed bad memories, finally resurface on our physical death bed in the form of what are known as "regrets of the past", or if they are good memories, "reminiscences of the good times". In terms of regrets of the past it is almost as if the Soul is trying to cleanse itself before it proceeds without our body on its cosmic journey.

Just to digress slightly but to give the reader greater understanding of how institutionalised religion has in certain ways corrupted the practical implementation of the truth of the Divine purpose. This cleanse the soul scenario is how an aspect of the Sacrament of Penance in the Catholic Church, known as Absolution or the Last Rites came into being supposedly to cleanse the Soul and prepare it before it journeys onwards, however in that situation it was cleverly contrived and implemented to give institutionalised religion final control over a person's death as they had maintained in life.

Approved by Pope Paul VI the Rite of Penance details the exact process that the church stipulates must take place for the person's soul to be cleansed so that they would gain entrance to "heaven" and so that God would in a sense take it easy on them on the day of judgement. And what did that process stipulate must happen? The churches' primary stipulation was that it can only be done by a priest of the Catholic Church, once again even in a person's dying moments tying the believer to institutionalised religion as an example for others to follow, or if they don't their soul will not be cleansed.

Someone asked a church spokesperson at the time, well what if the person is unconscious? The spokesperson's answer to that was. Well, the priest, if he thinks that the person would want absolution, he can give conditional absolution. Someone at the time asked does the priest have to be beside the person. The church answered, "well we think at least within twenty paces would be appropriate".

The church set the agenda on how it should happen, and who can allow it to happen, basically telling their followers that they the church held the keys to a person's eternity and that it could only be done their way. And that has been the continuing ongoing deception through the ages that has kept a Catholic person tied psychologically and thus financially to the Catholic Church. Jesus said, "I will give you the Keys of the Kingdom". He did not say the church will give you the Keys of the Kingdom. And Jesus was not referring to heaven when He said this.

With regards to our pre-physical death present life situation, the more we choose wisely in life the less ammunition gets locked away in the deep recesses of the mind for the ego to use in a negative way at a future time, which includes the final mental emotional torment of regret. All things physical, being immersed in time, evolve to a particular but still temporal state of existence, of having a beginning and having an end, and eventually dissolve into nothingness, but all things non-physical, all things of the spiritual dimension are birthed and stay in an eternal state of existence, a state of timelessness. They nourish us continually.

This is how the Book of Matthew Amplified Version in the New Testament in quoting Jesus puts it. "Do not store up for yourselves (material) treasures on earth, where moth and rust destroy, and thieves break in and steal. But store up for yourselves treasures in heaven, (mental and spiritual preparedness), where neither moth nor rust destroy, and where thieves do not break in and steal; for where your treasure is, there your heart (your wishes, your desires, that which your mind and life purpose centres on) will be also".

This is the catalyst for self-transcendence and with that a higher level of conscious awareness. We make a real and present moment choice, by asking ourselves the question; What is more important to me, this temporal state of existence or my eternal state of existence? Once we make the choice we then live psychologically, spiritually, and physically with the consequences. Will it be a life lived, supported, sustained by, and aligned with Infinite Intelligence, or a life lived in a state of alienation from Infinite Intelligence. The Bible puts this conundrum one faces, some finding it more difficult to navigate than others, due to the energetic pull of a temporal existence, in a stronger way where it says with God speaking, "I have set before you life (spiritual wisdom through insight), and death (spiritual ignorance)", and then encourages us to choose life.

Jesus said, "it is harder for a rich man to enter the Kingdom of God than it is for a camel to pass through the eye of a needle". Why did He say that? Because for a rich man their central purpose in life is to maintain or improve their monetary status and to ensure that they do not put the level of affluence and circumstantial experience that their monetary status buys in jeopardy.

Maintaining one's financial status and thus the temporal pleasure it buys subconsciously and consciously is the driving force and underlying sustained purpose in their lives. So, trust in God is relegated to second place through an "inbuilt fear of losing that financial status and the accompanying level of freedom to choose one's ongoing experiences that it gives them". That sometimes subconscious fear of lack or loss is simply the ego saying, "don't mess with my intent, or my way of doing things". But that level of freedom is purely physical and not the truth that Jesus promised would "set us free". Some of the richest people in the world have had mental breakdowns,. committed suicide or died from a serious illness.

When we choose spiritual life rather than spiritual death, we bring into play in our daily lives the omnipotent, omnipresent, and omniscient power of Universal Consciousness or Infinite Intelligence, thus our state of being or level of consciousness begins to evolve to a higher state, and our temporal state of existence begins to transcend all the old, wrong, rational mind based ways of thinking, emotionally reacting, and physically behaving. Our life is then blessed in far greater ways than it ever was previously, which includes Wisdom in all of life's circumstances.

So, nothing material is lost but everything spiritual is gained. A subtle joy, peace, and gladness about life, regardless of our physical circumstances begins to flower like a bud opening itself to the early morning sun rays. All old things quietly and without effort pass away, and all things become as new.

When we choose spiritual life, we will find ourselves becoming more intuitively wise in our thinking, which means our choices become more often than what was the previous case, the right choices. And we don't "shoot from the hip" as the saying goes, as we previously had done. We find little things begin happening, good things, that many in the early stages of their evolutionary journey through consciousness may dismiss as simple co-incidences, when in truth they are the hand of Infinite Intelligence coming into play. Our old self, now fuelled by Infinite Intelligence, renewed daily, is transcending to a new self to a new state of being and with that a new state of living.

The literal meaning of psycho-spiritual self-transcendence is:

"A human being's act of overcoming the limits of the individual self and its ego driven self-interested desires, through spiritual contemplation and reflection and ongoing practical application".

It's not just about asking God to change you, it's about your choosing to change and accepting the support of Infinite Intelligence in the process. For the Axial Sages that I spoke of in Chapter 1, self-transcendence was their number one priority. Self-transcendence is born out of humility and the logic of respect for the mystery of everything that we did not create, but which also emerged from the same Creative Source as ourselves, Infinite Intelligence, whether it be nature or another human being.

One of the very real and quintessential examples of true self-transcendence was in fact the life of Viktor Frankl, who, in spite of all the atrocities occurring around him, in spite of all the personal suffering and heartbreak he experienced, or perhaps in some instances because of it, he continued on and left in his final passing a wonderful legacy that continues to this day.

Frankl found a way to rise above his circumstances spiritually and psychologically and thus go on physically. He tied his life to meaningful goals. If you want to live a happy life, tie it to a meaningful goal, not to meaningless people or meaningless things. He chose to transcend his circumstances by focusing on a higher constructive cosmic purpose in his situation than that of the destructive carnal purpose of the German Nazi ideological agenda. His personal purpose was functioning at a higher vibrational level than that of the Nazis and consequently at a higher level of consciousness. He survived and continued to live a purposeful existence.

Hitler however died hiding in a bunker and his purpose to build a whole new world without a skerrick of ethnicity in it died with him. Which is probably something that those considering joining the current Neo-Nazi organization should quietly contemplate.

For those readers who feel that life has thrown them too many curved balls and that it is too late for change to occur in their lives let me say this. I believe it is possible to live your life as if you were living a second time, as if you had been born again, no matter what you have done or what has been done to you or how old you are. It's all in the state of mind you choose in your present moment circumstances.

In 1951 the American singer Eddie Fisher released a song which became a hit called Turn Back the Hands of Time written by Larry Wagner. When I was a child, we had a lot of music around the house which my mother and older siblings listened to on the radio or played on the record player. As a toddler around 4 years of age I still remember a particular part of the chorus of that song. Now the original lyrics said, "bring back that dream of mine", speaking of a lost relationship, but Eddie Fisher's version which is the one I remember said, "bring back the dream divine", and it was that version that has stayed in my mind all my life. The lyrics said, "turn back the hands of time, roll back the sands of time, "bring back that dream divine, let's live it over again".

The composer was talking in a type of karmic way about two acts of transcendence. Firstly, transcending psychologically backwards, setting aside, and forgetting our current circumstances and all the wrong choices that accompanied our journey into what we call our reality or our current "lot in life", and resetting our psychological time clock back to zero, back to the beginning, and from that point then starting over again and transcending forward.

But this time doing it again the right way, by forgetting everything about our first failed attempt at navigating life, and then, in a deliberate and purpose filled way, meaning the way of deliberate intent, moving forward purposefully in life for whatever physical time in life we have left.

Most people living in an unconscious state of being live their entire lives transcending backwards in their psychological state of existing, drifting back into the world of memory, they call it reliving the "good ole days", or remembering the "bad ole days", and they stay too long there, dwelling on the past. Spiritual law says forget those things that are passed and press forward. Now whilst the lyrics of that song had been born out of the composer ruminating on a physical relationship that went awry, they could equally be applied to the world of the spiritual dynamic as it did for those during the Axial Age.

The Apostle Paul in discussing this principle of forgetting the past with the Philippian people said, "brothers and sisters whilst I do not consider having completely taken hold of it," in other words I do occasionally slip back in my thinking, "the one thing I do however is to forget what lies behind and reach forward to what lies ahead".

He was talking about leading a purpose filled existence. In the spiritual aspect of humanity's existence more than ever we need to "bring back the Dream Divine" as Eddie Fisher sang, bring back healing and newness and a new purposeful unified level of thinking and behaving and responding to the circumstantial existence of our lives. That was God's original dream for humanity as witnessed in the Garden of Eden story in the Old Testament where everything was as one until it wasn't.

The Australian Aborigines have the longest cultural history of any group of people on earth. Educated estimates date this history around 65,000 years. Aboriginal philosophy is known as the Dreaming or Dreamtime and is based on the inter-relation of all things and all people in the universe. This philosophy, the Dreaming, explains the origin of the universe and the workings of nature and humanity. It shapes and structures life through the regulation and understanding of other people, other lands, and other spirits.

It is the story of events that have happened, how the universe came to be, but more importantly, it is a story on **"how human beings were created and how their Creator intended for humans to function within the world as they knew it,"** which included functioning with a continual attitude of spirit connectedness in their relationships with each other and with all of nature".

The Dreamtime refers to the religious-cultural worldview attributed to Australian Aboriginal beliefs, and this concept of Dreamtime, whilst difficult to explain, in terms of non-Aboriginal culture could be described as:

> "An all-embracing concept that provides rules for living, a moral code, as well as rules for interacting with the natural environment thus providing a total, integrated way of life, a lived daily reality".

An understanding of life not dissimilar at all from the pathway to a more progressive and humane society that the Axial Sages brought to the world. You know more so than any other generation in the past, this generation of humanity has the means to live life meaningfully and purposefully regardless of the past, but, in many cases, so many choose not to. Regardless of the means they have, or the means they don't have, life for many has still not attained a self-satisfactory level of meaning and purpose. We see this so often reflected in the lives of individuals who seem in all outside appearances to have the world at their feet, only to see in a news report an announcement of their apparent suicide.

You see, everyone has their own specific purpose in life that they are able to choose, but the most primary purpose for all of society over and above our individual purpose is our Divine Purpose. Our Divine Purpose on earth is in our physical daily lives to love God, to love our neighbour and love ourselves and spiritually in our Soul lives to successfully journey through consciousness back to our Source. The Dream Divine plan for the evolution of the universe and all it contains is a co-operative joint participation plan. We are all in this together and each must play their part. That's how plans evolve into practical reality.

First and foremost our primary purpose in life is to consciously evolve to higher state of being, and at any time can be evidenced or witnessed in the individual level of transcendence in our own personal lives, our wisdom in interpreting life events and responding to them. Then those physical purposes of our life are empowered and find the space to materialise. Humanity should take the example of the lilies of the field as Jesus put it, who neither toil nor spin, they just live in a constant state of "presence" or "being," not taking everything as a personal affront.

When we choose to with intent transcend in our thoughts and our subsequent behaviour, what will manifest out of that transcendence is evidence that we have evolved into a higher level of consciousness. Transcend in thinking and behaving first and then you will automatically evolve to a higher level of consciousness because you have "chosen life," not by words alone but through your actions also.

Institutionalised religion has put the cart before the horse when it says come to church and God will change you. No, it is "choose to change and God will sustain you" and give you the power to evoke continuous change or continuously transcend the old way of thinking and behaving, thus taking you to a new and higher level of consciousness. That higher level of consciousness then strengthens our resolve and enables us to further transcend in our thought life and subsequent behaviours.

This is what Jesus meant when he said, "you shall be witnesses for me". He was not talking about standing on street corners or knocking on doors handing out leaflets that say, "Jesus loves you", as well meaning as that may be. That does not help anyone one iota if they are in a situation where every person around them is demonstrating a lack of love for that individual. A transcended state of existence in word and deed is the only true witness for the prosecution of noticeable change that can occur in our life or our society's life as we move forward to a higher level or deeper state of consciousness.

The Axial Age proved the authenticity of this fact. The meaning of life is all about transcendence and evolution, continuous growing transcendence, and evolution, till eventually we all attain to what the Apostle Paul described as, "the unity or universality of the faith and in our knowledge of God, unto a perfect man (or woman)". If you are not psychologically transcending, then you are only physically decaying, sad to say that is your life in the present moment.

The classic Indian Vedic text known as the Upanishads in addressing the act of transcendence says:

"You are what your deepest desire is. As your desire is, so is your intention, as your intention is, so is your will, as your will is, so is your deed, and as your deed is, so is your destiny".

We all have a desire to fulfil what we call our destiny and at times it can be a very frustrating desire. And so we go about life starting things, not finishing things, and then starting new things and not finishing them all in a vain attempt to find that elusive destiny or purpose. What I am saying is that your primary destiny is to strive to obtain a higher and deeper level of consciousness and when that intent is embraced and acted upon, when you seek first the Kingdom of God, Grace, or the Creative Power of Infinite Intelligence is released to point you in the direction you should follow, whether that be in work, in a relationship or in life in general. Infinite Intelligence begins building a purpose filled existence for you.

It is not all about "finding your calling", a term religious institutions have carelessly taught to the frustration and psychological detriment of many, it's all about "choosing life". Once you "choose life", you automatically engage Infinite Intelligence to guide you into a purpose filled existence. Then when we are directed to a specific purpose, and we begin working towards achieving that purpose in a responsible manner, then the stage is set for a higher purpose to be achieved through us. As it did with Viktor Frankl. How do we find an initial purpose? Exactly as the Vedic text says, "first desire, then set your intention, and then do something about it or take action".

It is impossible to define the overall purpose of life or the meaning of life in a general way because we are all individuals playing our part. Life moulds and shapes and thus forms a person's destiny, hence life is different and unique for everyone, for everyone's destiny is different and unique. But the most important thing in the process is to be alert, aware and vigilant that when you initiate the process the ego mind will come out to play and to interfere.

No person and their destiny can be compared with any other person and their destiny, hence the soul-destroying habits of jealousy and envy, wishing we were someone else or somewhere else, are just a waste of time and merely hinder the realisation of our own personal destiny. No situation repeats itself, and each situation calls for a different response, and sometimes the situation in which a man or woman find themselves may require them to shape their own fate by their own actions. Whilst at other times it's more advantageous for them to use the opportunity for contemplation, reflection and regrouping and then re-prioritising, and then sometimes they need to just "let go and let God".

Sometimes, as we see occurred in the life of Jesus with the crucifixion, a person may be required simply to accept their fate. But Jesus didn't see it as fate, he saw it as His purpose, as part of His introducing the New Covenant to society, the new Law of Spirit. He expressed it with the words, "not my will, but thy will be done." And with regards to the physical harm He was about to experience, his cross to bear so to speak, He accepted it as His contribution to the fulfillment of the Divine redemption plan, the Atonement. Every situation is distinguished by its uniqueness. Suffering is not necessary to achieve a higher state of consciousness, but sometimes it can be part of a continuous unfolding purpose.

What we must remember is as the book of Romans tells us that we can have great confidence that God who is deeply concerned about us, causes all things to work together as a plan for good. There is always only one right answer to the problem posed by the situation at hand and the final say in the matter is held by Infinite Intelligence. When a person starts to think that they have nothing to live for except ongoing suffering, then they have set themselves on the pathway of a purposeless existence.

So, the only solution they have if they really want to move forward successfully in life is to find purpose in or through that suffering. There is no other way to go. Alternately they can suffer themselves into oblivion having wasted their one chance to turn their life around. The Muslim Sufi Mystic Rumi put it this way:

"These pains you feel are messengers, listen to them".

This is the central theme of existentialism, free will, the capacity to choose life or to choose death. To live may involve some suffering, but to survive is to find meaning in that suffering and through that a way past it, as Viktor Frankl did. To find the message in the suffering the first step is acceptance. If we accept that yes suffering of some kind is a part of everyone's life, then we must accept that it may be part of our life, and if we want to continue this experience of life, then that suffering was intended to be part of the solution and not just an inconvenient disturbance.

If you are suffering, ask the universe what the purpose is, the true purpose in it, what is the message in it. But ask with an attitude of really wanting to find purpose not in a tone of giving up. Jesus experienced incredible suffering not just physically but psychologically but came through to a new resurrected life despite that suffering. The Muslim Mystic Rumi wrote:

"Have you ever seen a seed fall upon the earth and not rise with new life? Why should you doubt the rise of a seed named human?"

Life is all about transcendence, transcending our current state of being and moving forward psychologically and thus consciously to a higher level of being, and if the universe in its desire to see us transcend allows some suffering to hasten us along, then why would we not want to rather than focus only on fighting it, try and find purpose in it by listening to the message it is bringing. If your suffering is of the emotional kind as in a breakup in a relationship don't just wallow in self-pity transcend that age old way of behaving the way of the lower nature and rather seek the true message in what has happened so as to not repeat it in your future relationships. That's what finding purpose is all about. And at times that may require you to be ruthlessly honest with yourself about your own shortcomings.

Friedrich Nietzsche the German philosopher who became one of the most influential of all modern thinkers, and whose attempts to unmask the motives that underlie traditional Western religion, morality, and philosophy deeply affected generations of theologians, philosophers, psychologists, poets, novelists, and playwrights, once said:

"He who has a "why" to live for, can bear with almost any" how".

The "why to live for" that Nietzsche is talking about is "a purpose", not "the final purpose" but rather "a purpose". Find a purpose in the present moment that you are functioning in as a sentient being. (Sentient beings are beings with consciousness). The well-known spiritual teacher Eckhart Tolle talks about focusing on the present moment. When you focus on the present moment don't do it begrudgingly, do it with an intent to find a purpose in it. There is a purpose in everything and if we will stop and pause and step into that gap of thought we will find it.

Frankl discovered in his own suffering that life in some circumstances but not all, through no fault of oneself does not necessarily always deal one the right cards. And whilst those around him were moaning and complaining and giving up on "life" in a revengeful and bitter way, because they felt that it, life, had failed them, and enough was enough, they were not going to give life any second chances Frankl saw it differently. Frankl, rather than embrace the same attitude refused to throw in the towel because his purpose was more important to him than the temporal circumstances he had found himself in. He realised that to press through this situation what those around him needed more than anything was a fundamental change in their attitude towards life, and to stop treating life as the enemy.

You see life is not the enemy, and whilst circumstances in life can appear to be the enemy, they can also be an ally if we choose to let them. Frankl realised that he had a responsibility to teach those despairing men around him that what mattered most was not what we expected from life but what life expected from us. The meaning and purpose in his existing circumstantial life that Frankl discovered for himself and then saw as his destined charter to try and help as many of those around him to understand too, was that life ultimately means assuming responsibility for our life, and then taking the right attitude and subsequent action to defend that life and thus fulfil the ongoing demands life sets before us. Which basically meant find a purpose in any and all given moments and respond to it.

Sometimes in my travels on the road I would pause and look at homeless people or sit on a park bench and observe a particular individual, and the thought that always came to mind as I paused to look at them was that they lacked purpose, which in most cases kept them locked in their present seemingly dire existence. When all the time most homeless people are thinking I live this way due to lack of finances, or because rents are too high, or because of my addiction to alcohol, these are the reasons I live this way. No, those things come out of a lack of purpose in the first instance, they do not cause a lack of purpose.

There are exceptions however, as I saw whilst visiting Santa Monica Beach in California where I found a homeless person who had found a purpose in his current seemingly dire circumstances. Every day he would "borrow" a shopping trolley from the local supermarket and would spend all day walking around the precinct picking up rubbish. He had found purpose in his current dire circumstances.

In his own way he was trying to make the world around him a little better, but from a spiritual perspective he had found a purpose and was manifesting it, and I am sure that when he slept under a piece of cardboard in the park that night, he would have felt a lot better about life than those who had spent their day drinking out of a flagon of wine under a tree. We are all put on earth for multiple reasons, not one singular reason, even though many would think that their current situation predisposes them to not having a reason. Not one single person can be replaced, not one single person can be repeated.

We all have our unique tasks and have been given through life specific opportunity to carry them out for the good of humanity and the betterment of ourselves. And subconsciously, without him perhaps totally realising it, this prompting the homeless man was receiving each day to get a shopping trolley and go and pick up rubbish, was in fact the universe prompting him to find a purpose in his everyday existence, because "from little things then big things can grow". It was Mark Twain, the American writer and author of two of the major classics of American literature The Adventures of Tom Sawyer and the Adventures of Huckleberry Finn who said:

> *"The two most important days in your life are the day you were born, and the day you find out why".*

But that does not mean that it has to be an "earth shattering why" at every stage. At times it might be just to "grab a shopping trolley and pick up some rubbish." This is where a lot of people with some type of spiritual bent get it wrong and live in frustration. The ego mind says, "you are called to be a teacher of God". Whilst God just wants you to love a certain person and be kind to them in their present moment of suffering, not to preach to them. It's a three-step process. Firstly, find your spiritual purpose, which is exactly as I outlined in Chapter 2, which is the spiritual purpose for all humanity, to in a unified way evolve in their level of consciousness to the highest level.

Then secondly find some purpose in the present moment, be attentive in everything you do. No matter how mundane your job may seem, focus on it, give it your fullest attention. And then thirdly having apprehended the first two, then "your purposes in life will find you".

The spiritual principle of having a deliberately chosen attentive attitude in all you do is written in the Book of Colossians where it says, "Whatever you do, whatever your task may be, work from the Soul, that is put in your very best effort as something done for the Lord and not for men. (Amplified Version). This is a Divine Principle that initiates the involvement of the Creative Spirit. You are fulfilling with energy your current purpose in life, the task at hand and then Divine Energy springs into action. You are putting Divine Principle to work, evidenced in your attitude to the task at hand, and Divine Energy will respond to its own Law or Principle.

People march in the streets protesting "all my freedoms have been taken away". Many are just doing it aimlessly or simply selfishly, and many I dare say are doing it solely out of boredom and not having purpose. Manifesting from their lower nature simply because they are bored with their current existence. So, in an attempt to find a purpose, they join up with some ideologically driven group who do in fact have a purpose, whose sole purpose is to disrupt society to unsettle authorities or governments. Why do people align with these groups? Because they have nothing else to do, no purpose to centre their attention on, so they substitute a visible reaction against life and their life circumstances for the purpose they don't have. But not all of them.

People such as Dr. Martin Luther King Jnr and his followers were different. They marched with a specific Divinely inspired purpose in mind, a purposeful intent, societal equality for black people, the unification of society no matter what the colour of a person's skin, and it was always done with a non-combative attitude and subsequent peaceful behaviour. Those who march to protest on their freedoms being all taken away are wrong. Not all have been taken, and certainly not the three most important ones. Regardless of what a person feels life has denied them or taken away from them, there are three things that can never be taken away, freedom of thought, freedom to choose our attitude, and freedom to choose our attitudinal driven response to a situation.

I mentioned earlier in this chapter the Old Testament scripture where God gave the people a choice between spiritual life and spiritual death and encouraged the people to choose life. That was the moment Infinite Intelligence demonstrated that humanity had been given free will, freedom to choose a specific life path. Divine Intelligence allowed for the possibility that we could choose the wrong way for free will creates duality, duality of attitude, duality of choice, duality of behaviour, one leading to Light and its opposite leading to darkness and psychological disorientation. If we want to walk towards the Light, we must eliminate from our lives any choices that may possibly detour us up the road of darkness.

Regardless of outward circumstances, we all have the capacity to live life through and despite our sufferings, and yet so many use their sufferings as an excuse for not living life, or alternately many are merely living life according to the level of their current suffering. The Axial Sages that I spoke of in Chapter 1 discovered that it was possible to transcend this habitual way of approaching life, that was coming from a thought-based attitude of suffering and lack and live an honourable way that would not only benefit humanity but achieve inner fulfilment and a sense of purpose and meaning for the individual at the same time.

Societies in this modern day have a get and get attitude, rather than a give and get attitude. Jesus said "give and it shall be given unto you. This is a Divine Principle threaded into the fabric of the universe one of the key principles that hold this universe together.

Jesus did not say get and it shall be gotten by you. Humanity has the capacity to transcend this innate sense of entitlement that has been built into its psyche, but it can only be totally transcended and subsequently removed from the psyche as a higher level of consciousness is reached. And I'm not talking about necessarily transcending their current physical situation whether that involves some sort of suffering or not, I'm talking about primarily transcending their current psychological situation.

Suffering in life to achieve a greater depth of spirituality and transcendence is not a necessity, but by the same token, it is not an obstacle to achieving a meaningful and purpose filled life. We not only live in a society that has a get and more shall be gotten by you attitude, but we also live in a society where individuals have become unforgiving of themselves, full of doubt about their own personal opportunity to achieve some sort of meaningful state of being. Viktor Frankl recognised that human beings bear a responsibility not only to the rest of humanity, but also to themselves, regardless of the suffering they might be going through, regardless of the lack, regardless of the pain.

Remember this man was living in circumstances at that time in a concentration camp, where, when every new day dawned, it brought with it a morning greeting that echoed the possibility of physical extermination. He had seen his mother, father, brother, and wife killed by the Nazis, he had little food and the constant threat of disease and abuse from his keepers. But Frankl accepted the fact that suffering, as well as satisfaction, are elements in life that we all at some various stage must embrace, and that as capable as most people are of weathering success, so too people have an innate ability in them to weather suffering.

The beginning of self-transcendence is when a person awakens to a sense of responsibility that life is theirs, life belongs to them, and that in the final run they have only been given one life and it is their choice and their choice alone as to whether they will live it meaningfully and with purpose, or whether they won't. The beginning of self-transcendence is when people accept that life is not based on temporal circumstances, but on a belief in one's own eternal and unlimited potential. Self-transcendence occurs when a human being realises their innate capacity to expand their personal boundaries in whatever area they choose, whether that be intra-personally, personally, or transversely, and thus correct themselves, correct the psychological and thus physical trajectory of their own personal universe, correcting their relationships with others and correcting their attitude towards nature.

A person then begins adopting an attitude that life is higher than what thoughts proceed out of the carnal mind and adopting an attitude that real life centres on the infinite potential we all have through our Christ Mind or Buddha Mind, the Mind of Infinite Intelligence.

Self-transcendence commences through our knowing that we are able through the pure potential that exists within us, to surpass the visual limits that appear on our horizons, the visual obstacles that occur in our lives, and to transcend past these things to a new state, a realisation of that quiet hidden Intelligence which lies on the other side in the sea of pure potentiality.

If you look at the life of Jesus, there is a story in the Bible about what is called his time of testing and subsequence transcendence in the wilderness, where Jesus was in that moment, able to take himself out of the mental torment that he was going through knowing his crucifixion was near, and to step into a new state of being.

He was able to transcend his existing psychological state, His state of mind, into a resolute realisation that his own Divine purpose was to be the implementer of the Atonement process for humanity, that this was his individual personal purpose, and that this was his Divine purpose over and above his daily purpose. His daily purpose was to fulfil his obligation as a human being to find purpose in everything he did. His specific Divine purpose was to initiate the Atonement and introduce Infinite Intelligence in the form of the Holy Spirit the Ruh al-Qudus into the world.

Know your Divine purpose, which is to journey successfully through consciousness, focus on your daily purpose, respond to it, as Jesus did, start living a life of purpose filled intent in all the minor or major things in life, then any Divine purpose that needs your assistance you will be directed to, and it may be just something as simple as to help an older person carry their heavy grocery bag, for remember with Divinity it's the little things that matter. Be faithful in the little things. We are all pieces in the great jigsaw puzzle called life, this evolutionary journey through consciousness, each with their part to play to complete the picture.

Am I saying that a one size attitude fits all in terms of everyone being able to tap into the meaning of their own life? No, I am not. There is an individuality of purpose and potential that is unique to every person's life. But you won't find it unless you first begin the habit of adopting a purpose filled mentality in every little thing you do. Don't just indulge in a thought, that's called day dreaming. Do you love the thought of being able to paint but don't paint because you "think" you couldn't, then how will you ever know? You see not all people have some grand earth-shattering destiny to fulfil, not all people are Leonardo di Vinci's or Picassos, but some are. And you won't know unless you "just do it."

Your purpose in life might be to leave a legacy of love and kindness to your grandchildren that will sustain them in life and influence their own lives for the better; a legacy that they too will pass on to their own children and grandchildren. The purpose for some may be to contribute to the field of science, the purpose for some may be in charity work or humanitarian aid that goes entirely unnoticed by the world around you. The purpose for some might be in healing or in medicine.

If you think that you must have a "special purpose" so that people will applaud you or to win the praise of people, then you are bringing the ego into your quest. The purpose for some may be in the creative arts, perhaps in writing, in music or entertainment, but you will never know unless you decide to deliberately self-transcend your rational mind that keeps telling you that you can't do it.

Don't doubt yourself. Doubt is the primary enemy of destiny, but when desire decides to realise itself into a purpose filled intent, and a person psychologically and physically embraces that intent, then through the intervention of Infinite Intelligence that purpose can be realised. You can do all things through the power that lies within you. We can't get to realise a purpose in life, whether that be a daily purpose or a Divine life purpose, purely through hoping and dreaming and wishing. Reflection is necessary in the first instance, but it must be followed by action. Remember what the ancient wisdom of the Upanishads say:

"You are what your deepest desire is. As your desire is, so is your intention. As your intention is, so is your will. As your will is, so is your deed, and as your deed is, so is your destiny".

We **set our intention and then we focus our attention** on that which we desire, that purpose that is on our heart. Then Infinite Intelligence, Universal Law or Divine Principle will do its part. Eckhart Tolle in his powerful book The Power of Now describes this as living in the "present moment". We do not allow our gaze to turn back on the inner turmoil, the doubt, but immediately when we feel those things coming to our mind again, in the instant that we feel their pull, we redirect our thoughts and actions to the outer purpose that is waiting for us. What is more important is not what lurks in the depths of our ego centred unregenerated thought pattern, that will always attempt to discredit, discourage, and subsequently destroy our confidence, but what waits patiently in the shadows wanting to emerge as our true purpose in the moment, that is what is most important.

We all have the freedom to find meaning in life transcending meaningless attitudes and meaningless situations. We all can find freedom even when we feel imprisoned in our own lack. Talk to yourself the answer is within you. But remember we are all individually unique, so what we purpose to do will not necessarily be the same as our neighbour or friend.

Compared to the conditions that society lived with in the pre-Axial Age years, in today's modern society, more and more people have the means to live purposefully, but rather choose to wallow in uncertainty, as if they had no meaning to live for. Everything can be taken from a person, but the one last thing that will never be taken is our freedom to choose whether we react against life or respond to it.

Perhaps one of the greatest examples of this philosophy of existence was remarkedly demonstrated in the life of Nelson Mandela. What mattered most to Nelson Mandela was not the meaning of life in general, but rather the specific meaning of a person's life at a given moment in time, and Nelson Mandela never lost that sense of purpose and sense of understanding of the meaning and purpose of his own daily life irrespective of his spending 27 years or 9,860 days in prison.

The song says as do many people in everyday conversation that "what the world needs now is love, sweet love", but primarily "what the world needs now is purpose, sweet purpose". For purpose brings peace, and without true peace, true love cannot thrive. If you have no purpose and spend all your time wallowing in uncertainty you are never in a state of peace, and if you can't find peace you are not free to love.

You see contrary to what many people think, Jesus did not come to spread love he came to spread peace, knowing that real love can only emerge from a place of peace within. How did he maintain that peace in his daily life leading up to his crucifixion? Simply through focusing purposefully on everything that passed before him. Jesus did not say "my love I give to you", he said, "my peace I give unto you". He preached "blessed are the peacemakers" not blessed are the love makers. While he was on earth Jesus did not say "my love shall guard your heart and your mind," he said, "the peace of God that passes all understanding through me will guard your heart and your mind." Then he left the Holy Spirit with us as the Comforter. What is a comforter? A comforter is one who brings peace midst apparent chaos.

> *"True peace is not the absence of trouble; it is a supernatural restful state of mind that is present even midst the extreme ego influences and antics of the enemy".*

The Prophet Muhammad of the Muslim faith came with the same message of peace as did Jesus of the Christian faith. Muhammad had great respect for Jesus as a prophet sent by God, and the Muslim extremists who in their jihadist rage kill and destroy lives and livelihoods in the name of Allah have got it all deludingly wrong.

You see our spirits are continuously striving against our lower nature, the lower qualities of the ego which are anti-peace. That is the great jihad of our life, not the violent jihad that is espoused by the extremists, which is emanating from the lower nature of each extremist. The literal meaning of Jihad is struggle or effort and means much more than a holy war. It relates primarily to the workings of the Soul.

True Muslims use the word Jihad to describe three different kinds of struggle, the primary one being the struggle to live their faith as well as possible and to build a good Muslim society, but to the true Muslim a good Muslim society does not mean an Islamic controlled world. If you look at places where Muslim scholars have broken down the concept of jihad you see that it has two parts. It has what is known as the lesser part, and it also contains what is known as the greater part. The lesser part, or what you could describe as the combative jihad, is the act of fighting yes, but here's the point, it is fighting only in defence of religious freedom where that freedom has been seriously compromised or curtailed, and fighting in defence of your home, or fighting in defence of basic human rights.

Muhammad's jihad was not about killing innocent civilians or others simply because they are not of the Islamic faith. However, the second and greater or higher spiritual jihad that Muslim scholars speak of is the striving against the ego and its lower desires and those manifestations of the ego that would bring unrest, lack of peace and alienation of some kind from your fellow human beings. The Qur'an when speaking of fighting in the cause of Allah, is talking about fighting for the cause or needs of those weak, ill-treated, and oppressed people who are being denied basic human rights and the blessings of God. Fighting those people whose ego driven desires would seek to harm the oppressed.

The Qur'an says, "and why should you not fight in the cause of Allah for those weak, ill-treated and oppressed men, women and children who cry out oh Lord rescue us from our circumstances and raise up for us from you, one who will protect us and who will help us". When we self-transcend, we develop new personality traits that involve the expansion of our personal boundaries, to exclude the combative attitude of our lower nature, and in terms of our level of consciousness this includes a greater understanding and expansion of our knowledge of spiritual things and of the spiritual world itself, which includes a deeper comprehension of the existing invisible oneness that permeates the universe and always will.

We must remember that all Christians and all Muslims, and all Buddhists, well, all people for that matter, are meant to live life in complete transcendence; to live a life of daily transcendence of the unnecessary and irrelevant aspects of the rational mind in our earthly life, leading to transcendence of consciousness in our psychological evolutionary life and transcendence of time with regards to eternal life.

This is what Jesus came to teach, this is what the Buddha came to teach, this is what Muhammad came to teach. This is the mystery sometimes hidden in their teachings. My life situation exists in time, but my life exists in timelessness. My life situation is temporal, but my internal life is eternal. Which is why it needs our attention. So this is how life works. There are three different aspects of transcendence or self-transcendence, three kinds of transcendence in life that we are all destined to participate in.

There is a Physical Transcendence, which sees the body grow and develop from the moment of birth. Then there is Psychological Transcendence, a transcendence of the mind aspect of the Soul, where we transcend or go beyond the restrictive confines of an ego-controlled self and transcend to an intuitive level of perception, where we begin seeing things not from our own pre-programmed or prejudicial viewpoint, not from our own imagined or real circumstances, but from the viewpoint of Infinite Intelligence. It can be simply initiated, as not done previously, by asking ourselves in every difficult situation, "how would Jesus' handle this, or how would the Buddha handle this, or how would Muhammad handle this?" The Apostle John in speaking of the transcendence of the Physical and the Psychological said as we read in 3 John 1 and 2, "Beloved I pray that in every way you may succeed and prosper physically just as your Soul prospers."

And thirdly there is Spiritual or Consciousness Transcendence which I have touched on and will touch on further in later chapters. In terms of Spiritual Transcendence you could put it this way also. When we change our way of thinking (psychological transcendence), and subsequently our way of behaving, we elevate the presence of God in our lives and the peace that comes with it, without doing anything else. Spiritual Transcendence is when we enter the dimension of timelessness, where clock time no longer has any value for us except perhaps in some everyday deadline we must meet. But the primary focus of our life should be to Psychologically Transcend first, because when this happens a transcendence in Consciousness, or Spiritual Transcendence automatically flows out of it.

When we Psychologically Transcend, we transcend the old egoic rational and emotion driven way of thinking and responding, that only asks, "well how am I going to handle this" or "how is this going to affect me," whilst subconsciously allocating blame to the other person. When I talk about ego transcendence, I am speaking about transcending or going beyond our hereditary or self-developed personality patterns that influence our habitual way of thinking and behaving and replacing them with new ones, even in just the present moment. Because until we change our ingrained habit patterns that we have continually embraced all our lives, the mind attacks will continue. Remember this is a psycho-spiritual warfare we are involved in.

People will notice the change, but they will be puzzled by your new way of interpreting events and behaving. Some will accept it, but some will also reject it because they felt very comfortable with your old ego-controlled self, your old way of interpreting events and behaving, particularly if it aligned with theirs. Your friends will either go through this inner transformation with you, supporting you, and learning from your example, or simply drift out of your life. Some relationships will dissolve but others will deepen.

Similarly, as it did in the Axial Age, it all starts with Psychological Transcendence, a change in our way of thinking and behaving. Infinite Intelligence won't force us to change, and religion won't cause us to change, we must of our own willingness, "choose to change". Biblical terminology puts it this way, God saying, "draw near to me and I will draw near to you".

How do we draw near to God? Firstly, we don't have to lock ourselves away in a monastery on a mountaintop. We start by aligning our thoughts and behaviours with Divine Principle, the God way of thinking and the Jesus way of behaving. It really is as simple as that. The result of this is that we become intuitively empowered by Infinite Intelligence and a change of nature and subsequent behaviour is automatically manifested. It is no good having a form of godliness but denying the power of it. Paul spoke of this in the New Testament in his letter to Timothy.

Will we always hit the right mark? Of course not, because our state of psychological preparedness, which includes living daily with a disciplined purpose filled intent, thus far has been way off the mark. But we will gradually with the help of Infinite Intelligence get better as we train ourselves to in all situations pause, reflect, and choose wisely. For in that pause or gap of thinking, in that stillness of the moment, Infinite Intelligence comes into play. As our mind leans more and more towards the prompting of our higher nature rather than the urgings of our lower nature as it has done all our life, our life then is progressively transformed. The New Testament says, "we are transformed through the renewing of our Mind."

The Apostle Paul describing this pathway to a higher level of consciousness and thus a more positive level of existence, referred to it as being transformed through the renewal of our mind or our thought process. So, there is a psychological transcendence where we transcend or go beyond egoic thought patterns, and with that comes a behavioural transcendence, which is where we transcend our own needs in favour of the needs of others, and there is a spiritual transcendence, where we transcend space and time, and the nature of true reality becomes clear to us. It is where we separate ourselves from the timebound and enter the realm of the timeless, which is a state of continuous Cosmic Consciousness or what some would refer to as a continuous state of "presence".

What is the purpose of self-transcendence? Its primary objective is to move us forward in our evolutionary journey through consciousness into a higher level of awareness and finally a return to our source, as I indicated in the previous chapter. Which automatically brings into our existing temporal physical life positive experiences and with that an emotional peace and harmony and a sense of well-being. Theologians over time, many having never really understood how they come about, have referred to these positive experiences as the "blessings of God" and spiritual masters of the East have referred this sense of well-being and feeling of peace as a "state of bliss".

Transcendence comes when we understand and acknowledge and adopt a new way of perception, which is when we begin seeing things or perceiving things as the God Mind perceives them, and thus our thoughts and subsequent behaviours begin aligning with God's Universal Law or Divine Principle, which brings the "power of the Spirit" into play to create right results.

For instance, when human law (human thinking) says, "don't give as you might not have enough left for yourself, Divine Principle (God's thinking) says, "give first and then more will be given unto you". Human law, the law of the egoic mind says, "curse the person that curses you", but God's Law or Divine Principle says, "bless those who curse you". A human being's way of thought says, "you know for what that person did to you, they deserve a piece of your mind". God's way of thought or Divine Principle says forgive and you shall be forgiven. We transcend our own feelings; we transcend our own rational thought process; we transcend our current emotionally reactive state of mind and begin living primarily out of an intuitive thought process.

In everyday language transcendent means going beyond. Going beyond our current state of practical existence, comes out of our transcending to a higher level in our psychological existence, our way of thinking, which leads to a higher state of consciousness. For many people this is a big and difficult step to take because it means stepping out of those habitual personality patterns that we have been accommodating all our life. It requires courage and self-discipline. But in terms of our spiritual journey, it is the true evidence of our transcendence to an altered state of consciousness, and it's marked by the conviction that one is beyond concern with the self and can now perceive reality with greater objectivity.

That higher level of consciousness may be evidenced in a newfound deep compassion for and sensitivity towards those who are suffering. I know it did for me. I changed from a person who would in many instances only give a sideways glance or a momentary thought as stories of an individual's, or a society's suffering in another part of the world or at home were being broadcast on the daily news. Now these stories always gain my full attention and when they occur as unfortunately, they do, I become immersed in a state of emotional compassion for those who are suffering, particularly if it is a little child, but equally applies to adults, to animals and other life form in general. Which causes me in that moment to ask of God a blessing for them in their time of need.

The evidence of having attained or evolved to a higher level of consciousness, in a practical sense can be seen in a person's life in many ways, but one thing for sure is that the practical change relating to their nature or behaviour will be identical to the nature and behaviour that Jesus evidenced in His life and work. The Mind of Christ having taken ascendancy in our life is manifesting Christ attitudes and Christ emotions in our attitudes and emotions. Transcendence involves the very highest in the most inclusive of the holistic levels of human consciousness. We relate and behave towards everything as ends rather than as means to an end, to other humans, to other species, to nature and to the cosmos.

True transcendence results in our saying and doing things that we have not done before, as if we had been born again as a new creation and started all over again. We have turned back the hands of time.

We look up into the night sky and feel connected to the stars and feel a subtle connection with the universe and feel at peace and in need of nothing. When we fully transcend, we have evolved to a realisation that we are and always have been a part of a universal consciousness, the creative essence of Divinity, the Word, existing as energy beyond our original mortal form. We know we are immortal; we know we will never die. Death or the fear of death loses its sting as the Apostle Paul described his own experience.

Many may be thinking now, but how. How do I transition? What do we have to do? I go into some more detail as this book progresses, and in the Spiritual Pointers section at the end of the book, but you don't have to wait until then to start. In the first instance, the simple answer to this is that we do what we know intuitively we must do now. We choose to change now, we start now. For instance, we encounter a difficult situation, it may be a conflict of some type, say in a relationship, we do not do what our mind "first" tells us to do because rest assured the egoic side of our nature, our habitual personality patterns that we have always given pre-eminence to will quickly respond.

We pause, we reflect and in the stillness of that moment we listen for the inner voice, that still small voice or prompting from Infinite Intelligence. In speaking of the still small voice, most people commonly call conscience and its war against the egoic side of our nature, the voice of the Ego Mind, Sogyal Rinpoche, in his book The Tibetan Book of Living and Dying said the following:

> *"Two people have been living in you all your life. There is the ego, which is garrulous, demanding, and calculating, and there is the hidden spiritual being, whose still voice of Wisdom, you have only rarely heard or attended to".*

As I discussed in Chapter 1, during the Axial Age, through psychological transcendence, visible changed personality patterns emerged demonstrating newfound expressions of compassion, kindness, love, empathy, courage, and solidarity of purpose, and from a cosmic point of view higher levels of consciousness. There was a consciousness transcendence from a state of Collective Unconsciousness to a state of Collective Consciousness. (I discuss this in easily understandable detail later in this book.)

But it was not for all, particularly for those tribes whose self-survivalist attitude had been over many centuries more deeply embedded in their tribal identity, who felt that self-interest was meant to be at the front of the pack not the back, and who continued to hang on to the belief that life was primarily all about self-survival, which of course had been the only experience that generations had endured up until this time.

In today's modern society, it is by and large not totally different. For many individuals due to the trans-generational transfer of old habits and beliefs even subconsciously are still focused on self-survival. And so we see in religion many "religious people" tinker around the edges of a true spiritual experience, whilst continuing to live life embroiled in physical and psychological chaos and confusion in a minor way for example in interpersonal relationships or major way as in doctrinal or worse still physical culture based religious wars.

For centuries and centuries philosophers, theologians, and a wide variety of intellectuals have set about shaping our beliefs with their influence ever present in many of our existing practices, institutions, and basic assumptions about ourselves and the world we thought we knew.

From the mystic's point of view, the philosophical perspective is that there is only one consciousness, one mind, and one field of truth that is the source of the entire universe, one creative intelligence which created all life, sustains all life, and which supports all life. That field of truth is an Infinite Intelligence, commonly referred to by many religions as God, because it is a "being or presence" that is invisible to the senses, and as such one that cannot be comprehended through normal intellectual intelligence or described in a language understandable to all.

I spoke of this Infinite Intelligence during this chapter as the Creative Spirit of God, that which powers Divine Principle or Divine Law causing it to manifest. I give greater understanding of how this Infinite Intelligence is interpreted by the most well-known religions of the world in the following chapter.

> "I know this world is ruled by Infinite Intelligence. Everything that surrounds us, everything that exists proves that there are Infinite laws behind it. There can be no denying this fact".
>
> *Thomas Edison*
> *Scientist and Inventor*

The Many Names and Different Interpretations of God

FOUR

> "I do not believe in the God of the theologians; but that there is a Supreme Intelligence at work in the universe, I do not doubt at all".
>
> Thomas Edison

Thomas Alva Edison was born February 11, 1847 and passed October 18, 1931, aged 84 years. He was an American inventor and a businessman sometimes described as America's greatest inventor ever. Born and raised in the American Midwest, Edison developed hearing problems at the young age of 12 years, the cause of his deafness being attributed to a bout of scarlet fever that he had experienced earlier during his childhood, that led to recurring untreated middle ear infections. Being completely deaf in one ear and barely able to hear in the other ear, it is said that Edison would listen to a music player or a piano by clamping his teeth into the wood to absorb the sound waves into his skull. Certain medical professionals in the day also suggested that he may have had ADHD, one of the most common neurodevelopmental disorders of childhood.

However, none of these things prevented him from pursuing a fascination, developed in his early childhood, with inventing things and creating new things. As he got older, rather than focusing on trying to change his health status, he developed the habit of looking on the positive side of his existence, in that his hearing loss was in fact a good thing because it allowed him to avoid distraction and concentrate more easily.

Edison commenced his working career as a telegraph operator the experience of which it is said inspired some of his earliest and most notable inventions. In 1876 at the age of 30 years he established his first laboratory facility in New Jersey where many of his earliest inventions were developed. Later, he established a botanic laboratory in collaboration with Henry Ford the car manufacturer, as well as another laboratory in New Jersey that featured the world's first film studio.

Being a prolific inventor, at one stage he held 1,093 US patents in his name as well as patents in many other countries. Edison went on to become known as the greatest inventor of all time inventing devices in fields such as electric power generation, mass communication, sound recording, and motion pictures. including amongst other things the phonograph or record player as it is more commonly known, the motion picture camera, the incandescent light bulb, the carbon telephone transmitter, and the rechargeable battery. Not a day would go by when all of us don't have to thank Edison for the many tools and conveniences of our modern life whose present design came out of his original inventive and creative genius.

To name a few, such as the fluorescent lamp, the nickel alkaline storage battery, the universal electric motor, the motion picture, and the basic principles of modern electronics, would be barely scratching the surface of his contributions to society, all resulting from painstaking trial and error experiments. Thomas Edison's life has much to teach and inspire. Much of his success and brilliance can be attributed to his unique outlook and personal philosophy, which resulted from the self-discipline developed during those painstaking trial and error experiments, and an indomitable spirit of perseverance that embraced each failed experiment as a positive step forward on the long road to success.

The Many Names and Different Interpretations of God

Each failed experiment which when questioned about, he would merely describe as not being a failed experiment but rather as 10,000 ways that just didn't work. When once questioned also by a reporter about the origin of his creative genius it is said he paused in a moment of reflection, and then quietly replied:

"I know this world is ruled by Infinite Intelligence. Everything that surrounds us, everything that exists, proves that there are Infinite Laws behind it. There is no denying this fact. It is mathematical in its precision".

In the early centuries of humanity's known existence, the concept of there being an Infinite Intelligence was central to most religious thought, and in everyday language this supreme intelligence was more commonly referred to as "God". However, progressively over time, as new religions, new philosophical schools of thought, and new discoveries in science burst forth into humanity's existence, the generalised term God was replaced by a new name, an individual name that reflected either the teaching of the new religion, the original mythos of that society, the specific language translation of the word God, or a combination of all three.

For example in the science of Quantum Physics, the phrase describing this unknown intelligence from which a discovery was birthed, was named "a field of pure existence" or a "field of pure potentiality". But a phrase still in essence referring to that same Infinite Intelligence commonly referred to as God. The English word God comes from the old Anglo Saxon word *god* which itself is derived from the Proto-Germanic word *gudan*. The language of Anglo-Saxon or Old English is the earliest recorded form of English language, and Proto-Germanic or Common Germanic is the reconstructed hereditary language of the Indo-European languages, which are native to Eurasia, Eurasia being the name given to all of Asia and Europe.

Throughout religion's history, it has not just been the naming of God that has created differences in religious approach, but rather, perhaps far more noticeable has been the emergence of different concepts of God that have come to the fore as different religions have individually birthed themselves into humanity's existence. For instance, to simplify it:

In Judaism, Infinite Intelligence is Yahweh, the God of Abraham, Isaac, (Abraham's first-born son by his wife Sarah), and Jacob, (Abraham's grandson also known as Israel). God is the supreme spiritual Deity who supernaturally and physically delivered the Israelites from slavery in Egypt and gave them the Law of Moses. Historically in Judaism God is evidenced as the Old Testament God of judgement and retribution but also the Old Testament God of blessing and cursing. You could call it a God of a dualistic nature or temperament.

In Christianity, Infinite Intelligence is seen as the eternal being who created all things and sustains all things and has three representations, the Father, the Son (Jesus) and the Holy Spirit. Christians believe God to be all knowing, all powerful, able to be everywhere at once, believing that God is of a different substance than humanity. In Christianity God is the New Testament God of love, compassion, and mercy. In Christianity unlike in Judaism, from which Christianity stemmed, God does not punish you in this lifetime, but will punish you in the afterlife, hence the heaven and hell scenario, in what Christians refer to as the Day of Judgement.

In Islam, Infinite Intelligence is Allah the Absolute, the God of Abraham and Ishmael (Abraham's first-born son by Hagar, his wife Sarah's maidservant). Allah is basically the Arabic word for the English word God. Whilst in Christianity God is what is known as a Trinity, meaning having three representations, the Father, the Son, and the Holy Spirit, in Islam Allah means deity or lone god, and like Christianity, believes Allah is not of visible form. Allah is the lone

The Many Names and Different Interpretations of God

God every Muslim must worship. Islam emphasises that God is all merciful, compassionate, and omnipotent.

In Islam however, whilst there is only one God, there are 99 names used for that one God and each of these names evokes a distinct attribute of God's nature. These group of 99 names are described as al-asma al-husna, which literally means "the best names". Muslims believe Allah created the world in six days and sent prophets such as Noah, Abraham, Moses, David, Jesus, and Muhammad to guide humanity into spiritual truth.

In Hinduism, the concept of Infinite Intelligence varies in different Hindu traditions. For instance, in **Sikhism** God is conceived as the oneness, the invisible Infinite Intelligence that permeates the entirety of creation and beyond and abides within every part of creation. The one who is indescribable yet noble and perceivable to anyone who surrenders the ego. Sikhism is a monotheistic religion which means Sikhs believe there is only one God, however they believe that this Infinite Intelligence called God is present in creation and whilst not being the universe, is the driving life force within it.

In Chinese religious history, Infinite Intelligence was referred to as Shangdi or Lord on High, or simply Emperor. Shangdi is the Chinese term for Supreme or Highest Deity. Historically Chinese civilization has hosted a variety of the most enduring religious-philosophical traditions, including Confucianism, Taoism (Daoism) and Buddhism. However, since 1949 China has been governed by the Communist Party of China, an atheist institution that prohibits party members from practicing religion while in office.

After the Cultural Revolution ended in 1976 religious organizations were given a measure of autonomy, but it was and still is strictly measured and monitored for its compliance to Communist ideology. Whilst the government states that it formally recognizes five religions, Buddhism, Taoism, Catholicism, Protestantism, and Islam, it is only within strict parameters they are allowed to continue, and regarding

Islam and Muslim minorities, in recent times it has adopted a very determined approach in "re-educating" Muslim minorities in the way of Communism.

In Buddhism, a religion that does not include a belief in a creator deity or any Divine personal being, in its doctrine of Samsara it is taught that there is a plurality of divine intelligences, beings or gods, heavens, and a cycle of deaths and rebirths, to which all life in the material world is bound. Unlike most other religions, Buddhism does not claim to have originated through a God in heaven. Nor did Buddha ever say that he was the son of God, the messenger of God, or a reincarnation of God. Buddhists however similar to Hindus, do believe in a Universal Consciousness or Universal Mind, it being a metaphysical concept suggesting an underlying essence of all being and becoming in the universe.

So in essence, the word God is simply an everyday word we use, handed down through successive generations to describe a Supreme Being who is higher than all, to describe a Supreme and Infinite Intelligence, the mother and birthplace of true Wisdom. Neither does God refer to himself as God, describing Himself in spiritual writings purely as "I Am". Human beings merely historically drifted into using the word God to refer to this Infinite Intelligence, because various cultures found this Intelligence not only difficult to describe, but also found it to be a being whose ultimate function and purpose they found even more difficult to agree on. But the one thing that they did all agree on unreservedly was that "God does exist".

So, to try to bring the concept of what God is into some exclusive religious, philosophical, or scientific arena is futile. What we must be prepared to simply accept is that **"God Exists".**

In this book I use certain words or phrases interchangeably when I am referring to this Being traditionally known throughout history as "God", words leaning more towards the cosmic non-ephemeral nature of God's existence. Whilst I primarily use the terms **Universal**

Consciousness or **Infinite Intelligence**, I may at times use the words the God Mind, the Creative Cosmic Spirit, the Supreme Creative Being, Presence, Being, the Creative Spirit, the Holy Spirit, the mother of Wisdom, and I often just use the word God itself, since most readers are familiar with it.

Putting God (Infinite Intelligence) purely into a Christian context, I would say:

"God is the source of humanity; Jesus the son is the avatar of God sent to lead a psychologically separated society back to that Source, and the Holy Spirit is the creative change agent given by Jesus to us, tasked with the responsibility of overseeing and supporting us in that psychological journey through consciousness back to our Source. All three separately are different aspects of Infinite Intelligence, all three together are the Trinity of Infinite Intelligence".

Putting God (Infinite Intelligence) into a non-partisan religious but inclusive meta-physical context I would say:

"God is an invisible, omnipotent, omniscient, omnipresent, omnificent, and omnibenevolent, energetic force, an Infinite Intelligence. The Brahman or Oneness in Hinduism, the Ruh al-Qudus in Islam, Universal Consciousness in Buddhism, the Holy Spirit in Christianity, and the Word in Judaism.

A loving energetic force, Being, and Presence that created, and continues to create, sustain, support and guide the transitionary and constantly evolving journey through consciousness and the accompanying ever changing psychological and ephemeral experience of all life in the universe".

The five "omni attributes of God" as listed above, characterise God as all powerful, all-knowing, constantly encountered and everywhere present being, all good and unlimited in creative power, each of them involving the other four and all providing a perspective on the all-embracing supremacy of Infinite Intelligence against any other form of intelligence such as human or artificial.

Omnipotent means that God is all powerful and in total control of himself and his creation, omniscient means God is the ultimate separator of truth and falsity, so that his ideas are always true, omnipresent means that since God's powers and knowledge extend to all parts of the universe, he himself is present everywhere, omnificent means that God created all things and has unlimited powers in creating. And omnibenevolent means that God is absolutely good, and that no action or motive or thought or anything else about God is not purely good.

Jesus himself asserted and confirmed to those around him the omnibenevolent component of God's character, when as we read in the Book of Mark, he stated that no one is truly good except God. That whilst human beings can do good things, at the same time they can also do bad things, but only God is omnibenevolent or wholly good in both thought and deed. Together these five Omni's define Gods supreme nature and yield a rich understanding of its creative, life changing and loving reach.

> "All of life is interrelated, we are all caught in an inescapable network of mutuality, tied into a single garment of destiny. Whatever affects one directly, affects all indirectly. We are made to live together because of the interrelated structure of reality. No lie can live forever, and as we continue to hope for peace and goodwill toward men, let us know that in the process we have cosmic companionship".

Excerpt from the final sermon of Dr. Martin Luther King Jr., Christmas 1967.

The Cosmological and Ecological Connectedness of The Universe

FIVE

> "Every man must decide whether he will walk in the light of creative altruism, or in the darkness of destructive selfishness."
>
> Dr. Martin Luther King Jnr.

Dr. Martin Luther King Jr. was born Michael King Jr. on January 15th, 1929, and passed April 4th, 1968, at 38 years of age. Dr. King was an American Baptist minister, but more well known for his activism and the stand he took on human rights and racial equality. In his role as the visible spokesperson for the Civil Rights Movement in America from 1955 until his assassination in 1968, he became well known for his passion in championing the cause of citizen equality for black Americans, using nonviolent protests and nonviolent civil disobedience. He once said that he was merely fulfilling his calling, having been inspired in his Christian beliefs by the nonviolent activism of Mahatma Ghandi, an Indian lawyer, social activist, and writer, who became the leader of the nationalist movement opposing the British Rule of India.

Under King's leadership, the Civil Rights Movement always practised the tactics of nonviolent protest with good success, mainly due to his strategic approach, with King always personally choosing the methods, times, and specific places in which protests were to be carried out. And whilst there were quite a few dramatic standoffs with segregationist authorities, who on many occasions themselves resorted to violence, the violence that did occur was more so due to the direction given by the then FBI director of the day J. Edgar Hoover, not because of the actions of the protesters, who were fully aware of the behaviour King expected from them.

Hoover, who it was later revealed was a closet homosexual, cross dresser and participant in wild sex orgies, and whose whole life and sense of morality was after his passing found to be seriously in question, continually branded King as a radical troublemaker, which gave him public licence to discredit King, and since Hoover was a man of questionable ethics that process often took form in false accusations against King and his followers.

Some argued that in fact King's untimely death was orchestrated by Hoover, believing Hoover had his FBI agents collaborate with James Earl Ray the man accused of assassinating Dr. King. Others felt it went further than this, believing Hoover had personally tasked his agents to kill King and that James Earl Ray was merely the scapegoat charged. Many believed that Hoover was capable of this, he wielded much power in government circles, with unproven rumour similarly seeing him linked to the assassination of President Kennedy, some 5 years earlier in 1963, who himself was an avid and vocal supporter of Dr. King.

Most people today, save those still alive who witnessed it first hand, have limited understanding of the intensity of physical and emotional abuse and destruction that was brought upon the Black American community during that time of official segregation. The policy of segregation involved separate housing suburbs and apartments, separate education, and separate social services for people of colour. Some of the extreme believers in segregation, many whose descendants have taken up the white supremacy battle in this modern day, felt that any push towards co-existence and equality between black and white people in society must be resisted at all costs. There were also many in the segregationist movement arguing for colonisation, either by returning the formerly enslaved people to Africa or creating their own reservation as was done with the American Indian.

The first steps they took towards officially mandating segregation came about in the form of what were called in those days, black codes. Black Codes, as in "code of life conduct for black people", commenced around 1865. They dictated a code of lifestyle that black people must adhere to, including where they could work, where they could live, and who they could associate with, which basically meant they were to associate with other black people only. It also ensured that black people made themselves available for cheap labour after slavery was officially abolished. It would not be long before state jurisdictions set about making these Black Codes law so they could become enforceable by lawful authorities meaning the police and the courts.

They eventually were legally sanctioned by the U.S. Supreme Court and officially, for legislative purposes named the Jim Crow Laws, Jim Crow being a name used as a derogatory term for black people. Legislators segregated everything, from schools to residential areas, to public parks, to public transport, to theatres, to pools, to cemeteries, to asylums, to residential homes for the aged. There were separate waiting rooms for white people and black people in professional offices. Not just doctors' surgeries but all professional offices. It was all about complete subjugation of the black people physically, emotionally, and mentally.

As part of the segregation movement, some cities instituted zoning laws that prohibited black families from moving into white dominant suburbs. Oklahoma became the first state to segregate public phone booths and public toilets. Colleges were segregated which saw new separate black institutions like the Howard University in Washington and Fisk University in Nashville being created. Virginia's Hampton Institute was established in 1869 as a school for black youth, but with white instructors only, teaching skills to regulate black people in service positions to whites. Basically, to teach them that their calling in life was to be as slaves to white society with a small pittance for payment.

One could in some way liken it to the current psychological and physical suppression through detention of the Uyghur Muslim minority in Communist China in this present-day, using indoctrination internment camps as an intermediatory device for re-educating them in the Communist way whilst at the same time utilising, according to the latest reports, at least 200, 000 of them to harvest cotton. Identical in fact to how Black Americans were conscripted and used to harvest cotton in the southern American states before slavery was abolished.

Midst all of this and more, around 54 years ago, Dr. Martin Luther King Jr. stood up to preach in his church, the Ebenezer Baptist Church in Atlanta Georgia and said the following. "In order for us to achieve peace on earth, we must develop a world perspective, a vision for the entire planet". He continued, "yes I understand that as individuals and nations on earth we all operate independently, but we need to more so recognize our interdependence on each other rather than our independence from each other, for all of life is interrelated".

On that morning during what was to be his last Christmas sermon before his assassination, in an almost prophetic way King anticipated much of the ecological, social and environmental breakdowns that he believed would occur in society over the coming 50 years, and his concerns regarding the apparent psychological disconnectedness between all, a disconnectedness that influenced and promoted not just diverse but also divisive differences in attitude to social justice, that need to be radically mended for the sake of humanity's present and future survival.

Whilst Dr. King's work to dismantle the hate filled intent of the white supremacy movement was rooted in his Christian beliefs and in what he believed was every individual's God given right to freedom, what is less known about him was his deep understanding of

The Cosmological and Ecological Connectedness of The Universe

the cosmologically unified state of our existence and the voice he gave many times in his sermons and Civil Rights gatherings to the cosmology of the interconnectedness of the universe and all it contains. For in that Christmas Eve sermon, he went on further to speak of the intrinsic cosmic connectedness of existence itself when he said:

> *"We are all caught in an inescapable network of mutuality, tied into a single garment of destiny. Whatever affects one directly, affects all indirectly. We are made to live together in harmony because of the interrelated structure of reality".*

On Christmas Eve 1968, exactly one year later, Colonel Frank Borman and his crew were on their fourth orbit around the moon. When he saw the earth swinging around the left side of the lunar horizon he exclaimed, "Oh my God, here's the earth coming up, wow that is so pretty". Those photographs taken by the Apollo 8 astronauts, the first widely available photos of a radiant earth hovering over the cratered grey moonscape alive with clouds and oceans, illuminated against the black cosmos, became an instant photographic icon, creating a new wave of cosmic mindedness and ecological awareness; photographs that were presaged twelve months earlier by Dr. King's prophetic message of interconnectedness on that Christmas Eve when he tied his vision for social justice to the interrelated structure of the universe, and in the final words of his sermon said the simple words:

> *"This is our faith, as we continue to hope for peace on earth, let us know that in that process we have cosmic companionship".*

Dr. King was of the Christian faith as we know when he spoke these prophetic words during what was to become his farewell sermon. Whilst using different terminology, remarkably similar in its purpose was the farewell sermon the Islamic religion's Muhammad gave to his followers. In Muhammad's final sermon in 632 A.D. he said, "an Arab has no superiority over a non-Arab, nor does a non-Arab have any superiority over an Arab. A white person has no superiority over a black, nor does a black have any superiority over a white, except in piety and good actions".

Here we see a perfect example of a common intent that regardless of religious affiliation, regardless of time and timing, two men from two vastly different eras, sought to convey to their own respective societies the interdependent calling for harmony and connectedness placed on all of humanity regardless of race, religion, or social status.

Both Dr. King and the Prophet Muhammad had demonstrated in their words a higher level of Cosmic Consciousness, much higher than most of the arguing, warring, combative, ideologically driven and belligerent members of society around them; a higher level that is still vitally needed to be seen in the rhetoric, actions and societally influencing behaviour of religious leaders in this modern day, if the world is to evolve collectively into its ultimate social, spiritual and cosmological pre-ordained destiny, thus understanding and accepting that we all exist as one whole and holy nation before God.

There are two key learnings about the functionality of the universe that it is necessary for us to clearly comprehend if we are to individually move forward in the three-stage evolution of our existence that I spoke of in Chapter 2, our journey through consciousness. A lack of understanding that will either stall completely our evolutionary journey through consciousness back to our source, or at a minimum hinder it, making it at times just seem difficult.

Those two key learnings are firstly an understanding of the cosmological metaphysical connectedness of all things in the universe, and secondly an understanding of the ecological connectedness of all things in the universe, meaning the relationships of living organisms to one another and to their physical surroundings. A relationship of connectivity and interdependence that must be maintained and not interfered with through humanity's predisposed disposition to selfish and greed fuelled intention and action.

Both these learnings when clearly understood and appropriated, have the potential to assist, guide, and successfully support and motivate us in our individual evolutionary journey to higher states of consciousness, or through non-appropriation interfere, perhaps in a minor or perhaps in a major way, with the progressive flow and fluidity of that evolutionary journey through consciousness.

Now whilst I will speak in far more detail in the following chapters on the nature of our cosmological connectedness and its alignment with our psychological interdependence, how it all works, I will however touch briefly on it here. I will then go on to focus on giving greater understanding to you the reader, on the importance of us knowing or having a greater awareness of the ecological connectedness of the universe we live in. A greater understanding of the ecological structure of this universe, not in any huge technical or intellectual way, just a simple understanding of how it comes together, and the importance of our maintaining the fluidity of that structure.

I use the word understanding because whilst it is said that knowledge is power, for me to give you knowledge alone is not profitable, knowledge without wisdom is profitless. There are many intellectuals out there in the world, full of knowledge, but extremely deficient in wisdom. Whilst knowledge is power, wisdom is our choosing the when and how to use that power, and wisdom emerges not at the point of receiving knowledge, but at the point of understanding that knowledge. One of the five wisdom books in the Bible, the Book of Proverbs says:

> "Get skilful and godly wisdom, it is pre-eminent, and with all your acquiring get understanding, actively seek spiritual discernment, mature comprehension and logical interpretation". (Amplified Version).

Understanding of any knowledge gained is necessary for us to form the right opinion or belief, and subsequently be motivated to then execute that opinion that is formed in a wise manner. The gift of understanding perfects a person's speculative reason in the apprehension and internal absorption of truth. In other words understanding opens us to acceptance of truth and our acceptance promotes the internalisation of truth so that it becomes part of our practical existence.

So firstly, touching on the Cosmological Connectedness of the universe. Even though Dr. King was of the Christian faith, the basic tenets of other religions would agree with his theory of a cosmic connection between all form and all sentient beings in this universe. For instance the religion of Buddhism teaches that there is an invisible web of interconnectedness in all things, between human and human, between nature and nature, and between humanity and nature, and that all beings and phenomena exist only because of their relationship and connectedness with all other beings and phenomena.

It teaches further that through **"attitudinal and behavioural engagement with this connectedness our true identity is established and enhanced"**, and we create an environment that not only sustains all other existence, but also creates a living cosmos, a whole. What we might call, a whole and thus Holy Universe. For when a wound is healed then the entire body becomes whole again. The religions of Hinduism, Sikhism, Taoism, Shintoism, also teach similar principles about the interconnectedness of all things created, a cosmological connectedness of each human being with the other, having the mind of a Divine and Infinite Intelligence present and participating as the glue that binds all together.

However spiritual teachers over the centuries have identified the tendency that most human beings living in an unenlightened or unconscious state of being have, to, in a sense disassociate themselves from the connectedness they were meant to embrace, and in its place take upon themselves the delusional belief that we are all

The Cosmological and Ecological Connectedness of The Universe

separate beings, not only functioning separately and independently physically from each other, but also separated psychologically and spiritually, living a totally separated existence from Divinity and all that Divinity has created.

This noticeably happens a lot with highly educated people and in the world of other intellectually focused groups such as in the scientific world. It is in some part one of the results of purely gaining much knowledge but without real understanding and wisdom that needs to accompany it.

But with certain scientists over the last few centuries there have been exceptions. There have been scientists with an existing measure of Cosmic Awareness, who, many times through their work and research, have come to an understanding and appreciation of the existence of this cosmological connectedness with a higher intelligence. Scientists such as Albert Einstein, Sir Isaac Newton, Thomas Edison, and Nikola Tesla are good examples. These were scientists who found that the world of science was indeed compatible with the teachings of these religions, and that it is possible to have both intellectual achievement and cosmic appreciation and understanding.

Albert Einstein for example once said, "a human being is part of the whole called by us the universe, a part limited in time and space, who experiences himself, his thoughts and feelings as something separated from the rest, a kind of optical delusion of his consciousness". Similarly Leonardo da Vinci, regarded as the greatest inventor of all time, whose designs it is said if they were built would have revolutionised technological history, regardless of his genius had a firm belief that everything in the universe connects to everything else and it was our purpose to maintain this "through our creative instincts". He believed that creativity was a type of metaphysical exercise programme given to us from the universe to keep the universe functioning at its peak level of connectivity. Sort of like how muscle exercise keeps the body functioning and flexible.

Nikola Tesla also, the American inventor, electrical engineer, mechanical engineer, and futurist, best known for his contributions to the design of the modern alternating current (AC) electricity supply system, once said, "the day science begins to study non-physical phenomena, it will make more progress in one decade, then all the previous centuries of its existence".

You see science is a systematic enterprise that builds and organizes knowledge in the form of testable explanations and predictions about the universe. That's how it seeks to gain understanding. Wisdom does not necessarily enter the picture at all. Science is based on a loop of observation, theory, experimentation, and validation. Science is based on facts. Science is based on empirical measurement (it quantifies) usually in terms of units of mass and energy velocity and position. Science is objective truth.

The problem for science though is that because science is based on objective measurement, it finds itself in a dilemma, because consciousness, that which connects humankind, cannot be directly observed, and measured. It cannot be measured because it is the one that measures.

It is a dilemma that many spiritual seekers of truth have difficulty with also because human beings are sensory beings, if it doesn't fall under the category of being able to be seen, touched, heard, felt, or smelt, meaning falling under the category of being easily identifiable or "knowable", we human beings have difficulty in accepting its reality. Similarly, some religious leaders have shifted this lack of knowing into the realm of the unknowable teaching that this level of cosmic awareness, this knowing of the unknowable, can only be ascertained or accessed through faith. And then when asked by someone the question, "well what if I lack faith", in replying without a measure of wisdom would say, "well ask for more faith", and leave the questioner bewildered. You know the type of bewilderment that says silently, "well I've been there, done that, and that didn't work, got anything else."

The Cosmological and Ecological Connectedness of The Universe

Many religious leaders have also stressed the incompatibility of religion with science as do many scientists stress the incompatibility of science with religion. Not so a cosmically aware religious leader such as Dr. Martin Luther King Jnr. who in speaking on this subject said the following: "Science investigates; authentic religion interprets. Science gives man knowledge, which is power; authentic religion gives man wisdom, which is control. Science deals mainly with facts; authentic religion deals mainly with values. However, the two are not rivals".

> "Science investigates and experiments; authentic religion, investigates, reflectively interprets, and experiments. Science gives man knowledge which to the world is power, authentic religion gives the world what I call "the trinity of power", which is knowledge, understanding and Wisdom which are all needed to give true power and control. Science causes man to understand that which is not known, authentic religion enables man to know the supposed unknowable".

You see the Soul of a human being has a magnetic quality about it, and therefore the need to be connected is the natural drive of our Soul. Whether that is to a Divine Being, to another person, to the abundance in this world, to success, there exists in all creation an overriding and sometimes overwhelming drive of the Soul to extract as much of the goodness of the universe as we can, and draw it into our lives, spiritually, emotionally, materially, and physically.

There is also inbuilt in our Soul, a subtle subconscious drive to make a connection with the world of the formless, to connect with consciousness, a drive to be connected to the unseen spiritual aspect of this universe, that is built into our being at birth, which is why some people with very limited involvement previously in any religious activity, will seek out a church to attend at Christmastime and Easter. This magnetic quality of the Soul is also why some people are drawn to meditation, or to a religion such as Buddhism, or always feel emotionally moved when they hear the song Amazing Grace.

Whether it be in a connected religious type of relationship with the God or spiritual deity of our choosing, or in making a connection through some sort of spiritually based activity such as meditation, or other spiritual involvement, there is a subconscious drive within all of us that moves our Soul in the direction of that which is sacred. The Buddha put it this way, "just as a candle's light cannot live without fire, so man cannot live fully without the fire of the Spirit involved in some way in the practical aspects of life".

Understanding our cosmic connectedness is not about us finding an ephemeral God that is distant and separated from us, even though institutionalised religion leans towards this type of teaching, you know the kind that says, "come to church and find God". Rather it is about understanding the reality of the Divine Conscious Presence, the Infinite Intelligence that permeates this universe, and the truth of our existing interconnectedness with it already; a truth that most are unaware of, but even if we have never stepped foot in a church in our life it has always been there. We are already immersed in Consciousness, and Consciousness is already in us, we don't have to go to a place to find Consciousness.

A phrase attributed to an archdeacon in the early Apostolic times named Stephen seen in the Bible's Book of Acts says, "the Most High does not dwell in houses made with hands," and the Gospel of Thomas, a Gnostic text containing the post resurrection teachings of Jesus, tells us that the Kingdom of God (Infinite Intelligence or Universal Consciousness) is within us, and surrounds us, for God does not live in temples of wood and stone." Jesus going on to say, "when I am gone split a piece of wood and I am there, lift a stone and you will find me," and it was Jesus who said, "I and the Father are one".

The Dalai Lama, Buddhist Monk Tenzin Gyatso has a conviction of that connection, Jesus and Muhammad had a conviction of

The Cosmological and Ecological Connectedness of The Universe

that connection, the Muslim Mystic Rumi had a conviction of that connection, Gautama the Buddha, and Mahatma Ghandi had a conviction of the existence of that cosmic connection, as did Dr. Martin Luther King Jr.

But it is not just confined to the overtly religious or spiritual people that we see this. Many other notable figures in history have come to understand this, people such as Nelson Mandela, Mother Teresa, Walt Whitman, Walter Bowman Russell, and Francis Bacon, who it is believed after his illumination, his realisation of his own cosmic connectedness with Infinite Intelligence, when writing under the nom de plume William Shakespeare, in a spectacular spirit influenced cosmic connected creative manner wrote all those wonderful Shakespearian plays and poems, and sonnets.

So, what is Cosmic Consciousness or Cosmic Awareness? Cosmic Awareness or call it intuitive awareness, is simply said the operational platform for Universal Consciousness. What is Universal Consciousness? It is Infinite Intelligence, the Mind of God, that keeps the world and all it contains energetically and thus physically and psychologically connected and interdependent on the other. It is a unifying energetic force. It is the Mind of God, or the Cosmic Loom of the universe, creating the new to replace the old and sustaining and upholding the existing.

People who know how to knit know what happens if just one single thread in a garment becomes separated, the whole garment has the potential to eventually unravel. A dropped stitch in a column in a knitting project can unravel a whole garment if not fixed speedily. We live in a world that right now is in a state of serious psychological "unravelling". It needs to move forward quickly in its evolutionary journey to a higher level of psychological existence, to a higher level of consciousness and with that a higher deeper level of awareness.

Consciousness is a psychological "state of Being", Awareness is the operational level, the perception level which we function at whilst evolving through a particular state of consciousness, a particular psychological level of being. Awareness is all about the perceptual functioning level of our mind, our analytical thinking process, how we see things at a particular time and place whilst we are continually evolving in our psychological journey through the different levels of consciousness or conscious existence.

There are three terms used in both Social Psychology and in certain spiritual writings, Social Psychology being the scientific study of what influences people's thoughts, feelings, beliefs, and intentions with regards to their social behaviour. These three terms are Collective Unconsciousness, Collective Consciousness, and Universal Consciousness, all being components of the "consciousness" or conscious existence of humanity.

All human beings from the moment of their very first thought become connected to the Collective Unconsciousness. We are all energetically connected and interdependent on each other for survival; and because all thought is creative energy that is sent out into the universe, one thought, one wrong or right thought affects all, sometimes in a most obvious way and sometimes in the most subtle way. In other words not noticed until it begins to unravel a person or a situation at a later time.

From this state of being we progressively evolve out of the Collective Unconscious state into a higher level, as we mature psychologically or grow in wisdom and knowledge. I say "wisdom, and knowledge" because when knowledge is received by whatever means the potential is there for a dropped stitch to occur if wisdom to support that knowledge is rejected, and knowledge alone is embraced. Because as I said previously wisdom is the catalyst for deep understanding, and understanding enables us to form the right opinion, which leads to right choices. Unfortunately, if wisdom is rejected and knowledge whether truth or false is all that is embraced, we all don't evolve at the same time, some get left behind. Which is why a

The Cosmological and Ecological Connectedness of The Universe

cosmic awareness of our interdependence on one another is vital, just as Dr. King stressed.

The collective responsibility of humanity to fulfil its destiny, is to evolve consciously together, to survive through Wisdom and understanding its initial journey through the realm of Consciousness known as the Collective Unconscious and emerge into in the first instance, a state of Collective Consciousness. And how do we do that?

We do it through Wisdom. The wisdom of right thinking and right and righteous behaviour according to the principles or laws of Universal Consciousness, that have been set in place by Infinite Intelligence, to guide humanity through its evolutionary journey. We use the tools or Laws of the Universe, Divine Principle, spiritual law, provided by Infinite Intelligence, to journey past the Collective Unconscious state of being, and onward through the Collective Conscious state of being, and then finally into Universal Consciousness and with that we are ready for our final date with destiny, the return of our Soul to its source.

The state of being, or 'state of mind', known as the state of Collective Consciousness, is purposed by Infinite Intelligence, as part of its cosmic plan to be the launching pad that takes people with their next transition completely away from both the Collective Unconscious and the Collective Conscious state of being, into a state of complete immersion in the Universal or Cosmic Consciousness of the universe. That Universal Consciousness could be described as God's own personal Collective Consciousness, God's Nature, the totality of God's Mind and God's thought processes.

When a person moves into a state of Universal Consciousness, they move into what is spoken of in Biblical terminology as "a life lived in the Spirit, a life of being led by the Spirit," and described in Buddhism as "the state of Enlightenment." Which brings us into complete psychological alignment with Infinite Intelligence.

How does this process of progressive immersion in higher levels of consciousness work? It happens through mind renewal, through the renewal of our thinking processes. It happens as we align our thoughts with God's thoughts or Divine Principle. We are choosing to become psychologically aligned with Infinite Intelligence which brings about a state of like-mindedness. As I spoke of in Chapter 3, we transcend into a new state of awareness. We continue to sink deeper into the ocean of Universal Consciousness through thinking intuitively about all things rather than simply rationally according to purely our level of knowledge.. by thinking about all things reflectively and wisely.

The process of mind renewal that the Apostle Paul spoke of is exactly the same process of striving for Buddha Mindedness that the Buddha spoke of. We are renewing our way of perceiving and thinking which results in a new way of doing and behaving. The Buddha once described the mind as a wild horse. It needs to be tamed. In the Eightfold Path, he recommends practising right effort by first avoiding and then clearing our minds of negative, and unwholesome thoughts. Once that is achieved, one perfects a wholesome, tranquil state of mind through the practice of ongoing disciplined positive thought patterns. When we have completed the process of mind renewal, we have completed the Atonement process as in Christianity and reached Enlightenment as in Eastern Religion. That's how it works. And it all centres on our state of mind.

It is a psychological spiritual thing not a physical thing. It's not about my works it's about my willingness to embrace how God works. It's the "not my will but thy will be done" attitude of Jesus on the cross. I am sure that if Jesus could have chosen his own way to die he would in the first instance have not chosen it to be through a crucifixion.

But the will of God was that the final sacrifice for humanity's past had to be a sacrifice of both the physical and the psychological, the

The Cosmological and Ecological Connectedness of The Universe

total slate had to be wiped clean. Jesus represented the sacrifice of the complete self that had dictated the attitudes and behaviours of humankind, since the original psychological fall, and Jesus accepted that as evidenced in his dying words, "not my will, but thy will be done."

Gershom Scholem, a highly regarded German born Israeli scholar, the first professor of Jewish Mysticism at the Hebrew University of Jerusalem, was greatly impressed by the sages and mystics of the Axial Age that I spoke of in Chapter 1, and their total dedication and focus on ascending through the various stages of consciousness, their unwavering commitment to transitioning through these psychological realms that were associated with the fullness of the Divine Light.

The Apostle Paul described his renewed life after completing these two transitional processes in this way. "I have been crucified with Christ, (the transition from the Collective Unconscious to Collective Consciousness), it is no longer I who live but Christ lives in me," (the transition from Collective Consciousness to full immersion in Universal Consciousness). This is the mystery hidden in the story of Jesus' baptism in the Jordan River by John the Apostle. He was fully immersed in the water, symbolic of God the water of life, He was immersed in the Universal Consciousness and a dove descended upon him symbolic of the Holy Spirit the Creative Spirit of God, and evidence to those around Him of His true Divinity.

That is what this transitionary life we live is all about and it only needs one thing from us to complete its evolutionary cycle, to take us out of the Outgoing, through the Involution and to the Return on the other side, and that one thing is our voluntary willingness. No one can force us to do this similarly as no one could force Jesus to stay on the cross. He did it as an act of His will. We choose spiritual life, or we choose even unintentionally, through ignorance or lack of understanding about life's purpose and priorities, spiritual death. We choose a life of Cosmic Connectedness a focus on Infinite

Intelligence, or a life of Carnal Connectedness, a focus on ourselves as being the centre of the Universe.

We choose a new way of living, according to Divine Principle, or we remain cosmically static at our old way of thinking and behaving. We surrender to Infinite Intelligence and its will and its way of doing things, so that whilst we are in the world we are not of the world, or alternately we just simply ignore the gentle promptings of the Spirit and stay immersed in the world of self.

Now remembering that all of life in the universe is connected and, in some irrevocable way, interrelating all the time, it is helpful in our journey to see how this works with regards to the interrelatedness of all animal life, and all vegetable and mineral matter. To gain greater understanding of the ecological connectedness of all life, not just within itself, but how the survival of the ecological side of our universe impacts on humanity's physical survival. Ecology, also called bioecology, bionomics or environmental biology, is the study of the relationships and interconnectedness between living organisms and their environment.

There is a term ecosystem used in Ecology. An ecosystem is a geographic area where animals plants and other organisms exist within their landscape, regardless of whether in an interconnected system of life or not. The term ecosystem was introduced into society in a scientific paper written by an English botanist named Arthur Tansley. The title of the paper was The Use and Abuse of Vegetal Concepts and Terms and was published in 1935. In that paper Tansley defined an ecosystem as a whole system including not only the organism complex, but also the whole complex of physical factors forming what we call the environment.

Since then, since the release of Tansley's paper, there has been a fascination by those in the scientific world who have a passion for the survival of the planet, to come to a greater understanding of the cosmology of ecosystems, how in fact individual components of it,

The Cosmological and Ecological Connectedness of The Universe

whether they be animal, vegetable, or matter, fit into its successful functioning in a co-operative and interconnected way. Doing it not from an ideological aspect, or a fear driven aspect, as we see occurring in some of the current climate change debate, but from a scientific aspect using visible facts and based on a loop of observation, theory, experimentation, and validation process as is all scientific analysis.

The attraction of the study of the ecosystem for scientists is all to do with the system part of the ecosystem. You see an ecosystem such as a coral reef, has very similar software to that of Antarctica or that of a tropical forest. Regardless of whether it is indeed in the arctic circle or on the coral reef, or in the Amazon jungle, the same basic large-scale processes can apply anywhere. They being that organic matter decomposes and becomes nourishment for something else. Whether that be in a grassland, in a jungle, or even in a mountain stream, there are nutrients such as carbon, and phosphorus, and nitrogen, and sulphur, invisible to the eye nutrients, that get passed around like Monopoly money everywhere. It just happens to occur a lot faster and there's a lot more of them being passed around in the tropical rainforest, than there are in the desert.

If a predator hapless organism is removed from the ecosystem say in the African jungle, or in the Andes mountains, the entire dynamic would change, just as it would if you removed certain animals from a national park. For example, bats play a very important role in ecosystems as pollinators, pollinators being animals of all types that visit flowers and take away their pollen. Pollen is a sex cell of plants. Insects such as honeybees and other animals such as birds, rodents, monkeys, and even humans are all pollinators giving something of themselves to enable the continuance of life or the evolution of life.

Insectivores, animals that feed on insects, such as hedgehogs and moles, worms, and other invertebrates, all play their part. And of course, some of humanity, having no understanding of how the ecosystem works, only see these things as pests and an interference in the dynamic of their economical and physical existence, that need to be eliminated. Such thinking merely reflecting the ancient self-survivalist nature buried deep within the psyche of a human being. But all these things, bats included, play and important role in the ecosystems as do many other animals and insects such as bees.

Bees are one of our most important pollinators. Recent research has found a nearly 50 percent decline in the areas occupied by bumblebees in North America, with bumblebee populations in North America plummeting because of extreme weather conditions. Pollination occurs when pollen is moved within flowers or carried from flower to flower by pollinating animals such as bees, bats, butterflies, and beetles, but even by the wind. Pollination has an environmental connection as well. The transfer of pollen between flowers of the same species leads to fertilisation and successful seed and fruit production for plants.

Pollination ensures that a plant will produce full bodied fruit and a full set of viable seeds. Around the world there are also roughly 1000 plants that are ground for food beverages, spices, and medicines that need to be pollinated by animals to produce the goods which we depend on. Goods such as apples, blueberries, chocolate, melons, peaches, potatoes, pumpkins, vanilla, and almonds.

Where would we be without our morning cup of coffee. New research has found that bee pollination can result in a 10 to 20 percent pollination effect in coffee, and whilst the Arabica coffee plant is self-pollinating, bee pollination enhances the quality of the yield, and the Robusta coffee plant depends on cross pollinating. About 6 to 8 weeks after each Robusta coffee flower is fertilized, cell division occurs, and the coffee fruit remains as a pin head for a period totally dependent on the climate.

Much of society simply just does not understand the role or the interconnected relationship these pollinators have in the ongoing survival of humanity or for some they just don't care because

The Cosmological and Ecological Connectedness of The Universe

their immediate self-survivalist nature dominates their thinking and behaving. We are seeing that worldwide there is disturbing evidence coming forth that many pollinating animals are suffering from loss of habitat through chemical misuse, and through human introduced invasive plant and animal species, all supposedly in the name of human progress. And all this has occurred simply due to one single reason, humanities lack of understanding of the relationship, the connectedness, between all of nature's life and their own.

This invisible state of connectivity in terms of the ecology of the universe is not limited to the world of plants and animals alone. It exists and has been seen to be evident in studies of the meteorological environment or atmosphere of the universe. Edward Norton Lorenz was a scientist, a meteorologist, and a professor at the Massachusetts Institute of Technology, a man described as a genius with the soul of an artist. In his lifetime he was the winner of many scientific awards including the prestigious Kyoto Prize for outstanding achievement in basic sciences.

Known affectionately in scientific circles as "the father of the chaos theory", Edward was lauded by his peers for his many scientific achievements, in particular the theory that later became commonly known as the butterfly effect. In layman's terms it was a concept that explained how small effects could lead to big changes. How something as minuscule as a butterfly flapping its wings in Brazil, could progressively change the constantly moving atmosphere of the universe in ways that might later trigger tornadoes in Texas.

Years before the first national Earth Day, before ecology and the environment and climate change became catchwords, before popular knowledge of "Gaia theory" and "systems thinking" emerged, Dr. King was "tying his vision of compassion, kindness, justice, and peace, to the interrelated structure of the universe" similarly as Jesus had done. Whilst Dr. Martin Luther King Jr. did not live to see those photographs taken by the Apollo 8 astronauts, the first widely available photos of a radiant earth hovering over the cratered grey moonscape alive with clouds and oceans, illuminated against the black cosmos, that created a new wave of cosmic mindedness and ecological awareness, because of his untimely death, his vision for equality and his understanding of the interconnectedness of all life that had presaged those space images lives on.

In this modern day some fifty plus years later, so many of our challenges represent a failure to understand our cosmic and ecological interconnectedness. White supremacists and neo-Nazis, emboldened in these times, preach a timeworn Hitlerian hatred that corrodes community cohesion and evaporates the fluidity of humanity's cosmic flow. Corporate and social capitalism, with its widening gulf between the ultra-rich and the millions of people born into and continually living in poverty, strains our social fabric, and blurs our sense of societal cohesiveness and psychological and spiritual connectedness.

While the worsening climate crisis, evidenced in droughts, floods, and famine, provides an unforgiving reminder of the earth's delicate and fragile interrelatedness with humanity and with itself, providing in themselves evidence also of the destruction that we can bring upon ourselves in allowing the purposeful intent of those self-survivalist and greed driven individuals to put their own selfish needs above those of our future generations.

It will be only through our understanding of our connectivity and the appropriation through wisdom of life principles and behavioural undertakings that promote and maintain an attitude of connectivity, will we then see both the individual and our collective society journey successfully in its evolution through consciousness back to its source.

" *"Mind is consciousness which has imposed upon itself limitations because it chose to separate itself from the Mind of Infinite Intelligence, creating a gap in the connection. You were originally limitless and perfect. It is within that gap that the God Mind waits patiently longing for us to return.*

Humanity's responsibility to itself is to close that gap that separates the finite mind and the Infinite Mind, the gap that separates the Mind of Man from the Mind of God, opening up each individual once again to Infinite Intelligence and the unlimited and unbounded potentiality it desires to express in a creative and selfless way through each of us".

Universal Consciousness The Creative Cosmic Loom Weaving the Fabric of The Universe

SIX

> "The day science begins to study non-physical phenomena, it will make more progress in one decade, than all the previous centuries of its existence".
>
> Nikola Tesla

Nikola Tesla, born 28th of June 1856 and passed 7th January 1943, was a Serbian American inventor, electrical engineer, mechanical engineer, and futurist, best known for his contributions to the design of the modern alternating current (AC) electricity supply system, a necessary component of our everyday existence. Futurists or futurologists are people whose specialty or interest is futurology, which is an attempt to systematically explore predictions and possibilities about the future, and how they can emerge from the present.

The term Futurist most commonly refers to people who attempt to understand the future through trend analysis, people such as authors, consultants, thinkers, organisational leaders, and others, who engage in interdisciplinary and systems thinking to advise private and public organisations of such matters as diverse as global trends, possible scenarios emerging, market opportunities, and risk management. We have seen much of this type of work at play in recent times as the Covid epidemic has spread and evolved with certain institutes advising governments of expected outcomes from various types of reaction to the spread of the virus.

Tesla Motors, the American electric-automobile manufacturer, formed initially by two American entrepreneurs to develop an electric sports car, was named after Nikola Tesla that Serbian American inventor, to honour his contribution in bringing what we simply know as electricity to the world and into our homes. Tesla once said, my brain is only a receiver in the universe, there is a pool from which we obtain knowledge, strength, and inspiration, and whilst I have not fully penetrated the secrets of that pool, I nevertheless know that it exists. He then went on in his creative career to tap into that pool. Tesla once described himself as a discoverer of hidden principles, equipped with a vivid imagination and focused by design to seek harmony in the human condition.

According to Tesla, inventors represent that branch of humanity who are responsible for the safe progress and well-being of the race and the preservation of our natural resources. That their primary goal should be to bring about a world where creativity, culture, and peace could thrive together. Similar in intent and based on his own personal experience and attained knowledge of traditional philosophies in India, was Pandit Gopi Krishna, a twentieth century teacher, who presented to the world not only a theoretical explanation of the evolutionary process of humanity, but a thorough roadmap for examining the evolutionary impulses and the drives that guide humanity on its path to higher consciousness.

Gopi once said, "Man is destined for a brighter and more glorious state of being than his present existence. It is a glorious state visualised as being solely due to a union with God and with that a biological transformation of the brain and nervous system leading to the emergence of a blissful expanded state of consciousness, the natural endowment of future man". Believing that this biological transformation of the brain witnessed the emergence of higher personality traits of the Divine kind, he went on to say, "these spontaneous transformed personality patterns are in fact representative of an evolutionary metamorphosis slowly taking place in humanity, through cosmic laws of which we have no precise understanding at present".

I will speak in the next chapter in more detail about awareness, about the concept of Simple Conscious Awareness and Cosmic Conscious Awareness, and how they surface in consciousness, that pool of consciousness that both Gopi Krishna and Nikola Tesla were referring to, but firstly, what is "consciousness" itself? What is this thing called consciousness? We need to have a clear understanding of what this thing called consciousness is, for in this current spiritual climate, there can be some confusion with the use of the term consciousness and the term conscious awareness or just awareness, with some spiritual teachers interchanging these two terms as if they have the same meaning. They are of course linked but refer to two different things.

In looking at the subject of "consciousness" firstly we must accept that life as we call it is a transitionary journey. We are continually evolving spiritually (soul), physically (body), and psychologically (mind). Life is not as many believe, simply a stop, start, and sometimes stationary and frustrating physical and emotional journey, and then that's it, we die and hopefully have a nice funeral where people will say nice things about us. We must come to understand and accept that there is a universality and eternality to our existence and not just be content with the individuality and temporality of our existence.

And that costs us nothing and it is not a hard thing to do. We simply accept that life, our life, does not end when we physically die. We must come to accept that there is a cosmic side to life that is with us when we are alive and continues with us when we are dead physically. We just decide to accept that there is a cosmic side to our life as well as the carnal side, and then seek to understand through knowledge and wisdom how it all works. This is how it works.

There is a single energetic force of mind or intelligence that pervades the whole universe. Now this is not just a religious idea or a philosophical thought bubble that has been passed down to us over the centuries, even though yes, it is the ancient teaching of spiritual masters since the beginning of known time. Rather it is an exact scientific truth. Tesla understood this, the renowned scientist Albert Einstein understood this, as have many other scientists, who told us that everything in existence is energy, and that all energy is part of a universal energy or energetic force, including the energy existing in human form, animal form, natures form, and all forms of material substance, everything. This hidden energetic intelligence is what Jesus was speaking of in a mystery when he said, "look under or at a rock and you will find me there."

It is an omnipotent energy force, meaning it is all powerful, it is an omnificent force which means unlimited in its creative ability, it is omniscient meaning it knows everything, and it is an omnipresent energetic force which means always present everywhere at the same time. This means it's in me, it's in you, it's around me, it's around you; it's in those pebbles on the beach, and in the sand that supports the pebbles, and in the ocean that moves those pebbles along. It's in the clouds in the sky, it's in the air we breathe, it's everywhere. It is all around us and it is inside us.

This Infinite Intelligence or energetic force is spoken of in the Bible in the Book of John as being with us, meaning in the form of Jesus and everything around us, and in us, meaning an invisible energetic force inside our being. It is a creative energetic force that sustains us and keeps us physically alive, whether we are conscious or unconscious, which is why people who fall into a coma can live for years in that comatose state.

It is known in Judaism and Christianity as the Word, and in other religions by various names including in the Islamic religion where it is called Ruh al-Qudus, the Spirit of Holiness (Holy Spirit), God's agent of Divine Action and communication. It is in all things created because all things emanated from it, the source, in the beginning, just as in a human being the DNA of the mother and father, those who participated in the original conception, is transferred, or reproduced in the child, so the DNA of Infinite Intelligence creation's source is within us all, no matter what religion we follow or whether we follow a religion at all.

Jesus also referenced this energetic force of creative life and change and its connection with us all when he said to the people, "when I am raised to life again, meaning his resurrection, you will know that I am in my Father, and you are in me, and I am in you. (New Living Translation). Meaning the eternality of the DNA of his heavenly father, Infinite Intelligence, would evidence through his resurrection, and be evidence that nothing, not even what is seen as the highest form of physical annihilation, physical death, could conquer him. The Apostle Paul in coming to understand this internally cried out, "death, where now is your sting."

This hidden intelligence is what is described in spiritual writings as Universal Consciousness or the Universal Mind or sometimes just simply termed Consciousness, terminology for a metaphysical (things outside human perception) concept suggesting an underlying essence of all being and becoming in the universe, of all that exists and all that can be creatively brought into existence in the future in terms of chronological time.

It is the energetic force that was and still is present in the ongoing implementation and practicalities of the three mysteries, the Outgoing, the Evolution and the Return, that I spoke of in Chapter 2. It is the same Outgoing of God that created the universe. That is the energetic force that we are speaking about here now. It is the energy force that is known as the Universal Field or Infinite Intelligence. There are different terms of expression for it, simply because the understanding of the existence of it and its activity surfaced in different places at different times, through different disciplines including religion, science, and philosophical thought, over the course of humankind's existence.

It was given different names at various times by different cultures, different religions and different sciences and philosophical genres, but nevertheless names all still referring to the same creative energy force. In his scientific research and investigation, it was referred to by Albert Einstein as "an unmanifest field of pure consciousness, of limitless intelligence and creativity", and if we look more closely at this "unmanifest field of pure consciousness" we see the following.

Spiritual writers, psychology writers and religious writers over the years have put forth what we might describe as a compartmentalised version of consciousness that breaks it down into three distinct and different functioning components. The terms used to describe the three are the **Collective Unconsciousness, Collective Consciousness**, and **Universal Consciousness** that I touched on in the previous chapter. They are three terms used in Social Psychology, Social Psychology being the scientific study of how people's thoughts, feelings, beliefs, and intentions influence social behaviour.

All these three compartmentations of consciousness participate in the development, structure and functioning of the universe and its involvement in the evolutionary spiritual and psychological journey of all individuals during their physical lifetime. Now I talk in more detail in Chapter 8 about the work of Carl Jung the renowned psychoanalyst, who did a lot of experiential work in one specific compartment of consciousness, the Collective Unconscious, in treating his patients who had some sort of psychological disorder such as bi-polar syndrome, but to give you this basic understanding of the three terms as a precursor to that chapter now.

There is a sequence of psychological transitions that occur in the minds (the thinking levels and intelligence levels) of all individuals as they journey through life. They are in fact three different States of Awareness, or you could call them three states of perception. Perception in this instance being the way we look at or interpret life circumstances in our thoughts. We would all have heard someone express that they seem to get wiser as they get older, or when commenting on a wayward child perhaps making bad choices they might say, "he's just going through a stage". That's what I mean by psychological transitions, we go through stages in our way of thinking about things or interpreting things that happen to us and those around us in our daily lives. And how we think or interpret a situation determines our behaviour or the action we may decide to take.

However, it does not necessarily totally depend on age as to when the psychological transition occurs. Sure our physical transition does depend completely on age but not our psychological transition to higher states of awareness or perceiving. There are still a lot of adults around making immature and sometimes simply dumb decisions.

Now as we psychologically sit in each state of awareness in this our psychological transitionary journey, we are also existing in a corresponding state of Being or Presence or Consciousness that aligns with that state of awareness, and from which that state of awareness "feeds itself". So here's the thing. Consciousness is fed by our current awareness and according to the degree of vibrational energy that our present state of awareness possesses determines whether or not our consciousness evolves or de-evolves or just remains at its existing level. But also our level of consciousness in reverse feeds our current awareness. They work together. So your state of awareness feeds your consciousness, and your state of consciousness dictates your state of awareness.

So, as we journey through life psychologically, as we move through the three levels of awareness, so too our level of being or existence, our level of consciousness that feeds it evolves. Feeds our level of awareness with what? Feeds our level of awareness with knowledge and understanding and a measure of wisdom. The **lowest form of consciousness** that the individual can be psychologically immersed in is the **Collective Unconscious. The highest level of consciousness** that an individual can be immersed in is **Universal Consciousness.**

The highest level of awareness a human being can attain is Cosmic Awareness and the corresponding level of being or consciousness that the mind is immersed in and is fed from at this stage is Universal Consciousness, or the Universal Mind, Infinite Intelligence. To have reached that level one has developed their minds' perceptive (awareness) processes, which includes both their rational thought processes, and their intuitive thought processes, to the "highest point of renewal", where it is able to tap into Infinite Intelligence as it so desires. Wisdom becomes freely available. One then becomes what is termed a **Cosmic Consciously Aware** person. You are functioning in the world but know in your inner being you are not of the world. It is what the Buddha termed a state of Buddha Mindedness.

The Apostle Paul spoke of this renewal process, the process of developing our perception processes, in addressing the Roman people when he said, "be ye transformed by the renewing of your mind". To evolve into a Cosmic Consciously Aware person is to be psychologically transformed, old things just pass away, including regrets about the past, and anxiety about the future. All perception and thought processes become as new.

To help clearly show the alignment between Awareness and Consciousness, I have placed a table of how this works at the end of Chapter 7. However, since this chapter as the title suggests, centres on Universal Consciousness, then that is what I will focus on here and leave the Awareness Consciousness connection to the next chapter.

Most religions have come to acknowledge the existence of this Infinite Intelligence, this Universal Consciousness, or the Universal Mind, this unmanifest field of pure creative potential, this field of pure consciousness, even if many fail to appropriate it. It is the creative and communicative aspect of God in all religions albeit described in many ways, but all pointing back to the Infinite Creative Intelligence that is God in Spirit. In Chapter 4 I spoke of the many names of Infinite Intelligence and each religions basic description or interpretation of what it is and or does, but let's just simply say for now that God in Spirit is Infinite Intelligence, which is Universal Consciousness, which is an energetic force, an unmanifest field of pure potential.

Now just to add to that and include some historical and cultural religious context, some examples but not all examples of how and where its existence was first acknowledged and continues to be recognized.

In ancient Judaism this Infinite Intelligence or Universal Consciousness is seen as the Divine Force, quality, and influence of the Highest God over the universe. In Old Testament theology it is referred to as "the Word". As we read in Genesis, "in the beginning was the Word, and the Word was with God, and the Word was God".

In early Christianity, similarly as in Judaism, this Infinite Intelligence or Universal Consciousness is known as the Word, but in New Testament theology its presence is more referred to as the Holy Spirit, the active creative component of the Christ Mind, which of course is the God Mind, Infinite Intelligence, since Jesus is described as God in flesh. The Bible says in the Book of John in describing Jesus, "The Word became flesh and made His dwelling amongst us. We have seen His glory, the glory of the one and only son who came from the Father". (New International Version).

It is saying that Infinite Intelligence manifested in human form and dwelt amongst us in the form of Jesus. Why did this happen you ask? So as to meet humanity at its existing level of understanding, that of Simple Awareness. The scripture then tells us that when Jesus knew His departure was imminent he told the people around Him that he would, after he was gone "send the Comforter", the Holy Spirit, who would teach them all things". The Holy Spirit is the voice of Infinite Intelligence that was given to us to guide and assist us through our evolutionary journey of consciousness.

The New Testament tells us that the Word in flesh, named Jesus, departed, and replaced himself with the Word in Spirit, the Holy

Spirit, Universal Consciousness. Because unlike Jesus in the flesh, who was confined to a body and thus confined geographically in who he could assist, so could only influence and instruct those close to him, the Holy Spirit on the other hand as an energetic spiritually creative force could be everywhere at once. Jesus came to introduce the spirit of Infinite Intelligence, the mother of all Wisdom, to humanity.

In Islam this Infinite Intelligence or Universal Consciousness is Ruh al-Qudus, the Spirit of Holiness and is God's agent of Divine Action and communication. The Muslim interpretation of this Infinite Intelligence is generally consistent with other interpretations based on the Old and New Testaments.

There are three dimensions to the Islamic religion (Ara.ad-din). They are Islam, Iman and Ihsan. Islam is the religion itself; Iman is one's inner faith, and Ihsan is an Arabic term meaning beautification, perfection, or excellence. To the Muslim it is a matter of taking one's inner faith (Iman) and showing it in Ihsan, in both deed and action, in a demonstration of social responsibility borne from religious conviction. And this is all done with the assistance of Ruh-al-Qudus, the Holy Spirit of the Islamic religion, God's agent of Divine action and communication.

In Native American this Infinite Intelligence or Universal Consciousness is known as the Great Spirit or as Wakan Tanka in Lakota, a Siouan language of the great Sioux Tribes in North Dakota and South Dakota, and as Gitche Manitou in the Algonquian peoples. The Great Spirit has at times been conceptualised as a celestial deity. A god of creation, history, and eternity, who also takes a personal interest in world affairs and might regularly intervene in the lives of human beings.

The Aboriginal First Nation people of Australia refer to Infinite Intelligence or Universal Consciousness as Baiame, the Divine single creator or the creator Sky Father who made the land and the rivers and who gave the Aboriginal people their laws. Many Aboriginal people easily mix Christian concepts with beliefs about the Dreaming or Dreamtime allowing them to reconcile two different viewpoints. The Dreaming or Dreamtime is a psychic deeply intuitive state in which or during which contact is made with ancestral spirits, or the Law given in the beginning. They communicate with Universal Consciousness, similarly as Christian Mystics do in times of reflection or contemplative meditation.

In Zoroastrianism which is one of the world's oldest continuously practiced religions, based on the teachings of the Iranian speaking prophet Zoroaster, this Infinite Intelligence or Universal Consciousness is known as Spenta Mainyu, and is the source of all goodness in the universe, the spark of life in all humanity, and is the ultimate guide for humanity in righteous behaviour and communication with God.

In Hinduism in ancient spiritual writings such as the Upanishads and Vedanta, Infinite Intelligence or Universal Consciousness is the Ultimate Reality and the Absolute. It is the all-pervasive, genderless, infinite, and eternal intelligence which does not change yet is the creative cause of all change. In Hinduism it is called Sat Chit Ananda meaning the root and ground of the universe and the source of all that exists, pure consciousness.

In Vedanta, which is one of the six schools of Hindu philosophy, one of the oldest spiritual philosophies, it is called Brahman. The Vedanta philosophy revolves around only one truth, the existence of Brahman. Brahman is the name of the transcendent power that exists beyond the universe, the creative energy that exists beyond all things. In Vedanta, **this** consciousness is **"the potential for the experience of true awareness".**

Similarly, as Christians see God's creative energy as the Holy Spirit or the Breath of God, but don't worship the Holy Spirit more so focusing their worship on God and Jesus, Hindus do not worship Braham, but they believe that the power that is Braham appears throughout the entire universe and sustains everything in it, as Christians, many only subconsciously rather than pro-actively, see the power of God at work. Hindus believe that Braham is an energy force, and the universe is a manifestation of that energy.

Different words than what Christians use, but basically the same meaning. The Bible says, "in the beginning was the Word", (an energetic intelligent creative life force, the Breath of God), "and the Word was with God, and the Word was God". A Hindu would probably say, "in the beginning was Braham, and Braham was with God, and Brahman was the creative energy that exists beyond all things and sustains all things".

Universal Consciousness, that same creative energy that Albert Einstein referred to as, "an unmanifest field of pure consciousness, of limitless intelligence and creativity", has over the centuries been variously defined by spiritual writers, religions, and scientific minds, of a variety of brands as seen above. It has also been called presence, being, unlimited potential, a sea of potentiality, an observing presence, a sense of something existing or watching beyond the realm of the mind, but regardless of what it is called, all roads lead back to the truth of the existence of this Infinite Intelligence and the energetic transforming elements it contains.

There are many noticeable elements to this state of consciousness apart from that already alluded to, the higher level of awareness, and the primary one you could say is a new capacity for intellectual enlightenment or illumination, or you could call it the getting of Divine Wisdom, which places the Cosmic Conscious individual on a higher plane of existence than the rest of humanity. They begin knowing the unknowable, that which exists in another dimension, a different time and space, and cannot be known through Simple Awareness which manifests in this existing time and space and uses as its vehicle the rational and many times irrational thought process.

In this state of consciousness, that state of Cosmic Consciousness, one also comes to an awareness or sense of their own immortality, a conscious awareness of the eternal life that is already theirs, where prior to this the tendency for a human being is to see themselves purely as a mortal human being who eventually will die and then that is the end of life, except perhaps if they gain entrance to that mysterious place called heaven.

Cosmically Aware individuals see immortality or eternal life as being theirs now, not as some sort of gift in the afterlife if you have been one of the good guys in the present life as institutionalised religion teaches, but an unshakeable realisation of their own immortality in their present existence right now. Death then becomes a thing not to be fearful of, rather something to be embraced as another ongoing cosmic adventure. The Apostle Paul, when he came to this realisation cried out, "death, where now is thy sting". In speaking of Jesus the Book of Timothy in the New Testament says, "who abolished death and brought life and immortality to light." The ancient Prophet Isaiah in speaking of the coming of Jesus said, "he will swallow up death for all time."

Despite millennia of analyses, different definitions, and explanations and debate by philosophers, religious leaders and scientists over the centuries, all might I say coming from different levels of their own existing state of consciousness, perhaps the only widely agreed notion of all of them is that "the intuitive thought process", the process of intuition which comes from a deeper or higher level of conscious awareness than that of Simple Awareness, does in fact exist in all sentient beings and thus has the potential to be experienced by all.

It is a field of potential creativity waiting and wanting to be expressed through a human being. What I am saying here is that what we refer to as being in a state of Cosmic Consciousness brings to our reality the capacity to tap into a previously unmanifest ocean of creative potentiality waiting and wanting to be expressed in form of some kind, whether that be thought form or some sort of visible structured form. Different methods have been given by writers and teachers over the centuries on how to access this energetic force, how to tap into it. Some say we can do it through meditation, some say it exists in stillness and silence so by surrendering to stillness it can be realised, and others would say it can be accessed through the process of mindfulness.

Some past spiritual teachers such as the Maharishi Mahesh Yogi, one of the well-known teachers of the transcendent capability of a human being in the early 70's, an Indian guru to celebrities such as the Beatles and the Beach Boys, regarded as the father of Transcendental Meditation, taught that the basis of all life, inner and outer, meaning our thoughts and experiences, is a field of pure existence, "pure Being", as he called it in the early stages, an unmanifest field of pure consciousness, of limitless intelligence and creativity that can be tapped into by all human beings.

However, having lived as a young adult at this time, I would suspect that in his practical demonstration of Transcendental Meditation in the classes he held, he would have included for some of that hippie era, a measure of support to achieve that goal in the form of a joint or alternately a hallucination inducing pill. But regardless of their individual approaches one thing they all agreed on is that this state of consciousness and the ability to tap into it does exist and is available to all.

When Dr. Martin Luther King spoke of the connectedness of humanity and the cosmic companionship, we all have, he was coming from a place of Cosmic Awareness, an awareness of and belief in the interrelatedness of all things in the universe, this ethereal connection we have in the invisible field of consciousness. When Albert Einstein described the intuitive mind as a sacred gift, and the role of the rational mind to be that of a faithful servant to that gift, he was speaking out of his own personal experience as a scientist in tapping into Infinite Intelligence and thus becoming in that moment a Cosmic Conscious creative individual, seen as one of the greatest scientific minds ever. Intuitive thought is the language of consciousness, the intuitive process is the communication process of Infinite Intelligence.

Gopi Krishna who I referenced earlier in this chapter emphatically believed that the creativity as expressed by certain individuals in history, those creative individuals exceptionally gifted who displayed certain characteristics common to an expanded state of consciousness in their particular branch of human activity, were unmistakable symptoms of a transformed personality and a high-level of cosmic awareness; a state of being thought by many to be far beyond the reach of normal individuals, but not by Gopi.

For Gopi believed that it was a higher level of consciousness that is available to all human beings, that is those human beings who are prepared to come to understand it, and then take the time and make the effort with Wisdom to develop a higher state of awareness by transitioning out of their existing state of perceiving into a whole new way of looking at life and understanding why things are as they are and what can be done to change them. I share this process of transitioning to a higher level of awareness in the following chapter.

" *The great challenge of a person's consciousness has always been to let go of the lesser in order to include the greater, to let go of the visible in order to make way for the invisible, to let go of the lower nature to give ascendancy to the higher nature, which simply is to let go of the ego's interpretation of things and allow the Spirit's perception of things to be the dominant influencer in our life.*"

Awareness The Operational Platform of Consciousness

SEVEN

> "A human being is a part of the whole called the universe; but experiences himself, his thoughts, and his feelings as something separate from the rest, a kind of optical delusion of Consciousness".
>
> Albert Einstein

Albert Einstein was born March 14, 1879, and passed April 18, 1955, at the age of 76 years. Einstein was a German born theoretical physicist who was widely acknowledged as being one of the greatest physicists of all time. More widely known for developing the theory of relativity, which gave physicists around the world a whole new understanding of space and time, Einstein also made important contributions to the development of quantum mechanics. Quantum mechanics is a fundamental theory in physics that provides a description of the physical properties of nature at the microscopic level of "atoms and subatomic particles", and it is the foundation of all quantum physics.

Classic physics on the other hand, which was the description of physics that existed before the theory of relativity, describes many aspects of nature, but only at an ordinary macroscopic (large) scale, while quantum mechanics explains the aspects of nature at the small atomic and subatomic level. Einstein's work was well known for its influence on the philosophy of science, and in 1921 he received the Nobel prize in physics for his services to theoretical physics and especially for his discovery of the law of the photo electric affect. This was a discovery which went on to result in the manufacture of specific electronic devices specialised for light detection, one of the most well-known being night vision devices that are used by defence forces and by law enforcement agencies.

With regards to his spiritual or religious beliefs, in 1929 Einstein, when questioned on the matters of God and the Soul, gave his viewpoint in this way. He said, "I see our God in the wonderful order and lawfulness of all that exists in both man and animal", and then when further questioned about the meaning of life, and what a meaningful life is, on several occasions he said the following. "The man or woman who regards their own life and that of their fellow creatures as meaningless will always be unhappy, one must find meaning. If you want to live a happy life, tie it to a meaningful goal, not to meaningless people or meaningless things". He went on to say that there are only two ways to live your life, one is as though nothing is a miracle and the other is as though everything is a miracle.

Einstein died in April 1955 from an abdominal aortic aneurysm, which is an enlarged area in the lower part of the major blood vessel the aorta, the one that supplies blood to the body. He died after refusing surgery saying, "I want to go when I want, it is tasteless to prolong life artificially. I have done my share it is time to go, I will do it elegantly".

Whilst at one time consciousness and awareness were viewed with scepticism by many scientists, in recent years it has become a significant topic of research both in spirituality, psychology and in neuroscience. Albert Einstein, this man whose achievements made the name Einstein synonymous with the word genius, this man who possessed an unbelievable intellectual capacity and used the faculty of his rational mind to the absolute limit, was the same man who believed that no single problem he encountered could ever be solved from the same level of "awareness" occurring when he discovered it, meaning the level of intellectual awareness, the level of Simple Awareness.

He believed that the truly valuable faculty influencing his successful achievements and the true measure of intelligence was in using his imagination facilitated through the power of intuitively tapping into a higher level of awareness, from a deeper level of consciousness, the realm of Infinite Intelligence. If you analyse his many achievements, you see that underpinning his work was a deep determination to understand the underlying unity of the universe and all it contains. As a dedicated scientist he profoundly altered the way many people think about themselves and the universe. He spent the last half of his life trying to develop a unified field theory, a description of the one energetic field, the one consciousness he felt underpinned and gave rise to everything in the universe, including all the forces in nature.

And he kept persisting, even though he received much criticism from his fellow physicists in his pursuance of what they saw as an impossible task. But Einstein was not deterred in his creative quest and continued attempting to discover that deeper level of awareness and knowledge which was invisible to the mortal eye, right up until the very end of his physical life. What he did not understand though was that he was attempting the impossible. He was trying to bring "that which is unknowable" into the "realm of the knowable." Because as a dedicated scientist he was used to bringing "the unknown into the realm of the known." We can't define the unknowable we can only be aware that it exists. That God exists.

Einstein in his later years once said: "The one thing I have learned in a long life is this. That all our science measured against reality is primitive and childlike, and that we still do not know one thousandth of one percent of what nature has revealed to us. It is entirely possible that behind the "perception of our senses" worlds are hidden of which we are unaware". Einstein was right. You see:

"Perception is the birthplace of awareness".

What does the perception activity of our senses produce? Perception, our way of looking at something and interpreting it, whether it be a person, a circumstance, or an event, produces awareness, but different states or levels of awareness according to each person's psychological development, their state of mind. These states of awareness are not identical states, for we all see or perceive things differently according to our individual psychological history, the programming of our mind over time including that which we have been hereditarily or genetically programmed with. We are not all programmed the same.

How we individually perceive something, or how we judge or interpret something, say a person, a set of circumstances, or an event is all influenced by the existing individual learnings we have psychologically absorbed and the individual opinions we have formed as fixed beliefs throughout our life thus far, from birth to the present moment. Which is why there can be so many different opinions formed in times of individual or societal crisis as to the cause or reason for the crisis, and why there is disunity of thought and suggested response.

You see Einstein's search for the underlying unity or unifying element of the universe was not just an intellectual exercise. He sought to understand through the methodology of science what he already knew and had experienced deep within. For Einstein that experience of Awareness and more specifically Intuitive Awareness or Cosmic Awareness, was far more important than the many accolades given him for his scientific discoveries. He once said, "the finest emotion of which we are capable is the mystic emotion. Herein lies the gem of all art and true science".

This mystic emotion that Einstein was referring to was not something mysterious and incomprehensible. He knew it was available to all and he aspired to have more of it for himself. I spoke of the

Awareness The Operational Platform of Consciousness

reflective habits of the ancient mystics in Chapter 1. The word mystic as he expressed it is derived from the Old French *mystique* and the Old Greek *mustikos or muein* which means "to close the eyes and then initiate". As it is meant to happen, and more commonly understood by serious practitioners of meditation than others, when the eyes are closed to the sense realm of sight and consequently to the goings on or thought influencers of the outside world, then the inside world, the intuitive world of spirit, has been given a small gap in thought to express itself, to initiate a thought that comes from a different spiritual dimension, and thus ignite a deeper level of awareness.

I mentioned in the previous chapter that in this current spiritual climate, there can be some confusion with the use of the term consciousness and the term conscious awareness or just awareness, with some spiritual teachers interchanging these two terms as if they have the same meaning. They are of course linked, there is a synergistic relationship between the two, but they are two different things. So, in simple terms to help us understand, I put it this way:

"Consciousness is a psychological "state of Being", Awareness is the operational level, the perception level which we function at whilst evolving through a particular state of consciousness, a particular psychological level of being".

You see spirituality or the spiritual life is a journey of awareness and the only direct experience we can have of Universal Consciousness or Infinite Intelligence is through enhanced states or a higher level of awareness. When a society increases its level of awareness, which gives all the ability to see things or perceive things clearly and objectively through reflection and introspection, it is evidenced in everyday societal life as a greater level of societal cohesion and co-operation, a more unified society with a central go forward purpose, rather than a fragmented individualistic and opportunistic getting nowhere state of existence.

To experience enhanced states of Cosmic Awareness therefore requires spiritual discipline, our getting to know the source of all knowing, as it did with the people during the Axial Age. An increased level of awareness doesn't just come like a flash of inspiration, a light bulb moment, it takes application, but not necessarily difficult time-consuming application. It is like a physical relationship, in the sense that good relationships don't just happen. They grow through awareness of what it is necessary for you to do to help the other individual thrive, and then subsequently applying yourself to the task. In other words, you become aware of the needs of the other person and then apply yourself to accommodate those needs.

This type of attitude, this "intent filled attitude", when applied to developing a higher level of awareness, is evidence to the world of spirit, the creative energetic forces in the universe, that you are in fact serious about wanting to get to know the unknowable, Infinite Intelligence.

So, it's not about the occasional perfunctory prayer, or the occasional dabble in meditation, or the occasional church attendance, which unfortunately is the habit of a vast variety of believers and seekers, it's about some sort of self-disciplined regular involvement and interaction with the formless or what is described in spiritual writing as "the unknowable", which is of course, Universal Consciousness, Infinite Intelligence. It is all about getting to know the unknowable. That doesn't take time, it just takes a determined measure of self-discipline. The spiritual life, our evolutionary spiritual journey is not about putting our soul into cruise control and hopefully eventually pulling into the heavenly carpark.

You see most human beings are primarily driven by and base their lives around what we describe as the known, and the unknown. The "known" being that which can be experienced and interpreted by our five senses (Simple Awareness) and known and understood by our intellect, and the unknown, being that which we can't experience with our senses and don't currently understand but believe we may some day in the future if we keep searching. This is why many people spend a lot of time on Google. They are trying to bring their unknown into the known via someone else's understanding of something.

This is also exactly how science works, dealing primarily in the realm of the unknown. The prefix "un" in unknown means "not", so naturally unknown means not known, which implies that by some means, perhaps through more scientific research, we may be able to bring it into the known at some other stage in the future, with the help of our intellect and repeated experimentation. This is how Einstein tried to come to an understand what he described as the unified field of pure potentiality, but in that situation, because he was trying to know that which is unknowable it was an unachievable task. Infinite Intelligence can't be found it can only be defined and intuitively tapped into.

But with everything else making the unknown known is the premise that underpins the drive of all scientists particularly scientific people in the medical research field. We saw this recently in the search for a Covid vaccine. They just have a firm conviction that the answer is out there somewhere in the universe or in some aspect of the universe's functioning and wants to be found, and that if they search long and hard enough intellectually and experientially it will be found. And that somewhere in the universe is the realm of consciousness. All that type of thinking comes out of an operational level of consciousness known as **"Simple Conscious Awareness"**.

Now the mystic, someone who pursues truth beyond the normal human experience, beyond the workings of Simple Conscious Awareness, as with those of the Axial Age, in terms of the known and the unknown, would say yes, they exist, but there is another realm of consciousness called the **"unknowable"**. Mystics or mystically minded people believe that whereas Simple Conscious Awareness comes out of a thinking process and perception birthed in human intelligence and influenced by individual personality patterns, there exists a state of perceiving through the unknowable, a way to tap into the unknowable, and thus greater wisdom and understanding by using a higher level of awareness called **Cosmic Conscious Awareness**.

This type of awareness is in fact commonly referred to as intuitive awareness or intuition. Cosmic Conscious Awareness involves a perceptual thinking process birthed not in human intelligence as is Simple Conscious Awareness, but birthed in Infinite Intelligence, the home of the supposed unknowable stuff, that which is not knowable through human intelligence.

Cosmic Conscious Awareness you could say is an intuitive thought process, a state of mind that enables one to "know the supposed unknowable". Cosmic Conscious Awareness is not about knowing something tangible and obvious, in other words something able to be experienced or perceived by one of the five senses. Cosmic Conscious Awareness, call it intuition if you like, is the experience of knowing that which is hidden from normal human intelligence. We see many examples of this in the Bible in the teachings of the Apostle Paul where he speaks of things "hidden in a mystery" that some people were not yet ready to receive because they were not spiritually mature enough, meaning cosmically conscious or cosmically aligned enough. They had not yet evolved to the necessary level of Consciousness that would enable them to tap into it.

Similarly with Jesus, which is why he spoke so much in parables, which were simple stories with a spiritual message behind them, able to be understood simply and easily through the level of Simple Conscious Awareness, the lower functioning level of awareness. Jesus was fully aware that the majority of those around him were operating at the operational level of Simple Awareness, so he spoke to them in simple language, knowing that having received it that way, in an easily understandable way, if they were mature enough to go away and reflect on the story he told, the light would go on, they would have a light bulb moment, and they would come to understand the deeper spiritual implications of the story.

Cosmic Conscious Awareness is about actively intuitively tapping into the intelligence and wisdom of Infinite Intelligence, the Creative Source of all things. When we focus primarily on this level of intuitive perceptual understanding, the "looking at life from God's point of view" level, we progressively evolve psychologically, and thus the inner and outer experiences of life blend together in a harmonious way, into a continuous subtle sense of our connectedness in thought to the intangible creator of the universe, Infinite Intelligence. And that really is a confidence builder.

One experiences a new harmonious confidence in the evolving life process, a "what is, is" approach to life, a que-sera sera, whatever will be will be approach. So that no matter what happens, we simply don't mind what happens, we accept it, and we deal with it, and a new way of living, a peace filled, relaxed joyous way of life materialises. Jesus in the Book of John put it this way, "I have told you these things, that My joy and delight (in life) may be in you, and that your joy and gladness may be of full measure and complete and overflowing". That's a lot of joy and gladness.

Cosmic Conscious Awareness is not about going to church, it's about Being, it is not about speaking pious theological phrases, it is not about donating money to the church to be used as they choose, for as St. Augustine the 4th century theologian said, "God has no need of your money, but the poor do". Cosmic Conscious Awareness is not about elaborate robes and formal ritualised acts of worship, it is all about "knowing the unknowable".

Knowing the unknowable is not like the principle of faith that is spoken of in the New Testament and taught more than anything with much conviction by leaders in institutionalised religion, using the words of Jesus where He said, "if ye have faith as a grain of mustard seed you can ask what you will, and it shall be done for you". Institutionalised religion has in many ways used this Bible verse to turn the principle of faith into a transactional experience.

Faith has become a currency in so much that many Christians are taught that the Christian experience of receiving God's blessing depends on how much spiritual currency they mysteriously possess, how much faith they have. Jesus was talking about having confidence in the Divine Principles or Divine Laws that govern the functioning of the universe, not faith in the outcome of a certain transactional experience. In some religious brands, when a Christian fails to be healed after being prayed for by a religious leader, they are in many cases told that they lack faith, implying that they lack the spiritual currency needed for this transactional process between them and God to occur.

Christianity needs to understand that the healing miracle is not given according to the amount of spiritual currency you possess, miracles are all about a level of consciousness, and come about through one's capacity to vibrate at the highest level of consciousness, in a harmonious continuous relationship with Infinite Intelligence.

The term **"Cosmic Conscious Awareness"** or to make it simple let's call it **"Awareness"**, is a term being used in more and more instances in spiritual teachings, but it does not have the same meaning as consciousness, and this is where some people get confused. But here's the link. Our state of "Awareness" refers to the "operational aspect" of our mind (how it perceives or interprets our life circumstances and experiences) and it aligns with whatever state of being or consciousness or presence we are existing in at that time in our ongoing evolutionary journey through the different levels of consciousness.

You see similarly, as there are three states of awareness we transition through or are meant to transition through, so there are also three states of consciousness or being that we evolve through during our life, each one aligning with our state of awareness at the time. The problem is though that for some people they come to a dead stop in Simple Awareness and their way of thinking remains separated from God's way of thinking, which is the primary reason that there is so much disunity in society, because everyone is operating from their individualised, pre-programmed, prejudiced, self-interested, and sometimes bigoted points of view.

These three states of awareness or perception are, **Number one,** Simple Awareness (note, this includes Self-Awareness which is commonly known as self-consciousness), **Number two,** a blend of Simple Awareness and Cosmic Awareness, and **Number three,** a complete state of Cosmic or Intuitive Awareness. Biblical writings refer to the second state of awareness, Number 2, the blended state, as one of double mindedness, the Book of James 1:8 saying, "a double minded man is unstable and restless in all his ways, in everything he thinks, feels, or decides", (Amplified Version). And describes the third state of awareness as a state of being intuitively led or guided by the Spirit of God. The Book of Romans 8:14 says, "for all who are allowing themselves to be led by the Spirit of God are Sons (or Daughters) of God. (Amplified version)

The three states of Being, or Consciousness, or Presence that these three states of awareness align with are, **Number one, Simple Awareness** aligns with Collective Unconsciousness, **Number two, the blend of Simple and Cosmic** aligns with Collective Consciousness, and **Number 3, Cosmic or Intuitive Awareness** aligns with Cosmic Consciousness.

When we are evolving through the Collective Unconscious state of existence, which is from the moment of our birth, Simple Awareness is the perception level we function at. When we are evolving through the Collective Consciousness state of existence, Simple Awareness plus a small measure of Cosmic Awareness is the perception level we function at. It is known as "a state of double mindedness". When we have evolved into a Cosmic Conscious existence the faculties of our

Soul and thus our perceptive abilities are fully aligned with the Mind of Infinite Intelligence, and the perception level we function at is that of Cosmic or Intuitive Awareness. To help one understand this a little better I have placed a table at the end of this chapter showing this sequence of psychological and cosmological events.

As we progressively evolve in our journey of consciousness, the state of awareness that we must pay particular attention to is Number two, the blend of Simple Awareness and Cosmic Awareness. Why? Because at this specific stage of our evolutionary spiritual journey we can either power on through, or alternatively, when we become the victim of adverse circumstances, we can regress to our previous ways of thinking and behaving, which is commonly referred to in Christian writings as back sliding, sliding back into our previous ways of perceiving and behaving.

It's like we have dipped our toes in the ocean of Universal Consciousness but have not fully immersed ourselves in the waters of the God Mind fearful of what is ahead, it might be too cold to fully immerse ourselves. You could say we are torn between God's world of thought and our own self-interested world of thought; we are torn between the Spirit's voice and the Ego Mind's voice. As an example, you often hear people say, "I was going to do a certain thing or act a certain way, but "my conscience" told me not to". That is a blending of Simple Awareness, the "I was going to" part, and Cosmic Awareness, the "but my conscience told me not to" part.

That state of mind, what is termed spiritually as a state of double-mindedness, or what people describe as "well I was of two minds about it", indicates some sort of ego mind orchestrated conflict of opinion with the still small voice of Wisdom within. Which does in fact show, that yes, we can evolve psychologically to the next level, if, and here's the big if, if we choose to respond to that still small voice of Wisdom and not reject it in favour of the ego's voice. If that still small voice is not responded to, if it is not acted on, we fail to nurture the soil of our Soul and either stagnate spiritually or regress spiritually and thus devolve further consciously.

I mean has anybody ever wondered what conscience is or where conscience comes from? Conscience is that still small voice of Wisdom that Sogyal Rinpoche, the author of The Tibetan Book of Living and Dying said "we rarely hear or attend to". Conscience is that still small voice that whispers intuitively to us, "now come on, do the right thing". It comes from Universal Consciousness, Infinite Intelligence, encouraging us to take a different path, the path of Wisdom, from the one which the ego mind is prompting us to take, so that we are not just making the same old wrong choices time and time again and slipping further and further back in our evolutionary journey through consciousness.

Conscience as we call it, that still small voice within, that voice of Wisdom is naturally still there, it will not desert us during that conflict with the Ego mind, it will not leave us nor forsake us, even if we in the moment reject it's Wisdom, and will wait for another opportune time to help us grow spiritually, because that is its role as our "comforter in crisis", continuously guiding us and sustaining us psychologically, supporting us in our evolutionary journey to a higher level of awareness.

You see God gives, and gives, and never gives up on us. We have that Spirit, that creative energetic force freely given to us to teach us and guide us in all our ways. It's there already, within us. We breathed it in at birth and we immediately cried in joy. And then after time passed we forgot that we had it.

But as conscience as we call it, is exercised more, as it is listened to more, and responded to more often, its promptings appear more regularly to guide us through difficult or challenging situations. However, if we reject its promptings, it does not try to force us to make the right choice, it just quietly sits back and waits for another opportunity to help us evolve to a higher state of being. The 'will

I' or 'won't I', the 'should I or shouldn't I', double-minded state of being is also seen in people who perhaps participate in random acts of kindness and compassion but are not fully committed to living a compassionate and kind life. In other words, it is not a complete attitudinal and behavioural change. They are torn between the world of spirit and the world of man.

When we have evolved into the Cosmic Consciousness state of existence, the final stage of our evolutionary psychological journey, Cosmic Awareness is the perception level we function at, always. Without hesitation, we automatically respond from God's perspective. We don't in a way need our conscience to tell us not to be angry at someone, we just simply don't get angry anymore. We don't need our conscience to tell us to forgive someone, we just simply do not hold grudges anymore. The pre-eminence of our lower nature has given way to the purpose of our higher nature, the nature of Christ. Life then psychologically becomes a harmonious walk in the park, or as the New Testament puts it, "we are walking every day in the Spirit".

In its practical application it means we automatically look at life from God's point of view all the time rather than our own self-interested and self-opinionated viewpoint, and perhaps only seek God's help or cry out to God in moments of crisis that we find impossible to manage by ourselves. This sees our human intelligence become the servant of Infinite Intelligence, no longer attempting continuously to be the master of it. In secular spiritual teachings this is simply what is termed as the transition from an ego led life to a spirit led life or becoming our true self. How did Albert Einstein put it in describing this dilemma that society finds itself in? He said:

> "The intuitive mind is a sacred gift, and the rational mind is a faithful servant. We have created a society that honours the servant but has forgotten the gift".

Consciousness or Presence as it is often described, is a psychological "state of Being" and Awareness is the operational level, the perception level which we function at whilst evolving through a particular state of consciousness, a particular psychological level of being. We do not have to attain the presence of God or find the presence of God or step into the presence of God; we simply align our thinking with the God Mind's way of thinking, and it automatically happens. To be in the presence of God does not require us to work harder it requires us to unlearn harder and work wiser. To let go of the old way of thinking and thus perceiving. To let go of all things or thoughts that hinder us in evolving to higher and deeper levels of consciousness through deeper more intuitive levels of awareness or perception.

Jesus said as we read in the Book of Luke, that if our eye is healthy, meaning how we perceive things, then our whole body will be "full of light". What does that bring about? It releases a manifestation of what is known as God's Grace. Both Jesus and the Buddha prioritised the "aware, awake, watchful state". What is that? It is a state of alertness to Divine promptings. Jesus even spoke about it, and it is recorded in the Book of Matthew in what is known as the parable of the ten virgins.

No different from what wisdom teachers from various eras have taught including in this modern-day Eckhart Tolle who continually speaks about "being present", which simply means being watchful. Or as the Apostle Paul described it being vigilant and alert. You see Divine Principle or Divine Law never dates; it is eternal. What the Apostle Paul taught during his time, similarly we see inspirational teachers like Eckhart Tolle 2000 years later teaching similar principles albeit using different terminology.

Awareness is all about the perceptual functioning level of our mind, our analytical thinking process, how we see things at a particular time and place whilst we are continually evolving in our psychological journey through the three levels of consciousness. This journey continues throughout our whole life, from birth to physical death. Human beings are continuously evolving creatures physically and psychologically.

Consequently, we find that our opinion on some societal issue, say our attitude to world poverty or the environment, or some other social issue, can dramatically change as we get older. We have evolved in our way of thinking about certain things and now see and interpret them from a higher level of consciousness and thus reflect on them at a deeper level of intuitive awareness. But the difference is that our physical body will progressively decay, for all things of form eventually rust or decay, but our psychological body, our Soul, is eternal.

In their practical outworking how do these three operational levels of awareness come into play?

*"**Simple Awareness** is a knowing awareness of our visible external existence and experience, and what is happening in our world, using our sensory perceptive abilities, our five basic senses, touch, sight, hearing, smell, and taste".*

Note: It includes Self-Awareness commonly referred to by most people as Self-Consciousness.

*"**Self-Awareness** is our perception of our personal individual structure, physically and mentally, our identity, and includes how we see that individual structure in comparison with other people. It is the self-conscious state of mind."*

*"**Cosmic Awareness** is our awareness or how we perceive our invisible internal existence and our outer external existence and experience, looking at the world and those in it from God's perspective through the perceptive lens of Infinite Intelligence. It is intuitive thought at its highest level.*

Further to this Simple Awareness involves only the use of our rational thought processes, our intellect, to interpret something in our mind, whilst Cosmic Awareness, does include our rational thought process, which too is part of the unified field of pure consciousness, but prioritises the use of our inner mind, our intuitive thought processes to inform and interpret. That same inner mind that is known in Christianity as the Christ Mind and its intuitive communication process known as the Voice of the Holy Spirit, (common term is conscience), and known in the Islamic religion as Ruh al-Qudus, the Spirit of Holiness and God's agent of Divine Action and communication.

Simple Awareness is a psychological state of perception, how we look at things, through the prism of our rational mind. **Self-Awareness** is the psychological state of how we perceive ourselves based on our inherited, circumstantially experienced and socially influenced prism of our rational mind. **Cosmic Awareness** is a renewed state of thinking and perceiving, that aligns with and gives pre-eminence to the intuitive God or Christ Mind within us, Infinite Intelligence. We prioritise looking at life from God's point of view and not our own or that of others unless their perspective or point of view aligns with God's point of view. Breaking those three levels of awareness down even further.

Simple Awareness is how we perceive and interpret all things around us, not just visible things but everything that is witnessed by one or more of our five sensory perceptions, touch, sight, hearing, smell, and taste, including how we perceive all human things, all material things, and all psychological things, our thoughts, and emotions. As any of these things enter our "sensory zone of awareness" we make an immediate judgement about them. You know the kind. "Wow he's good looking" or "wow that is a delicious pie", or "that makeup makes me look so good", or "this coat feels so warm", or "that story really makes me sad", or "you know that situation really makes me so angry".

Simple Awareness causes us to make an immediate judgement about something or someone. This perceptive awareness is subjective, meaning influenced by personal feelings, personal tastes, and personal opinions, and is unique to us. We are all conscious beings. Awareness is being alive or what is called sentient, which is to have the power of perception through the senses. Without awareness birthed in a particular state of consciousness there is no life. Life and awareness are synonymous. It is because of awareness that we have any experience whatsoever, so, if you don't have conscious awareness, in other words if you are unconscious, you can't see, you can't hear, you can't taste or smell, you can't cry, you can't laugh.

You are basically in a perception coma whilst still being physically alive. All perception is based on being conscious and aware. Without consciousness you can't think, you can't imagine, you can't remember. All our internal experiences, memories, desires, and emotions are dependent on consciousness. Our behaviour is dependent on consciousness, our personal relationships depend on consciousness, our social interactions depend on consciousness.

All of what we experience as our outer able to be seen environment, and our inner able to be thought environment, is dependent on our being in a conscious state of awareness. If you close your eyes and imagine yourself sucking on a lemon, you will find yourself salivating because of its "imagined" bitterness. What was real? Were you sucking on a lemon? No, you weren't. The only thing real in this scenario is that something unknown allowed you to imagine that scenario, the result of which was that you had an imagination induced physical reaction, you salivated. The same reaction albeit not as intense that you would have had if you had sucked on a real lemon and not an imaginary one.

This is the concept of all mindfulness, creative visualization, law of attraction type principles that we see being taught in webinars and seminars. Just because some teachers of these programs don't have a true understanding of the deeply spiritual role of consciousness, does not mean that the principles won't work. What happened in that suck a lemon scenario? Simply said I suggested the lemon scenario, you thought about it, and you had a "subtle intention" in response to your thought. You see:

> "Thought contains energy, energy to create after its own kind. Thought sets intention, and intention creates behaviour".

You thought of sucking on a lemon, a subtle intention, "I must salivate" came into existence, activated a salivatory gland, nerve signals are sent to our salivary glands and your body behaved according to that intention. The degree of subtlety of the intention depends on the food and your previous conditioning to it. If you have grown up loving the taste of donuts then walking into a bakery and smelling fresh donuts may bring about a lesser intense but still subtle intention, which activates a response physically (salivating) and a conditioned response behaviourally (you purchase a packet). Homer Simpson's frequent drooling over donuts and Duff beer became an iconic and instantly recognizable sound. A subtle intention is a very faint intention and because of that subtle intention you created an experience.

Intention, subtle or intense is the starting point of all our dreams and is an energetic force within itself that fulfils our needs. Intention is a conduit between reality and non-reality. You could say **"intention is what fuels Creative Consciousness"**. Everything that happens in life begins with an intention thought. Awareness is the birthplace of intention, and Cosmic Consciousness is the Divine Creative midwife who delivers the reality of that intention, who creates form out of the formless, who alchemises thought into reality.

The sages of India observed thousands of years ago that our life is shaped and impacted on by our desires, from which intention comes forth. The classic Vedic text known as the Upanishads declares:

"You are what your deepest desire is. As your desire is, so is your intention. As your intention is so your will. As your will is so your deed. As your deed is so is your destiny."

Now **Self-Awareness**, the second aspect of the three levels of awareness that I spoke of, does fall under the category of Simple Awareness, but operates in a specific area of our visible world. Self-Awareness is the ability to be aware of oneself as a functioning, physically alive body, an individual sentient being that is separate from all other sentient beings and different in form and appearance from all others, both human and animal.

What is a sentient being. In Buddhism, sentient beings are "beings with consciousness". Sentient beings are composed of the five aggregates of matter, sensation, perception, mental formations, and consciousness. Mahayana Buddhism teaches that all sentient beings contain the Buddha nature, the intrinsic potential to transcend the conditions of samsara (the cycle of birth and death to which the material world is bound) and attain enlightenment.

Similarly the Bible teaches that the human being has within them the Christ Mind or the Christ Nature, the intrinsic potential to transcend the rational mind way of life that stems from our lower level of awareness and create a new way of thinking and behaving stemming from our higher nature, initiating what is termed a Spirit led life. The Apostle Paul in speaking to the Corinthian people about this said:

"But we have the Mind of Christ to be guided by His thoughts (how he perceives things) and guided by His purposes (His intention). (Amplified Version).

Studies have shown that whilst Simple Awareness makes its appearance in the human infant within a few days after birth, Self-Awareness (commonly called Self-Consciousness) makes its appearance in a child at the average age of three years and then progressively increases its level of intensity, reaching its peak during the teenage years. However it can continue for some through adulthood, particularly if a teen doesn't grow out of their feelings of some sort of physical or mental shortcoming they think they have compared to their peers; which is a reality to that teenager that generates a subtle intention to behave in a certain way, to exhibit what is known as self-conscious behaviour.

Cosmic Awareness, the third aspect of the three levels of awareness, is a deep state of awareness of the cosmos, of the life and order of the universe and all it contains, and of the interconnectedness of all that life. It is a state of "being" that all human beings have the capacity to tap into. To be in a state of Cosmic Awareness is to have evolved through and out of the Collective Unconscious state of psychological existence, through and out of the state of the Collective Conscious existence and to have finally evolved into the psychological state of Universal Consciousness, a state of "knowing the supposed unknowable", or being able to tap into that which is not known to the senses.

It is a state of intimacy with Infinite Intelligence, and with that an ongoing ability to tap intuitively into the creative source of the universe, the all-knowing, all powerful, everywhere at once, creative thought domain of that Infinite Intelligence, the thought domain described by Einstein as an unmanifest field of pure consciousness, of limitless intelligence and creativity.

If you asked the question, where did Einstein's conviction of nature's underlying cosmic unity come from? What was it that drove this determination he had to continue in his scientific investigation into these things? What was it that made him feel compelled to continue despite ongoing opposition and criticism from his peers? Perhaps a clue as to the answer to these questions can be found in a letter he penned to the Queen of Belgium.

In 1929 Einstein had visited the Belgian Royal Court and a firm friendship developed between himself and the Queen of Belgium,

Elisabeth of Bavaria. They shared a mutual interest in music with Einstein being very proficient in classical violin and the Queen being an accomplished pianist, resulting in them having many magical musical moments together. For Elisabeth, Einstein and making music were a psychological way out of her golden cage. Music was like oxygen to her, and she enjoyed Einstein's lack of interest not only in protocol but also in his own apparent fame.

They corresponded regularly and a letter he wrote to the Queen included the following. "Still there are moments when one feels free from one's own identification with human limitations and inadequacies. At such moments one imagines that one stands on some spot on a small planet, gazing in amazement at the cold yet profoundly moving beauty of the eternal, the unfathomable life and death flow into one, and there is neither evolution nor destiny, only "being".

With these words Einstein describes an experience he had of the underlying reality of life, a unified field, not only beyond time and space, but beyond life and death, beyond the evolutionary theory of life and the singular destiny theory, and beyond every life form and every created thing and every theory and every imagination. The destiny theory or the idea of destiny is the belief recognised in Newtonian physics that in our universe everything happens because of simultaneous interactions of everything. Thus, destiny is not an individual concept, it is not my destiny or your destiny, it is our destiny. And what did Einstein say he experienced at this level, "only being".

This realisation was remarkably in line with the ideas of not another scientist but rather ideas held by one of the well-known teachers of the transcendent capability of a human being in the early 70's the Maharishi Mahesh Yogi, who I referred to briefly in the previous chapter, but who is worth revisiting and adding to. Maharishi was the Indian guru regarded as the father of Transcendental Meditation and worldwide leader of a new religious movement at the time. He was known publicly as the guru to celebrities such as The Beatles and The Beach Boys and actresses such as Mia Farrow.

The guru's teaching was that the basis of all life, inner and outer, meaning our thoughts and experiences, is a field of pure existence, "pure Being", as he called it in the early stages, an unmanifest field of pure consciousness, of limitless intelligence and creativity that can be tapped into by all human beings. He taught that this field of pure consciousness is the source of everything in the universe and that all the forms and phenomena in the universe are but vibrating energetic waves in the ocean of consciousness that he called "Being".

Moreover, he put forth his chosen method of tapping into this pure consciousness. He called it Transcendental Meditation, teaching that when we practice this technique in a simple, natural, and effortless way, our chaotic mental activity settles effortless inward, and the mind moves beyond (transcends) the rational thinking process and immerses itself in the ocean of pure consciousness within, Infinite Intelligence, the true Self. Simultaneously the body settles down to a uniquely deep state of rest, dissolving stress and restoring psychological balance. He called this new state of "being" Transcendental Consciousness.

The Maharishi emphasised that when we psychologically transcend, we experience or come into contact not merely with the source of all thought, but also with the ocean of intelligence (Infinite Intelligence or Universal Consciousness) from which the whole universe is born and sustained and the place in which all thought is energised. Then he emphasised, we gain what he called the support of nature to fulfill our desires with increasing ease. And as we progressively move into higher states of consciousness, we come to recognize, as a direct experience, the ultimate unity of life, the reality that everything in the universe is nothing other than an experience of the Infinite and Eternal and all experience is connected.

Who or what is used by Infinite Intelligence as the primary channel for communicating with humanity, for connecting the Mind of Infinite Intelligence with the Minds of Humanity. As previously mentioned, that creative communication agent in Judaism is called "the Word", in Christianity it is referred to as the "Holy Spirit", the Comforter and Teacher, in Islam it is called Ruh al-Qudus, the agent of Divine action and communication. The great American Sioux Indian nation calls it the Great Spirit Wakan Tanka.

It is referred to as the Sky Father by the Australian Aborigine, and in Zoroastrianism, the ancient pre-Islamic religion of Iran it is referred to as Speanta Mainyu, the source of all goodness, the spark of life in all humanity, and the ultimate guide for humanity. In Indian Hindu philosophy, it is known as Brahman, the transcendent power that exists beyond time and space, the creative principle which lies waiting to be realized in the whole world.

How can we tap into this Infinite Intelligence? We can do it by various means. The Maharishi spoke of the way of Transcendental Meditation, the Axial Age Mystics spoke of contemplative meditation and quiet reflection, Eckhart Tolle speaks of silence and stillness, but there are other more socially direct and societal connecting ways as well. It's easier than you think. And here is one very worth considering.

Einstein, a scientist with an unbelievable understanding of the "laws of physics" that are involved in the operation of the universe, publicly implored humanity to transcend this optical and psychological delusion that it has found itself in, this dysfunction and isolation from fellow humans that it continues to embrace as its way of life, and thus tap into this Infinite Intelligence, and discover in so doing our true reality. Describing humanity's current psychological condition and what it is necessary for humanity to do to enable it to transcend its current state of being and thus discover a new state of psychological existence Einstein said this:

> "The intellect has little to do on the road to discovery. There comes a leap in consciousness, emanating from a leap in perception, call

it intuition or conscience or what you will, the solution just comes to you, and you don't know how or why".

Then in describing a practical way on how humanity can get past this illusionary lifestyle and position itself to take this leap in consciousness he focused on selflessness rather than humanity's existing state of self-interest, when he said:

"This delusion is a kind of prison for us, restricting us to our personal desires and to affection for a few persons near to us. Our task must be to free ourselves from this prison, "by widening our circle of compassion". To embrace all living creatures and the whole of nature in its beauty".

Einstein spoke of "widening our circle of compassion". He took the road less travelled to Cosmic Consciousness the road of compassion, a primary functioning principle of Divine Intelligence, which has an inherent power within itself, a cosmic energy enabling us to connect with Infinite Intelligence and thus initiate circumstantial change and birth it into humanity's existence. And whilst it is a road less travelled to Cosmic Consciousness, it is one that has been chosen by many in the past including Mother Teresa, the founder of the Order of the Missionaries of Charity, considered to be one of the 20th century's greatest humanitarians.

Einstein spoke to humanity not in scientific language but at the level of Simple Awareness, with something they could simply grasp, to point them in the direction of Cosmic Awareness, similarly as Jesus did quite often in His time when He spoke in parables. Jesus also spoke to humanity at its current psychological level of existence, its rational self-centred isolationist thought-based approach to life, even though he was a Cosmic Aware individual himself. Einstein said that we need to widen our circle of compassion, indicating that when we embrace an attitudinal and behavioural change in relation to all other beings on the planet, as a deliberate choice, then we will deepen our understanding of the cosmological nature of our existence.

He was basically saying "God does not change us, we choose to change", by behaving as if we have changed our way of thinking, and then Infinite Intelligence supports us in our quest and transports us to a deeper level of consciousness, that will cause us to think differently and want to behave differently in the ongoing future. It is the "draw near to Me and I will draw near to you" principle as written in the Book of James in the New Testament.

Einstein spoke of our adopting in our practical temporal earthly life, behavioural changes in accordance with Divine Principle, God's way of thinking. and through that then cosmological change will automatically happen. No profound scientific or intellectual or philosophical perspective or formula was given by him. He instead simply said:

"We can take a 'leap' in consciousness, even by doing a simple thing such as widening our circle of compassion".

To have compassion or to show compassion means to empathise with someone who is suffering and to feel compelled to reduce that suffering. It's a fuller truer definition than sympathetic feelings alone, and it's a very spiritual interpretation of the meaning of compassion. Why did Einstein emphasise our choosing compassion and not perhaps choosing love, which is the common catch cry of many people who cry out "all you need is love" or "the world needs more love". He chose compassion over love in the first instance, because he understood that love is an intense feeling of deep affection surfacing through the sense realm, while compassion is the sympathetic consciousness or awareness of another's distress and a deep desire to alleviate it. A desire surfacing in the intuitive perceptive realm.

Love is associated with feelings like warmth, affection, caring, and attachment, whilst compassion is associated with feelings like sympathy, pity, and kindness, however what we can be mindful of is the fact that out of compassion a deep sense of true love can grow as a person's level of consciousness evolves to a higher level. We saw that occurring in the life of that well-known humanitarian Mother Teresa, who in her desire to help feed the poor and the sick coming out of a deep Jesus like compassion for the poor and hungry people of the world, she grew to love them as if they were her own children that she had given birth to.

"Compassion does not grow out of love, rather it is the birthplace, the womb from which love can emerge and blossom".

Compassion literally means to "suffer together". Those who spend time researching emotions define compassion as a feeling that arises when you are confronted with another's suffering and feel motivated to relieve that suffering. Compassion is not the same as empathy or altruism, although the concepts are related similarly as the concept of love and compassion are related. How would one know that one is a compassionate person and not just an empathetic person?

A compassionate person will always find commonalities with all other people rather than focus on the differences. A compassionate person will always look for a connective experience emotionally rather than a disconnecting one. A compassionate person will not put emphasis on their own needs rather will put emphasis on the needs of others. A compassionate person is kind to themselves, for if one can love oneself, one can love their neighbour.

A compassionate person has a high emotional intelligence and an attitude of gratitude for all they have. When we have compassion, it gives us the ability to not only understand someone else's situation, but also a deep desire to take action to improve their lives as it did with Mother Teresa. It is a quality of psychological makeup that allows us to step outside of ourselves and see the circumstances of others without prejudice, and cosmically it supplies the willpower to do what is necessary to make the world a more caring and unified place.

You see in what a potential opportunity may be to express compassion, many people bring prejudice and simple awareness judgemental thoughts into the equation and the opportunity to express and further develop compassion is lost. They mix the hint of compassion that arises in them with egoic thoughts of, "well they've only got themselves to blame". Or they see a young woman sleeping on a park bench, are touched intuitively by the sight of her, and immediately introduce prejudice into the equation remarking to their friend walking with them, or even just thinking to themselves, "probably a drug addict".

From his own understanding of how the universe works what did Albert Einstein say would be the benefit of widening our circle of compassion. He said that will enable us to "take a leap in consciousness", which means we move more quickly to a higher level of awareness of the existence of Infinite Intelligence and our connection with it, and with that a deeper level of cosmological existence, and a preparedness to receive Grace, the unmerited favour of Divine Intelligence.

Widening our circle of compassion involves both transcendence and evolution. We become what is known in Biblical text as "a doer of the Word", the Voice of Infinite Intelligence, and not just "a hearer only", deceiving ourselves. It involves us choosing to transcend our current attitudes and behaviours in relation to our fellow man, and to begin living according to Divine Principle. Which automatically brings Infinite Intelligence into play, seeing us evolve to a higher level of consciousness or presence, with a deeper understanding and awareness of our connection with the Divine Intelligence of the universe. I explain how this evolution occurs, and the sequence of psychological processes or changes that occur during this evolutionary journey, in the following chapter.

The Psychological and Cosmological Evolutionary Journey of Humanity

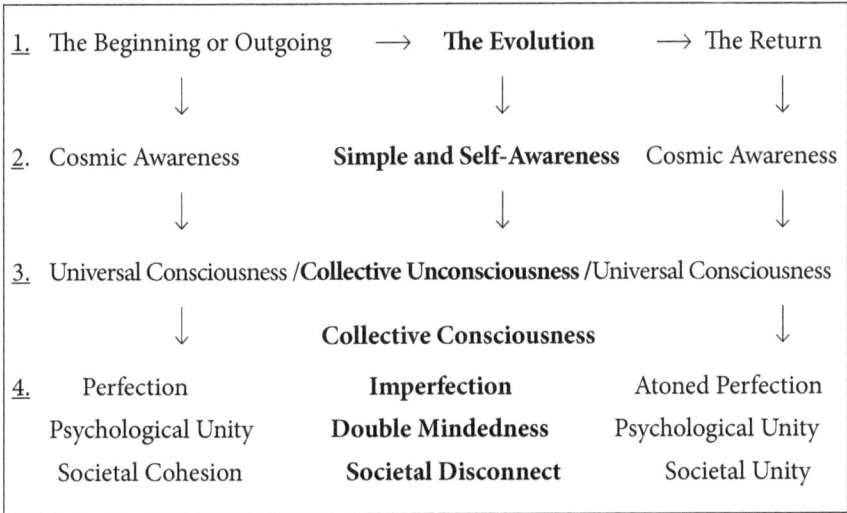

During the early stages of humanity's evolutionary journey, its journey of consciousness, its level of consciousness devolved seeing it descend into a State of Imperfection, one of Psychological Disunity, Societal Disconnection, and a lack of Awareness of its cosmological existence. When humanity returns or evolves to its original state of consciousness, it will be transmuted back into a State of Perfection, one of Psychological Unity, Societal Cohesion, and Cosmological Awareness or Knowing. It is what the Apostle Paul described as all of humanity coming to a unity of the faith, manifesting the stature and character of Jesus the Christ, a perfect and complete person.

Line 1. The Cosmological Mystery of Our Existence. The Three Stages. (Chapter 2)

In the Beginning after the Outgoing, humanity existed in a State of Perfection. One of Psychological Unity, Societal Connection, and a state of knowingness, realising its Cosmological Unity. Line 2. Our State of Awareness or Perception, the operational level of the mind during this time. (Chapter 7). <u>Line 3</u>. The corresponding State of Consciousness, or the State of Being that we have evolved to, and exist in, during our time living life in each individual operational level of Awareness. <u>Line 4.</u> The result of humanity's evolutionary unification process. Its state of being or perfection, its psychological condition or state of mind, and its relationship with the rest of society.

> "Although you appear in earthly form, your essence is pure consciousness. You are the fearless guardian of Divine Light, so come, return to the root, the root of your own Soul".
>
> *Rumi*

The Evolutionary Journey of Consciousness

From the Author.

During this chapter, you will see different words and terms used for the human mind, for what the average person would simply describe our one single mind, our rational thinking mind.

With regards to human thought processes, historically the spiritual teachers of most Eastern and some Western religion have spoken of a human being having not one mind but two minds, a dualistic nature, an upper mind, and a lower mind. The thoughts of our upper mind emanating from what is called our Higher Nature, and the thoughts of our lower mind emanating from what is called our Lower Nature. Traditionally both the upper and lower minds have been called different names in different spiritual writings and religions.

So as not to confuse the reader I have outlined below the words and terms I use in this chapter in reference to the two minds we possess, our upper mind and our lower mind.

When I talk about the Upper Mind and its workings, I will refer to it in either of the following ways:
As the Upper Mind, as our Higher Nature or Higher Self, as the Mool Mind, as the Christ Mind, as our Intuitive Mind, as the Voice of the Holy Spirit emanating from the Christ Mind, or as Conscience.

When I talk about the Lower Mind and its workings, I will refer to it in either of the following ways:
As the Lower Mind, as our Lower Nature or Lower Self, as the Maya Mind, as the Ego Mind, as our Intellect or Rational Mind, or as the Voice of Ego at work in our minds.

I trust this brings clarification.

EIGHT

> "Paradise is not a place; it is a state of Consciousness".
> Rumi

Jalal ad-Din Mohammed Rumi was born September 30th 1207 and passed December 17th 1273. More commonly known as Rumi, he was a Persian poet, Islamic scholar, and Sufi mystic whose influence transcended national borders and ethnic divisions; Iranians, Turks, Greeks, Pashtuns and other central Asian Muslims, and the Muslims of the Indian subcontinent have greatly appreciated his spiritual legacy for the past eight or more centuries. Rumi's poems have been widely translated into many of the world's common languages and transposed into various formats. He has been described as the most popular poet and the best-selling poet in the United States.

But whilst for the lover of poetry, this deep passion for life he expressed and his descriptions of true love and true peace in his poetic work are greatly appreciated and admired by many, when you look more deeply into his life you see that Rumi was far more than a poet. His place in history and his legacy is significantly broader than that of having just been a wonderful poet bringing enjoyment to many, for when one looks more deeply at his written work, one sees that he served as a beacon of light, a beacon of spiritual and psychological light, to not only those of his time, but also to many in the centuries following his passing.

Rumi continued even after his passing to lighten the path to cosmic consciousness for spiritual seekers desiring earnestly to better understand the conscious nature of humanity's existence. You see for Rumi the experience of consciousness he had been given, was far more important and far more a reality to him than his experience of the material world, the praises of men, and the appreciation generously given him in his role as an enlightened poet. It was an attitude very similar to that of Albert Einstein who received much attention and accolades from his scientific work, but never lost sight of the hidden intelligence at work in his discoveries and in subtle ways tried to convey this belief to the world.

You see Rumi fully understood that this mystic quality that people witnessed and were drawn to in his work, in its origin stemmed from a deep and profound creativity surfacing out of his own personal spiritual experience, which he then expressed in his writings. A type of poetic musing purposed to be put into print and given to others as a service, a musing on what he had come to realise deep within. So rather than just producing poems containing an intellectualisation of the spiritual process, he expressed a cosmic understanding, evidencing that he firmly believed in the evolutionary process of the Soul.

Some Islamic scholars, perhaps to their own spiritual detriment, would debate the credibility of his association with the Islamic religion because of the non-conformist nature of his writings, which to some of a theologically fixed mindset from an Islamic point of view would have been seen as a type of Islamist heresy. Similarly, as early Christian Gnostic revelatory writings about the spiritual life were deemed heretical by the Catholic founders of Christianity.

But this bothered him not, for Rumi having come to understand the cosmological nature of humanity's existence accepted that he belonged to that class of Islamic philosophers who were transcendental in their thought process. Rumi knew that his poems and stories with his main point and emphasis always being on the cosmic universality of our existence, were central to all people and indeed necessary for all people to enable their spiritual vision to extend beyond the narrow understanding and sectarian concerns of institutionalised religion.

Rumi also understood according to the Qur'an that the life of the Prophet Muhammad was an act of mercy sent by God to all worlds and all peoples, that he was a messenger similarly as Jesus was a messenger. Rumi once said about Muhammad, similarly as Muhammad had said about Jesus, that the Light of Muhammad does not abandon a Zoroastrian or a Jew, for the light of Muhammad, shines upon everyone, bringing guidance to all of those who are led astray, revealing a true pathway for humanity out of the desert wilderness of alienation from its source.

You see Rumi was a Muslim man of faith, who in his own evolutionary not revolutionary manner, progressed spiritually to a state of knowing the unknowable. I use the term "evolutionary, not revolutionary", because true Cosmic Consciousness is not about a 'religious revolution', as is the belief of some radical extreme elements of institutionalised religion in both Eastern and Western societies.

Rumi's life was a life lived with a deep understanding of the evolutionary journey of the Soul through consciousness, that commenced with humanity's devolution from its original source to the lowest level of Collective Unconsciousness, and then continued its progressive evolution from that level through the level of Collective Consciousness, concluding its evolutionary journey at the source from which it originally came, Universal Consciousness, the Creative Mind of God.

He has always served as a beacon of hope and light to the Islamic Muslim community in the centuries following his passing, and for many individuals his 'light' has helped and continues to enlighten the spiritual pathways of many. Unlike those Muslim extremists of his day Rumi understood that:

"True spirituality is not about revolution, rather it is about self-realisation through revelation".

The realisation intuitively that one's spiritual destiny does not follow the pathway of evil intent, rather prioritises the way of enlightenment, the evolution of one's state of consciousness, resulting in a state of psychological oneness with Divinity and a state of oneness of purpose with humanity. We start looking at life and perceiving all that happens from "God's point of view" rather than in the circumstantial way of Simple Consciousness. This kind of attitude, which you could describe as "a Divinely inspired way of thinking about life and responding to life", does not come about through one having a religious attitude to life whilst subconsciously denying the power of it.

It comes about through the process of consciousness evolution, the progressive psychological moving of a human being's mind into a deeper state of Cosmic Consciousness and thus Cosmic Connectedness, a state of "knowing the unknowable," and then consciously adopting whole new patterns of thinking and behaving that evidence one having come to understand the cosmological nature of humanity's existence and purpose; new patterns of thinking and behaving that are in line with the thought processes of the Mind of God.

But these understandings are not limited to just those of spiritual inclination, similar understandings about the nature of the universe have been discovered in both the scientific arena and in other fields of study such as psychiatric medicine, relating to the transcended personality patterns that quietly manifest out of a higher level of consciousness. In the next chapter I speak of the findings of one of these pioneers in psychiatric medicine Carl Jung. Carl Gustav Jung was a Swiss psychiatrist and psychoanalyst, recognized as the founder of what is known as analytical psychology.

The Evolutionary Journey of Consciousness

Of all the beliefs that Carl Jung held, perhaps more than any other, that motivated him and drove him forward in his quest to come to a greater understanding of how the human mind works, was his belief that there is a common deep substratum of the totality of all human minds known as the Collective Unconscious, which every individual is connected to, and which all individuals draw from continuously as each person's life unfolds.

For Jung the Collective Unconscious was seen as a grouping of minds, a collective group of minds comprising all the minds and their content that have ever existed. A group mind the contents of which we all share, something we are born with, that contain what you could describe as humanity's shared concepts or what I would describe as "humanity's shared personality profile." Jung believed that this Collective Unconscious or collective mind is the part of the mind containing everybody's ancestral memories and experiences, some perhaps in the form of specific archetypes and myths, that whilst having shaped a particular society are also common to all of humankind.

He believed that within the Collective Unconscious lies a force of instinctive nature that stays mostly dormant in functioning societies, but at certain times comes alive, usually during a time of personal suffering, or as societal revolutions or crises appear; a state of aliveness that brings us to a higher spiritual, moral and ethical level of being. Whilst Jung seemingly saw this as purely a psychological process, and never publicly acknowledged it as perhaps being a transitionary spiritual occurrence as well, I see it as being exactly that, as a primary component of God's cosmic plan for all humanity working through the creative instinct of Infinite Intelligence. I put it this way:

"In times of personal or collective turmoil, suffering or crisis, a powerful force, will always arrive at the right time to help. A force lying in stillness and supposedly dormant in the Consciousness of

the Universe, that powers people, through and past their suffering, into a positive unknown, transitioning them to a new and higher level of psychological existence. It is the force of Divine Light, that as the saying goes " brings out the best in people."

However, and this is important to know, in opposition to this, arising out of totally corrupted and misguided egoic driven thought patterns, stemming from a more deeply devolved state of the Collective Unconscious, we may witness a cosmic force of a confrontational and antagonistic nature, arriving to stall or destabilise the growth of humanity's Soul, a force that as the saying goes, "brings out the worst in people." We see this happening frequently in this current Covid pandemic crisis.

The deeper your current state of consciousness has devolved the more likely you are to oppose "right and righteous" thinking. Thinking that places emphasis on our shared humanity. The deeper your ship of life has sunken in its devolution in the ocean of consciousness, the more difficult it is to salvage it, but it is still of course totally doable, it is salvageable, through the miracle working power of Infinite Intelligence. It is just a bit difficult if we attempt to raise the deeply devolved ship of our own consciousness with our own winch and cable, our rational and mostly biased thought processes.

Is suffering necessary in this our evolutionary journey of consciousness? Will it always involve suffering? No, it is not necessary and no it won't. But for some people, sometimes the pain of suffering or even just continuing irritating circumstances, are a necessary motivational component of our spiritual journey, helping our Soul to grow in knowing. It tends to hasten us along, similarly as to how hunger pains are a motivator for us to eat food helping our physical body to grow.

In terms of our evolutionary journey of consciousness and the corresponding higher levels of awareness we function at, this initial psychological transitionary event from the Collective Unconscious state to the Collective Conscious state, perhaps initiated by some "suffering event", is the first pre-destined and pre-determined state of mind transition that occurs in every individual at some stage in his or her life.

If a person misses the boat so to speak because they choose to reject the opportunity to transition in their thinking process, they will at a future date and time be given another opportunity to do so, even if it is in another lifetime. Not necessarily through a "collective suffering" event this time but perhaps through a "personal suffering" event. Our own will is in charge from a chronological time aspect of how soon we transition or how much later we move forward in this part of our psychological evolutionary process.

After this first transition from complete Collective Unconsciousness to Collective Consciousness, the Collective Unconscious influence, still functioning but at a much lower level of influence and intensity, will be replaced by Collective Consciousness, which strives to take an individual or a society to a greater level of connectivity with humanity, and to a higher level of spiritual endeavour, which manifests in one's embracing a deeper social conscience. One tends to start thinking more of the needs of others than they do of their own needs, which sees for some deep expressions of compassion and kindness emerging in their persona, their personality patterns of behaviour. They become more selfless in attitude and deed.

The Bible references this as being in a behavioural state of good works or righteous deeds. But these emerging attitudes or acts of compassion are not simply passing trends, such as a brief social conscience prompting that might see a person "toss a few pennies in a homeless man's hat". They are fixed evolved states of awareness: new ways of perceiving or interpreting the events that come before us and certainly a new way of looking at the suffering of our fellow human beings, regardless of where in the world it is occurring.

This 'state of mind', the state of Collective Consciousness, as against the Collective Unconscious state, is purposed by Divine Intelligence as part of its cosmic plan, to be the launching pad that takes people with their next transition completely out of the Collective Conscious state of mind and into a state of complete immersion in the Universal Consciousness. Which is not only an expanded awareness of one's shared humanity, but also a complete and unshakeable awareness of a person's cosmic connectedness with Infinite Intelligence and the existence of something or someone higher than us, an energetic force at a much higher level vibrationally.

When a person genuinely moves into a state of Universal Consciousness, they move into what is spoken of in Biblical terminology as "a life lived in the Spirit, a life of being led by the Spirit," and is described in Eastern Religion as "the state of Enlightenment." But don't be confused. A life truly lived "in the spirit" is not just simply a life lived in good works alone or weekly church attendance and involvement in church activities. It is a life of cosmological proportions not activity proportions. Similarly as an enlightened life is not merely one of permanently sitting in a yogic position chanting pious phrases or mantras.

After this first transition, from a state of Collective Unconsciousness to a state of Collective Consciousness, the Collective Unconscious, will still be functioning but at a much lower level of influence and vibrational intensity, and unfortunately this is where a lot of Christians and other spiritually inclined seekers come to a dead stop in their spiritual journey. They cease progressing spiritually at the point of good works or selective acts of charity so to speak.

Consequently, in their ongoing thinking process they are still being partially influenced by the Collective Unconscious of humanity, or as I call it, "humanity's shared personality profile". So some will believe that the spiritual life is solely about good works and acts of service to their fellow man. Others may live in a continuous state of double mindedness with one foot in God's camp and one foot, if not firmly in the ego's camp, then wanting to be in the ego's camp, and wanting to get involved in the non-Godly and potential anti-societal activities of the world.

It is a wanting that manifests in one's perhaps only spasmodic, but nevertheless continued acceptance of ungodly thoughts and attitudes, and continued acting out behaviours that perhaps sees them knowingly attend what they know will be a "violent" protest demanding their rights on Saturday, abuse a few police officers, punch the odd police horse, and then off to the confessional and perhaps Mass on Sundays or the mosque for prayers, or simply off to the local church on Sunday with the family.

Thus, the enlightenment seeker is still drawn into the ways of the world and the things of self-interest, the things that give the lower nature a measure of pleasure. This is what can lead to spiritual regression in the life of a believer, or to what is commonly known in Christian terminology as backsliding, a state of sliding back into the ways of the world, or the unconscious state of being, which is simply succumbing to the wily influences of the ego mind. Jesus recognized the potential for this to happen which is why He taught that we should be in the world but not of the world. Being in both leads to a life lived in what the Bible describes as a state of double-mindedness, two minds and subsequently two thought processes pulling in opposite directions.

This spiritual regression can occur in many ways including sexual sin, which is an act of betrayal of one's holiness and the devaluing of the holiness or inner sacredness of another person. The sexual sin aspect is one of the biggest weapons in the arsenal of the ego adversary, particularly in its attempt to separate members of the clergy from their transitionary spiritual journey, or stall them in it, and unfortunately many members of the clergy willingly co-operate with the ego mind in this. We have seen this occurring continually with many high-profile leaders in both Catholicism, Pentecostalism and in Sikhism, and of course as seen in the activities of Muslim extremists.

In this spiritual warfare in which we are all involved, even for those in an existing state of unconsciousness with no spiritual inclination in the present moment, the ego will always direct its mode of attack towards something involving one of the three basic drives of humanity, greed, power, or sex. And with many clergy seeing themselves in positions of power to influence people we see the sexual control drive sometimes linking up with the power drive to bring them undone.

To help us to understand this state of double mindedness this shifting back and forth from our lower nature to our higher nature that is the platform for spiritual regression or "consciousness devolution", from both a combined spiritual and psychological aspect I share the following which may help.

Rene Descartes was a French philosopher, mathematician, and scientist, who lived in the 16th century, a man widely regarded as one of the most important founders of modern philosophy. In some of his more notable writings in the early 1600's Descartes presented a formulation for *dualism* that gave rise in most parts of the Western world to a philosophical approach to the association of the body and the mind in how they relate to each other. In simple terms dualism is the state of something having two main and separate aspects. Dualistic thinking for example is to take the approach when observing a subject matter that it has two separate and different realities to its existence.

These realities can be subjective or objective, subjective meaning based on personal interpretation or objective meaning fact based, measurable and observable. They are also usually seen to exist as opposites and in some cases live in an ongoing confrontational mode with each other, or as a minimum, functioning in an ongoing state of opposition to each other. A prime subject for the exploration of dualism with writers over the centuries has always been that of the inherent nature of humankind and the perpetual conflict that has always existed between the good and evil sides of human nature, that all human beings are often confronted with at various stages in their lives.

Sometimes even in a minor way such as when a choice is given to do either the right thing or the wrong thing, knowing all the time that to choose to do the wrong thing may in fact cause some psychological or physical injury to another human being. Descartes approach to dualism predominates still in this modern world we live in, its basic premise being that there exist two kinds of 'things' that make up this world. There are thinking feeling things, subjects, and non-thinking feeling things, objects. Subjects include the human soul and God, objects being material things or inanimate objects; and both exist separately from each other. The 'dual' in dualism means two. So, in dualistic situations we find that two things are set up in opposition and are separate in some essential irrevocable way.

A religious concept following along the same lines as Descartes formulation, also known as Dualism, is to be found in Eastern Religion. It is a concept that has been taught throughout the ages, long before Christianity came into existence, and long before Descartes scientific work was published. But it only talks about the 'duality of the mind' we possess, not the duality of all things in the universe as did Descartes theory. In fact, it takes a dualistic approach to mind but a non-dualistic approach to the Soul, believing in the existing oneness of all things in the universe including God and humanity.

However, with regards to the mind it basically teaches that we have two different operational aspects of our mind, two separate minds you could say. Two minds that not only continually seek our attention, but also influence and seek to control our behaviours. They are two minds who also live in a state of opposition to each other. One of these minds is described as the lower mind or lower self of the body-mind-intellect persona, and it is a mind that spends all its functioning time continually focused on the past, on the future, and on present moment experiences, activities, and achievements.

Over time this lower self-entraps our thought processes causing us to attach ourselves psychologically in our thoughts to things of the past, usually regrets or pleasurable events, to objects and forms in the present, usually relationships, achievements, and material possessions, and to things in the future, mainly dreams and desires that we believe will bring us happiness, peace, and contentment.

The consequence of this lower mind's onslaught of activity is that it continually fills in and absorbs all our thinking time, thus distracting us and diverting us away from any interest or involvement in gaining understanding of our higher self, the higher spiritual aspect of our nature. It keeps us buried in the Collective Unconscious and separated from the influence of Universal Consciousness.

This lower mind in its functional aspect is connected to *Maya*, a concept of "personhood," Maya in Hindu philosophy (Sikhism), meaning illusion. Maya connotes a type of magic show; an illusion where things appear to be present, but things are not what they seem. It is a spiritual concept connoting that life as it exists visibly to the senses is constantly changing and thus is spiritually unreal; it has no spiritual reality, and consequently it is capable of change or being open to change and influence over time, but the true invisible things of Spirit are changeless and thus timeless.

But more so Maya is the power or the principle at play in life, which I like to call the play of personhood, that conceals from us the true character or nature of the spiritual reality of our being, our existing oneness with the universe, by placing what you could call a psychological veil between the non-visible Infinite Intelligence and us. Consequently, we perceive all of life's events purely with our sense organs and thus interpret our visible circumstances, how we see things that are happening in the moment according to our pre-programmed mental beliefs, biases, and prejudices, failing to accommodate the understandings and Wisdom of Infinite Intelligence that is freely available to us. The play of personhood, the illusionary life of Maya, separates us psychologically from God.

Now here are the key points in relation to Jung's teachings that I briefly mentioned before.

The Maya Mind is in fact the Voice of the Collective Unconscious, humanity's shared personality profile, which we are being continually influenced by in our thinking. A compilation of many things that influence, mostly in a negative way, why we think as we think, and why we behave as we behave". However, further to this we have the second mind, known in Eastern philosophy as the higher mind or higher self. In its functional aspect this upper mind is connected to *Mool*, which is a concept centring on creation's origins, God's Creative Spirit.

In Christianity, the largest religion in the world, the Mool Mind is referred to as the Mind of Christ, and the Holy Spirit is the communicative link between our mind and the Mind of Christ. The Holy Spirit is the voice that brings the thoughts and instructions of the Christ Mind to us in our daily lives. As previously mentioned, that same voice, the voice of the Holy Spirit is known in Islam, the second largest religion in the world as Ruh al-Qudus, the Arabic term for the Spirit of Holiness, the spirit that is seen in the Islamic Religion as God's agent of Divine Action and Communication.

Now these next few paragraphs are very important for us to grasp, to give us greater understanding as to how all the major religions in the world do in fact, contrary to widespread theological discourse, complement each other with aligned belief concepts regarding the relationship of our nature with God's nature.

The Mool Mind as taught in Sikh Hinduism psychologically connects us to the thought processes of Infinite Intelligence or Universal Consciousness, the creative influencer and watchman of our lives. In its active or functioning mode, it is one and the same in all religions, known to exist in all religions, but simply referred to in spiritual writings using different terminology. For instance in the Christian religion this Mool Mind is the Christ Mind within a person, the Apostle Paul said, "but you have been given the Mind of Christ", functioning in its intuitive communicative process with humanity as the Voice of the Holy Spirit.

In the religion of Islam, the Mool Mind is the Ruh al-Qudus, the Islamic name for God's creative agent of action and communication. The Qur'an, the Holy Book of Islam, in fact references the Ruh al-Qudus as the Holy Spirit. The Holy Spirit (Ruh al-Qudus in Arabic) is mentioned four times in the Qur'an where it acts as God's Divine Agent of Communication. And in Sufism, the mystical branch of the Islamic religion that involves the deliberate seeking of the truth of Divine Love and knowledge through direct personal experience with God, Ruh in Arabic, is a person's immortal, essential self, pneuma, the spirit, and in one instance refers to Jesus.

"The Mool Mind or the Christ Mind is the storehouse in Universal Consciousness, containing all the positive elements of the Collective Unconscious; but a compilation of only the "positive aspects" of humanity's shared personality profile that align with Divine Law or Divine Principle; a library of all things that influence the way we think and the way we behave, in our everyday lives in a positive and Divinely purpose filled way".

Eastern religion teaches that those people who are attached to Mool alone, a non-dualistic state of mind, are in a state of full enlightenment, a state of total presence, of being in God's Presence, tuned in to the Mind of Infinite Intelligence continually, looking to it for guidance continually. To this enlightened person the thoughts of the past are ignored, the worrying thoughts about the future are rejected, and the focus is totally on the present moment and on perceiving it from the Mool Mind's point of view. The slate of the past has been wiped clean and the Mool Mind or Christ Mind is not inclined to return to the things of the past with regret, nor has the desire to escape to thoughts or worries about the future.

Consequently, in a person's daily life, thoughts of regret about the past and thoughts or worries about the future, as they attempt to break free from the shackles of their confinement in the Collective Unconscious, all fall on deaf ears. How so? Because the enlightened person's inner ear is tuned solely into the thoughts of God, and God's thoughts, and those Divine thoughts always align with Divine Law or Divine Principle, which is true Wisdom.

You see the unenlightened thoughts of the lower mind are non-existent to God, they play no part in God's thinking processes. The God Mind, that we have been given, cannot perceive them let alone entertain or embrace them. This is the mystery hidden in the teachings of Jesus as seen in the Book of Matthew, when in encouraging those around Him to not worry about the future or dwell on the past, He told them to consider the lilies of the fields. Often referred to as white apostles of hope, the white colour of the lilies is symbolic of the purity of the Christ Mind. Lilies represent rebirth and hope in what might seem a hopeless situation.

To see consciousness in its ultimate purity is to experience what is called Universal Consciousness. It is to experience the mind as pure consciousness. When you experience the mind as consciousness you experience full knowingness. However, to experience Universal Consciousness in its fullness the individual consciousness of a person must go through the ego dying process and then be re-born into Universal Consciousness, which can happen by choice or sometimes through suffering as already spoken of.

Alternately, the individual consciousness of a person can expand or grow or evolve to become as Universal Consciousness through adopting attitudinal and behavioural changes that align with Divine Principle, practical demonstrations of obedience. Which is what I was talking about when I spoke about embracing compassion. You see it is not possible to understand what Universal Consciousness is without experiencing it, because it is not compatible with the ordinary level of understanding, the level of Simple Awareness. The Book of James 1:22 (Amplified version) says:

> *"But prove yourselves doers of the Word, actively and continually obeying God's precepts, and not merely listeners, who hear the Word, but fail to internalise its meaning, deluding yourselves by unsound reasoning contrary to the truth".*

What is this basically saying? It is saying it is a waste of time and you are deceiving yourself if you think by attaching yourself to some sort of institutionalised religious practice that you are going to achieve a higher level of consciousness. If you think that by attending a church and sitting listening to the sermon, nodding your head in agreement, or alternately nodding off, and then leaving the church and doing your own thing that is contrary to Divine Principle, and to the teachings of Jesus, that you are going to achieve a higher or deeper level of consciousness, I'm sorry, you won't. The disciple James who wrote the above words says that you are only deceiving yourself.

> *"Institutionalised religious deception is a primary tool of the ego mind to place you in a position of unknowing complacency in your evolutionary journey of consciousness".*

However, when we through a disciplined approach to attitudinal and behavioural change, through personal practice and experience, embrace Divine Precepts, the death of the ego mind influence is automatic, resulting in an automatic expansion of our level of consciousness. We grow deeper in our understanding, or in our knowing, of Universal Consciousness. And what do we discover when that happens? We discover it is the elimination of psychological separateness, of any division of perception, perception being our thoughts and way of seeing things, between us and God.

Hence springs the Buddhist notion of "no self". The Buddhist say that ultimately then there is "no self", because in the embrace of Universal Consciousness you cannot experience a self. Buddhism holds that personal identity is delusional, that each of us is a self that turns out to not actually exist. The Dalai Lama said that clinging to, or being obsessed with the delusional self, is the major cause of suffering.

When your attitudes and behaviours in this visible physical world, in relation to other human beings and nature become fully aligned with the attitudes and behaviours of Infinite Intelligence (Universal Consciousness), as witnessed in the life of Jesus, relationships with others and with nature then become ones based on self-less-ness rather than selfishness, which feeds the growth of your consciousness further. Because when Universal Consciousness, the Mool Mind is embraced, existing consciousness becomes absorbed and recognizes being as one with Universal Consciousness and so can do nothing else but manifest God's Nature. We are able then to tap into Divine Power.

This is the meaning hidden in a mystery in the teaching of Jesus where He tells His disciples as seen in the Book of Acts, "but you will receive power and ability when the Holy Spirit has come upon you". What is the Holy Spirit? It is the creative agent of the Mind of God, Infinite Intelligence or Universal Consciousness. Whilst your consciousness has always been a part of the consciousness of the universe, it now recognizes it. It understands that it is not separate from God and God's power. The power of the Collective Unconscious to negatively influence us is then meta-physically negated, and we no longer have or need that existing non-negated consciousness we call the egoic self, being involved in or ruling our lives.

Certain leading figures in the world of psychiatric medicine knew this. Certain leading figures in science knew this. Certain leading teachers on the true spiritual life knew this. Carl Jung, the Swiss psychiatrist, and psychoanalyst, recognized as the founder of what is known as analytical psychology, in coming to understand this said:

> "Much of the evil in the world is due to the fact that man in general is hopelessly unconscious."

Albert Einstein, the genius of the scientific world, who by his own admission came to deeply understand the existence of this Universal Consciousness, the Infinite Intelligence as he described it, through his work experience, believed it was this and not his rational thought processes that enabled him to achieve his legendary status as the greatest scientific genius ever. He described this progressive revelation through experience that he had in the following way when asked where this genius came from. He simply said:

> "You can't solve the problem with the same level of consciousness that created it".

Jiddhu Krishnamurti, the 20th century Indian philosopher, speaker, writer, and teacher of contemporary alternative spirituality, in commenting on the attitudes and behaviours of his day and the need for a radical change in consciousness put it this way. He said:

> "How very important it is to bring about in the human mind a radical revolution. The crisis is a crisis in consciousness, a crisis that cannot any more accept the old norms, the old patterns, the ancient traditions. Considering what the world is now, with all the misery, conflict, destructive brutality, aggression, and so on, man is still as he was, still brutal, violent, aggressive, acquisitive, competitive, and has built a society along these same lines".

When we are totally attached to the Mool Mind, its egoic opposite the Maya side of our persona, the negative aspects of the Collective

Unconsciousness of humanity as Jung would describe them, no longer have any power or influence in our lives. They will still be there and occasionally come to the surface of our awareness, to taunt us or to try and influence us in a negative way, but have no power to influence our behaviours, unless, and this is important, unless we allow them to.

If we welcome this Maya side of the persona, and entertain it, it will influence us for the worse, similarly as in a physical setting the local gossip in our neighbourhood has no opportunity to influence our thoughts about or reactions towards our fellow neighbours, unless we invite her or him in for a cup of tea and a chat, unless we entertain their presence.

If we resist the Maya side of our persona, it will flee from us in the moment, and with continued diligence eventually disappear altogether. Because remember there is a stage that we go through in our evolutionary journey through consciousness that sees us hovering in our thinking and behaving between the Collective Unconsciousness influences and the Collective Consciousness and Universal Consciousness influences. A stage I referred to as a state of doublemindedness. We are caught or torn between two minds, between the negative interfering thoughts of the Maya (Ego) Mind and the positive influencing thoughts of the Mool (Christ) Mind.

The Bible in the Book of James succinctly puts it this way, "resist the devil and he will flee from you." It doesn't come any more straightforward and simpler than that. What does the result of our resisting bring about with regards to our evolutionary journey of consciousness? It means we do not experience any devolution in consciousness, our state of being or presence, by entertaining thoughts emanating from our lower nature. We don't lose ground in the consciousness warfare. We hold our position to the point we have already transitioned to and grow from there, as the positive influences of the Divine Nature witness practical expressions of itself in our attitudes and behaviours.

Now turning to the Maya Mind in more detail and what it is. We know that it involves the workings of the ego but how does this happen? The Maya Mind is the negative field of intelligence, as opposed to the Mool Mind, the positive field of intelligence. The Maya Mind can be likened in a physical sense to a gun that has the capacity to wound, in this case wound us emotionally or mentally, and thus influence us attitudinally or behaviourally, but it a gun with the bullets removed. However, if we choose to load the bullets of unhealthy thinking back into the gun it rearms it.

There is a distinct parallel or correlation between this Hindu philosophy and the Christian message, where in the Book of Corinthians we see the Apostle Paul saying, "if any man be in Christ", meaning living in a Mool state of mind, "he is a new creation, old things are passed away", meaning the old Maya Mind things, "and all things have become new." In other words, the slate of the old way of thinking, the old way of the Maya Mind that we have been embracing becomes psychologically wiped clean once we start living out of the Christ Mind's way of thinking and perceiving. After this it is up to us to keep that slate continually clean by not entertaining unhealthy thinking.

Most people are dualistic in their thinking to some greater or lesser degree, meaning they fluctuate between the Maya Mind (the negative influences of the Collective Unconsciousness) and the Mool Mind, (the positive influences of Infinite Intelligence) depending on their circumstances and depending on which mind they are tuned into more often and have thus formed habitual patterns of thinking. In other words which mind they have formed a working relationship with.

They fluctuate between personhood and presence, or between non-enlightenment and enlightenment, with most unfortunately leaning more towards a Maya Mind way of thinking as the cares of life ensnare them. And of course, those with little or no interest at all in the things of the Spirit, those totally immersed in the wiles and ways of the world, in the Collective Unconsciousness, usually becomes fully attached to the Maya Mind way of life.

Consequently, physical things that bring some sort of emotional satisfaction such as people, possessions, passion, relationships, activities, and pleasurable experiences become a primary point of interest and involvement, seeing the world of the spirit being pushed into the background, until perhaps when death approaches and a sense of one's immortality emerges with the fear of what is to come. This fear is what birthed the Catholic concept of the last rites, the absolving of all sin, as part of the absolution process, which is known in Catholic theological circles as one of the Sacraments of Penance.

The Catholic hierarchy of the early fourteenth century introduced the process of absolution or last rites as part of The Sacrament of Penance. It is based on the Catholic premise that the Catholic Church is the only true church of God, and that only a representative of the Catholic priesthood can grant a person pardon for all the indecent acts they have committed in their lifetime. So, what they are saying basically is that it's okay to function totally out of the level of the Collective Unconscious in your lifetime, being totally influenced by the ego mind, the Maya Mind, if you ensure you clean the slate of your mind just before you physically die. It is just a tool of institutionalised religion to keep a believer tied to the institution and a tool of the ego to keep an individual tied to the world of the Collective Unconscious.

The more one entertains the Maya Mind, the stronger is the emotional attachment to past doubts and regrets, and to future hopes and dreams. Their Maya Mind is always tempting them to either totally ignore or override through logic and reasoning what their inner Mool Mind the Christ Mind within is trying to tell them. The Maya Mind in fact chokes off the Voice of God, Infinite Intelligence, silencing it. Jesus references this play of personhood in a parable in the Book of

Matthew, where He talks about the good seed in the garden that is choked by the thorns or weeds. A parable is a simple story designed to illustrate a moral or spiritual lesson.

This choking off process could be likened in a physical sense to a person continually talking over the top of you to drown out your words. But in this case, it is drowning out the still small voice of the Holy Spirit, the voice of Ruh al-Qudus, because it knows that our old nature will always preference logic and reasoning over intuitive thought until we train it not to do so by adopting new attitudes and behaviours that align with the God Mind. The thought processes of the Christ Mind within, the way of thinking of the upper mind is then veiled through a person's deference or bowing to the will and to the reasoning and supposed logic of the lower mind, the Maya Mind. There is an obedience shift in relation to the workings of the spirit.

This ancient Hindu belief in the dualistic nature of the mind is completely in line with the New Testament teaching of the Apostle Paul, where he speaks of us having two minds. In one place he speaks of us having a mind that needs transforming and renewing, which is the Maya Mind, and in another place where he tells us that we have been given the Mind of Christ, which is the Mind of God, which is the Mool Mind which certainly does not need renewing.

Dualistic thinking, that is, leapfrogging between the Maya Mind and the Mool Mind, when continuously occurring in a person's life is aptly referenced in the Book of James as being in a state of doublemindedness, causing much instability in life. People even unconsciously use the phrase, "I'm of two minds about this" or "I don't know whether to go with my head or my heart" when thinking about making a difficult decision, not really understanding that probably their whole life is in fact one of two mindedness, or double mindedness or dualistic thinking.

The only thing that enables dualistic thinking to maintain its grip on one's life, the only thing that enables this constant movement or

The Evolutionary Journey of Consciousness

travel back and forth between the Maya Mind and the Mool Mind, the backwards and forwards between the Ego Mind and the Christ Mind to continue, and with that potentially causing a devolution in our state of consciousness, or if not then as a minimum causing our evolution of consciousness to remain static, is in fact us. We are the enablers. It is an energetic force but at the same time it is not some sort of secret spiritual power the Maya Mind possesses that enables it to distract and divert us away from the thoughts emanating from the Mool Mind or the Christ Mind within, so much so that we are unable to prevent it, it simply happens because we allow it.

We as an act of choice consciously or unconsciously, and mostly consciously, without proper reflection, allow the dominant nature of our Ego or Maya Mind to continually fill our cup with physical, emotional, and material desires in thought form, that continually influence us in the way we express ourselves, our way of speaking, and in the way we act, our way of behaving; and in doing so we continually reinforce to our thought processes, even subconsciously, a belief in the incompatibility of a spiritual life with those desires.

Rumi's views of course differed dramatically from those of the established religions who were present at that time, namely Judaism, Christianity, and Islam. These religions saw the original creative act as a voluntary and temporary one off or once in time occurrence. But for Rumi time was not part of the equation, because to him time did not apply to the realm of the spirit, for he saw time and space as being the basis of division in which the basic unity that the cosmic spirit desires for humanity is compromised and stalled.

Rumi believed the mind to be the key protagonist in that division of an individual soul with that of another, similarly, as did the Apostle Paul, which is why we read the Apostle Paul teaching the citizens of the City of Philippi, and those of Rome, "forget those things that are past" and "be transformed by the renewing of your mind", in other words if you continue to live in the past in your thoughts, you won't renew your mind. For Rumi, all these interfering things in the evolution of an individual's consciousness journey were seen as entities, spiritual forces emerging out of the cosmic ego due to the deep devolution of one's state of consciousness.

The process of devolution of our consciousness can be likened to the ongoing psychological separation of the mind of humanity from the Mind of God, or the ongoing deterioration of the alignment of our thought processes with God's thought processes. We first see an example of this in ancient writings as recorded in the story of "the fall" in the Book of Genesis in the Old Testament.

When that original devolution of humanity's state of consciousness happened, its way of thinking and interpreting life's circumstances dropped out of Universal Consciousness to the lowest level of consciousness which for Adam and Eve was self-consciousness, manifesting self-awareness and fear, for we read in Genesis 3 verse 10 in the Old Testament Adam saying to God, "I heard the sound of you walking in the garden, and I was afraid because I was naked, and so I hid myself.(Amplified Version). And from that point of conscious existence there is only one way to go which is up, that is of course if one desires above all else to participate in that evolutionary journey of consciousness back to its Source.

If you have ever watched a news report on television and looked at chaotic events involving groups of people using chosen aggressive behaviour to get their opinion across, you are watching a perfect example of a devolved state of consciousness in action, regardless of what their cause is. The positive driving force of the consciousness evolutionary process consists of the human soul's inbuilt desire to return to the original Divine Ground or Divine Source from which it came forth in the beginning, to remove the separation of time and space, and the illusionary gap between form and formless, transporting people from a sense of chaos and confusion to one of unified circumstantial and psychological peace and calm.

However, the driving negative force of the Collective Unconsciousness, the ego mind, will always seek a way of influencing or a way of preventing that from happening by initiating through a person's thought processes some sort of attitude or suggested behaviour that will drive their devolution of consciousness further. In the initial stage neither the body nor circumstance is the source of our chaotic existence, but rather chaos is created firstly in our thinking, and then reinforced by the body and circumstance.

The thoughts of our mind are either the instruments for the creation of positive vibration and positive matter or alternately for the creation of negative vibration and negative matter. The material or phenomenal or circumstantial only exists as it is relative to the perceiving mind. Neither God nor we exist because we go to church, or because we belong to a particular religious group.

> "We exist simply because God exists and the cosmic depth of our existence, or the level of conscious knowing we possess, our internal awareness of Presence, does not depend on us going to church, it depends on what we feed our consciousness".

If it helps simply look at it this way:

> "As our physical body grows and continues to exist because of the type of food we nourish it with, so it is no different with our Soul; our Soul matures and continues to function successfully in accordance with the Soul food it is fed. In both cases it is the "gigo" principle at work".

What is the "gigo principle"? In computer science, Gigo means garbage in, and garbage out, and it is the concept which says that flawed, or nonsense garbage input data, produces nonsense output or rubbish as a result. In relation to your Soul your consciousness operates by the Gigo principle. It simply accepts what you give it as input, it does not argue with you. If you give it negative input, garbage in, it will then give you negative output, garbage out. In terms of behaviours and attitudes if you give it positive input such as thinking in line with Divine Principle it will give you positive results according to Divine Law.

How did Jesus express it? He said:

"Man shall not live by bread alone, but by every word that proceeds from the mouth of God".

So, a simple example. If Divine Law says that we should forgive one another but we continually entertain unforgiving thoughts and attitudes towards another, we will eventually reap what we sow as our devolved consciousness manifests like for like. We are in fact punishing ourselves. You see the institutionalised teaching that God will punish us for our wrongdoing is a deception. God is a loving Intelligence and does not punish us, we in fact punish ourselves through wrong thought processes that manifest in the form of wrong attitudes and behaviours, as the principle of like replicating like comes into our individual circumstances.

We must always remember:

"Feed our body the right food and it will instinctively survive. Feed our Soul the right food and it will intuitively thrive".

Rumi's worldview was that the evolutionary journey of humanity centres on humanity's attainment of a deeper level of consciousness, and it is this which lies at the core of God's purpose for the world. Throughout history we have seen prophets, mystics and teachers emerge who were and are in tune with our cosmic purpose, teaching those who have an ear to hear. And even though most humans are still bound by their egotistic promptings and resultant biological urges, humanity is slowly becoming aware of its Divine origin and its Divine purpose and the free will it possesses to participate in that purpose. Free will being a significant reality that we should or cannot afford to pass up on.

Whilst we need to plug ourselves into life and feel all that it can make us feel, we also need to as the Dalai Lama expressed it, continue to elevate, and evolve through our life experiences and strive towards that re-integration of our purpose with the Divine purpose, and the reuniting of our Soul with its Divine source. You see Divine Intelligence deeply desires to see humanity transcend the psychological chaos and its dire state of discordance and disunity, that it did not possess in its original conception at the beginning of its evolutionary journey and so hasten its journey home.

One could rightly ask the question, so what changed? If humanity started off perfect and complete at the highest level of conscious awareness, why are we now living in this seeming state of psychological alienation from Infinite Intelligence and social alienation from our fellow human beings? What were and still are some key influencers that have brought us to this state of existence that causes us to think and behave as we do, sometimes for some in a seemingly irrational and societal disconnecting way?

I share some detail from a psychoanalytical viewpoint, a psychological viewpoint, and a spiritual viewpoint, all wrapped up within the blanket of the Collective Unconscious and the negative elements it possesses that continue to attempt to stall us in our journey of consciousness in the following chapter.

"There is a common deep substratum of the totality of all human minds known as the Collective Unconscious, which every individual is connected to, and which all individuals draw from continuously, sometimes without even knowing why, as each person's life unfolds.

It is both positive and negative in its overall content, containing all the past psychological experiences of humanity, including Indelible Mind Imprints of Joy and Gladness, Sorrow and Sadness, and Suffering and Pain, as well as Hereditary Hang-ups and Hurts, Trans-Generational Grievance and Grief, Intergenerational Biased and Bigoted Belief Systems, and Ancient Archetypal Activity.

These are all "present-day influencers" of our personas, some of which, specific ones, have taken deep root in the mind memory bank of certain individuals, making their presence felt at particular times, for the purpose of dictating one's present moment thoughts and attitudes, and thus directing one's behaviours and responses to life's circumstances and events".

This Unconscious Universe Why Humanity Thinks and Behaves as it Does

"An exploration into humanity's spiritual and psychological alienation from its Source, and the resultant attitudes and patterns of behaviour that emerged from it, leading to what we witness in the world today, the psychological separation, and the social and physical isolation of all individuals from each other".

NINE

> "No one can flatter himself that he is immune to the spirit of his own epoch, or even that he possesses a full understanding of it. Irrespective of our conscious convictions, each one of us, without exception, being a particle of the general mass, is somewhere attached to, coloured by, or even underpinned by the spirit which goes through the mass. Freedom stretches only as far as the limits of our consciousness".
> Carl Jung

Carl Gustav Jung was a Swiss psychiatrist and psychoanalyst, recognized as the founder of what is known as analytical psychology. He was born in July 1875 and passed away in June 1961, aged 86 years. Analytical psychology is the theory of psychoanalysis that focuses on the concept of the existence of a Collective Unconscious, and the importance of balancing opposing forces within the personality that emanate from it.

The concept of the Collective Unconscious sometimes called the objective psyche refers to the idea that "a segment" of the deepest unconscious mind is genetically inherited and is not shaped by personal experience as so many other aspects of our personalities are. I touched briefly on the concept behind the work and professional practices of Carl Jung in the previous chapter but explore his beliefs regarding why we think as we think and behave as we behave in more detail in this chapter.

According to Jung's teachings, the Collective Unconscious is common to all human beings and is responsible for many deep-seated beliefs and instincts including spirituality, sexual behaviour, and life or death instincts, or you could say survival instincts, which in turn are drives that lead to specific patterns of behaviour in life. Carl Jung brought to the world what you could describe as an almost mystical approach to analytical psychology.

For a while he was a close associate of Sigmund Freud the notable Austrian neurologist of his day, but over time with disagreements arising on a lot of Freud's theories on the functioning of the personality, Jung chose not to remain with Freudianism but rather carve a separate path for himself in the field of psychoanalysis. He subsequently developed his own set of theories, a blending of the natural laws of physics with psychological functioning, and with what some might say a little subtle metaphysical and spiritual influence.

Jung also introduced concepts surrounding the different personality types in society, some of his most notable work being done regarding the role of archetypal influences in the psychological constructs of a human being's mind. Having always been controversial as seen in the papers he published, he further alienated himself from the rest of his psychiatry brethren, who did tend to be a bit precious about their own theories, with his leaning towards a blend of religion and psychology. This was contrary to his fellow psychiatrists who preferred to pursue the subject of personality and mental illness purely from a scientific point of view, leaving religion or the spiritual side of a human being's existence totally out of the picture.

In his own personal practice, in dealing with clients with moderate to severe psychological issues at his clinic, over time Jung came to the firm belief that if we are to come to a greater understanding as to why we think as we think and subsequently behave as we behave in the physical realm, we must look not only at the known influencers of thought and behaviour, the visible and thus knowable circumstantial side of our existence, but also at the unknown influencers, the forces outside of ourselves, which have caused us to adopt certain mental attitudes and make specific behavioural choices.

It was an approach that similarly a medical practitioner might take in looking past the physical pain of the patient, to what is invisible to the eye, the internal medical problems the patient may have that are influencing the visible external situational pain. Jung's approach was to seek to find the unknown psychological and spiritually influenced causes of each patient's distress, that manifested in noticeable mental and emotional pain. Jung came to a firm conviction that for one to be not only circumstantially successful in life but psychologically as well, one must look at the spiritual side of their existence as well as the existential.

He believed that one must come to a greater understanding of the cosmological nature of one's existence, (the origin and nature of the universe), and the metaphysical nature of our existence (the nature of the Mind), looking at not only the obvious visible known influencers that cause us to think as we do and behave as we behave, but looking also at the unknown influencers, those things relating to the non-earthly realm. Those hidden cosmically aligned influencers that play perhaps an equal role in our choices and behaviours as do the simple hereditary or obviously self-developed ones. This you could say is the pathway Jung took.

So, in determining a pathway for this chapter, whilst there are many avenues we could explore in coming to understand "why people think as they think and behave as they behave" towards each other and towards the rest of society in general, in trying to incorporate only those things that are relevant to all of us and perhaps more readily able to be comprehended even from a state of Simple Awareness, I will particularly focus on understandings that have been important to me personally in my own spiritual journey.

The primary one being a deeper understanding of what you might describes as "the realm of the spiritual world", how it all functions, the cosmological and metaphysical or invisible side of our existence, both the positive and negative components of it, and secondly an understanding of the relationship between that spiritual world and what we call the ephemeral world, this universe of materialistic and human form in which we live in.

Because I feel for far too long society has been so self-absorbed with the form of life only, the dramatics of life, the sensationalised behaviours of human beings and groups, and the unpredictability of non-human form such as nature, that in some way has caused it to take its eye off the overall, what you could call, "game of life."

To truly come to an understanding of why the universe is as it is and consequently a greater understanding of why individuals and societies behave as they behave, to come to a more enlightened understanding, one has to be prepared to examine the whole functionality of the cosmos, yes the ephemeral or visible side of our existence, the facts as they happen on the ground, but also the invisible side of our existence, the meta-physical and spiritual side of our existence. Which we basically know exists because both scientific and spiritual leaders have been telling us for centuries that it does exist, and because so much undisputed evidence experientially and historically has emerged the law of averages tells us that it must exist.

And that is the premise on which I have lived my entire life, a belief that the world of spirit does exist and that the world of form and the world of "no form" both co-exist in the universe and are not exclusive to each other but rather inclusive of each other. So that being the case in order to come to a greater understanding of "why people think as they think and behave as they behave" it is not profitable to merely examine the behaviour, the form, but to come to an understanding of what things had to come together both visible and non-visible to cause that behaviour to manifest in the first place. As Albert Einstein said:

"You can't solve the problem with the same level of consciousness that created it".

This means to understand more deeply why people behave as they do we can't just look at the behaviour we must begin exploring the spiritual nature of our existence, the invisible world of spirit, and its relationship with the circumstantial side of our existence, how they both interact sometimes in a type of combative way, a war of opposites, but also how they are capable of co-operating with each other.

So many aspects of our human existence demonstrate a complete lack of understanding of the spiritual side of our existence, and for many evidence simply no acknowledgment of its existence at all, regardless of how "religious" some people believe they are. The ancient writings of the Book of Proverbs in the Old Testament say:

"Get skilful and Godly Wisdom, it is pre-eminent, and with all your acquiring, get understanding, actively seek spiritual discernment, mature comprehension, and logical interpretation". (Proverbs 4:7 Amplified)

Many "religious" people who attend a place of worship regularly still have no understanding of the spiritual world itself or even the fact that the physical world was birthed from the world of spirit. How do I know the spiritual side of life came first before the physical? Because it is written, "in the beginning was the Word, (the creative aspect of Divine Wisdom, Infinite Intelligence), and the Word was with God, and the Word was God". We exist only because God existed before us.

We will also look at gaining understandings as to why most people seem to live in a state of alienation from true wisdom and true understanding and thus wise decision making, and how this factor, the lack of true wisdom, can seriously influence the pathway our lives take not just spiritually, but psychologically and circumstantially as well. I describe this as "the alienation principle", our seeming psychological separation from Wisdom thinking and thus right and righteous thought processes and subsequent behaviour.

The Berean Study Bible, a new English translation of the Holy Bible based on the best available manuscripts and sources puts it this way:

> *"Do not forsake Wisdom, and she will preserve you; love her, and she will guard you. Wisdom is supreme; so acquire Wisdom. And whatever you may acquire, gain understanding. Prize her, and she will exalt you; if you embrace her, she will honour you."*

We will look at why certain present moment behavioural influencers are seemingly without hesitation given a rite of passage in some people, seemingly embraced without effort, character qualities of the positive kind such as love and compassion, kindness, and courage under fire, and why for some people those opposite character qualities of the negative kind such as biased, bigoted, and judgemental attitudes and behaviours, selfishness, and cowardice under fire are embraced by others.

We will also look at common internal psychological (mind) influencers that are to all appearances out of our control, that is of course until we dig deep enough and find them. Looking at specific "psychological influencers", indelible mind imprints including the generational transfer of biased and bigoted belief systems, and specific alternate spiritual influencers as taught by ancient spiritual leaders, that align with more modern theories in psychoanalysis, such as the theory of ancient archetypical activity that it is said influences our behaviour without our knowing it. And we will also look at specific recently researched psychological theories such as trans-generational trauma, including grievance and grief transferred thought patterns.

Most of the greatest psychoanalysts and spiritual teachers that have ever existed operated from one simple platform, a deeply embedded desire to assist people to navigate the experience called life in a more peace filled and successful way, and to throw off the shackles of failure and futility and thus discover life's true and common purpose. It was no different for Carl Jung and it was no different for the Indian teacher Jiddhu Krishnamurti who I quoted in the previous chapter.

Jung, in his life and work, from a psycho-analytic viewpoint held similar beliefs to Jiddhu Krishnamurti, an Indian Philosopher and teacher of alternate contemporary spirituality, who lived at the same time as Jung, albeit he was twenty years younger. You see out of all the desires that both Carl Jung and Jiddhu held, perhaps more than any other, which motivated them in their chosen work and drove them forward, was their quest to impart to others a greater understanding of how the human mind works, so that they could both become more effective in what each saw as their primary purpose in life, to be healers of the human soul.

Jung through his training and personal experience in psychoanalysis, was fully aware of hereditary and self-developed personality patterns that form and influence current behaviour but went one step further in looking past the singular hereditary experiences of his patient that were obvious, into the broader aspect of the influence of humanity's collective personality profile and its involvement as an influencer of a person's current behavioural patterns. A collective personality profile and potential influencer that he progressively came to describe as the Collective Unconsciousness of humanity, that which existed in the minds of all but was unknown to exist by all. I spoke of this Collective Unconscious in the previous few chapters.

For both Carl Jung the Psychoanalyst, and Jiddhu Krishnamurti, the Indian Teacher and Philosopher, underpinning their desire to be healers of the Soul, was the belief that there is a common deep substratum of the totality of all human minds known as the Collective

Unconscious, and that every individual is connected to it, but not only connected, they draw from it continuously as each person's life unfolds. They saw it as a unified field of awareness that influences the thoughts and subsequent behaviours of all human beings continuously in everyday life.

For Jung the Collective Unconscious was a grouping of minds, waiting in the deep sub-stratum of our psychological existence, almost I guess you could say like a psychological stalker, with individual aspects of it wanting or desiring to emerge at the appropriate time to influence us in our thoughts and subsequent behaviours. How very similar was in fact Jung's theory to the teachings of the Apostle Peter of the Christian faith who hundreds of centuries earlier had taught, "be sober, well balanced, and self-disciplined, be alert and cautious at all times. That enemy of yours, the devil, prowls around like a roaring lion, fiercely hungry, seeking someone to devour". (1Peter 5:8 Amplified)

Jung believed that this collective group of minds, comprising all the minds and their content that have ever existed, and a group mind the contents of which we all share, comes into play gathering data from the moment a child's perception or awareness processing ability they have been born with begins functioning.

A grouping of minds that contain what you could describe as humanity's shared concepts or what I would describe as *"humanity's shared personality profile."* In agreement with Jung, according to Krishnamurti, when one becomes aware of the existence of this shared personality profile, this Collective Unconscious, which is our collective mind conditioning, a common influencer of our thoughts and behaviours, one begins to understand the working of the entire cosmos.

Which basically means that rather than continually questioning the "why" of world events or individual behaviour we come to understand more easily and perhaps with slightly less judgement why certain individuals or societies think as they think, and behave as they behave, when previously we had in an almost judgemental way viewed that behaviour as totally bizarre, chaotic, and meaningless, and at times seemingly totally out of character according to what we know about the person.

As we gain this greater understanding of the workings of the cosmos, we also come to understand why a societal collective or group, comprising individuals who do not know each other, can come together under a common banner, in a unity of purpose, "like minded" people behaving combatively in certain situations such as in violent protests, or alternately calmly in relation to non-violent protests. When Carl Jung interpreted the dilemma facing society even in his day he said:

"Much of the evil in the world is due to the fact that man in general is hopelessly unconscious".

The words Consciousness and its variations such as unconsciousness and sub-consciousness fit into that character of existence that is known as "the meta-physical". The meta-physical world is a term used to describe the abode of things that transcend physical matter or the laws of nature, things that don't have a physically visible existence but do in fact still exist. A simple way of understanding this would be to say that a human body is of the physical kind, the non-metaphysical kind, but the human mind is of the metaphysical kind, its invisibility you could say indicating involvement of some unknown spiritual or energetic force.

Similarly, as with Jung, Krishnamurti saw consciousness as the total field in which thoughts, functions, relationships exist, and things happen, a non-ephemeral state, an invisible to the sense realm eternal world, continuous in its existence, or timeless, meaning that it can influence not only us in the present but was also involved in influencing our forefathers and their forefathers in previous centuries, and will be involved in influencing future generations.

As our physical world, this visible world we live in and all it contains can be perceived by either of our five outer senses, it is not the same with the Collective Unconscious. Human beings have five basic senses: taste, touch, sight, hearing, and smell. The sensing organs associated with each sense sends information to the brain to help us understand and perceive the world around us. Not so with the invisible world of the Collective Unconscious. The Collective Unconscious world cannot be perceived by our normal senses, taste, touch, sight, hearing, and smell, it can only be perceived and understood using spiritual sight, or "in-sight", internal sight, commonly known as "intuition". So we see that:

"The meta-physical world is timeless; the physical world is time bound. All things physical eventually rust, decay and disappear into dust, but all things meta-physical remain eternal".

However, what we must understand is that this ephemeral world is also in its time of visible existence in that field of consciousness, that unified field of existence that we are all attached to and influenced by.

If it helps you could liken our ephemeral experiences, our life circumstances at a given point in time, to the fish in the sea which are in their time of physical existence immersed in the sea, they are a part of the ever-evolving waters of the ocean, even though all are going their separate ways and making different choices. With certain species such as sharks making what seems to a human being to be violent and aggressive choices, but to the sharks they are simply self-survivalist choices, and other species such as certain oysters, around one in ten thousand it is supposed, eventually within themselves producing a beautiful pearl of great price.

But you see, to the sharks they are making the right choices because a shark's choices are made based on pure self-interest, either self-survival or self-sustenance which is a part of the survivalist instincts of all living creatures, human and non-human. We eat to give us energy in the moment, and to survive or prolong our physical life for the future. The sharks as they cruise in the waters of the ocean are simply centred on their own personal survival and it is no different with all living things whether it be a transmittable virus or a human. Survival is the basic instinct that dictates behaviour, it always has.

You see for humanity, whether it be psychological survival, in other words maintaining their sanity, or physical survival maintaining their life, since the original separation of the Mind of Humanity from the Mind of God, a predisposition towards self-survival has been the dominant driver in a human being's existence. Because protection by God was taken out of the picture. We see this reflected during the current Covid pandemic crisis, the self-survivalist nature of humanity has kicked in dramatically in the form of disputations, disagreements, vindictiveness and even violence.

Pro-vaccine attitudes and anti-vaccine attitudes, pro-lockdown, and anti-lockdown debates, witnessing different attitudes and behaviours emerging from ordinary people, those not in power, and consequently feeling not in control, desperate for their viewpoint to be heard, in the belief that if they are heard then others will respond and align themselves with that thought pattern, and so their own personal acceptable state of existence will survive and continue with the help of those other "like minded" people.

All experiences, motives, emotions, desires, pleasures, fears, aspirations, longings, hopes, sorrows, joys, and inspirations surface in that ocean of consciousness, a field which is divided into two parts, into the active and the dormant, the upper and lower levels, the upper being the surface or waves of the ocean and the lower being the deeper levels of stillness at the bottom of the ocean. All our daily thoughts, feelings, experiences, and activities are on the surface, (the ephemeral world) and below but still a part of the same ocean is the subconscious (the non-ephemeral world).

These aspects of consciousness with which we are not familiar, but nevertheless they are still there, lie dormant; either in a good way like a sunken ship wanting to float to the surface of our life to reveal its treasures, or in a detrimental way like a shark prowling around like a sea stalker, lying in stillness waiting for the right moment to attack. We personally are occupied with one little corner of consciousness, which is our own individual life; the rest, that we call the subconscious or the Collective Unconscious, we do not even know how to get into, however might I say this, "it knows how to get into us".

Our shared but mostly unconscious and unnoticed personality profile containing specific attitudes and patterns of behaviour, definitely knows how to express itself through us, in other words how to come to the surface of our ephemeral existence. It knows how to embed a particular aspect of itself into our life circumstances. It knows our weaknesses and our points of vulnerability. How does it know? Because it is the storehouse of all our thoughts and behaviours up until this stage of our life, as well as the rest of humanity's thoughts, behaviours and previously demonstrated vulnerabilities.

The Collective Unconscious is the oceanic library you could say of humanity's experiences from the first moment that humanity descended (the fall) or devolved from its state of perfection into its self-survivalist state and its self-interested independent existence. No longer co-dependent on its Source for survival, like a child who has run away from home thinking it will enable he or she to find the freedom of thought and expression that does not seem to be permitted in their present circumstances, but finding no place to lay their head, and perhaps through suffering they decide to return to their source, their home. This concept is analogised beautifully in the story of the prodigal son in the New Testament.

How might that happen? How might the Collective Unconscious take a particular point of vulnerability that we may have and manifest it in us in a socially inappropriate way or in a societally disconnecting way. The catalyst for it is always the attitude or behaviour of another human being. The energetic forces in life that descend on us whether for good or bad are not like a boogey man hiding behind a post that suddenly jumps out at us. Those energetic forces, the forces of goodness or evil will always express themselves through the thoughts, the spoken words, or the visible behaviours of a fellow human being.

Here's a very simple practical example. Two people are having a verbal disagreement and the next minute one person gets violent and physically assaults the other. Bystanders who know the two involved may comment, "I don't know what came over him. He's normally not like that". Others might say, "Oh yes I've seen that behaviour surface occasionally before". Surface from where? It had to come from somewhere. Surface from the Collective Unconscious or that part of it that has lodged itself into the person's own personal corner of consciousness, their personality.

The Collective Unconscious, our shared personality profile does exist, and parts of it, particularly those negative parts of it that we have entertained before in our pre-conditioned bigoted, anxious, and judgemental thoughts, perhaps even having broadcast them to the universe through our speech, and in our conversations with others, will in their desire to express themselves once again and multiply their existence in the universe, take advantage of every opportunity to do that.

When will they do that? They will do it in those moments you could say when we are only partly attentive to the truth of what is unfolding before us. They will sometimes to our own surprise and the surprise of others, come to the surface in a type of judgemental and emotion filled expression of our lower nature. And they can do that simply because we are not paying attention to the present moment. We are not alert to the possibility that they might intrude into our circumstances. In that anger incident just mentioned, the moment the verbal disagreement started our thoughts consciously or even sub-consciously move to a circumstance similar to it that occurred in the past, their effect still lying dormant in the Collective Unconscious, and all true awareness of what is happening goes out the window.

The Collective Unconscious is the active agent of the psychological triggering effect. What is a triggering effect? In mental health terms a trigger refers to something non-visible that affects your emotional state often significantly, by causing extreme overwhelm or distress. A trigger affects your ability to remain present in the moment, usually introducing specific thought patterns that influence your emotional behaviour, a flight or fight response.

A simple example of a triggering effect would be that if one starts crying during a sad movie it can cause others around to start crying. Other examples would be a panic attack coming upon a person in an unexpected moment perhaps if someone is in a lift (elevator) that suddenly shuts down or having a fear of heights which initiates panic amongst other users trapped also.. A common one is laughter. If you see someone or hear someone laughing uncontrollably you are drawn to join in the laughter even though you have no clue as to what they are laughing at.

In the example above with seemingly unpremeditated violence occurring, it may have been triggered by a current situation reminding someone of a similar past situation that occurred in the person's life that was quite distressing. Where did that trigger come from? It had to come from some realm of buried thought. You say well it came from memory. Okay then where are memories stored. Some would say the brain. But no scientific experiment or medical doctor in the course of performing a brain operation has ever discovered a little room in the brain with a sign on it that reads, "no entry storehouse of memories." Where are past memories stored that trigger something in the present? They are stored in the Collective Unconscious.

The triggering effect can also occur through involvement of any of the five senses. It happens a lot with the sense of smell. Most would be aware of the triggering effect of donuts on Homer Simpson as seen in the popular television series, that I briefly mentioned in the previous chapter, which causes a specific behavioural response, which in Homer's case is drooling and a deep desire for a donut. And most of us have been in a situation where the smell of the seaside reminds us of a happy childhood time. And what part of space and time do all these triggered memories come from? They come from the Collective Unconscious.

When one is aware of the totality of consciousness then one becomes aware of the importance of always functioning in a state of full attention, not partially attentive, but in a mental state that some spiritual writers describe as "being present". In such a state there is usually no friction. Friction, or the combative side of our lower nature only arises in life when one tries to divide one's consciousness, to partially isolate, totally separate, or just ignore the spiritual side of our nature at a given moment and preference the ephemeral or carnal side. When this happens, we live in what is known as a dualistic world, in a state of double mindedness as it is known in spiritual writings, a type of mental fragmentation. Which then creates ongoing psychological and thus circumstantial instability.

You see we all live our life in fragments. We are one person at work, another with friends, and another at home, fragmented particularly when our ego is threatened. A mind that is fragmented will never be aware of full consciousness, and thus the person with the fragmented mind lives a fractured existence. One must uncover the detrimental aspects of one's mind, those negative aspects of Collective Unconsciousness that we have habitually embraced and thus automatically given licence to function, layer by layer, not only to understand what they are, but to address and to deal with the fragments one by one.

Is this a difficult time-consuming task? No, it is not. How to we find them? They will arise in your interactions with others and when you have given them licence to function by co-operating with them, you will just feel extremely uncomfortable after they occur. An uncomfortableness that may even sometimes trigger an immediate apology. What is this feeling of uncomfortableness? It is your conscience, that still small intuitive voice of Wisdom within you that will whisper to you in its attempt to counsel you, to correct your behaviour or attitude, so that you do not continue in it and further devolve in your level of consciousness and thus find it even more difficult to dig yourself out. You see:

"Wisdom, Godly Wisdom, is the watchman of our evolutionary journey to a higher level of consciousness and consequently a higher level of psychological and circumstantial existence".

To uncover the detrimental aspects of one's mind is not a difficult time-consuming task; it simply involves taking a more resolute approach to be more present in our interactions with others, choosing to live daily in a new state of awareness in the first instance and giving Infinite Intelligence permission to do its work of reclaiming and restoring our state of right mindedness. I spoke on this in the previous chapter.

The Apostle Paul in the New Testament in speaking of this process described it as the "renewing or renovation" of our mind and taught that in doing so our life is progressively transformed. If we are physically renovating our physical dwelling, our home, in the process of that renovation we give full attention to the individual task at hand and the projected outcome we desire. So too in renovating or renewing our psychological dwelling place, our soul, we must give full attention to all the daily detail in it. You see, attention is not the same thing as concentration, so it is not as such energetically draining.

Concentration involves exclusion, while attention excludes nothing. We have all heard that common saying, "be quiet…I'm concentrating". Concentration encourages exclusion but attention encourages inclusion, but with a measured awareness of all inclusion. It is often that we concentrate on our own problems, our own ideas, and our own world, such that we are not objectively aware, and so we begin interpreting events purely from a "well how does this affect me" approach, drifting back into the self-survivalist way of thinking and behaving. We must:

"Concentrate on the true positive purpose or meaning in the moment and the desired perfect outcome for all, rather than the negative meaninglessness of the moment that the ego influenced mind attempts to convey to us to achieve its self-interested spiritual goal".

This is what it is to practice intuitive awareness or present moment mindfulness. We tap into some aspect of the workings of the Collective Unconscious though the intuitive thought process. One needs to be aware about everything in life in the present moment, not continually trying to remove what appears to be an unwanted intervention or relieve an ongoing state of boredom with some dreamt up future experience.

Awareness about how we walk, how we speak, how we talk, and how we think, and how we interact is necessary and with a little practice it becomes easier, and habitual, even though I know that in our interactions with some people it appears difficult. It is with a choiceless unbiased awareness however that spiritual doors can be opened, and one will know a consciousness or a state of being in which there is no conflict and no time, a state of Cosmic Consciousness.

Once we signify our willingness to be changed through deliberate action of some kind, we release Infinite Intelligence to do its part, and then we can effectively change ourselves, society, and the world in which we find ourselves. In referencing this principle of demonstrating our willingness to change with even a simple act of self-denial then Infinite Intelligence sets about playing its part. Biblical text says, "draw near to me, and I will draw near to you". Meaning if you draw nearer to me (Infinite Intelligence) in a practical way, my presence will envelop you and your desires. Similarly, the Qur'an says, "God guides to Himself whoever turns to Him". Different terminology, but with the same meaning in its practical application.

Until then our violent street protests will continue, our antagonistic and biased combative and prejudiced attitudes and behaviours towards others will continue, but will profit us nothing long term, merely giving us some sort of emotional satisfaction in the moment. Understanding ourselves marks the beginning of true wisdom because it leads us to a deeper understanding of others. Freedom is found in the choiceless and unprejudiced awareness of our daily existence and activity. This is the freedom that both Jesus and the Buddha spoke of. You see:

"To be truly aware is to be single minded, but universally conscious".

To be aware does not mean to give up on the life you know, but rather to look further for the internal truth, that enables one to live "peacefully" with a greater understanding of the life one leads, this life we have been so generously given, and the relationships one shares with one's environment, and one's family and friends. Which then releases Grace, which is the unmerited favour of Divinity, into our lives, for as Jesus said, "blessed are the peacemakers". He was saying God blesses those who seek peace. The three things that are most emphasised in the ancient writings of the Psalms and Proverbs are, "wisdom, understanding, and peace".

"Focused awareness, creates understanding, which releases Divine Wisdom, that when acted on restores peace into our lives, the peace of mind that was lost in the original psychological separation of humanity from God".

What is it that causes our state of double mindedness, our state of alienation from God Consciousness, and our susceptibility to the workings and influences of the storehouse of Collective Unconscious, the Maya Mind, and with that a deviation from a right way of thinking and behaving towards an individual or our fellow citizens of this universe? What is it that causes such intense societal disconnects that manifest in wars, violent combative protests, and connective breakdowns in personal, cultural, and social relationships, seeing many people respond to circumstances in a seemingly mindless way?

Visually it appears to stem from disagreements in opinions or beliefs, but what is the root cause of these disagreements and what is it that prevents people from being able to disagree without becoming disagreeable? It happens because life at the core of its existence, "is a spiritual warfare", manifesting in an orchestrated psychological warfare, a metaphysical warfare of the minds of men that is birthed in the first instance in the thoughts of men and then actualised in behaviours that align with those thoughts. Thought is a creative energetic vibrational force. As a man thinks in his heart, so a man becomes in his behaviours and actions.

The Invisible War Beyond the Veil of Normal Perception.

Much of institutionalised religion has in many ways failed humanity. Institutionalised religion has in most circumstances in its exegesis of the scriptures of the New Testament, failed to place sufficient emphasis on the metaphysical aspects of the functioning of the universe, particularly in relation to the concept of spiritual warfare and how it impacts on humanity's existence. The word "metaphysical" is derived from the Greek *meta ta physika* which means "after the things of nature", referring to doctrine, or posited reality, outside of human sense perception. In modern philosophical terminology, metaphysics refers to the study of what cannot be reached through objective study of material reality.

As a scientific concept, spiritual metaphysics is the study of the core principles of the spirit and of life on earth. It assigns classes to spiritual power. Nikola Tesla, the American inventor, best known for his contributions to the design of the modern alternating current (AC) electricity supply system, once said, "the day science begins to study non-physical phenomena, it will make more progress in one decade, then all the previous centuries of its existence." When humanity comes to a greater understanding of the metaphysical nature of its existence, it will easily come to understand the nature of its psychological existence, meaning why it, humanity, thinks as it thinks and behaves as it behaves, and what can be done to address that in order to prevent history repeating itself over and over again.

The first thing we must understand is this. Life is in fact at the core of his existence a warfare. Not a physical warfare but a spiritual warfare, and to know this is fact and to come to understand how it operates is the most important thing we can do as a pre-requisite to coming to a greater understanding of why people think as they think and behave as they behave. I am hopeful the following will explain in the most easily understandable way what this spiritual warfare is all about.

There is a war raging in the heavenlies. A war between the energetic forces of Light and the energetic forces of Darkness which flows down to this visible existence we commonly refer to as life, the life of humanity. In other words life as we know it, everyday life is continually being impacted on by these opposing forces of Light and Darkness both striving to achieve pre-eminence in the lives of all human beings. There is the visible side to our existence and there is a non-visible side to our existence. We live in an ephemeral world, and a spiritual world, a physical world, and a meta-physical world both co-existing with each other.

Now we all understand I am sure either through personal experience or by watching news broadcasts, much about how visible physical wars work, wars occurring on earth, but most people are totally unaware of how metaphysical wars work. Not so in ancient times, for Biblical records reveal two people who appeared to have a great understanding of the invisible wars in the heavenlies that impact on humanity's existence and experience. These two people were the Apostle Paul and the Apostle John.

Evidence of the Apostle Paul's understanding can be seen in the New Testament where he says things like, "for the flesh sets its desire against the spirit, and the spirit against the flesh; for these are in opposition to one another. (Galatians 5:17), and in reference to Jesus he said, "and having disarmed the powers and authorities, he made a public spectacle of them, triumphing over them by the cross". (Colossians 2:15). And further where he says", the weapons we fight with are not the weapons of the world. On the contrary, they have divine power to demolish strongholds". (2Corinthians 10:4).

There are dozens more references. You see Paul is trying to get the message across that the energetic forces of good and the energetic forces of evil are functioning realities of a human being's existence, not merely concepts or metaphors. There are two competing agendas for the control of the minds of humanity. The Apostle John's understanding of the metaphysical core of our existence is witnessed in the ancient Biblical group of writings simply known as the Book of Revelation which he authored. The Book of Revelation was said to have been written by the Apostle John sometime around 95-96 CE whilst he lived in isolation in a grotto type cave home on the Island of Patmos.

Patmos is a small Greek island off the Turkish coast located in the Aegean Sea. This grotto, now known as the Cave of the Apocalypse, is situated about halfway up the mountain on the island between two villages and is believed to mark the spot where John received his revelatory vision the contents of which he wrote down. These manuscripts were translated during the centuries following and included in the original construction of the Bible as the final book in the New Testament, The Book of Revelation.

The Island of Patmos had for a long time been originally inhabited by the Greeks, then later by the Romans for many centuries before Christianity finally arrived. However, by the first century A.D. due to the declining numbers in the island's population, the Roman authorities designated it as a penal colony for criminals. Then later when the threat of Christianity increased within the Roman Empire, those Christians who were deemed a threat to Roman authority because of their influence on the populace, were sent into exile on Patmos.

During this period savage genocidal persecutions under Roman Emperors such as Nero and Diocletian, saw slavery and exile becoming common sentences for Christians. Such was the fate of John the Evangelist believed to be the last survivor of the original twelve Apostles of Jesus, and history tells us that he was still actively evangelising throughout Asia even in his 80's. When the Roman authorities arrested him, while he was teaching near Ephesus in Turkey, he was sentenced to Patmos where he spent approximately 18 months in exile.

While he was serving his sentence, he received his prophetic visions and recorded them. Some years ago, I was privileged to visit both the ruins of Ephesus and The Monastery of St. John with this small grotto type cave home near it, called the Cave of The Apocalypse, now a shrine, and spent some time revisiting in my mind the circumstances of John's environment when he set about writing this scripture and others. There was an unmistakable presence or stillness that came over me when I sat on the rock bench and contemplated the profound writings that the Apostle John produced in his time in this grotto.

The Book of Revelation in particular Chapter 12, presents what may be regarded as history's primary explanation, of a great spiritual war raging behind the scenes of humanity's visible experience. It presents a mighty and terrible monster at war with Jesus Christ and all He stands for.

John presents an argument that beneath all the visible actions witnessed on the surface of history, beneath all the chaotic happenings, the wars, the suffering, the hurt, and the tragedies occurring in society, exists a determined spiritual entity and enemy seeking one thing and one thing only, to destroy the legacy of Jesus Christ and that of those who follow Him. John identifies this entity as that ancient serpent, who is called the devil and Satan.

Now whilst many people in this modern day dismiss the devil as a fantasy or myth, nevertheless one cannot take the ancient Biblical Scriptures seriously without believing that this personal and powerful spirit, said to be the fallen archangel and the enemy of Jesus and all He stands for, does exist, and that it has its own specific plan for the achievement of its goal. That a war is occurring in the heavenlies for the hearts, minds. natures and allegiance of all those whom Jesus would call His own. But more than this, one cannot make real sense of this world we live in and the secular madness that exists around the globe, as it is, without accounting for the existence of that opposing enemy of Christ and all Christ represented.

This entity is who the Apostle Paul was referring to when he said as we read in the New Testament, "for our struggle is not against flesh and blood contending only with physical opponents, but against the rulers, against the powers, against the world forces of this present darkness, against the spiritual forces of wickedness in the heavenly supernatural places. (Ephesians 6:12 Amplified Version). That being the case, in the first instance we must understand and accept, that as it is in any earthly physical warfare, where we see both opposing sides having their own chosen weaponry that they use against each other, so also it is no different in the world of spirit, in the metaphysical side of our existence.

The war in the metaphysical side of our existence is in fact a war of two natures. Behind the visible scenario of life there is occurring an invisible war for the ultimate control of every individual nature., and the weapons this entity uses to control our higher spiritual nature and devolve it to the level of its own, are the weapons of the Maya Mind, the world of illusory concepts, those things that don't consciously exist but still do exist in the metaphysical world, all things emanating from the negative components of the Collective Unconscious.

Conversely the weapons of our higher mind, our higher nature, seeking to continually defend the higher nature within us and with that the level of consciousness we have evolved to, are described in the scriptures as "mighty for the pulling down of the strongholds and the destruction of the attack mechanisms of this influencing entity".

It's a war of the opposing intent of two natures being played out through two minds, the Maya Mind, and the Mool Mind that I spoke of in some detail in the previous chapter. Biblical text puts it this way:

"The weapons of our warfare are not physical weapons of flesh and blood; our weapons are Divinely powerful through God for the destruction of fortresses". (2 Corinthians 10:4 Amplified).

Now the original text written above says that "the weapons of our warfare are not carnal". What are carnal weapons? Carnal weapons are weapons that oppose Divine Law. They are rational mind thoughts that oppose the thoughts of God's Mind, irrational thought patterns that oppose our intuitive mind patterns. They are thoughts and behaviours that are not aligned with Divine Principle. The Bible says in the Book of Romans that the carnal mind is enmity against God and is a mind that does not submit to God's Law. Other versions of the scripture describe those weapons of Divine Principle as "ones that demolish false arguments". False in terms of what? False in relation to Divine Principle and Divine Truth, the rule of law of Infinite Intelligence or what is known in the Bible as the Laws of the Spirit.

Most people believe, even from early childhood, in the existence of what is described as the devil, who represents the evil side of the spiritual world, but very few people consciously accept that this being, this metaphysical spiritual force or entity, could in any way be involved or have any participation in their own personal life and in societal events. Except of course those involved in occult religious organizations that pay homage to Lucifer. They welcome Lucifer's existence or presence and they certainly believe in the powers of darkness.

But many people, including Christians, give nary a thought to the reality of the existence of a dark side of the spiritual world, and its participation in the workings of our lower nature, and its involvement in the affairs of humankind. Similarly as most people are not aware of the "dark side of the internet" called the dark web, that publishes information that cannot be legally published on the normal internet.

Whether we like it or not if the basis or platform of all life is spirit, if we believe that in the first instance, in the Beginning was the Word, the Creative Spirit of Infinite Intelligence, and if we accept that God is Spirit, and that God created all things, and that God is the source and the one who sustains our present existence, then that being the case we must accept that those things that are good and beneficial to us must be okay with God, and those things that are not good for our Soul are not okay with God, and don't come from God, and thus must have come from somewhere else.

But many human beings, religious and non-religious, rarely give thought to where some of those things that are not good for us come from, things like the evil plans of men that result in wars and suffering, or the evil thoughts of individuals that manifest in evil acts that destroy people's lives if not physically then psychologically. They certainly don't come from God, God does not send us suffering to teach us a lesson, that's Old Testament religion. The God of the New

Testament or New Covenant is a God of love and mercy. And this is where it gets tricky for a lot of "religious people", particularly for those who have spent their whole lives drawing psychological sustenance from the negative storehouse of the Collective Unconscious, the Maya Mind, the carnal mind, whilst diligently attending church services every Sunday.

People are prepared to believe in a God in heaven, they are prepared to believe that this Infinite Intelligence is looking after us and guiding us and supporting us, they are prepared to accept that when we desperately need assistance, we can call out to God in prayer and that God will somehow supernaturally bring us help, thus meeting our needs, but this belief in God and occasional reliance on God, for many people of all religions, is brought into play usually only when everything else we have tried, when all our self-reliant and self-survivalist methods or choices have failed. In other words when we are desperate.

Most religious people will accept that the particular Holy Book of their faith was given to them to guide them in their spiritual life, but have little or no understanding as to what it contains to support them in their spiritual journey, whilst at the same time either consciously or subconsciously denying the existence of that which is written in their Holy Book creating awareness of the things that would oppose them in their spiritual life, and thus in their psychological evolutionary journey of consciousness.

Most Christians for example believe that Bible stories such as Jesus casting out demons and evil spirits are true, they believe that when the New Testament says things like, "resist the devil and he will flee from you", that this means that this spiritual entity or energetic force of darkness exists and is capable of intruding into their lives, to be true, but because of a lack of present moment or cosmic awareness, never expect it to happen or see it for what it is when it does happen to them. You see no one is immune to the workers of darkness. We all whether we call ourselves Christian or not are potential targets of the forces of darkness and are being influenced even in the most subtle ways at various times.

So, people of all faiths will attend religious services every Sunday, whether that be a church, mosque, or synagogue, embrace scripture that speaks of love, and kindness, and compassion, but ignore the other important parts that speak of warfare in the heavenlies and strongholds of evil and the necessity of mind renewal to enable these strongholds of the enemy to be torn down. And even after disciplined visits every week over years to their respective religious institution, they will still go out into the world, and because of their unregenerated imbedded thought patterns, get snared into verbally combative situations with others. Arguments, dissent, disagreements, disputations which all cause a devolution in one's consciousness.

The Bible says, "bring every thought in captivity to Christ", not Christ the person but the inner Mind of Christ, Infinite Intelligence; and to tear down every psychological stronghold that opposes the thoughts of the Christ Mind.

Well, you ask, "how do we know when we are being influenced or subtly attacked by these enemies of our higher nature?" Okay here is how. The practical expressions of this "carnal force that is enmity against God" only surface in two areas. In the thoughts first then in the subsequent responses. If we want to fix our behaviour, we must first fix our thoughts. First comes the thought, "he makes me so mad", and then comes the response, perhaps violence of some kind whether verbal or physical. If we train ourselves in the first instance in all our interactions with others, to be "present" as Eckhart Tolle describes it, which is really just remaining in a state of focused awareness on what they are saying, what we are saying, and any emotional reaction we feel surfacing in ourselves in the moment, we will eventually get to a sufficient level of consciousness that we become less as target.

The weapons of darkness work through the mind first and then manifest through behaviour of some kind. Darkness, the egoic side of our nature, works through thought, people, and circumstance. Which is why the Apostle Peter said, "be sober and vigilant for your adversary the devil prowls around like a roaring lion seeking someone to devour". He was not talking about something in skinny red tights with two horns on his head and carrying a pitchfork. He was speaking of that entity as it manifested through a person or a circumstance. That's the only way it can manifest, through the words or deeds of others. He was not speaking only in a purely metaphoric way. This was Wisdom teaching in a mystery.

You see our physical existence can be likened to a spiritual coin that comes fashioned with two sides. On the one side the Qur'an says that we are made in the best of moulds, (95:4), fashioned with the Breath of God's Spirit, (38:72), and chosen to be His representative of mercy upon the earth. (2:30). On the other side of the coin, the Qur'an describes humankind as fragile creatures made of dust from the same earth they walk upon (23:12); anxious, forgetful, ungrateful, vulnerable to the bite of a fly (22:73), a nothingness in the face of Gods' eternal reality; a mortal that is passing away a breath at a time, inching towards a death that will arrive without warning (31:34).

Dramatic yes, but with a message deeply embedded in it. A message from Muhammad to those of the Islamic faith about the importance of our being aware of the fragile state of our psychological existence and the necessity for our continual vigilance in terms of our thinking processes that impact on our psychological health. And so, a humanity that is unaware of both the spiritual nature and psychological nature of its existence and the inherent power for change in that, will take matters into its own hands through the physical.

Some people including Christians will do it by joining White Supremacist or Neo-Nazi groups, or other ideologically driven groups to try and force change, regardless of how that forceful attitude contradicts their beliefs. Similarly in the religion of Islam we see Muslim extremists deny the true teachings of the Prophet Muhammad about the power within to change behaviours. They try to force change by resorting to the carnal aspect of a human being's lower nature. What they don't realise is that ideological obsession is in fact a mind blinding weapon of the energetic force of darkness, a weapon which blinds a person to the realty of Divine Truth and Wisdom. And where does ideological obsession blind a person in the first instance. It blinds them in the area of their thoughts, in their mind.

Aleksandr Solzhenitsyn, the Russian novelist, a former inmate of the Gulags, the forced labour camps of the Russian dictator Stalin, wrote this about ideological insanity. "The imagination and spiritual strength of Shakespeare's evildoers stopped short at a dozen corpses because they had no ideology. Ideology, that is what gives evildoing its long-standing justification and gives the evildoer the necessary steadfastness and determination. (The Gulag Archipelago, Chapter 4, Page 17).

If we are to successfully evolve in our psychological evolutionary journey of consciousness, we must accept the fact that in the first instance life is not just a war on an earthly plain. Things are not as they seem to the senses. Underlying the manifestation of these warring and chaotic events on the earthly plain, is in fact the reality of an ongoing war in the realm of the heavenly plain. One side armed with the positive weaponry of the Mind of Universal Conscious, the Mind of God, and the other armed with the negative weaponry of the Collective Unconscious.

The Metaphysical Spiritual Warfare Being Played Out on Earth

How is this metaphysical warfare in the heavenlies played out on earth in the lives of humanity? There is a connection between the spiritual warfare in the heavenlies and societal warfare on earth, that causes people or societies to think as they think and behave as they behave, and for ease of understandability I approach it from the perceptual level of Simple Awareness.

From the moment a child is born, "awareness" of this life that they have been born into comes into play, their "perceptive abilities" kick in, usually noticed by those caring for the baby to occur within a few days after birth. This is purely Simple Awareness perceiving the conscious world and its goings on around them. At around two to three years of age Self-Conscious awareness, a component of Simple Awareness emerges and after this life in all its visible reality, the good, the bad, and the ugly of it begins to gradually unfold as the child's mind opens up a like a sponge to the continually growing flood waters of attitudinal and behavioural life rising around them.

They begin to continually collect from the present and also contribute to it, as they are taught and experience different events in their own personal lives and as they observe the reactions to circumstances in the lives of those around them, both the positive and negative elements of it. Everything is accepted and very little rejected because the thought processes of a young child are not developed enough intuitively to discern truth from fiction, and as such are easily influenced and manipulated from an early age. This is why children love fairy tales. They do not question the validity of what their minds are receiving.

Thus, the child begins building their own personal corner of consciousness, an individual library of attitudes, opinions, behaviours, all based on their own personal perspective of their own experiences. If they are brought up in a family environment of bigoted and biased beliefs and behaviours or from a spiritual aspect raised under the banner of institutionalised religious belief, those things are locked away in their own little corner of consciousness and become their very own framework of thinking and behaving though their ongoing adult life, unless some perhaps being recognized as unhelpful for the negative influence they have are subsequently dealt with and quickly discarded.

Has anyone ever asked of themselves the question, "why are some children bullies in the schoolyard and with others bullying is the furthest thing from their minds". Or perhaps the question, "what is it in a bully's psyche that drives them to choose a particular child to continually bully"? And what is it about that specific child that is different from others that causes the bully to single them out repeatedly, whilst with others the bully will stay as far away as possible? You know in this spiritual warfare we are all involved, wittingly or unwittingly, the forces of darkness are no respecter of age, ethnicity, or gender. If they find a pre-conditioned mind that suits their purpose that mind becomes an easy target for their destructive influence.

Much of the contents of a child's personal corner of consciousness in their evolutionary psychological journey come from key influencers in their lives from an early age, people such as their parents or a teacher, but can also come from that schoolyard bully. In the case of a child who is bullied continuously it might turn into a lifelong fear of overbearing or dominant personalities. Fear is the supa-glue that ties a person's thought processes to a particularly uncomfortable or hurtful event, fear of it happening again. For fear is a primary energetic tool of the egoic mind of a person's lower nature used to prevent you from journeying forward consciously.

The strength of this force of fear is not confined to humans though. We see it occurring in the animal world particular in relation to what are called "rescue dogs", dogs who through continual abuse by their owners can take years to be rehabilitated back to some semblance of sanity. I know from personal experience some never come back completely no matter how much love they have been given, so deep is the fear embedded. With animals however the fear usually embeds in sounds associated with previous bad behaviour so you can remove the dog from situational behaviour that caused the fear to originally be embedded, but a single sound associated with that behaviour of the past will trigger a negative response.

All influential beliefs and opinions that each child experiences will eventually be added to the Collective Unconsciousness of humanity, as each individual child through their own specific thoughts, words, and behaviours, their own personal reactions, and responses, vibrationally broadcast them into the universal mind, into the field of humanity's Collective Unconsciousness as they journey through life.

Many of the beliefs we now hold as adults came into our lives through our parents and our teachers in our early school years. It was a Jesuit priest from the Catholic Church, who famously said, "give me a child for his first seven years and I'll give you the man." Meaning I will embed into the child's untainted mind, into their personal corner of consciousness, a set of beliefs that will influence their attitudes, behaviours, and decisions throughout their whole adult life.

You see in most Western Christian organizations not all, that are based on Descartes duality theory, that I spoke of in the previous chapter, it is implied and taught that when we are born we emerge from the womb in a state of physical and psychological individualism, a state of separateness of soul and body from God. They teach that whilst we are able to ask God to come into our heart whilst we are alive here on earth, we will only become reunited, more so in a physical sense than a cosmic one, and at one with God when and if we get to that distant place called heaven after we die. This is not absolute truth but unfortunately that is what they teach.

In the meantime, we are encouraged to live the Christian life of kindness and compassion, carry on with our lives as best we can, be a good person, and try to keep in touch with "Our Father who art in heaven" by attending church and by praying as the need arises. This type of teaching always reinforces in the mind of the hearer a thought pattern shrouded with a continuous subconscious sense of separation and alienation from the creator, and a sense of individuality that causes one to see themselves as disconnected psychologically and socially isolated from the rest of humanity.

And here is my point. This spiritual warfare, originating in the heavenlies, but manifesting in the physical world in the present moment, causes a breakdown in both psychological and spiritual connectivity, resulting in the manifestation of continuous spot fires or full-blown bushfires of disconnection in both personal relationships, in spiritual relationships (the unity of religions) and in societal relationships. And that is how the Spirit of Darkness wants to keep it. It wants to maintain the existing personal, religious, and societal disconnect, and in doing so keep all in a state of alienation and disconnection from their true source of being.

To give a simple definition of what is the singular goal of the Force of Darkness as against the singular goal of the Force of Light, I would say darkness desires to create a disconnection of each individual mind in humanity, Light desires the reunification of all existing minds in humanity. Darkness promotes the individuality of the self; Light promotes the universality of all. Most historical spiritual writings, including stories in the Old and New Testaments contain a litany of stories pertaining to family disconnects, societal and tribal disconnects and disconnects in religious or spiritual beliefs. Stories of alienation, the alienation of one individual from another, or the alienation of one society from another. A continuous litany of stories of disconnect and of separation and division.

Have you ever asked the question "why is there such a disconnect between the two largest religions in the world Islam and Christianity, that has in recent decades led to so much suffering and death in the Middle East and around the world in terrorist attacks. Now I am going to give you the very simplified version. You could call it the brief humanised version. But firstly, remind us of this.

The spiritual warfare that I just previously spoke of, that exists in the cosmos, did not just commence recently or in the last few centuries. It commenced in that very moment when the original psychological disconnect of the Mind of Humanity from the Mind of God occurred. It commenced at that very moment when the thinking processes of humanity became separated from the thinking processes of God and thus became corrupted. This is the mystery hidden in the Biblical record known as "the fall" as referenced in the Garden of Eden story in the Old Testament Book of Genesis.

For aeons religious institutions have taught that that incident as recorded in the Old Testament was primarily about sin entering into the life processes of humankind, linking it to what they describe as humanity's fall from Grace, or blessing. No, it wasn't entirely in that sequence. It was primarily about the separation of the thought processes of humankind that subsequently caused humankind without any hesitation to embrace any attitudes and desires and behaviours that were not of God both willingly and without hesitation, including what are termed sinful acts.

Which then released individualised perception, individualised thinking, individualised interpretation, and individual reactions and responses based on those individualised perceptions, locking God completely out of the process. And that was the beginning of this self-driven world that we exist in now. It is not a recent occurrence, it occurred before religion came into the world, before Christianity came into existence, and before the Islamic religion was birthed into the world.

Underpinning that Garden of Eden incident, the psychological disconnect of the Mind of Humanity from the Mind of God, was the spiritual warfare that exists in the heavenlies, and underpinning every disconnect that has occurred in the universe since then, including the disconnect between Christianity and Islam we witness in certain world events, is the spiritual warfare that exists in the heavenlies, the warfare between the energetic Forces of Light and the energetic Forces of Darkness.

And until humanity comes to realise this, then wars on earth will continue, suffering will continue, the differences between the haves and have nots will continue, and the ongoing disconnect will continue, psychologically, socially, and religiously, including the disconnect between Christianity and Islam. The "false self", the usurper of the Mind of Humanity will continue to rule over the hearts and minds and subsequent behaviours of humanity.

So, bearing this in mind, this is how it played out in the original separation of Muslims and Christians, and I will keep it as simply as possible, in other words enabling one to understand it from the point of Simple Awareness. And note it was also the original cause of most of the wars that have occurred and continue to occur amongst the Arab nations in the Middle East that have witnessed the death of so many innocent people. To put it bluntly it was in its origin all about sex, power, and money, the three most formidable and basic human drives in the unregenerated minds of society then, as they are still now. Historical records reveal the following.

In ancient times there lived a man named Abraham. Abraham was the first patriarch of the Jewish people. Abraham was the first person to teach that there is only one God. Before that the people believed that there were many gods. Abraham is still the common patriarch of the Abrahamic religions which include Judaism, Christianity, and Islam. Abraham was married to Sarah. Sarah supposedly could not conceive children and so she encouraged Abraham to conceive a child with her maidservant Hagar, which he did.

Now whilst this information comes from the historical records in the Bible, and this is why Christians believe this, it is not only Christians, for Muslims believe it also. In Islam Hagar, Sarah's maidservant, is considered to be a full wife of the Prophet Abraham as is Sarah. This child, fathered by Abraham through Hagar, upon birth was named Ishmael However later Sarah did conceive a child of her own, and bore Abraham a son who was at birth named Israel. Then Sarah, concerned that Ishmael Abraham's firstborn might be the sole heir in the event of Abraham's death which was the custom, chose to banish Hagar and Ishmael to the desert so that Israel could become what Sarah saw as the rightful heir of Abraham's legacy since she believed that she alone was Abraham's lawful wife.

In the years and centuries following, Ishmael the banished first born son of Abraham became a minor figure in the traditions of Judaism and as such in the religion of Christianity which stemmed out of Judaism but continued to play a foundational role in the breakaway Islamic religion, history holding that Ishmael settled in Mecca and played an ongoing role in the origins of the Islamic religion. The Prophet Muhammad regarded as the founder of the Islamic or Muslim religion, came from the religion of Islam founded by Ishmael, the supposed illegitimate son of Abraham and Hagar, and the Prophet Jesus regarded as the founder of Christianity came from the religion of Judaism founded by Ishmael's half-brother Israel.

That was the first disconnect, surfacing out of institutionalised religious differences as to who were the true people of God, the Jewish people or the Arab people, Christ's people, or Muhammad's people. From that point in the centuries following, both religions became progressively institutionalised with their own sets of rules and governance instituted by the respective hierarchies of each religion. Each religion having their own sometimes ego driven mindset about that which was acceptable to be used to form their institutionalised religious belief structure.

And out of this what you could call in-glorious birth and ongoing religious, psychological, and societal disconnect, subsequently in the centuries following thousands of human beings have suffered and died, as each institution went about justifying its legitimacy. Darkness saw opportunity and darkness took advantage of that opportunity to further its own cause. But it was not just a disconnect in a theological way. It was more so,

> "A disconnection psychologically creating two different spiritual belief systems, leading to two different ways of thinking and behaving, leading to a disconnect socially and a disconnect societally, that led towards much suffering and many deaths then and even to this present century".

The forces of darkness had achieved their goal. Interestingly, in Arabic, the word for the Prince of Darkness or the Devil is *shaytan*, which comes from the root word *shatana*, which in its normal context, means "to take far away from or distance something or someone". In other words, the goal of the Force of Darkness is to create isolation or separation, and it can be implemented simply by one individual allowing the weeds of their ego, their unregenerated mindset to be watered and fertilized, as it did with Sarah, Abraham's wife.

The more we plant these seeds of pride and envy and greed and lust, discord, disunity, and distrust in the fertile soil of humanity's mind, the less Light will reach its heart. The more we plant Divine Thought into our minds the more we create connectivity. Like produces like. It's the Divine Law of Reciprocity that I spoke of in Chapter 1. Everything we do in this life eventually comes back on us, good or bad. The Qur'an puts it this way:

> "Whoever does an atom's weight of good shall see it: and whoever does an atom's weight of evil shall see it".

In other words, evil is a veil blinding or corrupting righteous human misperception. A veil that isolates us from God's Mind, separating us from the thoughts of God. We cannot do evil and be in the presence of God at the same time, and we cannot think hurtful evil thoughts, and at the same time draw on the true Wisdom of life. Wrong thoughts and wrong perception are from a lower level of consciousness. Just as cold indicates the absence of heat, so darkness indicates the absence of Light. The Bible puts it this way:

> *"For who has known the mind and purposes of the Lord, so as to instruct him? But we have the Mind of Christ to be guided by his thoughts and purposes.*
>
> (1 Corinthians 2:16 Amplified Version)

You see contrary to what both institutionalised Christianity and institutionalised Islam teach, except those of Christian Mystic and Islamic Sufi traditions, hell is not a place we go to; it is "a state of being or a devolved state of consciousness". Similarly, heaven is not a place it is "a state of being, or an evolved state of consciousness". But in our unregenerated or unrenewed mindset we think it is a place because we have been taught this concept by religious leaders from a very early age. A concept that we are currently psychically and physically separated from God and that we will eventually go to heaven to meet Him.

And so, humanity falls for the illusion of one's separateness or isolation from all other existence which creates a type of dualistic relationship between itself and Divine power, and all that this Divine power has created. It is an illusionary thought process that says God is way out there in the cosmos somewhere, and we are far away from Him, way down here on earth. What does that illusion do? It gives permission to the dormant but ever ready self-survivalist nature of a person to click in and do everything in its power to maintain that survival.

Thus in this life a human being knows of God, has heard about God, believes that God exists, thinks about God occasionally, prays when desperate, may attend a church or mosque regularly, but because of this mental or psychological sense of separateness only expects to get to meet God and be in the presence of God when they die and go to heaven, having never come to truly know God, to achieve an enlightened state of existence in this present lifetime, right here right now on this earth. That is why Muslim jihadist extremists are prepared to sacrifice their physical life to enable them to get to paradise which is the Muslim term for what a Christian calls heaven. What they don't understand is that as the Islamic Sufi Prophet and poet Rumi said:

"Paradise is not a place; it is a state of Consciousness".

Very little instruction has ever been given in the Christian religion or the Muslim religion, (excluding Sufism), the two largest religious organizations in the world, on the existing oneness of God and humanity, the non-duality of our spiritual existence, instruction that is paramount to a believer's working relationship with the Creative source of its existence.

Both Jesus and the Apostle Paul taught that regardless of our religious status, whether we are a priest or a parishioner, regardless of our personal status, whether we are a prince or a pauper, that the Kingdom of God is within us all. They taught that we are cosmically connected with Infinite Intelligence, and that all human beings have been given the Mind of Christ, which is the thought pattern and the perception processes of God. They taught that all human beings have been given the ability to see life from God's point of view rather than the egos, to see life from the Mool Mind point of view rather than the Maya Mind point of view.

Further to this both Jesus and the Apostle Paul taught that a person's life could be transformed now in the present moment through the renewing of the Ego Mind, through renewing the unregenerated Maya Mind that took over our lives after the original psychological separation. It is a renewal of the rational mind that corrects our thinking process, our way of perceiving or understanding things, re-aligning our perception with God's perception.

What is perception? It is our awareness, our way of thinking and interpreting things that happen to us in life. What is God's perception? It is God's awareness; it is God's interpretation of a situation which leads to Godly instruction (Wisdom) as to how a human being should navigate that situation. We then start looking at life and responding to life from God's way of thinking rather than reacting at life according to the ego way of thinking.

How does that happen? In the first instance it happens by us voluntarily initiating a working relationship with the Creative Mind of the universe, Infinite Intelligence, the Holy Spirit in Christianity, the Ruh al-Qudus in Islam. We begin as a deliberate act of our will to perceive, filter, and interpret the happenings of life through the Mool Mind of the creative source of our existence, rather than the Ego Mind, our separate and self-educated rational thought process, which on many occasions is not rational at all.

Why is it not rational? Because it is continually influenced by energetic sources and forces outside of our rational control. That's the warfare of the two minds. Those negative emanations from the Collective Unconsciousness of humanity are determined influencers. However, when our mind is renewed or regenerated, we begin living our lives looking at life deliberately from God's point of view, which brings a tremendous peace into our lives. The Bible describes it as the peace that passes all understanding guarding our heart and mind, meaning it is almost unfathomable how good it is.

You see from a very early age in our search for happiness, contentment and fulfilment, to restore the peace filled state, that peace of God that passes all understanding that was lost in the original psychological separation of humanity from Infinite Intelligence, we join the world of achievers, of collectors, of futurists and of potential becomers, earnestly leaning forward towards the next acquisition, experience or pleasure, and ever seeking to obtain more than our fair share of the success, happiness and riches that the unseen ego forces of the world temptingly beckon us toward.

This then progressively strengthens our individuality and our sense of separation from God, our independent nature, whilst subconsciously continuously reminding us that this is what life is all about, we are all on our own, survival of the fittest and fastest, this is reality so make the most of it, go for it.

We are born into this world as either a male or female with absolutely no psychological baggage at all, save perhaps the odd genetic influence, but certainly born with no self-inflicted mind baggage. From that moment on we start collecting what we could call 'thought things'. Thought things that will eventually turn into mind memories locked away in our individual corner of the Collective Unconscious, which will either continue to influence us throughout our life, if they are of value to the ego, or be discarded from our memory bank if they are of no further value. But here is the point. They are still lying dormant in the Collective Unconscious of humanity and more particularly in your little personal corner of it.

One type of memory that you can guarantee the ego will hold on to and continue to use to disrupt your life and side-track you with is any experience that you have had in the past that can be grouped under the category of fear. The Bible tells us that this was the first non-pleasurable emotion that Adam and Eve experienced in the Garden after initiating the original psychological separation of the Mind of Humanity from the Mind of God. Fear caused them to hide from God's presence. Why is fear important to the ego or the forces of darkness? Because fear is the one emotion that the ego mind can use again and again in a variety of different circumstances to influence or disrupt our lives. We see fear manifest in every area of people's lives, even in its most subtle forms such as anxiousness, worry, anxiety or depression.

Throughout our life, perhaps more intense though in the first half than the latter, this process of thought collecting and the depositing of each one into our personal little corner of the Collective Unconscious continues, contributing to our sense of individuality, our identity, and our sense of differentiation from each other, whilst strengthening our subconscious sense of alienation from the God Mind and psychological separation from the rest of humanity.

At the beginning of our life, we are given a name, John Smith, or Mary Jones or whatever, to identify us as a separate or individual person, and with that comes the impartation of the belief that this is who I am, I am Mary Jones, this is my true self. It is a name that is then used continuously throughout our life, as a reference point to distinguish us from other people and to keep the separation principle alive.

We inherit a nationality and a particular language that differentiates us geographically, socially, and linguistically from other societies on earth and for some we are upon our arrival into the world embedded into a specific culture, which can be visually identifiable as different from others in certain areas of lifestyle such as in religious practices, in dress, in dance, in music and in culinary choices.

Our culture then influences our lifetime habits and to some extent our relationships, accentuates our differences and demonstrates our independence from other cultures on earth, thus taking away any desire or notion of embracing the spiritual universality of humankind that is our cosmic destiny, or as the Apostle Paul put it, "coming to the unity or universality of the faith".

In terms of the spiritual life children born into some cultures are directed towards a particular religion, taught to preference its belief system, and shown how to participate in its rituals from a very early age. This is usually a hereditary bequeath, handed down either by the parents or through cultural influence. We find this happens more so in the East than the West, and for many people in the East this culturally inherited religious belief system becomes sole spiritual truth to them and remains a person's only spiritual perspective as they move through life. They are never really exposed to any other alternative religious viewpoint save their own inherited beliefs, and for many even if exposed to any different kind of spiritual truth they will fearfully reject it.

In Western society however, whilst there is no specific cultural influence directing a child towards a specific religion, there is a generalised misleading belief that Western cultures are all Christian societies, but this is not correct. However, many people who have no understanding or knowledge of the Christ within or of the Christian faith itself, save for the Easter and Christmas celebrations, will when asked about their religious beliefs, describe themselves as a Christian. I'm a Christian; my parents were all Christian they can be heard saying sometimes almost defensively.

It is also common practice in Western Christianity for allegiance to a particular Christian denomination to be handed down from generation to generation, more so with those of the Catholic faith, and to a lesser extent with protestant groups such as the Church of England or peripheral Christian groups such as Mormons and Quakers. But this is not primarily an allegiance to God, it is more so an allegiance to a particular religion's beliefs, systems ,and practices.

However this individualisation of groups in Christianity is no different from what occurs in the religion of Islam, albeit Christianity calls them denominations, Islam usually refers to them as tribes or the west calls them ethnic religious groups. In Islam there are many sects and groups with different understandings of Islam, the two most significant groups are the Sunni and the Shia, but there are also branches within individual groups for example with Sunni Islam there are groups like Barelvi, Deobandi and Najdi, with some of the differences between these groups going back to the first centuries after the birth of the religion of Islam, particularly in relation to the Sunni and the Shia; and with some of these differences inducing enough passion to result in bloodshed at certain times in Muslim history including in this present day.

We see this in recent times with the bombing of mosques in the newly Taliban controlled Afghanistan. There are also informal ideological movements such as Islamic modernism and Islamism, groups that are considered deviant and not truly Muslim by most other Islamic groups.

This division of Islam into groups or tribes are the contributing factor and primary reason why lasting negotiated peace and democratic style government with never be achieved by any western devised methods of peace making. It is a spiritual warfare fuelled by religious ideological obsession and differing institutionalised beliefs and practices embedded in the minds of the leaders and fed to the followers.

In more recent times we have seen the appearance of another ideologically insane group in the guise of Isis, a Salafist-jihadi organization whose adherents interpret the religion of Islam as a struggle against anyone who they decide has corrupted the ideals of Islamic governance, including other Islamic tribes, going about committing atrocities to support the beliefs of their tribe. So they are not just an Islamic tribe fighting another Islamic tribe they are an Islamic tribe fighting the world.

In its most simple definition, what is ideological obsession? It is a specific psychological influencer, pointing people to a way of perception that causes them to determinedly look at the world in a different way than the majority, to detach themselves from the ways and the minds of others and align themselves with "like minded" people, and to think as they think and behave as they behave, in ways that rarely benefit all of humanity, but are more so to the detriment of certain aspects of humanity who they feel are opposing them in their quest. Once again it is all about self-survival but in this case radically implemented.

It is a state of mind or fixed belief in a particular form of social, political, or religious philosophy in which practical elements are as prominent as the theoretical ones in its respective charter. In other words, if the theoretical ideology reads that the Muslim way of religion is the only way that society can survive, then practical elements such as murder and the blood shedding of all those deemed to oppose this must follow. Ideology subscribes to a system of ideas that inspires both to explain the world and if necessary, sometimes in a radical and violent way to change it. And why would one want to be like this? Simply to survive and continue in their own individual way of being and existing.

"Ideology is at its core based on a societal self- survivalist mentality".

The Formation of Our Identity

So in terms of why we think as we think and behave as we behave, no matter what our religion or even if we are not connected to any religion, over time, as part of the play of personhood, as our personal identity, the person we see ourselves to be, grows and develops, we will accept certain 'thought things' as truth, and they become our reality, including numerous false assumptions about ourselves and about our fellow human beings, about the rightness or wrongness of individualised cultures and religious beliefs and most importantly about who this person 'this identifiable me' really is.

Most of these assumptions about our personal self are linked to the physical, mental, and psychological aspects of our person; I'm good looking, I'm plain, I'm hot I'm not, I'm clever, I'm dumb, I'm good at Math, I can't do Math, I'm shy, I'm quite confident. Thus, the firming up of what is known as our identity, including aspects of our personality sometimes noticed and obviously recognizable by other people with comments such as, she's a bubbly person, or he's a moody person, or she's funny, or he's dour, aspects of our personality that continue to grow and solidify as we and those around us acknowledge that this is who we really are.

It is a personal identity being continuously shaped and reinforced through relationships, through our body mind experiences, the good and the bad of them, through our obsession with objects and forms meaning the material world, and through the continuous introduction into our minds of a conglomerate of supportive 'thought things,' for our ego mind is always on the lookout for thought things that more often than not reinforce our negative opinions about ourselves rather than the positive aspects of our identity.

Together all these thought things merge into our own personal identity, our personalised corner of Collective Unconsciousness, a fixed and hard to change belief system about ourselves, seemingly set like cement, that we guard dearly, consciously, or unconsciously with a type of, "don't think you can tell me who I am" attitude. An attitude that does not easily embrace corrective counsel.

It is an identity certainly containing some good things, but an identity also containing biased and bigoted attitudes or thought patterns and subsequent behaviours towards anything or anyone who would in our mind attempt to take any aspect of what we call our identity away from us. It is a personal identity that, having been seared into our minds, we guard dearly, and which will go on to influence the direction of the rest of our life sometimes in a positive and sometimes in a negative way, whilst continuously reminding us that this is who we really are, and that this is all there is to life, there is nothing else and we must live with that, you can't change it.

Thus, a platform for an ongoing self-absorbed, self-willed, and self-determined life, a life lived predominantly with a self-survivalist and sometimes selfish attitude has been established by early adulthood, with our day-to-day attention span, sub-consciously and consciously completely focused on all manner of things that affect or influence us "personally".

The Relationship of Archetypal Influences in Identity Formation

Jung in his research into understanding why societies and individuals think as they think and behave as they behave, whilst focusing on the role of the Collective Unconscious also highlighted the influence of archetypal patterns of behaviour that are a part of that Collective Unconscious. Now whilst the Greek philosopher Plato is credited with originating the concept of archetypes, in his research and writings it was Jung who coined the name archetypes for these shared mind concepts lying in the Collective Unconscious, these shared personality profiles.

Scholars would say the word archetype comes from the Latin noun archetypum, which means "the original pattern from which copies are made." However, the term archetype like so many words in the English language had its origins in ancient Greece, in the word archein, which means "original", and "typos", which means "pattern or type". Combine these two and you get the meaning of archetype to be:

> *"The original pattern from which all other persons, objects, theories, or concepts are derived, copied, modelled, emulated, or imitated".*

In Jung's world of psychotherapy, he used the term archetypes to refer to "personality patterns" that have existed since the beginning of time, patterns that influence the behaviour of people in a particular direction, theorising that as active components of the Collective Unconscious, archetypes serve to organize, direct, inform and influence human thought and behaviour.

People living out of similar archetypal influences sometimes unknowingly refer to someone with the same personality patterns as their own as being "like minded." Meaning the other person's mind thoughts and the behaviour emanating from specific thoughts, the way they think, and the way they physically or verbally respond in certain circumstances is the same as theirs. In Jungian psychology archetypes are seen as collectively inherited conscious ideas, images, or patterns of thought present in every person's psyche or mind.

And here an important point. The food sources that sustain these individual established archetypal personality patterns are in fact our behaviours, and the more repetitive a behaviour is, the deeper the personality pattern that first induced it becomes embedded in our psyche. It becomes what is commonly known as a compulsive mental addiction, and it is often labelled by those around us. "Oh, she's a worry wart," labelling a person who appears to worry about everything, to have worrying thoughts about everything, or "he's a hypochondriac" labelling with one word someone who continually thinks about the potential for them to experience some sort of sickness.

Our behaviours emanating out of our thought life or personality patterns energise and sustain these patterns, which then reinforces and maintains the same behaviour. So, it can be a never-ending cycle of either bad behaviour or good behaviour depending on the pattern resident in our personality. If we choose as an act of our will to no longer engage in a particular type of thinking that has been strengthening or sustaining that pattern it will progressively disable it. Which is also what the Apostle Paul was teaching when he said, "be transformed by the renewing of your mind." He was emphasising more than just a change of mind; he was talking about a transformation that causes others to exclaim "Wow."

Alternately, if we choose to approach it from the other end of the spectrum, the behavioural end, in other words if we take deliberate action to "fake it until we make it", this will also work because it too will eventually disable the thought pattern. You will become in actuality what you started off by simply faking. You see thought cannot distinguish between imagination and what is truth. I shared the example of how we saliva if we imagine ourselves eating a lemon. So it is either change your habitual thoughts or fake the change in choosing different behaviour, choosing behaviour that gives the appearance that you had permanently changed already. But you have to start somewhere if you want change to occur.

There are both the positive and negative aspects of archetypal egoic influencers the negative ones sometimes being referred to as shadow archetypes. These are many but here are a few examples. These negative personality patterns can appear in the form of "rumour mongering", backbiting, and thriving on the power generated by passing on secret or private news and misleading information, creating even more damaging rumours. Then we have the negative "victim" personality pattern. Its negative manifestations see the personality moving into the role commonly known as "playing the victim," because of the positive feedback it gets in terms of sympathy and pity, which reinforces a feeling of self-worth, a feeling of wow I am important, someone is listening to me and feeling for me.

Then on the positive side we have the "teacher" archetypal influence or personality pattern. The positive elements of this archetype are in that it freely communicates knowledge, experience, skills, and wisdom to those around them. We also have the positive "rescuer" personality pattern. We see it manifesting in someone who always provides strength and support to others in a crisis. One who acts out of love or kindness with no expectation of reward.

Jung was also very interested in the way societies and different cultures for hundreds of centuries have used archetypes in myths, attaching a specific archetype to a mythological story to enable a culture or tradition to be easily passed down, almost in storybook mode, from generation to generation. We often see this in various types of religious writings including the Bible, but whilst in Eastern Religion they are readily embraced, not so in Western Religion.

Some over superstitious elements of Christianity are very reluctant, similarly as they are with the spiritual warfare component of our cosmological existence, to entertain the possibility that some stories in the Bible may in fact be of a mythological nature to teach some moral or spiritual lesson; stories such as the serpent appearing to Eve in the Garden of Eden or the story of Jonah and the whale in the Old Testament. The definitive meaning of a myth is that it is a traditional story mostly centred on the early history of a people or society, explaining a natural or social phenomenon typically involving supernatural beings or events.

Jung also spent some time investigating and studying the similarities in the symbolism used in different myths and in religious and magic systems, symbols that have continuously occurred in many different cultures through the world's known history, cultures with absolutely no historical connection. To account for this similarity of symbols used throughout different ages in different religious myths, he suggested that there were two layers in this Collective Unconscious, two layers in this group mind that we are all involved with. Firstly, there is a personal layer coming out of individual personality patterns of behaviour that we have acquired throughout our life mainly through all our interpersonal relationships and experiences, and then a second layer that contains memory traces of experiences that are common to all of humankind.

These second layer personality patterns when formed are what he referred to as archetypes, and archetypes when embedded into a storyline become what are known as a myth. George Walton Lucas Jr., the Filmmaker, Philanthropist and creator of the Star Wars and Indiana Jones franchises once rightly said, "I've concluded that mythology is really a form of archaeological psychology. Mythology gives you a sense of what a society believes, and what they fear."

Archetypes are in fact pre-conscious psychic dispositions or in simple language subconscious attitudes of thinking that form the substrate, the underlying layer, from which the basic themes of life in particular religions occur. Archetypes that we see present to a greater or lesser degree in most religious writings and in certain religious brands, particularly in Eastern Religions such as Hinduism, and in specific cultures such as the Australian Aborigine and the American Indian, are with their inclusion into what is called a myth, used to explain the original pattern or model from which that society, tradition or religion first sprang.

The problem for a lot of people though in considering this is as the saying goes "separating truth from fiction.' Discerning what actually or literally happened and what is merely myth designed to share a truth, principle, or theory, but this really does not have to be a problem. For instance, with Christians this happens a lot with regards to some Biblical stories such as Noah and the flood, the serpent speaking to Adam and Eve in the Garden of Eden, and the trials of Job, which some use as a point of debate. Are they true stories or is there some form of life lesson buried in them that the universe wants to teach us? I think, well does that really matter, if there is a life lesson in it take it, if not move on.

Jung believed that the same archetypal images that reside in certain stories in the Bible also reside in the human soul, and manifest in the lives of people causing them to do psychologically inspired things such as love and hate, and to carry out heroic deeds, and in certain circumstances causing them to do things which they would not ordinarily do as a matter of conscious will. We have all heard people use the expression, "Honestly I don't know what made me do it." Nothing made them do it, but something of a cosmic nature may certainly have influenced them to do it.

Archetypal myths in literature can be described as an action, event, or situation, that with the involvement usually of a specific character or characters represent a universal pattern of human nature and subsequent human behaviour. Sometimes called universal symbols, in certain myths different archetypes arise representing opposite character qualities, positive and negative you could say. For example, an archetype representing a hero and one representing a villain, both these characters then are blended into a singular story to create a theme of behaviour for certain individuals or indeed societies who oppose each other.

This relates closely to Descartes Principle of Dualism, which I spoke of in Chapter 8, which sees two opposite life forces such as good and evil existing in a combative environment opposing each other. The storyline in myths and in most fairy tales, which are equally a form of myth, is usually centred on the character of a person or thing exhibiting a quality of goodness or righteousness, referred to as the hero or heroine, going up against a person who predominantly exhibits evil, referred to as the villain, to restore harmony and justice to society.

Some years ago I attended the opening of the musical stage production called Wicked: The Life and Times of The Wicked Witch of The West, in St. Louis Missouri, which was an adaptation of L. Frank Baum's children's novel The Wonderful Wizard of Oz. Amongst the characters representing both sides of the coin, goodness and evil, we have Glinda the good witch of the south and then the opposite archetypal character, the wicked witch of the north. More modern day perhaps is what we are seeing in the Marvel series of films, with heroic figures such as Batman going up against enemies of goodness such as the Joker, similarly Superman going up against the arch villain Lex Luther. Even board games can emerge out of the world of myth. If one looks at the history behind the much-loved Snakes and Ladders board game, one will discover the mythological overtones behind its creation.

When Carl Jung used the concept of the archetype in his theorising on the workings of the Soul, he was mostly referencing what he saw as timeless, ageless, universal mythical characters that reside within this invisible Collective Unconscious of people and societies all over the world. In their functional role you could say that they manifest in our personalities and subsequent thoughts and behaviours as motivating factors and are specific recognizable types. Aspects of our personality that cause us in our thinking, communicating and behavioural processes, to be as we are, say what we say, and do what we do, and with regards to the emotional side of our nature to feel how we feel.

Archetypes have been recognized as being present in humankind since the time of Plato, who probably went a bit further than Jung believing that these pre-existing personality influencers were present in all manner of visible things, whether that be of the humankind or material objects such as sunrises and sunsets; the archetype or character quality in that instance being "beauty." Archetypes are said to provide the foundation of a person's personality and can explain why some people are seen as being quote, "such a kind and generous person," without effort, whilst another person can be typed as "a mean selfish ole bastard."

People unknowingly use the phrase when talking about a particular person's attitude or behaviour and perhaps semi-excusing it, "oh well he's just that "type" (archetype) of person." When understood, archetypes can be universally used to help us understand why different people think like they think and behave as they behave, whilst at the same time not justifying bad behaviour. Jesus on the cross expressed it this way, "Father forgive them, for they know not what they do". When we can come to accept and embrace that thought process of Jesus also, we will come to a greater level of forgiveness toward those who offend us, not only for their sake but also to our own psychological benefit as well, for to the measure we forgive shall we also be forgiven. Like produces like.

We must understand however that archetypes are only mind influencers in terms of thought patterns, they do not force us to behave in certain ways as we do, such as being kind or being unkind, that still comes back to free will, our choice. Free will always has the power to overcome mind influences. In relation to spirituality myths with their archetypal lead characters are stories of an imaginative type that are eternal and mysterious, and that seem to fulfil in various cultures a need to find a deeper meaning and understanding of life as we know it.

Many spiritual myths give clues as to the spiritual potential of human life and are sometimes used as an excuse for what does or doesn't happen in one's spiritual life. In many ways you could say that myths are stories that link together the outer with the inner, the experience of life on the physical plane with the human mind's need for an explanation of the spiritual or inner life of a person.

Perhaps partly from having witnessed the horrors of World War 2, Jung believed that society was crying out for balance, rather than the mental imbalance that seemed to be present in the ideologically inspired insanity of the war, particularly in Nazism. He also suggested that even though some religious organizations were aware of this mental imbalance in society, by them establishing their own philosophical outlook they were in fact still contributing to the imbalance in their teaching rather than trying to lessen it.

This differed from the orthodox church in the fact that as the church evolved into a more institutionalised state, it also evolved into a religion of pure form, ceremony, and ritual only, to the exclusion of the quest for an inner knowing; it adopted a purely externalist approach to Christian worship and practice and ignored all aspects of the internal approach. Similarly in Islam except in the mystical branch of Islam called Sufism. But as we see in the Gospel of Thomas, part of the Nag Hammadi archaeological finds, that Jesus came to make the inner as the outer and the outer as the inner, to make the above as the below and the below as the above, that all the internal aspects of humanity and all the external ways may be as one.

Jesus came to draw together the mind of humanity and the Mind of God. So, Christianity, rather than being fearful of Jung's work owes him a debt of gratitude for his dedication in bringing both the theological world and the psychological world into a state of connectedness. Jung in his role as a healer of the soul saw himself as a healer of the mind and the emotions, guiding a person through a process of thinking correction, of understanding what was illusionary in their life particularly in the emotions, emotional things that they had experienced in their interpersonal relationships that brought storms to their personal corner in the ocean of consciousness.

However, the process of psychotherapy unlike the workings of consciousness cannot be eternally creative, and whilst it can substitute in the mind one sane thought to replace one insane thought and circumvent for a while the resultant behaviour surfacing out of insane thinking, it cannot in the long term create a new person. Only the Christ Mind or Infinite Intelligence within can accomplish that kind of lasting psychological and subsequent circumstantial change.

Transgenerational and Intergenerational Trauma and Grief

Now lastly looking at some things that are seemingly out of our control, or that we are not consciously aware of, things that you could say we have not deliberately chosen to embrace, that influence how we think and how we behave. Out of our control in the sense that until we become aware of them, we can't deal with them, like a burglar hiding in the basement of our mind that quietly and surreptitiously in the dead of the night robs us of our identity, our immediate destiny, and even our potential. These burglar like things being transgenerational and intergenerational trauma and grief.

Transgenerational and intergenerational trauma are psychological terms that have in recent years come more and more to the fore in studies and research into why certain individuals or societies or races or conglomerates of people think like they think, and subsequently behave as they behave. It is a psychological term, which asserts that trauma, pain, and hurt, experienced in one generation can have an emotional impactful consequence that can be transferred ongoingly from generation to generation. That a survivor of a traumatic experience can even unconsciously transfer that trauma to their children and to their children's children, and to future generations in the family lineage.

When these findings came to light, certain members of the psychological profession found the idea implausible, but many of those early criticisms have been negated through increasing evidence gained, revealing many identifying markers that prove this to be true. Not necessarily psychological markers through birth, but more interesting markers obtained by research into social behavioural patterns.

Scientific research has discovered that DNA methylation, which is the molecular modification that alters gene expression without changing the DNA sequence, can be modified by stressful and socio-economic factors and that apparent DNA methylation has been associated with a variety of stress related neuro psychiatric disorders, such as depression, schizophrenia, bipolar disorder, and autism. DNA methylation has provided or may provide a mechanism through which early life adversity becomes biologically embedded in mental illness in future generations.

Accumulating evidence, from both experimental and human studies, has shown that adverse childhood experiences can induce significant and persistent changes in DNA methylation and other epigenetic modifications and that the stress induced epigenetic alterations can cause stable changes in the expression of genes involved in the stress regulation system, thereby contributing to neuropsychiatric diseases which includes depression.

A greater understanding of intergenerational trauma first came to light and was recognised in observation of the children of survivors of the Holocaust, the event in history that I spoke of in Chapter 3, when in 1966 a group of psychologists began to observe and monitor large numbers of children of Holocaust survivors who were seeking mental help in clinics around Canada. These were grandchildren of Holocaust survivors, and in terms of numbers they were overrepresented by 300% amongst the doctor referrals to a psychiatric clinic, in comparison with their representation in the general population.

Since then, as further research has been conducted, transgenerational trauma and hurt and the impacts of it have been noted amongst descendants of Afro-Americans who were forced into slavery, in native American Indians and in Australian Aborigines who were genocide survivors, and also in war survivors, in refugees, and interestingly in the children of survivors of continuous and ongoing domestic violence. Trans-generational trauma is a collective experience that can affect individuals or groups of people because of their cultural identity, ethnicity and nationality, or their religious identity, and because of its collective nature the term is not usually applied to single families or individual people.

Like survivors of individual child abuse, direct survivors of the collective trauma of subsequent generations have been found to develop complex post-traumatic stress disorders. Researchers have discovered that the transmission of trans-generational or intergenerational trauma between parents and children can be broken down into certain areas including communication conflict, lack of family cohesion, lack of parental warmth and parental involvement, with common symptoms in children consisting of depression, antisocial behaviour, delinquency, and disruptive behaviour in school.

Symptoms also differed based on ethnicity and the type of original trauma. For instance, enslavement and genocide, domestic violence, child sexual abuse, and extreme poverty were all common sources of trauma that led to intergenerational trauma. Survivors of unresolved trauma for example African Americans, when faced with racism motivated abuse or violence will react as if they were being subjected to the original trauma that their forefathers had experienced, with symptoms of trans-generational trauma having in recent years been identified among many black Americans in relation to the effects of slavery and racial discrimination.

Trauma rooted in the psyche of successive generations, leaves lasting effects that can remain for centuries, examples being seen in black children's internalisation of reactions to their skin colour, causing behaviour to manifest that was previously suppressed by their ancestors who originally experienced it, like a genie in a bottle desperate to emerge after centuries of confinement. In many ways this is similar in process to how bigoted and biased belief systems of say adult White Supremacists and Neo-Nazis can be passed down from generation to generation through the children. I say similar because these attitudes can be picked up by a child through their domestic environment, through what they hear and see in their everyday home life.

In this way biased and bigoted belief systems fall under the computer science concept called Gigo, meaning, garbage in, and garbage out. The word Gigo references the fact that flawed input data produces non-sensical output. In other words, no matter how intelligent artificial intelligence or human intelligence is or thinks it is, if wrongly programmed it will not give reliable outcomes or produce right or truth filled information. Programming is key.

However, in our journey of understanding as to why we think as we think and behave as we behave in a sometimes fluctuating and conflicting manner, we must look at it not only from the peripheral psychological perspective. The key to understanding these things that influence our behaviour lies in understanding the platform that supports and sustains the emergence of these psychological influencers, and that all comes back to the concept of the Collective Unconsciousness of humanity, that concept of the Collective Unconscious state of our existence and humanity's exposure to it that I spoke of in the previous chapter. As Carl Jung so succinctly put it:

"Much of the evil in the world is due to the fact that man in general is hopelessly unconscious".

The life lived in the realm of the Collective Unconscious is what I would describe as a life lived in a state of personhood, a life influenced by personal mind things, mind thoughts, specific mind responses according to what we have programmed in over time, and thus a life of psychological separation or alienation from Divine Wisdom and Godly principles. It is a life influenced by many personal things that we have tucked away in our own little corner of the Collective Unconscious including hereditary hang ups and hurts, trans-generational trauma and grief, biased and bigoted belief systems, past memories and future desires, and even inherited personality patterns of the archetypal ancestral kind.

All residing in the Collective Unconscious, and all attempting to influence in some way or another our patterns of thought, the state of our emotions and the resultant behaviour that emanates from those thoughts and emotions. And all being potential tools to be used by the egoic side of our nature as it weaponizes itself in this the "war of two spiritual worlds", the war between our lower nature and our higher nature.

Since all human beings were psychologically separated from the Mind of God in the beginning, all human beings have since been born and lived in the Collective Unconscious state of being, their lives lived purely out of and through logic and reasoning, which springs into action as thoughts, feelings, and emotions that manifest according to our everyday life experiences. In other words, we use logic and reasoning at the level of Simple Awareness to interpret and sometimes justify those everyday experiences. We use the intellectual side of our thinking process to try to understand why life is as it is without any input from the intuitive side which is in fact the place where many of these things are conceived before they are birthed into our awareness.

We are all born into a life lived in and subject to the influences of the Collective Unconscious which causes us to, regardless of whether they are archetypal, hereditary, tans-generational, or purely habitually self-developed, in our early stages of physical and mental growth establish fixed base line modes of behaviour.

Our lives are further shaped and influenced emotionally by those who have loved us or those who have refused to love us. Which of course continually reflects in our emotional life responses and behaviours with those close to us, triggering certain responses. These things particularly have a significant effect in establishing personality patterns that influence our ongoing behaviour and choices with regards to future relationships.

A point to note is that Jesus was not born into this state; Jesus being God in human form or in flesh as described in the Bible, was spotless and sinless and was born into the state of mind, one level higher than us, He was born into the state of Collective Consciousness. He was never influenced by the Collective Unconscious, even though as we see recorded in his wilderness experience with the force of darkness he was sorely tempted. But his response to these influencers was always to directly turn to Divine Principle as we see when he prefaced his reply to each temptation with the words "It is written", and then quoted that Divine Law that would negate the power of that egoic influence.

Which is also why from the get-go history records that Jesus went about doing good works. How? Because His level of conscious existence as the Mind of God in flesh was just a little lower than the Angels, but not as low as humanity, so the Bible tells us. Why did He appear this way? So that He could approach humanity at the point or level of its current perceptual existence, that of Simple Awareness, and guide humanity to a higher state of conscious existence. This is also why He was driven to do good works to give evidential truth of His state of Collective Consciousness.

This is the mystery hidden in Hebrews 2:9 in the New Testament. Jesus being God in flesh started at the point of Universal Consciousness and then descended to Collective Consciousness. But purely to pick our minds up, to pick us up at our existing level of understanding and put us back on the right consciousness evolutionary track. To in fact lead us back to our Source. Our mission or destiny is to go the opposite way. Jesus descended to Collective Consciousness to meet us, but we are to ascend, to ascend to a higher level, from Collective Unconsciousness through Collective Consciousness to Universal Consciousness, back to Him. Jesus, Infinite Intelligence, removed His robe of glory, and descended to meet us, to teach us, and to escort us to the highest level of consciousness, the bosom of God.

To teach us, through his example on how one should journey onward through the Collective Conscious lifestyle, always preferencing Divine Law over human ego driven intent. Jesus continually prefaced his replies when asked something about behaviour or life with the phrase, "it is written", referring to the fact that everything he believed in and every behaviour he embraced, and every teaching he gave was centred on directing people back to Divine Law the Law of God, the Law of The Spirit, our New Covenant with Infinite Intelligence.

Jesus came to lead us back home to the Creative Source of all things, the Word, Universal Consciousness. How did He do that? He did it by showing us through His own behavioural and emotional lifestyle, how to think, look and behave towards all of life in a compassionate kind way, and with his selfless crucifixion, how to put Divine Will ahead of self-will. He did it by living and behaving in accordance with every word that proceeded from the mouth of God. He lived every day in accordance with the Law of the Spirit, Divine Principle, the God way of thinking.

As discussed, "faking it until making it" used quite often in modern day mindfulness programs to good effect, can give us a temporary psychological reprieve, but it is only when people change their way of thinking and perceiving to the God Mind way of thinking and perceiving, will they automatically "psychologically alchemise that re-educated or realigned thought process into specific lasting behavioural change". In other words, if society starts doing things differently, doing things according to Divine Law, Divine Principle, God's way, or Infinite Intelligence's way of thinking and doing, they will most assuredly experience a permanent, not temporary positive enhancement to their humanity, and a true understanding of the Cosmic nature of their existence camouflaged in their present illusionary individual and self-serving existence.

It's about becoming liberated from the old way of thinking and behaving, to a new way of thinking and behaving, the Mind of Christ way, using the Divine Laws that control this universe as our guiding behaviour and true-self inducing self-transformational light. This then releases the Creative Principle of Grace into our lives.

I share more on what Divine Principle or Divine Law, or the Law of the Spirit is in the chapters ahead, and more on how by our adopting these attitudinal changes and behavioural principles into the practicalities of our life, the power of Infinite Intelligence is switched on thus bringing to fruition the miracle of change in our life, the freedom of body and mind, that we have long been desperately searching for.

❝ *"Life is not all about finding 'your purpose', we know what that is. It is to evolve consciously. Life is all about discovering a purpose filled existence as you are progressively evolving, using what the Universe is giving you in the present moment. It is about being faithful in the little things.*

It is in the first instance all about disciplining your mind to always find meaning in the moment, in the existing circumstances the Universe has placed you in. Find meaning in everything you put your hand to and from that point, the point of faithfulness, Creative Grace or Creative Life Changing Energy is released to flow. Be faithful in small things because it is in them that your strength lies".

Christianity and Jesus Islam and Muhammad and The Three Reasons Jesus Appeared on Earth

TEN

> "The Atonement process, of which the renewal of the mind process is a prime participant, teaches me how to escape from everything I have taught myself in the past and everything I think about myself in the present, and reveals to me the true reality of who I really was in the past and who I truly am now in the present."

Jesus, the historical figure, also referred to as Jesus of Nazareth or Jesus Christ, was a first century Jewish preacher and religious leader who was born c.4 BC and who passed AD. 30/33. Jesus became the central figure in the religion of Christianity, the world's largest religion. He is believed by most Christians to be the Son of God, the human incarnation of God and the awaited Messiah, the Christ, as prophesised in the Hebrew Bible, or the Tanakh, and as recorded in the Old Testament. The Old Testament is the first component of the Christian Bible that contains a collection of writings that were first compiled and preserved as the sacred books of the Jewish people.

Christianity is an Abrahamic, monotheistic religion, (a religion who teaches that there is only one God), and the Christian faith is based on the history, life, and teachings of the man Jesus of Nazareth and of those who followed Him. Adherents to Christianity make up most of the population in 157 countries and territories around the world, all believing that Jesus is the Christ, whose return as the Messiah (a leader regarded as the saviour of a particular country, group, or cause), was prophesied in the Hebrew Bible. This return of the Messiah also known as the second coming or the second advent is a Christian belief regarding the return of Jesus after his ascension to heaven around 2000 years ago.

Muhammad ibn Abdullah was an Arab religious, social, and political leader born 570 CE who passed 632 CE. He was the founder of the religion of Islam. Similarly, as in Christianity, Islam is an Abrahamic, monotheistic religion, that began in the seventh century BC, but through its roots it is believed to date back further. According to Islamic doctrine Muhammad was a prophet, divinely inspired to preach and confirm the monotheistic teachings of Adam, Abraham, Moses, Jesus, and other prophets, and believed to be the final prophet of God in all the main branches of Islam, although some modern Islamic denominations diverge from this belief.

Muhammad united the Arabian Peninsula into one single Muslim polity, which is an institutionalised political and religious entity, using the Qur'an as well as his own beliefs, teachings, and practices to form the basis of Islamic religious belief. It is the official religion in 26 countries in Asia, sub-Saharan Africa, North Africa, and the Middle East, and is believed to be growing faster than any other religion worldwide.

Christianity and Islam

If you asked the average person in the street which two religions in their opinion are the most combative in their relationship with each other, whilst some might say it would have to be Catholics and Protestants in Northern Ireland it is more than likely that most would answer, "well that would have to be Muslims and Christians". And in looking at it from a historical context in terms of the high number of ideologically driven religious clashes we have seen over the centuries that would basically be right.

Most people however regard the idea of a religious or holy war as a contradiction, for killing thousands of people and causing wholesale destruction seems to be as far from holiness as one can get. But religion and war have gone together for a long time witnessing opposing armies going into battle against each other, both sides believing that God is on their side, and that God is with them and supporting them. Sometimes armies have gone straight into battle after prayers and sacrifices have been offered to keep God on their side. In ancient tribal cultures including in Biblical times, when a leader and his tribe lost a war, they often had to change to the worship practices of the winners' gods. Gods and human ungodly behaviours have been closely linked for hundreds of centuries.

Wars themselves are sadly a constant, tragic fact in our world. People have long since spoken of the impending war to end all wars, Armageddon as it is referred to, or the Apocalypse, in a seemingly excitable anticipation of the final war that supposedly sees the destruction of society as we know it. More specifically though, Armageddon is the place where supposedly the final battle will be fought, whilst the Apocalypse are the reading of the events that lead to this world ending battle.

Today, perhaps more so than at any time before, due the explosion of the digital age, the subject of war is covered in more detail than ever before by the world media, usually accompanied by horrific visual images of death and destruction being inflicted on certain sectors of society. These visually disturbing images of man's inhumanity to fellow man and the pain and suffering that is left in its wake are being regularly broadcast into individual living rooms, causing some people to become erringly emotionally immune to the pain and suffering that war causes. More so in recent years we have seen with the renewed growth of these political religious differences certain sides advocating a retaliatory response as the only means of dealing with a nation whose beliefs and attitudes conflict with their own.

But herein lies the problem. People see these reports, these news broadcasts with their horrific visual imagery, and immediately come to the assumption that it's all about differentiating religious belief, when in reality it is far more than that. You see people use simple terms such as Muslims and Christians and religious extremists and religious differences to describe what is almost a hopelessly complex web of shifting power relations, of feudal alliances, ethnic sympathies, and historical grudges that shaped much of early European history in the past and continues in the present. All fuelled by the inherited beliefs, attitudes, and behaviours of people in political or religious leadership and a myriad of trans-generational prejudices.

It has nothing to do specifically with the true teachings of either Jesus or Muhammad, even though certain people mostly those of political persuasion have manipulated the historical record of these teachings to gain ego driven advantage and justification for their evil ego driven deeds. Here is a simple example.

The Ottoman Empire was a state that controlled much of south-eastern Europe, western Asia, and northern Africa, between the 14th and early 20th centuries. In the year 1683, a vast Ottoman army was camped just outside the gates of Vienna. For centuries thereafter, the siege and final decisive battle that took place, would be cast as a defining moment in the clash of two civilisations, a defining moment when the forces of Islam were halted at the gates of Christendom. That has been the narrative that most historians have continued espousing since that incident in history first occurred.

However, when you look a little closer at which parties were involved in that supposed decisive battle, you see that that specific narrative just does not hold water. For that great Ottoman siege had been coordinated in league with the French King Louis the 14^{th,} consequently perhaps more than half of the soldiers seeking to capture the Austrian capital were in fact Christians themselves not solely Muslims. There were Greeks, Armenians, Hungarians, Bulgarians,

Romanians, Serbs, people of many ethnic and religious backgrounds, all fighting under a common flag alongside the Muslim Arabs, Turks, and Kurds, in the Ottoman ranks.

One of the main figures joining the Turkish campaign and fighting alongside the Muslims was a man named Imre Thokoly. Imre was the son of a rich Protestant Christian family born in what is now Slovakia, and he was an avowed Hungarian nationalist. This nationalist movement was comprised of tens of thousands of Hungarian peasants who were angry at the rapacious behaviour of the Catholic Church in Austria. His alliance with the Ottoman's helped facilitate the rapid Turkish march of his nationalist supporters toward the Austrian capital.

That siege, lasting for centuries, had far more relevance to the activities of the Catholic institution than it did to differentiating beliefs between Muslims and Christians. That siege, which resulted in around 20,000 people dying, was not about Muslims versus Christians, but more so all about institutionalised religion's influence in politics and dynastic warfare.

However, through the manipulation of historical events that incident like many others have been used to construct the theory of the essential threat posed to a society when an invasion of people whose cultural identity is wholly alien to their own is allowed to happen. We saw this attitude continue to happen when another Hungarian nationalist the country's current Prime Minister Viktor Orban, cited the legacy of that Ottoman conquest to justify keeping Syrian refugees from passing through Hungary's borders so as to escape their war-torn homeland and find a better future. Orban has not been alone with this historical hysterical hype, and politically biased rhetoric.

A conglomerate of Eastern European leaders representing right-of-centre, nationalist governments have agreed with Orban's line painting a picture of the looming existential threat that an invasion of people whose cultural identity is wholly alien to that of Europe would bring about, with some even warning of the potential of an Islamic invasion of Europe if this is not prevented at every opportunity. What they don't understand with this ill-informed racial and politically inspired rhetoric is that by merely suggesting it, they are in fact feeding the frenzy and fuelling the fires of political activism and religious extremism, for extremism loves widespread exposure it's part of the egoic nature that underpins it.

Further west, from France to the United States, Conservative politicians, including Republican presidential candidates, have gestured at a clash of civilisations when proposing laws on refugees with some even suggesting the ceasing of Muslim migration altogether. Now in saying all that, why is it that in relation to religious wars most people if asked the question as to which two religious institutions they see as being the most antagonistic towards each other and the most combative, most would probably say it has to be Christians and Muslims. Why is this so? Why would the majority of people say that. It is simply due to a "lack of understanding" born in a blanket acceptance of what they have been told through the media, through politicians, and through the institutionalised mind influencing teachings of certain extremist religious leaders.

The Book of Proverbs in the Old Testament in addressing the need for a higher level of "understanding" says:

> *"Blessed is the one who finds wisdom, and the one who gets understanding, for the gain from her is better than gain from silver and her profit better than gold. She is more precious than jewels, and nothing you desire can compare with her. Long life is in her right hand, in her left hand are riches and honour. Her ways are ways of pleasantness, and all her paths are peace".*

The fact remains that in the history of Europe, for hundreds of years, Muslims and Christians shared common cultures, spoke common languages, and did not necessarily see one another as incompatible, and the starkest proof of that lies in the battlefields, where Muslims and Christians died next to one another over many centuries. The problem lies not with the incompatibility of the teachings of Jesus and Muhammad, but rather in the institutionalised interpretation of these teachings that brought with it differentiating opinion and human interpretation of the Laws of the Divine Nature rather than common cosmic awareness or intuitive understanding of the Laws of the Divine Nature.

When the institutionalisation of both Christianity and Islam occurred, it opened the door to disunity with the implementation of differing man-made law to direct the followers of both religions. The implementation of the ego driven attitudes of the hierarchy of both Catholicism and Islam through the establishment by the Catholic Church of what is known as Canon Law and the establishment by Islam of what is known as Islamic jurisprudence, took the responsibility for intuitive conscience inspired communication with the Spirit, vital for wise thought, wise understanding and right life guidance, away from the individual believer and gave it to the "church institution."

Which then systematically set about replacing the Wisdom of God and Godly Principles as the primary source for behavioural guidance, with institutionally, many prejudiced and ego driven, manufactured life or behavioural laws, codes of conduct you could call them. Rather than it being "this is how God says you should behave," or "this is how Jesus said you should behave", or "this is how Muhammad says you should behave," it became, "this is how the church says you should behave." Divine Wisdom was replaced by the human interpretation of Godly Wisdom with all the prejudices it contained.

Consequently, in this battle of two minds, in this spiritual warfare of the minds, the power of the ego mind was given preference over the power of the Christ Mind, and the Old Covenant way of thinking and behaving, the retributive justice way, was given preference over the New Covenant way of thinking and behaving, the way of forgiveness and mercy and love.

Thus the primary focus on the commonalities in religious belief that were in fact many, were set aside in favour of a deliberate focus on the differences. And this did not only occur between one specific religion and another such as between Islam and Christianity, but it also led to disunity and disagreement within each individual religion. Which saw splinter groups come into being. For Christianity it witnessed the birth of Protestantism firstly in the form of the Church of England, and with Islam it saw the emergence of the Sunnis and the Shiites.

Then came the attitudinal changes with many Christians and Muslims believing that the Bible is a totally different set of truths from those in the Qur'an, with some Christian churches even teaching that for a Christian to be in possession of the Qur'an is a sin against God. I don't accept that. I have several versions of the Bible and both a copy of the Qur'an and commentaries on the Qur'an, and my life is blessed in having them both. Muslims progressively forgot that Jesus who lived long before Muhammad, was revered by Muhammad as a true prophet of excellence.

The significance of the life of Jesus in Islam is reflected in the fact of His being mentioned in the Qur'an in 93 verses with various titles attached such as Son of Mary, Spirit of God, and the Word of God, and mentioned directly or indirectly over 187 more times with relational titles such as Isa or Masih. The Qur'an mentions that Jesus was born without sin to Mary as the result of virginal conception exactly the same as do the writings in the New Testament.

Ibn Arabi (1165-1240), an Andalusian, (Andalucía being the former Islamic states based in modern Portugal and Spain), was an Islamic philosopher and scholar, considered to be the greatest of all Muslim Philosophers. In his meeting with Rumi, the Sufi Mystic, Philosopher, and Poet, when discussing the conception and the birth of Jesus he said the following. "From the water of Mary or from the Breath of Gabriel, in the form of a mortal fashioned of clay, the Spirit came into existence in an essence, purged of nature's taint. Because of this, his sojourn was prolonged, enduring by decree more than 1000 years. A spirit from none other than God, so that he might raise the dead and bring forth birds from clay".

This description of the conception and birth of Jesus by Ibn Arabi was included in the Sufi Muslim Rumi's Bezels of Wisdom, a twelfth century book and Rumi's own spiritual doctrine of belief. The Qur'an also mentions Jesus as a deity (having a Divine status), in several verses including one that mentions that Jesus himself did not claim to be divine.

According to the Qur'an, Jesus was not crucified, but was rather "saved" by God, but Muslims do believe as do Christians, that He was raised alive to heaven. (The Resurrection). Over the centuries, Muslim writers have referred to other miracles Jesus performed like casting out demons, as do Christian teachings. In the Islamic religion, Jesus is believed to have been the precursor to the Islamic Prophet Muhammad. According to the Qur'an the coming of Muhammad was predicted by Jesus. Thus early Arab Muslims claimed legitimacy for their new faith in the existing religious traditions and the alleged predictions of Jesus.

Like all prophets in Islam, Jesus is also called a Muslim, as he preached that his followers should adopt the "straight path". What is this "straight path?" To a Muslim it is one of the three key components that a Muslim must "**assent**" to, and also follow, to remain under the religious umbrella of Islam. It is a rule of law that is not dissimilar in its intent from those instituted in the Catholic religion during its reign over early Christianity. I say similar in intent, but it is not necessarily similar in content.

As the Qur'an is the holy book and guidebook of what is known as "**The Assent**", the way of the straight path, so too the Holy Bible is the holy book and the guidebook of the Christian belief that "Jesus is the way." The opening chapter of the Qur'an says everything you need to know about **The Assent"** as a way of life that a Muslim must "assent" to, to remain a Muslim. It says:

> *"In the name of God, the Almighty, the most merciful. Praise be to God, the Lord of the world. The Almighty, the most merciful. Possessor of the day of judgement. You alone we serve and you alone we seek for help. Guide us to the "straight path". The path of those whom you have blessed, not those who have incurred the wrath, nor the misguided".*

According to that passage, the Qur'an assumes that the reader of its contents is a Muslim who follows three specific criteria. In looking at the Assent, the way of the straight path, with regards to what commonalities it holds with Christian teaching we see the following. Those criteria that a Muslim must agree on or "assent" to are:

1. To believe in the Existence of God. Christianity also teaches this.
2. To believe in the Final Justice. Christianity also believes in this, calling it the Final Judgement.
3. To follow "the straight path". Similarly, as in Christianity, and known in Christianity as "the way", meaning the "way of Jesus". Many Muslims strictly follow this straight path, and many don't. Many Christians strictly follow "the way of Jesus" and many don't.

The first criteria, to "Believe in God" for a Muslim as with a Christian basically means that one is of the conviction that something, some force of intelligence, either knowable or unknowable, either natural or supernatural, does exist, and that that force of intelligence creates and maintains the planets so that they survive and don't crash into each other, and creates, maintains and sustains all life that exists on these planets so that they survive and do not destroy themselves in that process of surviving.

The second criteria is to "Believe in the Final Justice", and for a Muslim this basically means that one assumes that no evildoers will get away without paying for their crimes, and that all doers of good will be rewarded for their actions. Christianity also believes this. However, in both Islam and Christianity, whilst this belief is held, there are also many who also believe in the Old Testament ego dominated teaching of "an eye for an eye and a tooth for a tooth", and in doing so in many cases adopt a way of thinking and behaving that evildoers must be dealt with in the present moment rather than wait for the final justice. It is a way of thinking and behaving that sets themselves up as the arbitrary judge and executioner of Divine justice.

The third criteria, to be a Muslim is to "follow the straight path", which is to follow the right path, or the way that pleases God. Christianity also believes this. One of the key aspects of the mission and ministry of Jesus was to lead people or direct people towards the straight path. When Jesus said, "I am the Way", he was saying my way is the straight path to God Consciousness. What was Jesus's way? It was the way of Divine Principle or Divine Law, which as we see in the scriptures, it was the pathway he continually demonstrated in his attitudes and behaviours, and in his relationships and interactions with others. By the fruits of his work, his attitudes, and his behaviours, he bore witness to this truth.

Spiritual law is law that has always been regarded as being above all man-made law, even though at times it has been used as a guide for the establishment of certain man-made laws. But unfortunately the tendency for human beings is to drift back to the old lower nature or egocentric way of thinking and doing things, because most human beings believe they are merely mortal, commonly known as taking the law into one's own hands.

So as we see in both Christianity and in the Islamic religion, even though the prophets such as Muhammad and Jesus taught Divine Principles of conduct and behaviour to be adhered to in order to create and sustain an orderly and unified society, over time both the Islamic Church hierarchy and the Christian Church hierarchy took it upon themselves to set themselves up as both judge and jury to meter out punishment to those who they deemed had betrayed or disobeyed the articles of the covenant, those Divine Principles. Which really is just a drift back to the Old Testament Law of Sin and Death method of dealing with societal issues.

With the death of the Prophet Muhammad in 632, the Islamist concept of a human being's capacity for direct communication with the Divine to obtain understanding and Wisdom ceased, and the existing revelatory communications that stemmed from the Abrahamic days became fixed and immovable. Thus, much of the metaphysical aspect of Muhammad's teaching was lost. Although some offshoots of the Islamic religion such as Sufism do in fact maintain a focus on the metaphysical component of their religion, the concept of the oneness of all. The fact is, as scientifically proven, neither the physical of the universe, nor the psychological of the universe, nor the spiritual of the universe, nor the metaphysical of the universe can be separated. We are all functioning as one whole, we are all part of the one cosmological Divine Dance of the Universe.

If we have the physical wrong the metaphysical cannot function. In other words if we have the internal wrong the external cannot function how it should. If our attitude is wrong our actions will be wrong and if our actions are wrong, it just reinforces wrong attitudes. That's how the world works. It's all cyclical and reciprocal. Physics cannot be separated from metaphysics. To everything there is both an inner and an outer dimension. Metaphysical causes, plus physical causes, lead to consequences. Moral causes, plus physical causes, lead to consequences. Meta-physics plus physics leads to consequences.

It is a reminder that whilst society has made tremendous advances in science, all scientists must come to understand that in the quest for increased scientific knowledge, that there is a force beyond physics which governs and controls the physical circumstances they are attempting to change or influence. Scientists of an earlier century such as Albert Einstein and Sir Isaac Newton understood this and gave credence to it. This force is what we call Infinite Intelligence, the Universal Mind of the cosmos, and the catalyst for it to move into functional mode can be initiated by us using a Divine Principle that it is creatively programmed to respond to.

Divine Principle or the Law of the Spirit as it is called in Christianity and the Law of Karma as known in Eastern Religion, does not discriminate or discern between a righteous deed and an unrighteous deed, or a righteous thought and an unrighteous thought, it is simply operating under the law of cause and effect, and will through "a change in vibrational frequency", return to a person in like kind whatever they have sent out into the universe, whether it is sent through thought or through their behaviour. Send out thoughts of unforgiveness and unforgiveness will be returned to you. Send out thoughts of bitterness and hatred and bitterness and hatred will be revisited upon you, now or at some further stage in your life. Display anger and anger will be revisited upon you.

It may be immediate, it may come later, but it will come. Your words and behaviour will be returned to you, psychologically or circumstantially. Send out love and love will be returned to you. This is what both Jesus and Muhammad taught. Send out generosity and generosity will be returned to you. That's the simplicity of how it works. The Law of the Spirit, Divine Principle is our God given mechanism for a peace filled blessed unified existence on earth. This is how we all come to a "universality of the faith" that the Apostle Paul spoke of, and "the stature of the fullness of Christ".

Everything starts with a thought, every intent we actualise begins with a thought, and every action we take begins with a thought. Get our thoughts in line and we get our behaviours in line. It's as simple as that. In line with what? In line with God's thoughts as evidenced in the nature and behavioural characteristics of Jesus and Muhammad. And as Rumi so simply put it:

"As you start to walk on the way, the way appears."

The Three Reasons Jesus Appeared on Earth

There are three primary reasons for the appearance of this man Jesus on earth. And in their simplest form they are as follows.

Reason number 1. To repay all of humanity's karmic debt, thus ending for all time what is known as the Old Covenant or Old Testament way of atoning for humankind's failings. His was the final sacrificial blood offering for the sins of society, past, present, and future. Ending for all time humanity's way of thinking, behaving, and relating to God, and ending for all time the reign of the Old Covenant Law of Sin and Death. Which was in simple terminology the Law of Crime and Punishment, the eye for an eye and tooth for a tooth way of dealing with individual or societal behavioural failings, behavioural failings deemed by those in religious authority at the time, the tribal leaders, to have fallen short of Divine Expectations.

After Christ, religious jurisprudence, the punishment by the people principle, was done away with, or at least meant to be done away with, and cosmological and metaphysical laws of Infinite Intelligence were introduced into humanity in their entirety. Cosmological law relates to the physical universe, its structure, dynamics, origin, evolution, and fate, metaphysical law relates to the invisible world, call it the world of spirit, and the fundamental principles that underpin this world and those things it contains, principles that cannot be discerned through merely rational thought or observed by the senses.

Both cosmological law and metaphysical law were originally introduced in the beginning into the universe through the Word, (God in Spirit in Christianity and Brahman in Hinduism), with Jesus (the Word made into flesh who dwelt amongst us) coming to introduce to humanity that same creative spirit of Infinite Intelligence, who this time would not be regarded as simply a universal creative force out there in the universe, but this time as Jesus came to teach, it would be a creative energetic force who would not only be with us, but in us. This energetic force is termed the Holy Spirit in Christianity or the Ruh al-Qudus in Islam.

Reason number 2. To reveal the power a relationship with Infinite Intelligence through the Spirit brings. The revealing of this unique metaphysical power we have been given was demonstrated by Jesus not only through his teachings, but more so through his personal attitudes and behaviours, all primary examples of the capacity for a human being to make metaphysical contact with the life-changing power of Infinite Intelligence, through our right and righteous attitudes and behaviours towards one another. The overall concept of this power was referred to as the Law of the Spirit of Life in Christ Jesus.

Reason number 3. To release the Spirit into humanity's existence and thus restore humanity's psychological relationship and method of communicating with Infinite Intelligence. The Spirit was released to sustain and assist humanity in its evolutionary journey through the ascending realms of consciousness back to its source. Jesus in announcing the impending arrival of the Creative Spirit of

God said in describing this Spirit or essence, "who will comfort you, who will teach you all things, and who will bring "all things" back to your remembrance." No more sacrificial or ritualised petitioning was necessary.

Bring what things back to our remembrance? Bring the Divine Laws of Infinite Intelligence, the life laws of thinking and behaving that were written on our hearts (minds) at that moment we took our first breath and were birthed into consciousness. Metaphysical energetically empowered Divine Principles that now lie in stillness in our temple within, waiting to be summonsed to action through our thoughts and behaviours.

To give further clarity on these three Divine Purposed reasons for Jesus coming to this conscious universe and how He fulfilled their purpose:

Number one, the re-payment of karmic debt, occurred in the incident that is known as the crucifixion of Christ. What is karmic debt? We have all heard the saying "what goes around comes around". Karmic debt is the unnecessary baggage that your Soul, (body, mind, spirit), carries with it on its trip through life during its evolutionary journey of consciousness. It is stored in your little corner of the Collective Unconsciousness. Now unfortunately unlike the luggage you might take on an overseas trip, this baggage never gets lost, which means you're stuck with it until you can open it up and sort through its ancient content, and deal with and subsequently dispose of it as an unnecessary psychological, spiritual, or physical influence or interference in your current existence.

I spoke of these unnecessary baggage "influencers" in the previous chapter. When you come to understand what this unnecessary baggage you are carrying with you is, you are then able to confront your outstanding karmic debt and in doing so lighten the energetic load on your Soul. A simple example might be long held unforgiveness regarding a previous relationship, that is influencing our capacity to successfully create a new relationship.

Now when we use the expression "what goes round comes around", we tend to think of it as only relating to bad things in our life, but the reality of it is, that karma is far more expansive than just our need to atone for our bad deeds, for positive karma exists just as abundantly as negative karma exists. The difference however is that you don't have to atone for your positive karma. You just anticipate the blessing that comes with it. Remember like produces like. Jesus came to teach us also the positive benefits of "good karma,' using terms like, "give and it shall be given unto you," and "as you forgive, so shall you be forgiven." He came to atone for our bad karma, and to teach us how to receive the grace or blessings of God, through the banking of positive karma.

In other words, if you steal from others, others will steal from you, if you deceive others, you will eventually be deceived yourself, if you insult others, then others will insult you, not necessarily to your face but perhaps make insulting remarks about you behind your back to others. If you cause pain and suffering to others, pain and suffering will eventually follow you. However, if you love you will be loved in return. If you nourish you will be nourished, if you give you will be given to, if you show compassion, then compassion will be shown towards you when you need it because you have banked that positive karma, and if you demonstrate purpose in your life, your life will indeed become purpose filled.

When the crucifixion occurred as part of what is known as the atonement or reparation process, Jesus atoned for all bad karmic debt that had built up since the beginning of humanity's existence and wiped the attitudinal and behavioural slate clean. The Light that was Jesus came to atone for humanity's darkness. The Old Covenant way of doing things of thinking and behaving and worshipping was over, the New Covenant or New Testament way of doing things had now begun. The previous Law of Sin and Death was finished, the new Law of The Spirit had begun.

But it is important that you understand the following, particularly if you were a child and are now an adult of institutionalised religious teaching, because institutionalised religion has not taught it correctly. Some of that teaching is seen in the workings of the Catholic institution's confessional. When a Catholic priest asks a parishioner "how long since you made your last confessional," they are really saying, "how long have you been carrying around this bad karma that is destroying your life," but they don't. Consequently they leave some parishioners with an after pay attitude, a "sin now pay later" subconscious attitude. The basis of the confessional is to reconcile a person with God, which is fine, but it is also taught to be a means of reconciling the "sinner" with the church, with the institution, and I will leave the reader to discern the true reason for this.

In the previous instance regarding karmic unforgiveness, whilst your karmic debt in relation to unforgiveness past and present was wiped clean through Jesus's atonement, if you accept that and then continue holding unforgiving thoughts or embracing unforgiving behaviours, for example holding grudges, you then negate the power of the cross and bring the metaphysical law of reciprocity, the law of "like produces like" back into your life, which is simply opening up the gate once again to bad karma.

Which is why Jesus said when you come to God in prayer first forgive others if you have anything against them, otherwise you have no power. Which is why the Lord's prayer that Jesus gave us says, "forgive us our trespasses," and then comes the important part, "as we forgive those who trespass against us." To the measure we forgive others so is the measure of forgiveness handed metaphysically to us. That is Divine Law or Divine Principle, or the New Covenant metaphysical Law of the Spirit at work. To the measure you extend forgiveness, so shall Divine forgiveness be measured out to you.

With the ending of the Old Covenant we can no longer be judged by God or through church jurisprudence, with the introduction of the New Covenant, the Law of the Spirit, we become the judge of our own attitudes and behaviours and the automatic sentence passer on ourselves. It happens metaphysically and automatically with "like producing like." The karma we send out to the universe is returned right back to us.

The karmic debt that Jesus repaid was not just a debt concerning the sins of humankind alone. It was a debt of the Soul. It was a debt of the complete person of humanity. It was a psychological debt, the debt owing for all of humanity's ungodly thoughts, all of humanity's ungodly behaviours, and from a physical point of view a debt repaid for all ungodly sickness and disease that humanity has allowed to impact on its Divine earthly existence. The crucifixion was both a psychological and physical crucifixion, and not just a physical one as has been long taught.

It was the price that Jesus (God in flesh) paid on the cross to terminate the contract of the Old Retributive Covenant and to replace it with the New Covenant of Love. This is how the ancient prophet Isaiah prophesied the coming of Jesus and the significant role he was to play in atoning or making reparation for humanities past. He said:

"But in fact he, (meaning Jesus), has borne our grief's, (psychological), and He has carried our sorrows, (psychological) and pains (psychological and physical); yet we ignorantly assumed that he was stricken, struck down by God, and degraded and humiliated by Him". He went on to say that this wasn't the case, rather Jesus was "wounded for our transgressions, (attitudinal and behavioural), He was crushed for our wickedness, (behavioural), our sin, (behavioural), our injustice, (behavioural) our wrongdoing; (behavioural), the punishment, (karmic debt owing according to the Old Covenant Law of Sin and Death) for our ongoing and complete well-being fell on Him, and by his stripes, his wounds, we are healed". (both psychologically and physically). Isaiah 53: 4 and 5 Amplified with bracketed parts by author.

> *"Jesus redeemed or bought back the Soul of Humanity, he wiped clean its karmic debt, clearing the way for its return to its unhindered consciousness evolution."*

Number two, to reveal the power a relationship with Infinite Intelligence brings was done by his example and through his teachings on the capacity a human being has to influence the metaphysical through their thoughts and behaviours and instruction about the power they would receive when the Holy Spirit had come upon them.

Number three, the release of the Spirit into humanity's existence to restore humanity's psychological relationship and method of communicating with Infinite Intelligence occurred when Jesus ascended back to His Source, Universal Consciousness, and released the Divine Essence into the lives of humanity to replace himself and to continue his work. He had pre-told his disciples he would do this. As the active communicative agent between Divine Intelligence and humanity, the Holy Spirit in Christianity and the Ruh al-Qudus in Islam, is the Divine Light sent to continually dissipate the spiritual, physical, and psychological darkness that lies in wait ever ready to attempt when the circumstances are right, to devolve humanity's progressive evolution of consciousness. The Qur'an 5:46 says:

> *"And in their footsteps, we sent Jesus the son of Mary, confirming the law that had come before him: we sent him the gospel: therein lies your guidance and light."*

So how do we step out of this state of the progressive devolution of our state of being or consciousness? It happens through our thoughts and behaviours. When the world comes to understand the character and nature of Jesus and live life accordingly, a merged consciousness will occur. And what does that entail? It means we must train ourselves to copy Jesus because Jesus lived through His Divine Nature, hence his thought processes and behaviours were identical to those of Infinite Intelligence, the Mind of God. He was God in flesh and as such simply imitated the God of Spirit, the Word.

You see it is natural for children to imitate their parents. Children often have their parents' nature, and thus will exhibit their behaviour, and their actions. You can be around a child, and you can see their parents in not only their appearance, but in the way they walk, in the way they talk, and in some of the things they do. The Apostle Paul we read in the book of Ephesians put it this way he said, "be followers of God", the word followers here means to mimic, to be an imitator.

We are called to mimic the characteristics of the nature of God as exemplified in the thoughts and behaviours of God in flesh, Jesus. In other words if necessary we "fake it until we make it." This is a true catalyst for raising our level of cosmic awareness thus deepening our immersion in the consciousness of Infinite Intelligence. The Apostle Paul said as we read in I Corinthians, "imitate *me, just as I imitate Christ*".

But you know you cannot imitate a person if you don't know anything about them, so to successfully imitate someone we must be first guided by the behaviour and attitudes of the person we desire to imitate. We must put into practice everything we know about that person. We are to do the things we see or saw that person doing and we avoid the things we see that person avoiding, no matter how habitual those things that we should be avoiding may have become. In an attitudinal and behavioural sense it is as I said, "we fake it until we make it", until we are progressively changed into the image of the person we are imitating. Then all our attitudes and behaviours will become automatic.

And whilst that is impossible at times to do through our own physical and psychological strength all things are possible when we apprehend the power of the Mind of God, which is why Jesus in his parting words to his disciples said the following, "and you shall receive 'power' when the Holy Spirit has come upon you". Power for what? Power to change our thought processes and behaviours.

But again, what did some elements of institutionalised religion do with its interpretation of that scripture. It handed it right over to the ego mind by initiating a focus on what they termed "the power gifts," the casting out of demons, and healing, and the self-glory that many ministers can gain through impressing others with this supposed "act of power". Pentecostal churches in Christianity were the biggest offenders in this area, seeking self-glory over God glory. The power given us was a power to overcome in the first instance vain thoughts and imaginations, and become imitators of Christ, not to build mega-churches on the back of supposed miracles.

How does it happen? How do we become imitators of Christ?
It all starts simply through our making a conscious decision to change our state of awareness, to change our perception abilities and subsequent behaviours, to the God way of perceiving and behaving, which is according to Divine Law, because God only responds to His own law that He has set in place in the universe. Then we will be progressively changed into the image of Christ, and it will eventually become automatic to respond from God's point of view rather than our own biased and perhaps sometimes bigoted point of view. First, we change our perceiving, how we look at things and interpret things that happen in life, which influences our way of thinking and then our behaviour falls into line.

I share what some of the key attitudinal (thought initiated) and behavioural (our way of responding) ways of Jesus were in Chapter 13. So, what does all of this bring us to? It brings us to Divine Principle, the God way of thinking and behaving. In the next chapter, as I have in previous chapters, you will see me use the terms Divine

Principle, Divine Law and Divine Thread. Please note that all three terms are interchangeable, and most importantly note that when I speak of Divine Law, I am not referring to institutionalised church or religious law, that Old Covenant thing is gone.

From a spiritual perspective when I speak of Divine Principle, I am referring to the operational platform of Infinite Intelligence, that which causes the creative Nature of God, to spring into action, or that which causes Divine Intelligence to respond. A hidden intelligence that the notable scientist Albert Einstein referred to as "an intelligence of such superiority that, compared with it, all the systematic thinking and actions of human beings are but an utterly insignificant reflection".

> "When we adjust our attitudes and behaviours in our daily thoughts and actions, aligning them with Divine Principle or Divine Law, which is the rule of law governing this universe, Infinite Intelligence has undertaken on our behalf to bring blessing to our lives.
>
> This is the life-changing supernatural covenant that Infinite Intelligence has established with us, whereby God transforms the useless into the useful, the meaningless into the meaningful, the purposeless into the purpose filled, and the temporal into the timeless".

Divine Principle
The Vibrational Pulse Sustaining and Supporting the Fabric of The Universe

"All the great masters who have ever existed lived their faith in different forms, but the one thing that they all perfectly aligned on with each other, was the belief that there are two fundamental and irrevocable truths that govern this universe."

> **Truth number one** pertains to the existence of Universal Consciousness, a Supreme Creative Infinite Intelligence that exists beyond the veil of separation, which is the true reality of our existence, our cosmic destiny that we are meant to know, understand, and psychologically transition into.
>
> **Truth number two** speaks of Divine Principle or Divine Law that this Supreme Being has set in place, that you could say powers the evolution of consciousness in our lives. Principles which when acted on, enable this transitionary earthly journey to our cosmic destiny, back to our source, to be a blessed one, lived in power, love, joy and unity, and a peace filled successful co-existence with all of humanity.

ELEVEN

> "Every soul that has perception is, even though in different times and in different organs of sense and motion, still the same individual indivisible person. Every man, so far as he is a thing that has perception, is one and the same man during his whole life, in all and each of his organs of sense. He is indivisible in space with all other particles in space".
>
> Sir Isaac Newton

Sir Isaac Newton was born December 25th, 1642 and passed March 20th, 1727. He was an English mathematician, theologian, physicist, astronomer, and author. Widely recognized as one of the most influential scientists of all time, whilst being responsible for hundreds of scientific discoveries, he is more commonly remembered for formulating the laws of motion and universal gravitation. The "laws of motion" in simple terms describe the relationship between a body and the forces acting upon it, and its motion in response to those forces. Whilst the universal "law of gravitation" basically says that every particle attracts every other particle in the universe with a force that is directly proportional to the product of their masses, and inversely proportional to the square of the distance between their centres.

Still to this day his work in this field is usually pictorially categorized in a cartoon showing Newton trying to explain the birth of his passion through the image of a young boy, standing under an apple tree watching an apple fall to the ground. This portrayal of his early insight into gravitational forces came from a common myth that Newton as a child saw an apple fall from a tree, leading him to search further as to why it fell straight down rather than at an angle or upwards. But probably lesser known was he for his work on separating white light into the colours of the visible spectrum, which resulted in him building the first practical reflecting telescope.

A reflecting telescope was one that used a concave primary mirror and a flat diagonal secondary mirror. In simple terms the visible spectrum is that portion of the range of wavelengths that are visible to the human eye and are commonly known as visible light. The visible spectrum does not contain all the colours that the human visual system can distinguish, for example unsaturated colours such as pink or purple, and variations like magenta are absent because they can only be made from a mix of multiple vibrational wavelengths.

Now most readers have probably come across in their spiritual journey teaching or talk about the subject of vibrations and other teaching such as the Law of Attraction or various types of mindfulness approaches. Many secular teachers on this subject have in many ways separated it from the subject of spirit or spirituality, more so using it purely as a thought enhancing tool for one to enhance their state of wellbeing, and their psychological and physical lifestyle.

However as Newton's Law of Motion sees outside invisible forces impacting on visible present circumstances, so similarly in both ancient spiritual teachings and in the philosophy of metaphysics, from which many of these secular teachings on mindfulness are based, we have come to understand that our thoughts, themselves waves of energetic force, are when occurring, impacted on by two opposing energetic forces.

There is the force emanating from Infinite Intelligence, the Mind of God, our higher nature, a unifying force of peace filled intent, and the force emanating from what has been termed the egoic side of our mind's thinking process an opposing force of our lower nature. A force which draws its content, or you could say its mode of weaponry to be used in this contest of energetic forces, from the wide field of the Collective Unconscious, the complete library of humanity's thoughts since its original conception.

What I intend to do in this chapter, is to show how this whole concept of vibrational influence does in fact exist and does in fact align with spirituality and spiritual writings that speak of our journey of consciousness back to our source. But more than this I will show how this earthly sojourn that we are experiencing during that evolutionary journey, can be enhanced through better managed vibrational functioning to achieve better outcomes, including all those outcomes that Jesus said we would be gifted if we follow in His ways and abide in Him.

Outcomes such as peace and joy, and comfort and wisdom and calm, regardless of our circumstances. Which unfortunately many "faith filled" people are not achieving due to their current dualistic mindset which lowers overall vibrational frequency. A mindset that is being buffeted by both the energetic forces of the higher nature and those of the lower nature, simultaneously, simply because it, the mindset, has failed to align itself completely with the higher nature, the nature of Infinite Intelligence.

In spiritual writings these two energetic forces in opposition or competition with each other are referred to in different ways including the Forces of Light and the Forces of Darkness, the Forces of our Higher Nature and the Forces of our Lower Nature, the Forces of our True Reality or True Self and the Forces of our False Reality or False Self. It is believed that when we think, speak, or behave and act in a certain way, we activate one of these energetic vibrational forces that will receive it in that specific moment we broadcast it into the universe, and then react according to that part of our nature it aligns with, meaning our higher or lower nature, and then respond and create or recreate according to what that thought, word or deed that has been presented to the universe specifically is.

Our higher nature will only respond to those thoughts, words, or deeds of a higher vibrational wave frequency, whilst our lower nature greedily grasps those of a lower vibrational frequency, or you could say those that align with the egoic side of our nature. This overall creative concept alive and hovering, but dormant, is spoken of in many ancient teachings, and it is recorded that it became activated in the first instance in the creation of the world.

The Old Testament reads, "the earth was formless and void, and darkness was over the surface of the deep. And the Spirit of God (an energetic force) was hovering over the surface of the waters. And God said, let there be light, and there was light". This was the original creative principle at work. God had a thought, God spoke that thought, and in the first instance light overcame the darkness that was present and thus the existence of this material world, what we call the universe, and all it contains was created in alignment with that thought. All things, including the human beings that were created, being simply extensions of that thought of the Spirit, like spiritual arms, extensions of that energetic force with the same energetic DNA.

So the human being that was created was a living, breathing, vibrational, creative, energy field. This has in fact been proved in modern centuries to be a scientific fact. Which means that the human being also has unlimited potential to create. Science including Quantum Physics has discovered the following. Our body is composed of energy-producing particles each of which is in constant motion, vibrating, dancing together, creating something, or creatively changing something, sometimes for the better and at other times for the worse, depending on the instruction it receives from our thoughts.

When these particles or molecules vibrate, they can move back and forth or up and down. Sound energy causes the molecules to move back and forth in the same direction that the sound is travelling. This is known as longitudinal wave, so named because the energy travels along the direction of the particle's vibration. For a vibration to occur, an object must repeat a movement during a specific time interval. A wave then occurs which is a disturbance that extends from one place to another through space and time.

Light and sound are vibrations that move through space. Light and sound are vibrational waves. Sound waves, visible light waves, radio waves, microwaves, water waves, (the ridge of the wave as opposed to the waters that oscillate), sine waves (waves of a pure sound, all sounds in nature), cosine waves (similar to sine wave except they occur earlier), stadium waves, (synchronised or mechanical), earthquake waves, waves on a string, and slinky waves (back and forth), are just a few of the examples of our daily encounters with waves.

Vibrational wave frequency is measured in what is known as hertz. (Hz), named after Heinrich Rudolph Hertz (1857 to 1894), the first person to provide conclusive proof of the existence of electromagnetic waves. Hertz in the International System of measuring is defined as one cycle per second. One Hertz equals one vibration per second. The number of cycles, or times that a wave repeats in a second, is called frequency. Frequency is measured in the unit hertz referring to the number of cycles per second.

Vibrations are energetic waves all having specific rhythms and happen on a grand scale in many things such as seasonal changes, but in a less obvious and more subtle way in terms of how and when they occur and can be recognized and categorized in our bodies and life events. To explain this in the terminology of Simple Awareness you could say:

"As vibrational rhythmic wavelengths are broadcast to the universe in our thoughts and behaviours, including our silent attitudes and expectations, then our inner bodies or outer physical circumstances, will respond accordingly and creatively change to align

with those specific thoughts or behaviours that we have broadcast into the universe".

You see "thoughts produce our reality", but it is not random reality. It is reality aligned with those thoughts. In other words, like produces like. Habits, which are really manifested thoughts that we have repeatedly entertained, when consistently applied produce what is to us reality, and through continuous repetition cement that reality into our being into our state of consciousness. Thus a habit is formed.

To us it is real, and our self-survivalist nature tells us that that is all that matters. Similarly, "attitudes produce our reality", because attitudes are simply thoughts that have been consistently held onto for so long, that they have also become embedded in our consciousness. All attitudes and all thoughts have their own specific vibrational frequency, which in turn energetically induces a specific behavioural response. A perfect example of this can be seen in the emotion inducing thought pattern of fear, that I spoke of in the previous chapter.

Fearful thoughts or fear filled experiences will induce a psychological and physical response of either aggression, meaning to fight back, known as the "fight syndrome", or produce an anxiousness to escape, known as the "flight syndrome". Our heartbeats, breathing rates and circadian rhythms, are all commonly known functions of our everyday existence and are also examples of physiological vibrational wave rhythms that we can see, feel, and measure, and that are open to influence and change. Circadian rhythms are 24-hour cycles that are part of the body's internal clock, running in the background to carry out essential functions and processes. One of the most important and well-known circadian rhythms is the sleep wake cycle.

But there are much smaller and less obvious vibrations happening in our bodies too, inside each one of our cells, cells being the basic building blocks of all living things. The latest scientific research estimates the total number of cells in the human body to be around 30 trillion, with about 30 billion of them dying and being renewed daily. All these cells work in harmony to carry out all the basic functions for human beings to survive and most human beings just take them for granted.

This means that the average human being at any given time has 30 trillion vibrational waves operating throughout their body, a huge energy field. The vibrations generate what are known as electromagnetic energy waves. Researchers have found that vibrations and the electromagnetic energy associated with them causes changes in our cells which can affect how our bodies function psychologically and physically.

Hans Berger was a German psychiatrist. He is best known as the inventor of electroencephalography in 1924, which is a method used for recording the electrical activity of the brain, vibrational waves of energy, commonly described using the term brainwaves, and as the discoverer of the alpha wave rhythm, which is a type of brainwave. Researchers have also known for a long time that thoughts and behaviours affect the vibrational rhythms in the body. Anxious thoughts trigger the release of stress hormones that stimulate the heart rate.

Likewise, the sound vibrations of music, affect our thoughts and emotions. That's why some people use certain types of music to relax, and others use certain types of music to perhaps vent, or to mentally escape from their current emotional state, or to enhance their current emotional state. Enhancing our emotional state is a habit which strangely at some time in our lives we all more than likely have embraced. By this I mean if we are going through a period of sadness due to a relationship break up, we play our favourite sad song as an adjunct to our desire to wallow in self-pity, which lowers our vibration further enhancing that existing emotional state of sadness and the vibrational frequency it produces.

However alternately, if we have lost a loved one through death, and are going through a period of grieving, we will play songs like

Amazing Grace to change our emotional state, to give our emotional state a sense of comfort which is of a higher vibrational level, because the act of comfort is a spiritual act. This is why Jesus called the Holy Spirit, the Comforter. The hymn Abide with Me, a hymn which induces a sense of comfort and peace vibrationally and thus psychologically and emotionally, is one of the most common hymns sung or played at funeral services and was also the hymn played by the ship's band as the magnificent passenger liner the RMS Titanic sank, and thousands met their death.

This change of vibrational wave frequency in our cells through music, thus influencing our physical and emotional responses, is all about the vibrational wave frequency of the specific music and specific lyrics we are listening to, which alters our existing individual energetic wave frequency status, and converts it to the higher vibrational frequency that our cells are absorbing through the music. Depending on the type of music we are listening to, we are either vibrationally energised or vibrationally deenergised. It was Einstein who said, "energy cannot be created or destroyed, but it can be transformed."

You see everyone's individual wave frequency hungers to operate at a higher vibrational level. Why? Simply because it makes us feel better. It gives us a specific emotional vibrational stimulus that our being is hungering after in that moment. What is our being really doing from a spiritual perspective? It is hungering for "a higher or deeper level of consciousness" or spiritual presence. Matthew 5:6 speaks of our soul hungering for right standing with God to become satisfied with life. King David we read in the Book of Psalms cried out, " my soul thirsts for God."

Our soul wants to get closer to "the God frequency". How do we know what vibrational frequency God is? We don't, it can't be measured. But what we do know is that God is love, the scriptures tell us this, and love has one of the highest vibrational frequencies. Research conducted by Dr. Leonard Horowitz, an internationally recognized authority on public health in his study of brain waves, has ascertained that the emotion of love generates a vibrational frequency of 528 Hertz, which becomes very desirable to our emotions, considering the average human body functions at a vibrational frequency of 3 Hertz to 17 Hertz.

Jesus was at the peak of vibrational frequency, and because Jesus was God in flesh, and because God is love, we know that Jesus was at a minimum vibrating at a frequency of 528 Hz, but was probably realistically much higher, because he was able to in his creative instincts and abilities discern and do things at such a high level, to the point of transforming the body energy of a person to raise that person from death to life. Because he was God, he was vibrationally at one or equal with God. Which is part of what he was referring to when He said, "I and the Father are one".

This is why Jesus was able to perform creative miracles, such as healing the sick and raising the dead. Jesus was given to us as an example of the hidden potential that lies in the consciousness of all humankind, for we read in the Book of John in His parting words to His disciples He said, "these things and greater works than these shall you do, because I am going to the Father". And when his disciples looked at him incredulously obviously questioning how that could be possible, we see he went on to say, "and I will ask the Father and He will give you another helper, comforter, advocate, intercessor, counsellor, a strengthener, standby, to be with you forever".

In the words of Einstein, he was talking about Infinite Intelligence, in the words of the New Testament he was talking about the Holy Spirit, in the words of the Qur'an he was talking about Ruh al-Qudus, the active on earth agent of Infinite Intelligence. Jesus said, "if you remain in me, and my words remain in you," that is, if we are vibrationally united because our attitudes and behaviours are aligned with those of Jesus, when we ask for something that is aligned with Divine Principle it will be done for us. Others during his time and since his time have increased their vibrational frequencies as they came to understand these things, naturally none to the level of Jesus, although many religious charlatans over time have professed to.

But certainly, other human beings who have increased their vibrational wave frequencies to a very high level have managed to create and achieve wonderful things for humanity in spirituality, in science, in psychology, in medicine, in literature, and in. art. From a spiritual perspective the Buddha was at that level, Rumi was at that level, and it was a level that some of the greatest creative minds ever such as Edison and Einstein were at. And a level that literary genius's such as William Shakespeare were at.

Now it is important that we understand that every cell in our body has the vibration of life in it, whether we are fully aware of it or not. Every cell in our bodies is comprised of energy that has the potential of fully resonating with and ascending to the highest vibrational frequency and at the same time, every cell in our bodies has the potential to descend to the lowest level of vibrational frequency, and the catalyst for this is the existing emotional vibrational frequency that we manifest at a particular time, which is intrinsically linked with our thoughts and subsequent behaviours at that time.

Emotions have voltage, the vibrational frequency of emotions are always on either an ascending and expanding vertical dimension of some sort, or alternately on a descending and contracting vertical dimension, all relative to the vibrational voltage of a particular emotion we are experiencing at a specific time. This is a scientific fact. Remember, "like produces like". Emotions resonate with the vibrational frequency that they generate. The higher the vibrational frequency, then the higher the expansion, and the greater life force in our cells. The lower the vibrational frequency, then the greater contraction, and the lesser life force is in our cells. The brainwaves of a fully enlightened person have been proven to vibrate at the highest frequency of 700 Hz and at what is considered by researchers to be the greatest potential degree of energy expansion.

Scientific research measuring brainwave activity with the use of an electroencephalograph has shown that the vibrational frequency of joy is 540 Hz and is expansive, meaning it can be increased and increased indefinitely in the right circumstance. Jesus said as we read in John 15:11, "I have told you these things so that my joy and delight may be in you, and that your joy may be made full and complete and overflowing". In other words, fully expansive to the degree that our body and mind have trouble containing it.

On the other side of the coin research has found that the brainwave vibrational frequency of fear is 4 Hz. Not far off zero. No vibration, no consciousness, no life. Perhaps this is where the common saying "scared to death" came from. And fear is the emotional feeling that the ego mind uses over and over again to interfere with and stall our evolutionary journey through consciousness. Which is probably why Jesus said, "God has not given to us a spirit of fear, but of power." Which indicates that when fear grips us it is emanating from a force that opposes God's power.

If you likened the whole vibrational expansion contraction thing to say a day out on the river, a ripple on the river does not necessarily affect us emotionally or behaviourally in a major way if we are out paddling our canoe up a river, but the energy vibration of a torrent that comes down on us can dramatically affect our emotional well-being and behavioural instincts, particularly when the emotional state of panic or fear emerges. Emotionally induced energy vibration in extremely fearful situations can become an intensifying charged current like a psychological tsunami that hits us with its full force.

We see this with the emotion of grief pulling some people down psychologically to despairing levels, and likewise the emotional energy of depression and loneliness can cause a person to feel so heavy and lifeless to a point that if it is severe enough, lifelessness is all that person can see in their future, which then leads some to contemplate suicide as the only solution and a preferable option. Fear causes the energetic life to drain out of us.

Research has shown that higher frequency vibrations are associated with things like gratitude, love, joy, spending time in nature, sunshine, yoga, raw whole foods, beautiful music, and lower vibrations can come from things like envy, jealousy, toxic people, toxic relationships, electronics, arguments, violence, junk food, drugs, and alcohol, resentment, and anger. The higher the frequency of your energy or vibration, the lighter you feel in your physical, emotional, and mental bodies. You experience greater personal power, clarity, peace, love, and joy. You have little, if any, discomfort or pain in your physical body, and your emotions are easily dealt with.

Now the following is very important for us to understand particularly if in our spiritual search we have been confused or conflicted by the variety of different teachings and different mind therapies such as positive thinking, mindfulness, law of attraction, being present, and others, and perhaps also if you have been concerned that these type of teachings may conflict with your religious beliefs. What I have just been talking about in terms of vibrations, can cause one to become conflicted because we think or have been influenced by others to believe that as a Christian or Muslim, we should not be embracing these metaphysical and psychological type concepts. Some religions, perhaps even yours, teaching that they are all of the devil.

But this should not be so, rather these teachings should be seen to complement Christian and Muslim teachings not to compete with them, because they are in fact present in both Christian and Muslim teachings, but many are hidden in a mystery in those teachings. Jesus often spoke spiritual truth hidden in a mystery in the form of parables, simple stories about life with a spiritual principle buried in them. You see Jesus was fully aware that many who came to hear him were immature in the faith. They were not spiritually mature enough to hear teachings about metaphysical concepts, things like how energy and vibration work. But not so the Apostle Paul who speaks of being caught up into what he termed paradise (the realm of God) and heard things so astounding that they cannot be expressed in words.

It is important we understand that over time the above scientific truths about vibrational influence and the impacts they have on our wellbeing both physical and psychological, have in fact been evidenced in the teachings of a variety of faiths albeit in some faiths being hidden in a mystery or in the form of a parable. All simply referring to the same thing, Creative Vibrational Energy Centres in our body and mind that we need to be aware of, and completely understand the role they can play in influencing our life for the better or for the worse, regardless of our "religious brand." The following will give you simple understanding on how this concept of the existence of energy centres has been expressed in different religions over time.

In Hinduism, the word used to describe the overall concept of energetic forces flowing through the body is prana. The different locations in the body and mind that that energy collects, or groups together are called the chakras. What exactly is prana? Prana is the Indian Sanskrit word for **"breath"**. Prana is energy, vitality, power. Prana is the foundation and essence of all life; the energy and vitality that permeates the entire universe. Prana flows in everything that exists. Furthermore, prana is the connecting link between the material world, consciousness, and the mind. You could call it the "Breath of God." In the beginning was the breath, and the breath was with God, and the breath was God.

This word chakra is a widely used concept in Indian religion that underpins many spiritual practices and philosophical systems. Within some forms of yoga, the chakras refer to energy or vibrational centres found in the body, located at major branching's of a human being's nervous system, beginning at the base of the spinal column, and moving upwards to the top of the skull. Chakras are points of metaphysical and or biophysical energy in the human body, which provide a nexus, one or more connections for the linking and flow of energy.

Chakras are also considered to be graduations of consciousness that reflects states of the soul, with chakras seen as energy centres wherein subtle electromagnetic forces connect to the physical, emotional, mental, and spiritual aspects of a person, vital force, material force, matter energy, organic material energy, or pneuma, describing the psycho-spiritual energies that permeate the universe. The word chakra itself is the Sanskrit word for wheel because chakras are said to be the spinning forces of energy in the body. In the Hindu teaching on this subject it is said that sometimes certain energy centres become blocked, and the process of clearing the blockage happens through specific yoga postures, breathing practices, or meditation.

From India, the notion of chakras as separate energy centres was taken to China, where it was introduced into the religion of Taoism, absorbed, and harmonised with Chinese concepts of the flow of energy known as Qi. The word Qi means **"air or breath"**. In Chinese medicine, traditional Indian chakra locations correspond to Chinese acupuncture points. So, we see many people turning to regular Tai Chi practices to get a subtle taste of this energetic force or getting some acupuncture treatment for bodily ailments. What are they doing? They are raising their vibrational frequencies and subsequently their sense of wellbeing. Qi is breath, vital energy.

In Taoism, Chi is the force that animates the universe. Chi is the force that sets the world and everything in it into motion. Chi is also the force that sustains all things once they are created. Chinese Taoist influences made their way to Japan and were absorbed into Shintoism, Japan's native belief system, and a religion which around 80 percent of Japanese citizens follow. In Shintoism Chi is known as Ki.

In the Islamic religion of Sufism there is a process called Sufi Healing. Sufi healing is an advanced ancient spiritual healing method resolving trapped emotional, physical, and spiritual energies. It uses the process of chanting sounds of erratic prayers for deep healing of ingrained patterns and trauma. These ancient sounds are said to carry a powerful healing vibration into the cells and energy fields of the person, to deliver healing at a profound level, well beyond the reach of the human mind.

In Sufiism, the mystical branch of the Islamic religion, the goal is awakening and self-realisation. It is taught in Sufism that each one of us possesses an energy field or an aura that surrounds and penetrates the physical body, in a way you could say, guarding it. It is a psychological and physical creative influence associated with the physical and mental wellbeing of a human being. It is taught that the more we are optimistic in our thoughts the more we generate positive energy or higher vibrational frequencies you could call them, while the more pessimistic we are in thoughts the more we generate negative energy, lower vibrational wave frequencies.

This mantra type chanting in Islamic Sufism is based on the same principle that forms the basis of mantra chanting in the Sikh religion which is a branch of Hinduism. The intention of mantra chanting in Sikhism, is to create vibrational energetic change in various energy centres known as the chakras that I just spoke of. The healing process both strengthens and relies upon spiritual growth and understanding that can lead us to a closer relationship with the universal life force regardless of our religious path or the spiritual framework we honour. And because of the inherent creative instincts, resident in all vibrational frequencies regardless of how high or how low they are, those creative instincts will ultimately affect our life circumstances either for the better or for the worse.

Now in terms of the early Christian writings, **pneuma** was the ancient Greek word used for **breath**, similarly as Qi is in Taoism, and Prana is in Hinduism, and Ki in Shintoism. Pneuma in both ancient philosophy and religion, refers to the vital spirit, soul, or creative energetic life force of a person. We see in the Christian religion, in translating the word pneuma into English in the Greek New Testament there are 254 instances where the word pneuma, meaning breath, was used in the original ancient writings to refer clearly to what has been normally translated in the Christian Bible as the Holy Spirit or more simply spirit.

What is the Holy Spirit? It is the Creative Breath or Spirit, an energetic creative force. It is Infinite Intelligence, the God Mind, in spirit form. An example of the use of pneuma in the New Testament Book of John, is where we read that Jesus **breathed** on His disciples and said, "receive the Holy Spirit". Meaning receive the vital spirit or creative force. Jesus was transferring the spirit that he had received to the disciples to empower them. We see also the Apostle Paul when in addressing the citizens of Philippi as we read in the Book of Philippians said to them, "for it is not your strength, but it is God who is effectively at work in you, both to will and to work, that is strengthening, energising, and creating in you the learning and the ability to fulfil your purpose for his good pleasure". (Amplified Version).

There is a distinct correlation of understanding and belief between the major religious institutions of the world on the existence of a singular creative energetic force involved in the affairs of humankind, albeit taught and practiced in different ways according to different hereditary influenced religious teachings. All referring to the scientific truth that the human being is a living, breathing, vibrational, creative, energy field, composed of energy-producing particles each of which is in constant motion, vibrating, dancing together, creating something, or creatively changing something, sometimes for the better and sometimes for the worse. How did the scientist Albert Einstein regard it? He said:

> "I have a rapturous amazement at the harmony of natural law, which reveals an intelligence of such superiority that, compared with it, all the systematic thinking and actions of human beings are but an utterly insignificant reflection"

He also said:

> "Energy cannot be created or destroyed; it can only be changed from one form to another".

What did Einstein mean when he said energy can only be changed from one form to another? Quantum physicists believe it's possible to speed up or slow down the vibrations that occur at the cellular level by changing our thoughts, behaviours, and even our surroundings. Scientists agree with this, psychoanalysts agree with this, and the ancient spiritual masters who spoke of the use of mantras to change our vibrational structure agreed with this, and the Islamist Mystic Rumi agreed with this albeit poetically in his poem the Poem of The Atoms that I spoke of at the very start of this book where he says, "the atoms in the air and desert are dancing."

It's all about the vibrational electromagnetic waves changing the cells in our bodies and brain structure, which then influence the physical and emotional energetic levels of our body and mind . This is why many people choose the seaside to go for a holiday because they have proven before that the surroundings destress them against their everyday life surroundings which can bring many stresses. What does a holiday at the beach do? It changes a person's vibrational influence, it changes their "vibe".

Other researchers of both the psychological, spiritual, and medical kind have discovered that certain thought patterns such as gratitude, joy, peace, love, and acceptance create high vibrational frequencies, while other mindsets such as anger, despair and fear vibrate at a much lower rate. We all vibrate energetically at a particular frequency, and this determines how we feel about our circumstances and how we react to our circumstances. The lower the frequency, the denser your energy, and the heavier your problems seem, and the more exhausted you can become physically. Here you may experience pain and discomfort in your physical body, and experience heavy emotions and mental confusion, or just plain old tiredness. Psychically your energy is darker. Overall your life takes on a negative quality. And it all comes back to our state of mind in the moment, our thoughts.

The concept of vibrational influence for change is based on the scientifically proven idea that all matter in the universe is made up of energy that vibrates. This includes everything, it includes you, your pets, your house, your favourite food, your possessions, liquids, everything is made up of matter and all matter is just a conglomeration of energy particles vibrating at a certain frequency. As well as this, all thoughts and emotions have their own vibrational frequency or wave frequency with peaks and troughs.

So, in other words, all matter and all psychological thought, meaning our beliefs, our attitudes, general thoughts that have a particular emotional flavour for example happy ones, bigoted ones, critical ones, bitter ones, revengeful ones, jealous ones, envious ones, grieving ones, sad ones, guilty ones, and on and on, are all composed of energy that is being broadcast into the universe from that moment we select each individual thought and begin entertaining it. And it will continue being broadcast into the universe as a steady stream of energy of a particular vibrational frequency, until we stop thinking that particular thought and move on to the next one.

To break this down further in the simplest way possible on how this process relates to our own human body and life experience; every atom, molecule, cell, tissue, and body system, is composed of energies that when superimposed on each other, create what is known as the human energy field. Many forms of energy exist, but they all fall into two basic categories. These are described by physicists as **"potential energy. and kinetic energy"**.

Potential energy is the type of energy an object has because of its position, or its location, meaning where it currently sits. It is stationary with stored energy waiting to be released. It is something with potential energy and with the capacity and potential to get moving, but it is just waiting for a push or a shove to do its thing. This is the opposite of kinetic energy.

Kinetic energy is energy derived from something currently in motion, actively using energy for movement.

In other words, potential energy is stationary, with stored energy ready to be released, kinetic energy is energy in motion, actively using energy for movement. In relation to thoughts and behaviours you could say thoughts are of the "potential energy kind" holding the potential to create a certain type of behaviour or action, and that action or behaviour when it does happen, after having been birthed in a thought first, is of the "kinetic energy kind," energy actively using that thought to create a response.

"Potential energy is the energy of "what can be". Kinetic energy is the energy of "what is".

For instance, an example would be that a spring has potential energy when it is compressed, and that potential energy transforms into kinetic energy when the spring is released. Energy transfer or transformation can also take place when energy moves from one place to another. Energy can move from one object to another, for instance when the energy from your moving foot is transferred to a soccer ball, or energy can change from one form to another. So, it can be transferred or transformed, but energy cannot be created or destroyed, it can only be transferred and transformed. It can be passed on, or vertically expanded or contracted.

Now energy also vibrates at different frequencies according to the specific matter it is contained in. Vibration is a fancy way of describing an overall state of being. Everything in the universe is made up of energy vibrating at different frequencies. All things in the universe are constantly in motion vibrating, dancing, even objects that appear to be stationary are in fact vibrating, oscillating, and resonating at a specific frequency. This is a scientific fact. When you change your vibration, you essentially cancel out the characteristics of the original wave frequency by overlaying a new exact opposite type of energy or a new size of peaks and valleys on top of it and thus you change the vibrational or wave frequency.

The American pop group the Beach Boys had it right, albeit coming from a slightly different angle when in the 60's they wrote and recorded the song Good Vibrations which said, "I'm picking up good vibrations, she's giving me an expectation, gotta keep those loving vibrations happening". They were describing an emotional attraction that was starting to occur that was going to initiate subsequent change in a physical relationship.

Interestingly though, the Beach Boys who both wrote and recorded that song were followers of the Maharishi Mahesh Yogi, one of the well-known teachers of the transcendent capability of a human being who I spoke of in Chapter 6. And as such were in fact practitioners of his process of Transcendental Meditation, a spiritual discipline designed in the first instance through the practice of a silent meditation to initiate vibrational change in a person's body and mind.

Vibrational change is the key component of consciousness change, through promoting an evolutionary change in consciousness (our state of being), that takes us to a higher level of conscious awareness of our inherent Divinity and the power within, or conversely moving us to an even lower level of conscious awareness and alienating us even further from an awareness of the Divine presence, thus lessening our potential for psychological and circumstantial change. For you see synchronisation of the vibrations of different elements is as at the heart of consciousness and physical reality. That's the link.

Jesus spoke of this synchronisation in a mystery in the Book of John when he said, "if you abide in me and my word abides in you," meaning if we are energetically united because his thoughts which contain his vibrational energetic life are in our thoughts, "you can ask what you will, and it shall be done for you." He was speaking of the power of Divine Principle at work if we synchronise our thoughts with his thoughts. How do we know his thoughts. We read the New Testament. And synchronization is what we all unconsciously hunger after. Our soul desires oneness with the universe and all it contains.

Many Christian people would never entertain the idea of embracing any ancient "religious concepts" in their health regime and daily practices. Yet we do see for example some Christians in their unconscious search for an understanding of this hidden vibrational influence, turning to various forms of yoga or mindfulness disciplines or things such as Tai Chi, because they have found that these things help them cope with the everyday circumstances and stresses of life, both physically and psychologically. And regardless of what institutionalised religion would say, there is absolutely nothing wrong with that, as all things work together for good. That's why 35 percent of the adult population in India practice yoga, and the total population of India is around 1.4 billion people.

What many people don't completely understand is that the spiritual concept of vibrational influence lies at the heart of yoga and certain other popular new age teachings. If they did, they would be less likely to find that weekly trip to yoga or a meditation session tedious, but rather see it for what it truly is, a magnificent tool given to us by our Creator as a psychological Support System, given to us by Infinite Intelligence, to help us achieve a higher level of consciousness and an enlightened state of being.

An interesting phenomenon occurs when different vibrating things or processes come into proximity; they will often start, after a little while, to vibrate together at the same frequency; they sync up sometimes in ways that can seem mysterious. Like produces like or creates something that appears to be new, but in fact it can be something that was existing within each object already, each having "potential energy" that just needed to be brought close to enable synchronization to occur and create something. A scientific example would be in the creation of laser beams. Laser beams are produced when photons of the same power and frequency are emitted together. This was an area that Sir Isaac Newton who I spoke of at the beginning of this chapter did a lot of work in.

Life is all about vibrational influence, but it's also about the type of vibrations that we release in our life, and most importantly about synchronised or shared vibrations that have the power to transform or recreate. Ervin Laszlo, a Hungarian philosopher of science, systems theorist, integral theorist, originally a classical pianist, and an advocate for the theory of quantum consciousness, twice nominated for the Nobel Peace Prize, said the following:

> *"Vibration is the language of consciousness, and we can control and thus consciously use vibration to make changes in our states of consciousness".*

This of course initiates circumstantial change. This is the theory behind all the psycho-spiritual teaching that has emerged over this last century, teaching such as the Law of Attraction, The Power of Positive Thinking, and Meditative Mindfulness and the teachings of Esther and Jerry Hicks, just to name a few. It is also the theory behind the teaching of the chakras that I mentioned previously, which are the physiological spiritual practices of certain forms of Hinduism and Tantric Buddhism, the word chakras referring to the various energy centres in your body that correspond to specific nerve bundles and internal organs. There are seven major chakras that run from the base of your spine to the top of your head, and when any one of these energy centres get blocked through some sort of negative input in thought, you may experience physical or emotional symptoms as a result.

All emotional states we participate in have their own specific vibrational or oscillating frequency. Vibrational wave frequencies are measured in what is termed as hertz (Hz) which is the rate at which vibrations and oscillations occur. So, an atom that is vibrating at a faster rate would be considered a higher frequency than one that is vibrating at a much lower rate. Take the vibrational frequency of fear for instance.

According to recent studies, your brain learns and expresses fear at a certain brainwave frequency and by changing the frequency we can change the feeling. Research has found that the brainwave frequency of fear is 4 cycles per second or four hertz. It has a low vibrational frequency in the realm of the emotions, but as with all frequencies is open to change and transformation, because all emotional energy vibrations being initiated in a thought are of the "potential energy" kind, that I just spoke of, and as such can be changed if the right steps are taken.

How in the case of fear would that happen? How could the vibrational frequency initiated by a fear thought change? Through what is known as synchronization that I just spoke of. Synchronisation is used to lock an object down or out for any shared resource. When a thread invokes a synchronised method, it automatically acquires the lock for that object and releases it when the thread completes its task. In other words, in terms of fear, fear is not destroyed because it is a separate vibrational wave, but it can be set aside or locked down. It is locked down until what we have replaced it with for example love, is able to complete its task. Fear will dissipate when synchronised with the higher vibration of love or gratitude or surrender or even enthusiasm.

The word enthusiasm is derived from the Greek word "entheos" which means inspired or possessed by the God within. When I was an instructor with the Dale Carnegie Institute we taught a session on how to use enthusiasm to negate the paralysing effect of "the fear of public speaking." Which involved in the first instant "faking it", using enthusiasm with our words and actions until it became habitual, and it worked. People eventually overcame completely their fear of public speaking because enthusiasm locked down the fear in the moment, and with habitual practice it became an automatic response whenever fear raised its ugly head which would become less and less.

What I didn't realise at the time because we were not teaching vibrational principles in the class, but realise now, was that the change happened because we were getting the client to embrace enthusiasm rather than entertain fear, which locked down the low fear vibration and substituted the higher vibrational frequency of enthusiasm in the moment, resulting in the manifestation of an inner calm. The vibrational frequency of enthusiasm was overlaid on the fear vibration, transforming it.

This is the mystery hidden in the Biblical teaching in the Book of Timothy that says, "for God has not given us a spirit of fear but of power and of love and of a sound mind". You see fear is a tormentor. It intends to keep you from fulfilling the destiny that God has on your life, to prevent you from living a joyful, spirit lead existence, where you give to others out of the overflow of love in your life.

Fear will keep you awake with nightmares. But fear is merely a specific brainwave frequency response to a particular thought, that when synchronised or superimposed you could say by the emotional brainwave vibration of love or surrender or gratitude, or enthusiasm, gets locked down, not destroyed just locked down, because as previously said wavelengths can't be destroyed but they can be transformed. So, it gets locked down or its free flow blocked until the higher vibrational frequencies of love or gratitude, or surrender can fulfil their purpose and clear the blockage.

In terms of how it works in our body chemistry. Brainwave frequencies correspond to emotional states in the brain, which in turn instruct the body to create a bath of chemicals. In the case of fear, the brain's response to fearful thoughts cause your adrenal glands to send cortisol and adrenaline into the bloodstream, which initiates the "flight or fight" syndrome. Although our bodies release these chemicals to ensure our survival in response to danger, they are not intended to linger. None of these things are good for our systems over the long term. If glucose, cortisol, and adrenaline remain too long in the bloodstream they can become perhaps like houseguests who have overstayed their welcome and create all sorts of unintended and unpleasant consequences.

Remember, our nervous system is a wave rhythm. Fear has an emotional response and can be successfully approached as a rhythm, and that rhythm can be changed. All rhythms are capable of being changed. Think of how you feel when you listen to Metallica music versus the music of Mozart. You feel two totally different rhythms. Think of how you feel if you have lived your whole life listening to classical music and the neighbour puts his favourite heavy metal rock album on at night at full blast. But he's alright with it because he has probably lived his whole life at that lower level of vibrational frequency, never perhaps having associated it with his present psychological and physical circumstances.

Think of how you feel when you listen to the song, We Will Rock You as against listening to the song Amazing Grace. It can be any sound from a rippling stream to a fast-moving horn blowing freight train going past our back fence line causing a rhythmic effect on our nervous system and our psychological or physical wellbeing in the moment. How do we know what rhythm we are functioning at in the present moment? We only need to look at our emotional state in the present moment.

What does that involve? It simply involves the process of awareness and reflection. Change your state of awareness or perception, how you see and interpret life circumstances, get to "know yourself" and your vibrational frequency will move to a higher level, and you will initiate circumstantial change your life. It really isn't that hard. But in the first instance it requires a measure of observational discipline as do all bad habits we are trying to change.

> *"Synchronize your existing vibrational level with thoughts that contain a higher vibrational frequency, and you change your life. This is the wisdom of the workings of Infinite Intelligence hidden in a mystery in the teachings of all the great prophets particularly evident in the teachings of Jesus and in the wisdom of ancient sages and mystics".*

Fear has the power within it to manipulate the masses. However, fear is an illusion born in the ego minds of human beings, and it can be dissipated through the higher vibrational frequency of love. The first instance we see of the emergence of the emotion of fear into humanity's existence is recorded in the Old Testament story of Adam and Eve in Genesis 3 in the garden, where it says that "fear came upon them, and they hid."

I spoke in Chapter 2 of the mystery of our evolutionary journey and the mysteries hidden in the teaching of the prophets in parables. Prophets such as Jesus when they spoke of love, and compassion, and gratitude, and giving, and kindness, and peace, even when through parables, were speaking in a mystery of the process of aligning our thought energy processes our attitudinal wave vibrations with the thought energy processes of God, Infinite Intelligence. A good example would be one in the Book of Luke Chapter 17 where Jesus speaking in a mystery about the power of the Divine Principle of Gratitude at work, told the story of ten lepers who were healed and only one of the ten came back to thank him.

How do the thought processes of God work? They work through Divine Law or Divine Principle set in place before the foundation of the world? This is the mystery hidden in the teaching of Jesus when He said, "man shall not live by bread alone, but by every word that proceeds from the mouth of God". The mouth of God speaks the purposeful thoughts of God. Who is the spokesperson of those purposeful thoughts? It is Infinite Intelligence, or the Holy Spirit in Christianity, the creative breath of God.

This is the mystery hidden in what is known as the Sermon on the Mount in the New Testament, the contents of which are sometimes referred to as the "ethics of the kingdom". It teaches the way of living an ethical life and consequently a successful life. The sermon teaches the mystery of using Divine Principle to raise our vibrational level and thus bring about change in the Soul, in the minds and emotions, thus leading to circumstantial change, which by the way includes our existing health circumstances. It is holistic in nature.

The Buddha spoke of these things in the same way in what is called the Noble Eightfold Path that leads to the end of suffering. Those eightfold paths are right viewing, meaning the right way of perceiving or seeing things, which means God's way, right thought, right speech, right action, right livelihood, right effort, right mindfulness, and right concentration.

The higher the wave frequency of your energy or vibration, the lighter you feel in your physical, emotional, and mental bodies. You experience greater personal power, clarity, peace, love, and joy. You'll have little, if any, discomfort or pain in your physical body, and your emotions are easily dealt with. And whatever ailments for whatever reason persist, you will be able to successfully deal with. Your energy is literally full of light. Your life flows with synchronicity, and you manifest what you desire with ease. Overall, your life takes on a positive and more peaceful quality. When we raise our vibrational level, we live a more wholesome life. When we vibrate at a higher frequency, we feel happier, mentally, and emotionally.

Even if we have had what is described as a bad day, we will bounce back faster and the bad things in our life whilst not being completely eliminated, because remember this is a spiritual warfare we are involved in, stop affecting us as much as they once did. The idea of successfully living at a high vibrational level centres around adding more positive vibrations to life and taking active steps to eliminate by locking them down, those negative ones that we may have hung onto such as anger, bitterness, apathy, greed, malicious intent, or single mindedness that are detrimental to another's wellbeing, thus automatically raising or transforming our existing personal vibration. When we are vibrating at a higher frequency, we feel better, lighter, full of love, we just feel happier and at peace, and we experience a greater sense of self-worth.

We hear a lot about having or desiring a spiritual awakening. The process of having a spiritual awakening is not about us having a vision of Christ appearing in our kitchen. An awakening automatically happens when we begin to clear certain things out of our life, wrong thoughts, wrong habits and relationships, and wrong belief systems birthed in the egoic mind of humanity, that operate from a low level of vibrational frequency. And then in the void that has been created by their removal, invite and embrace new enriching things that operate from a higher level of vibrational frequency.

The resultant evidence of that awakening having happened will be the gaining of an increased tendency to "just let things happen" rather than continuously trying to make them happen. We will find ourselves sometimes smiling at the absurdity of some of the things that occur around us and the things people say and do, and there will be greater feelings of compassion and connectedness with others and with nature and frequent thoughts of thankfulness and appreciation.

The renowned Indian philosopher, teacher, and mystic, Jiddhu Krishnamurti put it this way when asked the question as to what his philosophy about life was. He simply replied:

"I just don't mind what happens."

That is the essence of inner freedom. It is a timeless spiritual truth. Release attachment to outcomes, deep inside yourself, and you'll feel good no matter what". Gautama Buddha of the Buddhist faith put it this way:

"The basic cause of suffering is the attachment to the desire to have, and the attachment to the desire not to have."

Attachment to the desire to have, is called a "craving". Attachment to the desire "not to have" is called aversion". If you want to revolutionise your life, "seek aversion", the desire not to have. Then you will find that your genuine needs are met. It works, I know it works, because I personally live my life that way, and I am now more at peace than at any other stage of my life. Seek detachment rather than attachment. All forms of attachment have the potential to cause suffering. Attachment to a person, attachment to a circumstance, attachment to money. Manage your money but don't attach your existence to having more of it.

This is the mystery hidden in the teachings of Jesus when He said things like, "sell all you have and follow Me," or where He said things like, "let the dead bury the dead." He was not saying that you had to be poor to follow him. He was talking about relinquishing attachment.

Jesus also put it this way. "Therefore, do not worry or be anxious perpetually uneasy, distracted, saying, what are we going to eat? Or what are we going to drink? Or what are we going to wear? For the pagan eagerly seek all these things; but do not worry, for your heavenly Father knows that you need them. But first and most importantly seek and strive after his kingdom and his righteousness, his way of doing and being right, the attitude and character of God, and all these things will be given to you also". (Matthew 6 Amplified Version)

When we make an intent filled decision to give greater attention to right thought, it becomes more and more real to us over time, and has more and more power over our life, to change our overall vibrational frequency. All thought triggers an emotion, which then triggers a bodily reaction of some kind, which then motivates or drives us to behave in a certain way, and that is how "**your thoughts shape your reality**".

You see most thoughts arise without our choosing. We might think we choose our thoughts, one by one, but if we take a moment to observe our thoughts as they come up, we see that they just come up without any warning or "conscious preparation" put into them. They are either completely random or in some way attached to or a follow on from the previous thought. What we are unaware of is that there is however "unconscious preparation" put into them through the subtle influence of the Collective Unconscious of humanity, with many of our thoughts being chosen for us by the garrulous, demanding egoic side of our nature.

How do we counter that?

We counter it by ensuring that our present moment thoughts and behavioural tendencies are trained to be in line with Divine thought. We renew our minds and behaviours, and so progressively our thought processes turn towards the Christ Mind within in all circumstances, rather than just subconsciously being influenced by the encyclopedia of the Collective Unconscious.

And we also as the Apostle Paul said, "bring every thought into captivity to Christ", or bring every thought captive to our Mool Mind, which is the Mind of Christ within as soon as we find ourselves drifting over into ego driven thought patterns. The Book of Corinthians encourages us to, "cast down imaginations, and every high thing that exalts itself against the knowledge or Wisdom of God and to destroy every proud obstacle that prevents one from truly knowing God".

How do we do that?
We simply say out loud, or to ourselves if in company, "I bring all thoughts into captivity to my Christ Mind within". The current thought will dissipate and after a while the process will become habitual as through heightened levels of awareness it registers immediately if we are entertaining wrong thought processes. But it is all up to us. If we find all that too hard and are prepared to live every day out of a low vibrational frequency and subsequent low level of peace and harmony and happiness that is our choice.

What is the Christ Mind?
It is that still small Voice of Wisdom within you. It is that voice that we rarely listen to or give attention to. People who catch a glimpse of it not knowing the spiritual significance of it may refer to it as conscience, a little voice advising them to do the right thing. It is as simple as that. It is the "breath that whispers" in many religions, it is the Holy Spirit in Christianity, it is the Ruh al-Qudus, the Spirit of Holiness and is God's agent of Divine Action and communication in Islam, it is the Oneness in Hinduism, and it is the hidden Intelligence that the scientists Albert Einstein and Thomas Edison spoke of.

How do we know we have this hidden Intelligence, the Christ Mind within us?
All the great spiritual masters have spoken of it, and some of the greatest scientific minds in history have believed in it. And if that is not enough for us, we read in the Book of John in the New Testament Jesus saying, "but the helper, the comforter, the advocate, the intercessor, the counsellor, the strengthener, the standby, (who is) the Holy Spirit, the Father will send in my name in my place to represent me

and act on my behalf, who will teach you all things and will help you to remember everything that I have told you". (Amplified Version)

What does this Holy Spirit, the still small voice within convey to us?
God's Wisdom and Divine Understanding and interpretation in and for every situation.

What is the container holding all this Wisdom of Infinite Intelligence called?
It is called the Mind of Christ within us, the Mool Mind. We read in the Book of 1 Corinthians in the New Testament, written by the Apostle Paul, "but we have the Mind of Christ to be guided by his thoughts and purposes".

What is the container holding all that which is opposing the Wisdom of Infinite Intelligence.
It is called the Collective Unconsciousness of humanity and its active agent is the Ego or Maya Mind.

What is the Christ Mind within us filled with?
It is filled with Divine Principle, the thoughts, and purposes of Infinite Intelligence, Wisdom in every situation, all vibrating at the highest levels of vibrational frequency. We begin responding to life from the highest point of wise thinking, God's point of view, from God's perspective, and not from the level of our unregenerated state of mind, responding always out of our pre-disposed and habitual thought patterns. Consequently, our vibrational level increases and our consciousness grows, and our circumstantial and psychological existence changes.

Research into the brainwave wave frequencies that impact on our emotional state has shown that our (E)motions which are simply energy vibrating at a certain frequency, all have rates of wave frequency in a graduating scale and have in many trials discovered the following. Enlightenment is 700Hz, Peace is 600, Joy is 540, Love is 500, Reason is 400, Acceptance or Surrender is 350, Willingness is 310, Courage is 200, Pride is 175, Anger is 150, Desire is 125, Fear is 100 but can descend as low as 4 in extremely fear filled situations, Grief is 75, Apathy is 50, Guilt is 30, and Shame is 20.

With peace and joy showing vibrational frequencies of 600Hz and 540 Hz respectively, perhaps do you think this may have been the reason Jesus said, "blessed are the peacemakers", and also said "My peace I give unto you". Jesus also said, "these things I have spoken to you so that my joy maybe in you and that your joy may be made full to overflowing", referencing two of the highest emotional vibrational frequencies, peace, and joy. What was he referring to when he said, "these things"? He was referring to Divine Principle, the New Covenant Laws of The Spirit, that he was continually instructing his followers in.

How are those thoughts of the Christ Mind conveyed to our current thoughts?
They are conveyed through the still small voice of Infinite Intelligence mentioned above. The voice of God that Jesus was referring to when He said, "man shall not live by bread alone, but by every word that proceeds from the mouth of God". That still small Voice of Wisdom that we rarely heard or give attention to. Call it intuitive thought or conscience if you like. But we must cultivate a desire to hear it and not fight it, an attentive attitude towards it and a willingness to embrace it. It will not force itself upon you. Force is the way of the Ego Mind in this the war of two minds.

What does our embracing of it do?
It initiates through changed thoughts and behaviours a change in the vibrational frequency of the moment, which then introduces a

new and higher vibrational frequency that brings about right results. As mentioned in the scientific field where with scientific law, say for instance with Newton's Laws of Motion, we witness outside invisible energetic forces (vibration) impacting on the existing vibrational level of visible present circumstances, so from a psychological and spiritual point of view, within the human mind there are invisible vibrational forces acting on and influencing our visible life circumstances.

Two opposing energetic forces, one force emanating from the Christ Mind within, which is Infinite Intelligence, the Mind of God, the still small voice of Wisdom, and the other force emanating from the Ego Mind. This is the creative force of Light from the Christ Mind, and the destructive force of darkness from the Ego Mind, the energetic force of our higher nature and the energetic force of our lower nature, both attempting to impact on our how we perceive and thus behave in our visible reality, the society we live in.

You see when we think, speak, behave, or act in a certain way, whether a good way or a bad way, we produce a creative vibrational energy response and subsequent visible circumstantial reaction, capable of being seen, heard, or felt, and then physically experienced or psychologically internalised, not only by the person we are addressing, but also by us as we witness our own behaviour and imbibe and internalise that vibrational wave it produces as it is sent out into the universe.

A response not necessarily noticeable immediately but it has happened, and at some stage it will manifest into some sort of form in our life, whether that be physical form or psychological form. Do unto others and it shall be done unto you, in other words as you give so shall you get returned to you. Disrupt someone else's peace and your peace will be disrupted. Give kindness whether in thought, word, or deed and in some way and at some stage kindness will be returned to you by someone. Give compassion and compassion will be rendered to you. Show love and love will be shown to you.

This is Divine Principle or Divine Law, the Law of the Creative Spirit or Creative Energies of God at work. It is the vibrational pulse that binds the fabric of the universe at work. This is the way the "vengeance is mine; I will repay says the Lord", that the Apostle Paul spoke of works. It's not some supernatural sword wielding arm reaching out, it's a vibrational law or wave coming into effect, a law set in place before the foundation of the world by Infinite Intelligence itself. If you have ever asked yourself the question as I know many people probably have, as to how God manages the affairs of every single person in the universe. The answer is, God doesn't. It is we who manage our own affairs for better or worse through our thoughts and behaviours.

We set the primary agenda for what happens in our life and in part for what happens in the lives of those around us. Sure Divine Intelligence can intervene with a miracle if necessary, but in the first instance that is not how the Grace of God manifests. In the first instance it is we who initiate the manifestation of Divine Grace.

God has set these infinite vibrational laws in place as the platform of our existence, and our attitudes and behaviours determine the frequency at which they operate in our lives, and the frequency at which they operate in our lives determines the circumstantial state of our existence, both psychologically and spiritually and materially. When Jesus said, "the Kingdom of God:" is within you, he was talking in a mystery about Kingdom Law being written in the hearts of humanity to guide its thoughts and behaviours. So, here's my point. If we have ever asked ourselves midst all the chaos and suffering in the world where was God when this was happening? The answer is that God was there all along, we just did not perceive the presence. The irony of it is that God is a God of love, so God does not directly harm us or punish us, we simply punish ourselves.

Most people would be familiar with the Easter story of the crucifixion of Jesus, how when Jesus on the cross looked down at His tormentors and saw the anger and hatred coming forth and said, "Father forgive them for they know not what they do". Jesus was not just being gracious or kind when He said those words. He knew that they knew what they were doing. What he was saying was **Father forgive them for they know not what they do to themselves**, for they do not understand how Divine Principle works and how in particular the Law of Reciprocity works.

This Law of Reciprocity, what some people would describe as the Law of Cause and Effect, which you could describe as one of the overarching Universal Divine Laws, was put in place not as a means of punishing us, but rather as a teaching process to raise our vibrational level and thus our level of consciousness. Different from the manmade jurisprudence laws that are meant to be a form of punishment.

When Jesus said, "give and it shall be given unto you," He was teaching society of Divine Principle or Divine Law that applies equally to the giving of good things and the giving of bad things. Because vibration is no respecter of the positive or negative it just vibrates and creates. He was saying be kind and kindness will be visited upon you, be nasty and mean and these attitudes will be revisited upon you at some time or place by some person or other.

This is how the New Covenant (New Testament) law between God and humankind, set in place after the Atonement process has been implemented, and how it operates in our daily lives. The Old Testament covenant laws were more so jurisprudence laws set in place as a means of punishment by the people, the New Testament covenant laws are the Laws of the Spirit of life in Christ Jesus, and they are laws of Grace that were set in place out of love and as a means of life guidance for conduct and behaviour that brings with it blessing and reward.

Doing good to others brings goodness upon ourself, alternately doing wrong to others results in our punishing ourself automatically. The same energetic vibrational force that you send into the universe whether in thought or deed to attack another, will turn back when finished and attack you. It will return to the source from whence it came. The same energetic frequency force that you send into the universe to bless another will turn back when finished, return to its source, and bless you.

This is the power that every human being has but rarely realises it, the same power that Jesus was speaking of when he said, "ye shall receive power when the Holy Spirit has come upon you". What is this Holy Spirit? It is Infinite Intelligence, the original and highest vibrational frequency overriding, transcending, and transforming our current energetic vibrational frequency.

This is where institutionalised religion got it wrong. They took God's Principle out of the everyday life of the believer and substituted a man-made rule of law, in the case of Christianity it was Canon Law, and in Islam it was Islamic Jurisprudence, as the behavioural priority of the believer, and thus the believer became a powerless person, protected, as well as punished by man-made law. This is what Timothy was speaking of as recorded in the New Testament where he tells the people that whilst they have a form of godliness, in other words they appear to be Christians, they lack the cosmic power of their faith.

Certain religions did however hold on to and continue to advocate an understanding of this vibrational component of our existence, religions such as Hinduism and Tantric Buddhism, that I spoke of, where emphasis is placed on giving greater understanding on what are known as the Chakras, which are psychic energy centres of the body.

I spoke a little about chakras previously but the following bears repeating. Literally speaking, the word "chakra" from Sanskrit (the ancient spoken and literary language of India), translates to wheel, or disk, but references **several spiritual energy centres within the human body, each vibrational energy centre corresponding to specific organs in the body as well as physical, emotional,**

psychological, and spiritual states of being, that influence all areas of a person's life.

It is taught that when these energy centres are blocked your vibrational energy is blocked and you suffer various emotional and subsequent physical imbalances such as anxiety, depression, anger, grief, and fear. It is also taught that you can clear these blockages that are like a spiritual dam blocking the flow of spiritual, physical, or psychological wellness in our life, through meditation, yoga or even with the food you eat. And of course, when spiritual blockages are removed, Divine Principle or The Law of The Spirit is released to go about its life changing work. The Spirit is enabled to re-continue its flow.

Divine Principle or Divine Law is that "which initiates the out-working of Infinite Intelligence" causing it to override our existing vibrational frequency. As a spark plug emits across a small gap a spark of electricity that creates the ignition for the combustion needed to start your car and get it moving, that mobilises it, so Divine Principle, moving across a small gap from the time bound to the timeless, is the spark that ignites the power of Infinite Intelligence, that will cause it to spring into action and successfully propel your life forward.

A principle is a fundamental truth as well as a proposition. A principle serves as the foundation for a system of belief for a behaviour or for a chain of reasoning. Divine Principle is that which expresses universal truth; it inhabits and builds upon core spiritual and metaphysical truth that encompasses and reveals the existence of a Divine Intelligence and the creative power for change that is embedded into its character and nature. A power that works continuously at removing the effects of humankind's psychological fall from Grace and restoring the mind of humanity back to the relationship and position that God originally purposed it to have in its creation.

What does it mean to embrace Divine Principle in ones' life, and thus start or initiate the process of positive vibrational change in our lives? In its simplest meaning you could say it is to embrace in all our thoughts and behaviours, the personality patterns of the Mind of Christ. To in fact in all our thoughts and behaviours become you could say "an imitator of Jesus Christ". The book of Ephesians in the New Testament Chapter 5 verse 1 says, "therefore become imitators of God, copy him and follow his example, as well-beloved children imitate their father".

The ideal of the imitation of Christ has long been an important element of Christian theology, ethics and spirituality and the concept and its practice were found in the earliest Christian documents, but in most cases it is an ideal and not a personal priority. Saint Augustine a theologian and philosopher of the fourth century recognised as a saint in the Catholic Church, was among the earliest religious leaders to examine the legitimacy of the laws of man and attempt to define the boundaries of what laws and rights occur naturally instead of all laws being arbitrarily imposed by mortals. even saying that all the supposed worldly wisdom and its conscience should not attempt to force people to act or behave in a certain way.

I share a brief story in the following chapter about a more modern figure in history, not deemed a saint, but one who understood the necessity for humankind to begin living more Godly principled lives and who in his life and work dedicated himself more and more to becoming both an imitator and an instrument of Christ, and an advocate of societal change in attitudes and behaviours that were vitally needed if society was to emerge from its psychological and spiritual alienation and progressive consciousness devolution that he was witnessing all around him. The man's name was Charles Dickens.

> "You are part of my existence, part of myself. You have been in every line I have ever read since I first came here. You have been in every prospect I have ever seen since, on the river, on the sails of the ships, on the marshes, in the clouds, in the light, in the darkness, in the wind, and in the woods. In the sea, and in the streets, you have been the embodiment of every graceful fancy that my mind has ever become acquainted with, your presence and influence has been everywhere".
>
> Charles Dickens

Becoming Imitators of Christ

TWELVE

> "Every traveller has a home of his own, and he learns to appreciate it the more from his wandering. Reflect upon your present blessings, of which every man has many, not on your past misfortunes, of which all men have some".
>
> Charles Dickens

Charles John Huffam Dickens was born in February 1812 and passed on 9th June 1870 aged 58 years. He was an English writer and social critic. Dickens created some of the world's best known fictional characters and is regarded by many as the greatest novelist of the Victorian era, the Victorian era being the period of Queen Victoria's reign from 20th of June 1837 until her death on 22nd January 1901. The writings of Charles Dickens enjoyed unprecedented popularity during his lifetime and still do. By the 20th century critics and scholars had recognised him as a literary genius. His novels and short stories are widely read today and have been at various times translated into movies and stage plays.

During his life, despite his lack of formal education, he edited a weekly journal for 20 years, he wrote 15 novels, and five novellas. A novella being a short novel of narrative prose fiction, whose length is shorter than that of most novels, but longer than most short stories. He also wrote hundreds of short stories and non-fiction articles and lectured and performed readings extensively. His most well-known works being David Copperfield, Oliver Twist, A Christmas Carol, Great Expectations, and A Tale of Two Cities.

Dickens plots were always carefully constructed, and he chose wide elements of them from topical events, and from past historical events, turning them into his own special and compelling narratives. The novella A Christmas Carol remains especially popular and continues to inspire adaptations in every artistic genre. As with many other works of Dickens, that book titled A Christmas Carol was written as a work of social commentary. You see Charles Dickens had a lifelong devotion to helping the under privileged, believed to have been birthed in his experiences as a child, when his own family underwent difficulties with finances seeing them faced with debtors' prison.

A debtor's prison was a prison for people who were unable to pay their debts in Western Europe. In the 18th century, debtors comprised over half the prison population; some 945 of London's 1500 prisoners in 1779 were debtors and out of these 945 people 753 were in prison for debts under 5 pounds, a prison sentence of between 20 and 100 days. Through the mid 19th century, debtors' prisons, usually similar in form to locked workhouses, were a common way to deal with unpaid debt. His own family's plight forced Dickens to drop out of school and work in a factory.

In terms of his own religious beliefs and faith Dickens was born into an Anglican home but his parents were only nominal Anglicans who did not attend church services regularly. He was baptised in the Anglican church and for a while was a member of it except for a brief period in the 1840's when he joined and attended the Unitarian Church. Perhaps this was because we know for certain as evidenced in his letters, speeches, and novels, that he hated dogma and any kind of doctrinal beliefs. It was also obvious in his novels and any other writings and speeches he produced, that Dickens always avoided making any direct statements about his own personal religious beliefs, because to him being a Christian meant something positive rather than negative, something that emphasised morality and love.

It is evident in his writings and speeches however that he saw the attitudinal and behavioural life of Jesus as the best example one could imitate to have a truly spiritual experience. It is said that so fixed was he in this belief, that in his last Will and Testament he left instructions to his children that they must guide themselves by the teachings of the New Testament, but to only be guided by those teachings in their "broad spirit", and to put no faith in any one man's narrow reconstruction or interpretation of certain aspects of the New Testament's teachings.

And to this end he saw the only real answer to institutionalised religion's sometimes wrong interpretation of some of the ancient teachings of the prophets, drawn to fit into their institutionalised bias in favour of church law, was to be simply guided by one thing and one thing only, the life and practices of Jesus Christ.

Always having a subtle leaning towards specific types of social activism, as a young man Dickens expressed a distaste for certain aspects of organised religion and as such in 1836, he wrote a pamphlet titled Sunday Under Three Heads, using the pseudonym Timothy Sparks. In the pamphlet he addressed his words respectfully, but with a hint of sarcasm, specifically to the Bishop of London. In this short article he vigorously defended the people's right to the pleasure of family, friends and social interaction on a Sunday, and his strong opposition to a proposed government plan, initiated by the church, to prohibit games and pleasurable social and family recreational activities on Sundays.

In reminding the bishop of the disparity between the affluent and the poor, both in attitude, affluence, and influence, at the commencement of his article he said the following. "Your elevated station, my Lord, affords you countless opportunities of increasing the comforts and pleasures of the humble classes of society, not by the expenditure of the smallest portion of your princely income, but by merely sanctioning with the influence of your example, their harmless pastimes and innocent recreations."

He continued, "that your Lordship would ever have contemplated Sunday recreations with so much horror, if you had been at all acquainted with the wants and necessities of the people who indulged in them, I cannot imagine possible. That a prelate of your elevated rank has the faintest conception of the extent of those wants, and the nature of those necessities, I do not believe. For these reasons, I venture to address this little pamphlet to your Lordship's consideration".

He then goes on further in the article saying amongst other things, the following. "Look into your churches, diminished congregations and scanty attendance. People have grown sullen and obstinate and are becoming disgusted with the faith which condemns them. They display their feeling by staying away from churches, and rather turn into the streets on a Sunday to celebrate the rigid gloom that rains over everything around". You see Charles Dickens honoured not just the figure of Jesus Christ, but more importantly he honoured his principles and ethical behaviour, particularly those behaviours that focused on social justice, which Jesus exemplified in his life's work and purpose.

Having always been regarded as Christian in his faith, he was often described as someone who possessed deep religious convictions. Dickens consequently came to be recognized as a man who upheld and honoured the attitudes of social justice that Jesus practiced, rather than just being a Christian, who merely had a singular obsession with theological matters of doctrine and dogma that the religious institutions of the day seemed to be engrossed in, whilst most of them only demonstrated a token leaning towards the common needs of the less fortunate of society.

During his life, Dickens was an indefatigable letter writer and campaigned vigorously for children's rights and education and other social reforms. He disapproved of Roman Catholicism and 19th century Evangelicalism seeing both as extremes of Christianity, likely to limit the personal expression of one's faith, and was critical of what he saw as the hypocritical behaviour of religious institutions, all of which he considered deviations from the true spirit of the Jesus type of Christianity.

Dickens once referred to the Catholic Church as "that curse upon the world", seeing the Catholic Church as the main protagonist in the ongoing story of the institutionalisation of religion since Christianity's original inception. Dickens also rejected the evangelical conviction that the Bible was the infallible word of God. His ideas on Biblical interpretation were very much like those of the liberal Anglican Arthur Stanley of the day, who believed passionately in the doctrine of "progressive revelation".

Progressive revelation is not a movement from error to truth, which is in fact the basis of all supposed theological truth and has been the basis for the rising up of splinter religious groups separating themselves from mainstream religion. Progressive revelation is in fact the movement from truth to truth, the lesser truth to the greater truth, the provisional to the permanent, the inadequate to the perfect. From a Christian perspective the Old Testament is the beginning of God's "progressive revelation of Himself", but it is not a full revelation. Similarly in the Islamic religion the Qur'an is said to be a progressive revelation of God as revealed to the Prophet Muhammad, but it is not a beginning and an end of Islam's understanding of God and God's revealed purposes regarding humanity.

And that has been the biggest problem for the Islamic religion since its origin also, in that certain extremist sects within the religion believe that the Qur'an is in fact both the beginning and the end of God's unfolding revelation to humanity. It emphatically is not, because before Ishmael the son of Abraham set the framework for Islam that Muhammad laid hold of, Ishmael was in fact influenced by the revelation given to his father Abraham, from whose religious lineage Christianity emerged. As it is with the Qur'an, so it is with the Bible, there is still more revelation to come. Infinite Intelligence is a God of progressive revelation.

In my previous book "Everything's Gonna Be Alright, The Holy Spirit Knows What She's Doin', I spoke extensively on a group of believers during the initial birth of Christianity known as the Gnostics. The Gnostics believed in the process of progressive revelation and paid the ultimate price for this belief with their lives, because of the Catholic Church's opposition to progressive revelation, deeming it heretical. Catholic law of the day stipulated that heresy was an offence punishable by death, which gave the Catholic Church licence to exterminate all Gnostics. But both Dickens and Arthur Stanley were right, progressive revelation is a part of God's plan. We read in Hebrews 1 in the New Testament that God revealed himself at many times and in many ways in the past.

Adam received a little of God's truth, and so did Noah. God spoke more fully to Abraham, unveiling more of himself and his purposes, and then spoke through Moses and through various prophets since then, including Jesus and Muhammad. You see:

> "Progressive revelation is a movement from truth to more truth, and so eventually to full truth".

In describing this principle of progressive revelation, the New Testament's Book of Hebrews 1:1-2 says:

> "Long ago, at many times and in many ways, God spoke to our fathers by the prophets, but in these last days he has spoken to us by his son, whom he appointed the heir of all things, and through him also he created the world".

Jesus was the bearer of progressive revelation, and then in his departure handed that responsibility over to the Holy Spirit, who he said, "will teach you all things."

On 9th of June 1870, Dickens suffered a stroke at his home after a full day's work on the book Edwin Drood. He never regained consciousness and the next day he passed away. Contrary to his wish to be buried at Rochester Cathedral in an inexpensive and non-ostentatious strictly private manner, he was eventually laid to rest in the Poets Corner of Westminster Abbey.

A printed epitaph circulated at the time of the funeral with no emphasis by his own choice on his wonderful literary achievements simply read, "To the memory of Charles Dickens, England's most popular author, who died at his residence on the ninth of June 1870, aged 58 years. He was a sympathiser with the poor, the suffering, and the oppressed; and by his death, one of England's greatest writers is lost to the world".

Some of Dickens most notable works included A Tale of Two Cities, which was the first book as a child I ever owned. I still have it on my bookshelf having carried it with me for more than sixty years, albeit slightly worn. It was a bound copy of one of the original prints, and my first initiation into the social conscience of Charles Dickens and a glimpse into the Collective Unconsciousness of humanity. With A Tale of Two Cities, a fictional work with an historical basis, Dickens wrote the book as a type of cautionary tale to those in Russia who were desiring a revolution, because at the time of his writing the book he was witnessing the same conditions in Russia, particularly in the area of social discontent, that had occurred in England that led to the revolution in France, commonly known as the French Revolution.

And although Dickens wrote A Tale of Two Cities in 1859 as a cautionary tale to Russia its message was not heard and that Russian revolution did in fact occur taking place in 1917, during the final phase of World War 1. It removed Russia from the war and brought about the transformation of the Russian Empire into the union of

Soviet Socialist Republics (USSR), replacing Russia's traditional monarchy with the world's first Communist state.

The concerns of Dickens proved correct. The goals of the Russian Revolution were to take the power out of the hands of the aristocracy, but the outcome was a Communist government that was just as oppressive as the previous regime, and in terms of freedom of thought and expression still is. Dickens also wrote the book because he wanted to explore the redemptive power of love. The moral of A Tale of Two Cities is that experience and tradition provide greater stability than revolutionary uprisings. In the storyline of A Tale of Two Cities experience is represented by London, the capital of Britain, and revolutionary uprising is represented by Paris the capital of France.

Dickens portrays Paris as first dying under the corruption of the aristocrats, who with no social conscience continually ignored the ever-increasing plight of the poor leaving them starving and dying in the streets. But their behaviour is proven to be no better than those of the poorer citizens of Paris, who during the revolution participated as an act of revenge in terrible atrocities, witnessing many descending into moral decay, chaos, and unspeakable acts of violence.

The two main moral themes in the book are firstly "a potentiality or a possibility of redemption", if one chooses to change, and secondly "the importance of the role of compassion in the evolutionary journey of societies". Compassion being a primary Divine Principle that I have mentioned through the book that Albert Einstein also saw as a tool for the evolution of the consciousness of humanity. The storyline deals with the major themes of duality, double mindedness, revolution, and resurrection.

Some other works of Dickens that underpinned his desire for social justice and subsequent social cohesion, and to shine a light on the lack of it that was evident in the society of his day and the pressing need for change were Oliver Twist, in which Dickens exposes the sordid underbelly of Victorian England, where ruthless young innocents are at the mercy of both brutal institutions and the corrupting forces that watch over the streets. And Great Expectations in which Dickens examines class, social mobility, and the corrupting power of money. Where Pip, the central protagonist in the story, who having received a monetary windfall seeing his expectations regarding life raised, comes to realise that the windfall proved to be no panacea for the difficulties of life, because wealth altered his values and brought little psychological contentment in his life journey.

You see although from a personal perspective Dickens wanted to be popular and gain wealth through his writing, wealth was not his primary objective. He always had only one primary goal as a novelist. He wanted his novels to be parables, stories that would emphasise the importance of living and expressing the attitudes and behaviours of Jesus Christ in every interaction that human beings have with every other human being. Dickens firmly believed that he had been given a God-given responsibility as a creator of literary work to make clear to his readers what it meant to live a moral and ethical life, and he believed that through his own beliefs, reflected in his novels, that he could achieve this.

He once wrote a note to a good friend expressing exactly how he felt about this calling to write. It read, "With a deep sense of my great responsibility always upon me when I exercise my art, one of my most important, constant, and most earnest endeavours is to exhibit in all my characters some final reflections of the teachings of our great master Jesus and lead my readers up to those teachings and behaviours as the great source of moral goodness. All the good people that I speak of in my books have the character qualities of humility, charitableness, faithfulness, and forgiveness, and repeatedly I claim them for myself as a disciple of Jesus".

His thoughts on these matters were very similar to those of Leo Tolstoy, the Russian novelist writer, philosopher, and religious reformer, an admirer of Dickens, who stressed the ethical and moral side of Christianity, but turned away from Russian orthodoxy by rejecting the notion of a personal relationship with God. Regarded as one of the greatest authors of all time nominated for a Nobel peace prize, responsible for such epic novels as War and Peace and Anna Karenina, in reading the works of Dickens, Tolstoy described him as a great Christian writer, once stating that he found there to be something infectious about the love and goodwill that Dickens exuded in his writings, love and goodwill that Tolstoy believed was particularly evidenced to him in the book Dickens wrote for his family titled A Christmas Carol.

On December 19th, 1843, Dickens published a book titled A Christmas Carol, which he made no money from. The first edition sold out by Christmas Eve. By 1844, the novella (short novel) had gone through 13 printings and continues to be a robust seller more than 178 years later. The full title of the novella is A Christmas Carol in Prose, Being a Ghost Story of Christmas. Under extreme financial pressure at the time, Dickens reportedly wrote the story while taking numerous hour-long night-time walks around the streets of London simply observing people at work and at play.

Though it was a runaway bestseller, additions to the final book's presentation that Dickens demanded because of his fastidious nature regarding the appearance of the book and how the book was to be bound, saw the price of the materials to produce it take a big chunk out of his potential profits, which appeared to be of no concern to Dickens if the presentation of the book was acceptable to him and was giving aesthetic value to the purchaser.

Dicken's wrote A Christmas Carol to once again as he did with so many of his novels and novellas, alert society to the truth of its existing psychological dysfunctionality in both its attitudes and behaviours, most people having scant or in some cases no regard for the plight of their fellow citizens, never more evident to him at Christmastime, which was supposed to be a time of goodwill to all. It has been said that Dickens wrote A Christmas Carol to bear witness to the plight of the poor and thus powerless, and to encourage the prosperous and powerful to be kind and generous towards them. But there is a spiritual mystery hidden behind the storyline in A Christmas Carol, which goes beyond the actual events that happened in the lives of the characters that Dickens writes about.

You see A Christmas Carol is an allegory, in that it features events and characters with a clear, fixed symbolic meaning. The main protagonist in the book is Ebenezer Scrooge who represents all the values that are opposed to the idea and true spirit of Christmas. Opposing values such as greed, selfishness, and lack of goodwill towards one's fellow man. But because of Scrooge's attitudinal dysfunction that manifests in his personality patterns, he is explored at different times as both the protagonist and the antagonist. A protagonist in a book is not only an active participant in an event but also seen as a leader, a proponent, or a supporter of a cause, a champion. Whilst an antagonist in a book is the opposer or combatant working against the protagonist's or leading character's goal, antagonising them, and creating the main conflict.

The antagonist can be one character or a group of characters but in traditional narratives the antagonist is synonymous with the bad guy involved in either a psychological or physical warfare with an opposing person or viewpoint. We see this a lot in the Marvel series of stories with characters of the like of Superman (the protagonist) and Lex Luther (the antagonist), or Batman (the protagonist) and the Joker (the antagonist).

The thing that makes Ebenezer Scrooge such an interesting character in the book in spite of his reputation as a greedy and uncaring person, is that Dickens represents him as a perfect example of every individual human being who is unconsciously yearning for redemption and consciously striving after or seeking to find the secret of what makes a life "purposeful and thus meaningful". He then goes on to portray him as a human being who eventually has a type of epiphany and realises what it is that is going on. That he was experiencing the birth of a higher state of awareness through an emerging deeper social conscience. You could say that Scrooge comes to experience an epiphany, a moment of sudden realization or revelation that raises his state of being, his level of consciousness, taking him out of the Collective Unconscious state of mind, and into a Collective Consciousness state of mind.

Dickens interpretation of Scrooges redemption becomes evident at the end of the novel, where we see unlike the unredeemed Scrooge at the beginning of the story, where Dickens described him as a "squeezing, wrenching, grasping, scraping, clutching, covetous old sinner", he now describes the personality attitudes of the redeemed Scrooge as those of a changed person. He says, "he went to church and walked about the streets, and watched the people hurrying to and fro, and patted children on the head, and questioned beggars as to the cause of their circumstances, and looked into the kitchens of houses, and up to the windows, and found that everything could yield him pleasure. He had never dreamt that any walk, that anything, could give him so much happiness".

The themes of A Christmas Carol include the possibility of redemption no matter how unworthy of it one feels, or how unworthy others believe a person to be, the damaging effects of isolation, and the importance of love and compassion. All themes being a picture of the attitudes, beliefs, and behaviours of Jesus. Each of these themes is displayed through Scrooge's transformation from a miserly, greedy, and lonely man into an empathetic and kind individual. As the triumphant and touching end of the story goes, Scrooge is able to defeat a lifetime of selfishness in the worship of money, to become a new man with an entirely new outlook on life. He learns how to be patient and kind and generous. He is transformed in thought and deed.

The structure of the novella is set out in what is known as staves, five staves to be exact. This is an unusual structure that mimics the way in which a musical piece is put together such as the way in which someone might write a specific Christmas carol. Or a musical piece of the type of hymns that are popular at Christmas time, those primarily dealing with story of the birth of Christ, or other themes that are associated with the Christmas season, such as joy and the spirit of giving to others. Each stave in his book follows the actions of the storyline with the first stave setting the scene, the middle stave showing the turning point for Scrooge, with the final stave concluding the story by presenting Ebenezer Scrooge as a changed man.

The five staves pertaining to the storyline are Stave Number 1, Marley's Ghost, Stave Number 2, The First of The Three Spirits, Stave Number 3, The Second of The Three Spirits, Stave Number 4, The Last of The Spirits, and Stave Number 5, The End of The Story. The end of the story reminds us of the forgiveness and tolerance that was shown by one of the characters named Tiny Tim regardless of his circumstances.

Those two-character qualities revealed by Tiny Tim's example were thus learned by Scrooge and evidenced in his changed attitudinal and behavioural life, seeing Scrooge's transformation saving Tiny Tim's life. This is the lasting message of the story, that goodness and its attendant charity can overcome suffering in poverty and bad will, both spiritually and in all circumstances of life. It is a perfect picture of the central attitudinal and behavioural characteristics of Jesus Christ.

In Stave Number 1, Marley's Ghost, we see that the chains that Scrooge's deceased partner wear are important because of the material they are constructed from. Whereas normal chains are forged from metal, Marley's chains are constructed from what he valued in life, versions of material wealth. Dickens uses this as an example that our actions during our lifetime may have inescapable consequences if not now then even in death, depending on the value systems we have embraced throughout our life.

In Stave Number 2, The First of The Three Spirits, The Ghost of Christmas Past, this first ghost visiting Scrooge is meant to symbolise the experiences and self-absorbed and self-survivalist attitudes and behaviours that have turned Scrooge into the callous, mean spirited and self-interested person he is today. The spirit's glowing head suggests the location of the bitter memories Scrooge holds. They are locked away in his mind, his own personal corner of the Collective Unconscious.

In Stave Number 3, The Second of The Three Spirits, called The Ghost of Christmas Present, this second ghostlike apparition appears to Scrooge bringing with him visions of feasts and a transformed room in Scrooge's house. A picture of a redeemed life. It contrasts Scrooge's existing cold home with the abundance of other families and the type of home that could have been his if he had chosen a different attitudinal and behavioural path. Though the others do not have material wealth, they are rich in happiness and familial warmth.

The ghost also carries a scabbard but with no sword symbolising that lasting peace is the result of embracing right attitudes and behaviours through life not by embracing wrong attitudes and combative behaviour. Embracing aspects of God Consciousness which takes one out of the Collective Unconscious and into the Collective Consciousness state of being, and as such a deeper awareness of the existing unconsciousness that exists in society.

In Stave Number 4, The Last of The Three Spirits called The Ghost of Christmas Yet to Come, this final spirit, silent and clothed in black, is meant by Dickens to symbolise the uncertainty and fear of the future that comes when one has embraced primarily ego driven attitudes their whole life. The presence is itself mysterious and without identifiable features, showing that the future is not yet set and that there is still opportunity albeit for Scrooge short, for redemption through changed attitudes, behaviours, and a more righteous and ethical value system.

In the final Stave Number 5, The End of The Story called Scrooge's Gravestone, shown to him by The Ghost of Christmas Yet to Come, the gravestone symbolises Scrooge's potential fate if he does not change his ways: a lonely death, inconsequential to those who know him, with no lasting legacy.

So, The Ghost of Christmas Past, with his glowing head symbolising the mind, represents all our life experiences sitting silently, but still indelibly printed on our consciousness, many of which still influence our attitudes and behaviours in the present. I spoke of some of these in the previous chapter. All requiring our immediate focus and attention because they are still there influencing our attitudes and behaviours in the present, and we cannot move forward into the joy and peace brought by the Ghost of Christmas Present fully until some of them in particular are dealt with.

The Ghost of Christmas Present represents generosity, empathy, and the true Christmas spirit of goodwill towards all as recorded in Biblical teachings, where, when speaking of the impending birth of Jesus the angelic beings clothed in celestial light appeared before a group of shepherds and cried out, "peace, good will toward men".

And the "The Ghost of Christmas Yet to Come, is used by Dickens to represent the fear of death and of moral reckoning. We see that before this ghost leaves Scrooge it shows him two children who are hiding under its cloak. These two children are called "ignorance and want" and are a warning to Scrooge to change his ways. These two children, who cling to the ghost of Christmas present, represent both the rich man and the poor man's struggles. While the poor person is weighted down by want, ignorance the plight of the rich man is the more dangerous of the two because it leads to spiritual complacency and that ignorance is Scrooges main vice, since he has not bothered to learn more about his employee's conditions.

Ignorance in its basic meaning is simply lack of knowledge. In referencing this problem of ignorance, the Old Testament Book of Proverbs 4:7 says:

"The beginning of wisdom is, get skilful and godly wisdom it is pre-eminent and with all your acquiring, get understanding, actively seek spiritual discernment, mature comprehension, and logical interpretation".

Another character in the novella is Bob Cratchit. Cratchit is Scrooge's clerk and works in unpleasant conditions without complaint. He obeys Scrooge's rules and is timid about asking to go home to his family early on Christmas Eve due to Scrooges frequent irrational behaviour. Bob Cratchit represents the working poor in Dicken's novella. He is a man who cannot get ahead even though he is a diligent worker. He has a young child with a disability and other children to support as well. Poverty is represented by his character and Dicken's uses his lifestyle to emphasise and symbolise the existence of two opposite classes of society that exist in the world, the rich and the poor, the privileged and the under-privileged.

In one instance he does it through the symbol of coal. You see in the 1800's in England, coal was used to heat dwelling places during the cold months of winter. Scrooge gets as much coal as he likes and gets the bucket to top it up, but Cratchit only gets one piece and is reluctant to ask for another for fear of having his employment terminated by Scrooge.

But Bob Cratchit is always represented as a man of charitable nature. When he is celebrating Christmas with his family, he offers some kind words as a toast in honour of his employer Scrooge. But his wife is not as charitable describing Scrooge as "an odious, stingy, hard, and non-feeling man". If Bob hadn't reminded her that it was Christmas Day, a time of joy, and to calm herself down in front of the children, she would never have raised her glass to toast Scrooge, although she did do it in a somewhat scornful and sarcastic manner. In the storyline of A Christmas Carol Cratchit sees the Christmas celebration as a time of rejoicing in the blessings of the present moment and all it contained, and not a time to reflect on past grievances.

This is contrasted with the picture given of Ebenezer Scrooge who is always reflecting on past grievances and in terms of Christmas he hates it, because he sees it as a disruption to his business and money making. But he also hates Christmas because that happy time of the year emphasises how unhappy he is. Why is he unhappy? Simply because he spends most of his time recalling memories he would rather forget. He lives in the past psychologically and not in the present.

However, of all the characters in the book it was probably Jacob Marley who had the most influence on Scrooge, because he created the opportunity for the transformation of the character and attitudes of Scrooge. And in terms of the three ghosts that visited Scrooge, in the final analysis the Ghost of Christmas Yet to Come had the most impact on Scrooge, because it made him fear what was yet to come and motivated him to change in any way possible. The Spirit also pushed him over the edge making him realise he must change his ways to not end up like Marley forgotten and alone.

Now whilst the staves are the primary symbolic part of the novel in relation to the life of Scrooge, the story does contain other points of symbolism. Similarly, when you explore the writings that centre around the teachings of Jesus in the New Testament and in Gnostic text such as the Gospel of Thomas, you see that Jesus as did Dickens communicated with those around him at times using words or phrases easily understandable through the faculty of Simple Awareness, phrases such as love one another, bless those who curse you, forgive one another, and at other times spoke in a symbolic mystery that would come in the form of what was called a parable.

A parable is a story which in the first instance can be understood with Simple Awareness, but a story with a psychological or spiritual mystery hidden in its content. A story that relates to everyday life, but with a deeper spiritual meaning that could only be understood through quiet reflection. That was Charles Dickens' purpose and method in writing A Christmas Carol as was similarly his purpose with all his other books. They were wisdom hidden in a mystery, hidden in an allegorical mystery and in symbolism, that only those with a measure of discernment would understand, but believing that with other non-discerning readers, simply by hearing the story they might see something, and in seeing something, that they might come to believe the hidden mystery behind the story.

A symbol can be defined as a thing that represents or stands for something else and has a hidden meaning that helps portray a theme. In A Christmas Carol Charles Dickens uses obvious and discrete symbols to portray to the reader the themes his book has to offer. Some general themes in A Christmas Carol being social isolation, chances not taken, and redemption and rebirth. They are commonly used in stories of an allegorical nature. An allegory is a story within a story, it can be hidden in a parable.

For example, the surface story told in a parable might be about two neighbours throwing rocks at each other's homes, but the hidden story would be about a war between two countries. Some allegories are very subtle, whilst others like the rock throwing example can be more obvious.

So, A Christmas Carol is an allegory in that it features events and characters with a clear, fixed symbolic meaning. In the novella, Scrooge represents all the values that are opposed to the idea of Christmas, such as greed, selfishness, and a lack of goodwill towards one's fellow man and the eventual result of this kind of behaviour as the Universe takes its course. That was Dicken's end game in his pursuit for social justice, using his public profile as a gifted writer to subtly get his message across of a huge change needed in existing societal attitudes and behaviours to those more closely resembling the character and ethics-based life of Jesus if society wanted to prevent its current devolution and transcend its current detrimental social and spiritual shortcomings.

Similarly, as with Jesus when Jesus spoke in parables, He was telling stories with an end game in mind to impart to his listeners a moral or spiritual lesson. But Jesus spoke quite often in both allegories and parables. You see the difference between a parable and an allegory is that whilst a parable is a short story that teaches a moral or spiritual lesson, an allegory is rather a work of art that can reveal a hidden meaning, usually of moral importance. An allegory uses plants, animals, forces of nature, and inanimate things as central characters to tell a story, whilst parables use human characters to tell the story or the moral lesson of a story.

The problem for many Christians in their evolutionary journey into cosmic consciousness is that they fail to take the time to reflect on the mystery hidden in these allegories and parables of Jesus. Not so with those mystics of the Axial Age that I spoke of in Chapter 1 who took "time out" for meaningful reflection. We see this emphasis on the danger of not taking time to reflect deeply brought to the attention of his followers by Jesus when he shared with them as seen in the Book of Matthew what is known as "the parable of the sower". The Parable of the Sower is an allegory about the Kingdom of God within. In other words, it can be interpreted to reveal a hidden meaning, with everything in the story representing something else. It is a growth parable. .

In everything he thought and in everything he said and in everything he did, Jesus was always completely aware, alert, and vigilant that the enemy of Light, the ego mind lies in wait in the rational but mostly irrational minds of all human beings, lurking, garrulous and demanding, ready to snatch His teachings away from those who were susceptible to the ego driven biased and opinionated mouths of others. Anything that is beneficial to your growth in consciousness the ego mind will attempt to snatch away before it can take root. It can be something as simple as the words or teaching in a book you are reading.

I know this happens as I witnessed it with a friend who I gave my copy of Eckhart Tolle's book The Power of Now to as I felt she would benefit by reading it. She couldn't quite understand it in the first instance, so she just gave up. This is exactly what the mystery hidden in the parable of the sower is explaining. In the "parable of the sower" a man went out to sow grain. The man represents God, and the seed is the message Jesus brought from God pertaining to the will and ways (Divine Principle) of God.

A planted seed starts to grow or evolve from the moment of its initial planting, if it falls on a surface that is open to receiving it. So too the true message of Christ starts to deepen and grow within a person from the moment a particular aspect of it is heard by the person if they are sincere and open to receiving it. However, as we see in the parable some of the seed that was sowed fell on the path and the birds ate it. The birds represent the workings of the ego mind emanating from the energetic forces of darkness snatching away the seed and rendering it useless in terms of producing an abundant result after its own kind.

For example if intuitive thought or that silent voice within speaks to you pertaining to a state of unforgiveness you are holding against someone, and immediately you allow the "blame factor" (judgement) to enter the picture, it is as a bird snatching away the life changing power of forgiveness and with that snatching any potential the power of forgiveness has to raise your vibrational standing and your state of being or consciousness to a higher and deeper level. Which is why so many people after being given some revelation on some aspect of spiritual truth when trying to appropriate it in their own lives, either turn it into a self-serving religion or after a while simply discard it and go seeking something else.

So they bounce around the world of consciousness looking for another way to find peace or purpose. A perfect example of this can be seen for those who might be really led to take up the spiritual discipline of some sort of Meditation Programme, but without a true understanding of it and the resultant steadfastness that true understanding brings, they eventually bail out of the class as the cares of life ensnare them.

One of the most common weapons the ego mind will use in its war to contain a person's level of conscious evolution is "discouragement", which then brings about the "lack of time factor" as a psychological justification to ourselves for quitting. Because the ego is an entity that is time bound, whilst the spirit is an intelligence that is timeless. The ego looks at the present moment always, the spirit is focused on the end game that can be achieved through the present moment.

Why does the ego use the time factor as its primary influencer in the war of two minds? Because in its own realm of existence, from a cosmological perspective it knows it is an energetic force living on borrowed time, and in the time bound zone. This is similar to the perspective that humanity has about itself. Humanity generally believes it is just mortal and living in a time bound life, and so the entirety of an individual's existence is time based, focused on getting as much as possible "out of life" in the time it is here. It knows not that it is immortal, living in an eternal state just as its creator Infinite Intelligence is, both existing in the zone of timelessness.

In the parable of the sower the seed on the path represents those who understand the message from a point of Simple Awareness but leave it at that, failing to reflect more deeply to gain a cosmically aware understanding of the mystery hidden in that part of the parable. Usually because they are simply prioritising other things, mostly pertaining to the ephemeral nature of their existence. Things subtly emanating from the Collective Unconscious of humanity that the ego mind uses to divert and distract a person from their evolutionary journey into a higher level of consciousness. The birds represent the weapons of the ego mind, the seed on the path represents that portion of humanity who hear the message, but it is immediately snatched away as they divert their attention to the machinations of the ego mind.

Some seeds fell on rocky ground where there was little soil. The seed sprouted but when the sun came up it burnt it to its roots. The seed that fell on the rocky ground represents those people who respond in the early stages with great enthusiasm, but the revelatory experience they have been given is not allowed enough time through reflection to sink in deeply. So, when the ego mind brings its weapons into play, represented by the sun, they become discouraged and give up on the process as the ego influenced cares of the world ensnare them. The good soil represents those who receive the revelation and in a disciplined and steadfast way act on it in their lives.

You see Divine Principle once initiated by a human being, once launched into the conscious existence of humanity, and finding a home in fertile mind soil, will continue to create after it has been released. It is the Law of Reciprocity continuing its journey. It will move on continuing to express itself when it touches another fertile or receptive mind. Kindness will continue to beget kindness. The vibrational energy it contains cannot be destroyed. That is a scientific fact. As I said in the previous chapter it was Einstein who said, "energy cannot be created or destroyed, but it can be transformed." So kindness once given will continue to grow and be enhanced or used in different ways, it will continue to beget more acts of creative kindness.

To beget something is to reproduce or procreate, give birth to something. Love when broadcast into the universe and automatically stored in the field of the Collective Unconscious through an individual's conscious application will continue to beget love. Generosity when expressed will continue to beget generosity. This is why when given a Christmas present people will be psychologically influenced to give a gift in return. You see the Creative or Divine Principle once expressed in form has a life of its own and will continue its creative journey for eternity, it is timeless not time bound.

This happened with the works of Dicken's which in their full context, through his characters, emphasised the practical application of Divine Law, and the resulting positive change that can happen when Divine Principle the principles of Light are embraced. But not only this, Dickens also showed in some of his characters the chaos that is engendered when Divine Principle is rejected in favour of Ego Principle, the principles of Darkness. We see with A Christmas Carol it continued its creative journey in the lives of many, influencing them for the better.

One special individual whose life was influenced by Dicken's A Christmas Carol was a man named Carl Banks. Carl Banks, as he once described himself, was the least known but best loved cartoonist of his day and for many still to this day. An anonymity forced upon him through his employers self-serving preference to take all the credit for the characters Carl created for themselves. Born in 1901, Carl started off his working life in a variety of jobs, at one time seeing him holding jobs such as a logger, a steelworker, a carpenter, and a railroad repairman, before becoming a freelance artist which was his true passion in life.

When given the opportunity for a job as an apprentice animator with a film studio he jumped at the chance and went on to become the creator of many of Disney's famous characters including Scrooge Mc Duck, a cartoon character whose life and antics became an inspiration and a joy to children around the world. A cartoon character as admitted by Banks whose name and character qualities were all based on those of the key protagonist in Dickens A Christmas Carol, one Ebenezer Scrooge. Under the Disney umbrella he went on to create some of the most loved cartoon characters including Huey, Dewey and Louie and the scouting organization they belonged to which was named the Junior Woodchucks as well as the similar organization for girls called the Littlest Chickadees all of which Walt Disney took credit for.

In a perfect description of the world that he lived in and the delights to be found in certain aspects of it, plus the possibility for future change through quiet reflection with no judgement on past mistakes, in 1999, shortly before his passing Carl Banks wrote the following poem using some of his cartoon creations as symbols and examples to express his understanding of what it is that makes for a better world. It deserves considerable quiet reflection as it indicates his own attitude to life, an attitude very similar to that of the author Charles Dickens from whom he borrowed the character of Uncle Scrooge McDuck. Carl Banks wrote:

"The world is full of clans and cults abuzz as angry bees, and Junior Woodchucks snapping jeers at Littlest Chickadees. The ducks show us that part of life is to forgive a slight, that black eyes given in revenge keep hatred burning bright. So, when our walks in sun or shade pass graveyards filled by wars, it's nice to stop and think of ducks, whose battles leave no scars. To read of ducks who parody our vain attempts at glory, they don't exist, but somehow leave us glad we bought their story".

This is the wonder of the Divine redemptive plan of humanity releasing Divine Principle into the world through Jesus, showing that as we become imitators of Christ His words might reproduce and continue to reproduce after its own kind. The umbrella law that oversees this begetting activity is the primary Divine Law, The Law of Reciprocity at work. You see a principle is a proposition or value that is a guide for behaviour or evaluation. In law it is a rule that should be followed or is an inevitable consequence of something, such as the laws observed in nature or the way a system is constructed.

The principles of such a system are understood by its users as the essential characteristics of the system reflecting the system's designed purpose. You see all behaviour has a consequence of some kind, and since it is a scientific fact that everything in the universe is metaphysically connected, then both physical behaviour and psychological behaviour, whether deemed good or bad, lead to inevitable parallel consequences rebounding back on its practitioner. Like produces like.

Jesus had in his own life experience trained himself not to embrace corrupt understanding but only to embrace Divine Principle, as is seen in his wilderness experience. An alert attitude, that, if embraced by all of humanity would see a far greater proportion of people through progressive revelation come to a fixed understanding of the things of God and the workings of the spirit and save many people hours and hours of frustrating trial and experiment with different spiritual disciplines and different religious organizations, which we know leads some to just give up on spiritual things altogether. It just becomes too hard.

We must always remember that thoughts are vibrational wavelengths that produce our reality, but it is not random reality, it is reality aligned with those specific thoughts. Like produces like. A habit is simply a manifested thought that we have embraced continuously that manifests in our attitudes or behaviours as our need arises. As our vibrational rhythmic wavelengths are broadcast to the universe in our thoughts and behaviours, including our silent attitudes and expectations, then our inner bodies or outer physical circumstances, will respond accordingly and creatively change to align with those specific thoughts or behaviours we have broadcast into the universe and thus deposited into the sea of the Collective Unconscious".

Change the thought and you break the habit, keep fertilizing the thought and you sustain the habit and further entrench its negative influence in your life.

What are some of these Divine Principle we should prioritise in our thoughts and behaviours. They are those that promote the unity of humanity and not the individuality of it. Principles that were evident in the words and behaviours of Jesus are a good guide. Embrace the life principles of Jesus and you become an imitator of Christ that we are called to be. Attributes such as purpose, peace, love, compassion, kindness, and forgiveness. And a point to note is that most of these key principles are linked and begin to flow effortlessly in sequence as the previous one is embraced, for instance if you have no purpose, you have no peace or are unable to find peace. How are they linked?

The Scripture says, "without a vision you will dwell carelessly". When we dwell carelessly, without purpose, we have no peace, for purpose begets peace. When we have no peace we are not able to love fully for true love can only flow from a place of peace and rest. Without love compassion cannot be felt nor purposefully express itself, and without compassion true kindness will not flow. Through kindness forgiveness is able to be extended because you can't be genuinely kind to someone whilst embracing bitter or antagonistic thoughts towards them, but forgiveness can flow when genuine kindness is embraced and likewise kindness will flow when forgiveness is extended. The Bhagavad Gita 2: 66 says:

> *"There is no wisdom for a man without harmony, and without harmony there is no contemplation. Without contemplation there cannot be peace, and without peace there cannot be joy."*

That above passage links the Divine Principle of Harmony, with the Divine Principle of Wisdom, with the Divine Principle of Reflection, with the Divine Principle of Peace, with the Divine Principle of Joy. Everything in the universe is energetically connected.

Remember thought creates our reality. Think always in accordance with Divine Principle or Divine Law, or if it helps think thoughts that only align with the nature and behaviours of Jesus, and Divine results will be produced that are in accord with that attitudinal thought. Think purpose filled thoughts and meaningful results will occur. Think thoughts of a compassionate nature, and compassionate behaviour will be manifest. Think thoughts of a peaceful nature and peace filled attitudes and intent will emerge, and peaceful behaviour will manifest.

Control your conscious thought behaviour so that the unconscious behaviour of the universe does not intrude into your life. It really is as easy as that.

> *"Nobody chooses dysfunction, conflict, pain. Nobody chooses insanity. They happen because there is not enough presence in you to dissolve the past, not enough light to dispel the darkness. You are not fully here. You have not quite woken up yet. As long as your mind with its conditioned patterns runs your life, as long as you are your mind, what choice do you have? None. You are not even there".*
>
> *Eckhart Tolle*
> *The Power of Now*

The Shift The Death of Institutionalised Religion and The Resurrection of Authentic Life Changing Spirituality

THIRTEEN

> "Humanity is faced with a stark choice: evolve or die. If the structures of the human mind, (meaning our way of perceiving and thinking) remain unchanged, we will always end up re-creating the same world, the same evils, the same dysfunction."
>
> Eckhart Tolle
> A New Earth

Origen of Alexandria, born c184 and passed c253, also known as Origen Adamantius, was an early Christian scholar. Early Christianity is generally recognised by church historians to begin with the ministry of Jesus and end with the First Council of Nicaea, (325).

The First Council of Nicaea was a council of Christian Catholic Bishops convened in the City of Nicaea, by the ruling Roman Emperor Constantine 1 in AD 325. This ecumenical council was the first effort by the leaders of the Catholic Church and the governing Roman authorities to, by consensus, gain common agreement on two things. Firstly what were acceptable beliefs to be promulgated to all Christians in the Christian world, regarding the issues of the Divine Nature of God, of the Son, (Jesus), and regarding Jesus' relationship to God the Father, and secondly to gain agreement on the construction of the first part of the Nicene Creed, the Catholic statement of belief used in liturgy, the church pattern of worship.

The First Council of Nicaea also had on its meeting agenda the finalisation of a mandate regarding a set date for the observance of Easter, and the promulgation of early Canon Law. Canon law being a set of ordinances and regulations to be used to govern and control the church and its members. I spoke of Canon Law in previous chapters describing it as Catholic Jurisprudence, similarly as the religion of Islam has its own Islamic jurisprudence. Both Islamic and Catholic Jurisprudence, whilst being similar in purpose, that being a means of controlling and measuring the people, Canon Law is in this day not as intense as some aspects of Islamic Law, although in its early implementation it did involve brutal acts of punishment including, stoning, burning people alive at the stake, torture and crucifixion for certain offences.

Between the years 325 and 787 there were seven Catholic councils held. Some convened by the ruling Roman Emperor in conjunction with the Catholic bishops. They were: The First Council of Nicaea in 325, the First Council of Constantinople in 381, the Council of Ephesus in 431, the Council of Chalcedon in 451, the Second Council of Constantinople in 553, the Third Council of Constantinople from 680-681, and finally, the Second Council of Nicaea in 787, back to Nicaea where at that first council, the progressive institutionalisation of humanity's relationship with Divine Intelligence had its beginning. Back to where humanity's evolutionary journey to Cosmic Consciousness was hijacked by the mandated implementation of church law with its accompanying pomp, ceremony, doctrine, specific dogma, ritual, robes, and rules of conduct.

Some of the early church fathers had known better than this for a long time, but because of the unholy alliance between the Catholic hierarchy and the ruling Roman government, they were unable to prevent its progression, and after the physical passing of these enlightened Christian beings their concerns and teachings were mostly ignored.

Origen of Alexandria was one of them who had grave concerns about what he saw as the progressive misinterpretation and institutionalised interpretation of ancient scriptures, a man who had some seventy years earlier voiced those concerns with the following words.

"The present inequalities of circumstances and character are thus not wholly explicable within the sphere of the present life. But this world is not the only world. Every soul has existed from the beginning; it has therefore passed through some worlds already and will pass through others before it reaches the final consummation. It comes into this world strengthened by the victories or weakened by the defeats of its previous life. It's place in this world as a vessel appointed to honour or dishonour is determined by its previous marriage or demerits. It's work in this world determines its place in the world which is to follow this". He was speaking of the spiritual nature of a human being's existence.

Through this message of Origen's above and other teachings of his we see and understand that some of the institutionalised interpretations of the scripture that began to come forth from this institutionalised Catholic Church were totally wrong. A simple but profoundly important one was where the scripture speaks of the "resurrection from the dead" with the Apostle Paul saying, "if there is no resurrection of the dead, then Christ has not been raised", or where Jesus in John Chapter 11 says, "I am the resurrection and the life".

The institution's teaching brought forth the concept of the physical resurrection of Christ, not necessarily a problem, but what was the problem was the teaching that came forth from it that was based on the story of the resurrection of Jesus. One in particular that was troubling was teaching about a subsequent physical resurrection and eventual ascendency of all believers to a place called heaven, a place containing streets of gold, mansions for all of us to live in, with all our loved ones waiting with open arms to greet us and live with us physically forever, and as for the non-believers, well its off to hell for you.

Teachers such as Origen with understandings gleaned from the spiritual masters who had gone before him and complemented by his own spiritual insights through progressive revelation, understood that these scriptures regarding resurrection were not referencing a return from physical death, but rather the deadness of humanity's spiritual nature, until through an evolution in consciousness the hidden Christ Nature once buried by humankind's descent into unconsciousness will rise again. You see both the words sleep, and death are associated with the spiritual condition of the living in many passages throughout the Scriptures, not solely with the physical condition of the dead. Institutionalised religion has turned these metaphysical teachings into a heaven and hell scenario.

But this is not the only instance of the institutionalisation of the truth of the universe we live in. There are many others that have seen humanity continue to devolve in its state of consciousness, resulting in the confusion in thinking and bizarre behaviour we are witnessing in the world today. Those things are all the witness to that devolution. We on the other hand were called to be witnesses by our individual life example of our evolution not our devolution. In the first chapter of this book Chapter 1, I introduced the subject of the Axial Age, and in this the last chapter I reintroduce it and add to it.

The Axial Age was a time when there was a "fundamental shift" in the way the religions of the day and society in general functioned. The previous way of functioning, which mostly centred on the institutionalised expressions of ritual, pomp and ceremony, were displaced in favour of a new way of religious expression, a more authentic life changing way, a practical way. It first surfaced through "a shift" in both the teaching of the mystics and sages and the practical behaviour they exhibited that focused on the character qualities of compassion and kindness.

It became a process of using character qualities of Christ rather that religious ritual to fertilise the soil of religion. The mystics and sages were basically teaching people to "become imitators of Christ." The mystics and sages of the day had experienced a Divine revelation that religion itself without these two elements of compassion and kindness at the forefront of its existence would only enable the weeds of self-interest, self-servitude, and apathy, to quickly grow, choking off the flowering of the fruit of the Spirit that true religion was designed to produce in abundance. Spiritual fruit such as love, joy, and peace, gentleness, goodness and compassion.

The Axial Age was a pivotal moment in the spiritual development of humanity occurring between the years of 900 BCE to 200 BCE, trickling down to the Common Era or CE, which saw some of the world's great spiritual traditions come into being to nourish and serve humanity. (CE is the secular equivalent of what was originally A.D. from the Latin, anno Domini, meaning "the year of our Lord"). Traditions such as Monotheism in the Middle East, the doctrine or belief that there is only one God, Hinduism and Buddhism in India, Confucianism and Daoism in China, and philosophical rationalism in Greece.

These were the traditions which witnessed the emergence of timeless teachers, prophets, mystics, and philosophers, such as the Buddha, Confucius, the author of the Dao De Jing in China, the great Hebrew prophets such as Jeremiah, Hosea, and Amos, and the mystics of the Upanishads in India, along with the great fifth century philosophers such as Socrates, Plato, and Aristotle; all timeless teachers and all espousing an entirely new type of human experience. Note that the spiritual traditions such as Rabbinic Judaism, Christianity and Islam were all latter-day flowerings of that Axial Age.

During this time, we saw the birth of what is known as Axial Consciousness, which is a sense of identifying as an individual spiritual being as distinct from purely embracing a tribal identity. If this happened in this modern day, we would see people no longer identify themselves as a Catholic, or a Protestant, or a Muslim, which religious people have seemingly become obsessed with. There would be "shift from institutional identity" to identifying with Christ in a more personal individual way, and a more intimate and emulative way. For those of the Christian faith they would be simply Imitators of Christ, or if of the Islamic faith they would be Imitators of Muhammad, rather than Shiite or Sunni.

After the end of the Axial Age we very quickly saw this old trend of institutionalisation working its way back in, for the ego mind of institutionalised religion had only departed until a more opportune time. It was for some, put on hold until the way of the mystics had run its course. So it is not new, this trend of branding oneself with the name of the religion, you know the "I'm a Catholic" phrase, or "I'm a Muslim." With the institutionalisation of Christianity, and later with the institutionalisation of Islam, individuality or psychological attitudes of separateness began to flourish once again, which saw the individual self and attitudes of self-interest and self-survival become more important than the selflessness that flourished during the Axial Age.

Even as early after the Axial Age as in the time of the Apostle Paul, we see it was happening as recorded in the Book of Corinthians 1:12 with the Apostle Paul in chastising the bickering Corinthians saying, "each one of you says I am a disciple of Paul, or I am a disciple of Apollos, or I am a disciple of Peter, or I am a disciple of Christ. None more so eventually that those of the Catholic Church who believed that their institution and theirs alone had inherited the mantle of the Apostle Peter to control the Christian church.

This is still reflected in the attitudes of many in the church today who see their own religious identity being the identity of the particular church institution they are members of. For a lot of people when the subject of "are you a Christian" comes up, they might say, "Oh yes I am a Catholic or I'm an Anglican", or when discussing someone else in an almost critical way say, "you know she's a Jehovah's Witness".

You just never hear anyone simply say, "yes she's a Christian with different institutionalised beliefs than mine."

The Axial Age was different. It was a pivotal time in human history when human beings began to reflect for the first time about individual existence and individual responsibility for one's spiritual life, and the meaning of life and death. If there was one noticeable thing that all those movements involved in the Axial Age had in common, it was this. All of them had an acute awareness and concern for the ongoing suffering they witnessed, not only the suffering present in their own respective societies, but suffering holistically, suffering of the mind, body, and spirit. Suffering that was an ongoing condition and an ever present reminder of a spiritually, politically, and economically evolving yet unstable world.

Societal strife and turmoil infect people's thoughts, their dreams, their relationships, their desires, their ambitions, and their behaviours. Not one element of their physical life is left untouched and for many not one element of their psychological life as well. The Axial Sages knew this, and so devised and taught principles rooted in the deeper, less conscious levels of the self, the Soul, the inner person, that which is without form. The fact that they all came up with such similar solutions regardless of their spiritual brand, whether they were Buddhist, Confucianist, Indian Mystic or Christian Mystic, demonstrated that they indeed had discovered something transcending human rational thought (intellectualism) and the way human beings internalise the visible, (interpret their circumstances and experiences).

They all came to the conclusion that if people made a disciplined effort to re-educate themselves and realign their thinking with God's, or Brahman's or the Infinite Intelligence way of thinking, or whatever name they had for God, if people changed their way of thinking and perceiving to the God Mind way of thinking and perceiving, and then subsequently alchemised (transmuted or converted) that "re-educated or realigned thought process" into specific behavioural change, in other words if they started doing things differently, doing things according to Divine Law, God's way of doing, they would most assuredly experience a positive enhancement to their humanity.

When the Axial Age and the concepts embraced by it lost their footings in society, primarily through the greed driven intent of the local governments aligned with the power driven drive of institutionalised religion, we saw the evolutionary consciousness trajectory stall, as religion lost its ethical foothold, seeing the behavioural characteristics of societies deteriorate and their level of consciousness devolve. Except for those believers who held onto and continued to practice these enlightened concepts such as the mystics and sages. But in the main the life changing and life enhancing power of an authentic living religion was predominantly lost to the world in most societies at the time and to this day, save for small pockets.

But a "shift" is coming. The authentic religion of the future will not be a new institution or a new ideology, but it will give us a clear understanding of what was taught by the mystics, sages, and seers of all ages that actually worked in unifying societies, some understandings of which we do already have literary records of, and much we don't. Perhaps out of all the existing religions, the teachings that come closely to that previous Axial Age tradition of authentic spirituality and will in a new religion of the future, are those recorded in both the Upanishad's of the Hindu religion and those teachings of Jesus as recorded in the New Testament.

True spirituality and authentic religion is not about institutional alignment of the self, it is all about cosmic alignment of the Soul with Infinite Intelligence. Whether we understand it or not the fact remains that at every point of humanity's evolutionary journey, whether that be as a physical being or with regards to its mind or whether it simply be in the deepest recesses of its consciousness, in some way every individual has always touched the universe and derived their very conscious existence from that which is set above the universe.

The great heresy of institutionalised religion centres more than anything on its misunderstanding of "the fall", teaching traditionally that "the fall" as it is known, was simply a fall from Grace as sin entered into the world. Thus ignoring the most important aspect of "the fall", the psychological chasm that was created between humanity's consciousness and the consciousness of Infinite Intelligence, the separation of the Mind of Humanity from the Mind of God, which then redefined the relationship between humanity and God, and between individual and individual.

Humanity's understanding of its oneness with the universe was lost. Resulting in what we see in present day society, not only a huge divide between religions one with another, but also a huge psychological chasm between each individual and another, as each individual pursues their own individualised way of self-survival and self-satisfying selfishness, resulting in all the bitter strife, turmoil, and conflict we see in the world today. Authentic religion, but let's call it authentic spirituality, is all about re-establishing an understanding of the existing oneness of all living things in the universe and at its core involves our understanding the Divine plan for the return of humanity to the same consciousness of God's Divine spiritual nature and powers.1 Corinthians 15:22 puts it this way:

> *"For just as all people die to the consciousness of their true nature because of the union with Adam, in the same way all will be raised to God consciousness to life because of the union with Christ. "(Good News Translation).*

Formal religions are the outcome of the existing mentality of the race, the community, and the age in which they arise. We must always make allowances for this, and not expect any one form to be universally acceptable, or even understandable. When one examines the path of history it becomes clear that mankind is continually learning and evolving. Although we are still animals in a biological sense, what separates us from them is the evolution of the mind. This evolution of a human being moves through three stages: the physical, the mental, and the spiritual. Most people are still in the mental stage. Our religions reflect this shortcoming, but as we become more spiritually aware, our understanding of the spiritual life and of religions themselves will have to change.

There are two courses open to formal institutionalised religion, which really in many cases is simply inauthentic spirituality: either to strip itself of its pagan accretions and get back to the simple religion of Jesus, the "be imitators of Christ religion", or to recognise the allegorical nature of its present literalised scriptures, and to through reflection, contemplation and subsequent revelation come to understand and teach the real and original Divine Wisdom from which these teachings sprang.

From my own personal perspective I have an equal respect and admiration for the devotees of each and every religion who sincerely endeavour to practice what they sincerely profess to believe, even if some of the teachings they have embraced are not right interpretation of the scriptures, and to live the life indicated by the original founder or founders of that particular religion. A good Christian would have made an equally good Buddhist if they happened to have been born in a Buddhist community.

However, with respect to ethical behaviour, there is little room for choice, particularly if in that religion "conscience compromised behaviour" is embraced purely through blind allegiance to the institution or its corrupted way of interpreting the truths of God and the universe. All religions and spiritually based organizations worthy of the name must necessarily teach the fundamental principles of right ethical conduct, and unfortunately most don't, or if they do they merely skim along the surface.

But ethics alone by themselves are not what I deem to be authentic religion or authentic spirituality, and as for belief and creeds, and certain dogmas and doctrines, and ritual and robes and pomp and ceremony, these are merely the outer garment in which the religionist dresses up according to the conventions of his time and his community, covering up that which lies within the heart of the individual, both good intent and for some careless intent.

Both the truth and the mischief hidden beneath these outer garments is that these garments are not commonly assumed to be the real thing by most wearers, but merely modern physical copies of historical institutionalised thought and behaviour, and largely woven and subsequently worn for mere convention, respectability, and marketability of the brand, too often masking insincerity, and hypocrisy, and used as a cloak for unrighteousness, self-interested control and institutional governance.

These things as well as certain modern beliefs, dogmas, and creeds, which have been carried over and have survived from a far less enlightened age or period, can no longer be valid in the light of our modern knowledge and spiritual and scientific discoveries. For more recent scientific discoveries and more modern philosophical thinking tends to confirm the teachings of the ancient mystics and Jesus to a far greater extent that it does the beliefs, doctrines, and creeds of institutionalised religion.

Unfortunately a great many religious or spiritual people have not as yet developed any real appreciation of their spiritual nature and faculties, nor have they even attained to the mental capacity of which humanity through Infinite Intelligence is clearly capable, as seen by the attainment of a few, many of which I have used as examples at the beginning of each chapter of this book. Where it otherwise, the world would be a very different place from what it is today. In matters of religion the great majority still speak as a child, feel as a child, and think as a child as the Bible expresses it in 1 Corinthians 13:11.

Humanity in the main as it has been in times past, is today, superstitious, and distrustful of itself which causes it to find the concept of a universality of authentic religion an impossible task to attain. But the Apostle Paul in an almost prophetic way predicted that it will in fact happen when he wrote to the people of Ephesus and said the following: "until we all reach oneness in the faith and in the knowledge of the Son of God, growing spiritually, to become mature believers, reaching to the measure of the fullness of Christ, manifesting His spiritual completeness, and exercising our spiritual gifts in unity". (Amplified Version Ephesians 4:13).

Authentic religion itself, as an effort of the individual to realise his relation to the metaphysical or spiritual world, is both a person's highest effort and most deeply rooted instinct, yet for much of humanity there exists a profound ignorance of the laws and nature of the physical world they live in, let alone the metaphysical. Over and over again these laws have been presented to humanity as revelation, back from the remotest time of which we have any literary records. But always and ever the great majority of religions that have materialised through these metaphysically based revelations have then gone on to base their ongoing teachings only, on the purely visible that can be discerned through the senses alone.

Except for those revelatory teachings of the Upanishads, the sacred scriptures of the Hindu religion and the teachings of Jesus. They have been unable to literalise these. How do you literalise, "bless them that curse you," or "love one another." But due to the childlike natures and immature thought processes of some of his hearers, in his day and to this present day, due to the depth of their devolution from Divine Consciousness, Jesus spoke many times merely in mysteries and parables, because he knew they just could not grasp the truth. But those mysteries can be understood if one is prepared to seek to find the hidden mystery with sincerity.

Authentic religion is not a mere matter of individual salvation as much of the institutionalised teaching professes. It is in reality a cosmic process, from which the individual can in no wise separate themselves.

Many religions nowadays in so far as their institutionalisation, are simply a definitive set of beliefs, creeds, dogmas, and ritual, and are mostly departures from authentic religion: they are perversions of the original pure spiritual teachings. And over time since the end of the Axial Age institutionalised religion has progressively abandoned the simplicity and intention of their founders such as Jesus and Muhammad and become involved in endless doctrinal theological disputes.

After the Axial Age religion quickly lost its spiritual life changing characteristics, and became hardened, materialised, literalised, and secularised. Religions became worldly institutions, with exclusive, individualistic, and proselytising aims. They became the slayers of truth rather than the exponents and exemplars of right attitude and righteous behaviour. For this very reason we have witnessed certain supposed authentic meaningful religious organizations, originally borne out of one man's highest effort and deepest instinct, become powerful financially and politically from committing the greatest evils as well as carrying out acts for the highest good. The nature of the institution became inherently dualistic.

And being dualistic in their outworking, they have thus become both the originator and nourisher of the grossest superstitions and the cruellest practices, as well as of the idealistic supporters of saintly lives. Throughout history the dualistic nature of some religions has drenched the world in blood and claimed their own personal holocaust of tortured victims, seeing fire and sword and persecution, the rack, and the stake, being the operational components of what claims to be the supreme religion of love and peace. And in case you are wondering in this instance if I am only talking about radical Islam, I am not. I am also talking about early Christianity. In its institutional and hierarchical forms Christianity too has even to this day fostered the continuance of superstition and ignorance for the benefit of a shameless priest craft; and has served as a cloak, and even as an excuse, for the grossest sensualism.

My question is then, not as to whether religion as such will survive, it will, there can be no question as to that, for the hidden instinct of the human being is to reach out to the root and source of all being and becoming, and the hidden powers of his own nature which he feels himself capable of developing to an ever greater and greater degree.

This belief has been witnessed in abundance in recent decades with an explosion of teaching on the subject of the power of the mind and imagination and what can be achieved materially through harnessing the power of it. But whilst these teachings do have a metaphysical aspect to them, they can't be classified under the title of a journey into the oneness that the ancient masters spoke of.

What I would argue is that all genuine scientific and psychological investigation is a necessary part of the journey to authentic religion and that this distinction between the religious and the secular, between science and spirituality, between psychology and religion, has been for the most part purely artificial contrived by some leaders in those field who are more concerned with ego driven exclusivity, than with genuine inclusivity and connectedness. But not all. Which is why throughout this book, primarily at the beginning of each chapter, I gave examples of certain scientists in times past, who had a deep understanding and conviction of the involvement of an Infinite Intelligence in the ongoing evolution of the universe and in their own discoveries, one such scientist being the man regarded as the greatest physicist ever, Albert Einstein.

For scientific successes are in many ways a visible demonstration of the expansion of the human consciousness creatively at work. The human being's consciousness will inevitably expand. New faculties, or rather faculties now latent but with unlimited potential will come into play, and ever and always this evolutionary expansion will bring the individual nearer and nearer to a realisation of their own inherent spiritual nature and the ongoing life changing potentiality of it.

As such there are two courses open to inauthentic institutionalised religion. It must either strip itself of its pagan origins and get back to the simple religion of Jesus, or to recognise the allegorical nature of its present literally interpreted scriptures and gain understanding and subsequently begin teaching the real and original revelatory knowledge from which it sprang. Revelation from the ancient masters of the Upanishads, the mystics, sages, and seers of old, and the truth of the hidden mysteries of teachers such as Jesus and Muhammad, and not the corrupted teachings of those that followed.

But it will be harder for institutionalised religion to abandon its present ground than for a rich man to enter into the kingdom of heaven; for any potential reformers would have to reckon not merely with a deep rooted popular tradition, but also with a great institutional hierarchy, loath to depart from the sumptuous edifice which shelters and enriches it. So it will be interesting to see how the truth of Paul's teaching on the unity of the faith eventually comes to fruition in the future, but one thing we can be sure of is, it will.

However the good thing is that the concept of a personal Deity, the term sometimes used in evangelical circles for this being "my Lord and saviour", with the relationship being referred to as "a personal relationship with Jesus," taught in most Western institutional religious organizations has with both philosophical thinkers in the West and religious traditions in the East already gone.. Its place is taken today in philosophy by the concept of the absolute or reality, a fundamental reality which is the universe. This one fundamental eternal reality can be described as a principle, but never as a person.

It may seem strange to many minds to have religion without a personal God; but that already can be seen in many eastern religious philosophies, more particular in the Vedanta and in Buddhism, and it is these impersonal religions which are the freest from the rancour, strife, and persecutions which accompany more or less all religions in proportion as they degenerate into dogmas and formulas thus self-devolving their state of consciousness. It would appear, indeed, in the general history of religion, that in proportion as the personality of the Deity is accentuated so are the evils of the institutionalised forms. And in proportion to the degree that the impersonal nature of that which is the universe is recognised, so do these evils vanish, which sees freedom of thought and tolerance take their place.

All theological propositions about God are found on analysis to be self-contradictory, but it is essential to remember that every teacher has to adapt their teaching to the level of intuitive understanding of their hearers, and the general notions of the time and the community culture to which they belong. The teachings of Jesus, the founder of Christianity, had to be adapted to the crude Jewish conceptions of a personal God, who required above all things to be propitiated and worshipped; and it would appear that His presentation of a heavenly father was the most reformative one that his hearers were capable of understanding since the Jews have been throughout history a patriarchal society.

The Buddha, the founder of the religion of Buddhism, on the other hand, had to deal with minds of quite another order, and accordingly we find that he refused to personify or in any way define the Absolute. When questioned as to the nature of this Absolute Principle he was silent. So also with the religion of Hinduism. In Hinduism the Upanishads, the religion's sacred scriptures would simply reply "neti, neti," which is Sanskrit for "not this not that" to answer all attempts to give some sort of attribute to the Absolute, negating everything that the nature of God is not, but this negation is really the expression of a much larger affirmation.

You see the primitive or unregenerated mind requires a gospel, good news, something which adapted to the mental capacity of the hearers, to their current level of awareness, and something that would appear to console them for the evils and trials persistently plaguing their lives. Yet what may be a gospel for one individual, or one community, is very far from being so for others. Whatever it may have been for the ignorance of that part of the world in which the Christian theology was formulated, the statement that one had risen from the dead, and become the first fruits of them that slept, could be no gospel or good news, to those in possession of the ancient wisdom of the east.

What sort of gospel could it have been to Plato or Socrates, not to mention Confucius, Lao Tzu, the Buddha or Adi Shankaracharya, or others who lived and wrote centuries before Christ. What sort of a gospel can it be to ask these teachers and their followers if taken in its crude materialised form to believe that the dead do not sleep but are simply awaiting the resurrection of their physical bodies. We could say that Christian theology, far from being a gospel of good news, has done more than anything else to put the fear of death and hell into the hearts of untold millions. Some of the early church fathers knew better, but their teaching has been ignored.

But when we understand the spiritual meaning of resurrection from the dead, when we understand that it is not physical death that is referred to at all, but the deadness of man spiritual nature until his Christ principle has risen again in him, it having been dead and buried by his descent into matter, whereby also hangs the meaning of "the fall", we are no longer in conflict with a wider and deeper knowledge of these teachings of the ancient masters.

There are a great many references in the New Testament to the resurrection from the dead which have a deeper spiritual and metaphysical meaning, but they are commonly taught and taken as if they refer to a physical death and resurrection. Both sleep and death are associated with the spiritual condition of the living not the dead. Romans 15:11 says "now it is high time for you to awaken out of sleep". Paul was not speaking to a graveyard of dead people, he was speaking to a living, breathing, functioning group of believers. As there were in the time of Jesus and the Apostle Paul, there are still primitive minds in these matters who can only be fed with milk in the form of parables, but not with strong meat, the language of metaphysics, the language of the unseen world of spirit.

Institutionalised religion in its teachings moves within the narrow circle of its own rational mind, limiting the scope of that teaching to ensure it keeps strictly to the doctrinal position it is aligned with. It has neither the will nor the capacity to enquire into other modes of thought or other religions. Believing that it already has the truth, the whole truth, and nothing but the truth, and indeed believing that it would be a sin to question the basis of those beliefs, it goes on its way perhaps some with a slightly arrogant swagger, even pitying those whose beliefs and teachings differ from theirs. But the close and intimate experience of divine guidance and communion which is so real to many devotees, saints, and mystics, comes from the depths of one's own being, the Divine within, not from any institution, and as such can never be pitied rather envied.

Institutionalised religion has created its own personal gods and its own personal devils, and its own personal theological theories, but we clearly see that in all ages there have been those seekers who have transcended the crude popular notions which are attached to these theories, and which for the most part, because they are based on a simple realism which takes the objective world to be exactly what it seems and denies the concept of the metaphysical, they cannot possibly survive.

And religious beliefs based on accrued realism cannot possibly survive the present explosion of scientific knowledge through Quantum Physics in relation to the universe and how it functions. That is not to say that religion itself will be destroyed. But something much more real and much more fundamental will certainly take the place of the present crudities. Concerning institutionalised religion, the comedian and social activist George Carlin amusingly but correctly once said the following.

"Religion has actually convinced people that there's an invisible man living in the sky who watches everything you do, every minute of every day. And that invisible man has a special list of 10 things he does not want you to do. You know those ten commandments. And if any of you do any of these 10 things, he has a special place, full of fire and smoke and burning and torture and anguish, where he will send you to live and suffer and burn and choke and scream and cry forever and ever for eternity. But remember he loves you. He loves you, and by the way he needs money, so go to church and give. He always needs money. He's all powerful, all perfect, all knowing, and all wise, but somehow, for some reason he just can't manage his finances".

Every advance of knowledge, every new scientific discovery, every new metaphysical understanding attained, brings us nearer to true reality. That is to say it brings us nearer to a clear apprehension of the real nature of the problems of our life and our lack consciousness that underpins them. And the more that happens the more we come to understand that the appearance of "things", are simply veils which hide from us, rather than disclose to us, the one eternal reality. Which is why we must through greater understanding of the metaphysical aspects of our existence penetrate those veils that are simply hiding the true reality of who we are. This is authentic spirituality at work.

If I am was asked to define reality, I would say that reality is that which endures and does not perish when it comes into contact with time and space. It is that which changes not amidst all the visible changes occurring around it in the objective world, but also in the subjective world. To find it, a person must through reflection and moments of silence penetrate to the depths of their own being. They must find within themselves that which "endures"; that which is independent of the phenomenal; the deepest self which has never not been, nor will ever be seen or understood with the senses. The Bhagavad Gita 2:67 says:

"For when the mind becomes bound to a passion of the wandering senses, this passion carries away man's wisdom, even as the wind drives a vessel on the waves. The man who therefore in recollection withdraws his senses from the pleasures of sense, his is a serene wisdom."

One must find their true self and that can only happen as one lets go or detaches themselves of the phenomenal changing personality to which at present they cling so desperately. What is it that does not endure and what it is it that endures? We see Jesus in the Book of Matthew compared the two, as did Isaiah the ancient Prophet and Peter the Apostle. They said:

"All flesh is like grass, and all its glory like the flower of grass. The grass withers and the flower falls off, but the Word of the Lord endures forever".

What is the Word? It is the Absolute as spoken of in ancient religions. It is Infinite Intelligence as described by Albert Einstein; it is true reality. In the very beginning it was the Word and the Word was God. Institutionalised religion took these words of Jesus speaking about the Word, the Creative Spirit of God and turned them into their own reality, teaching that it meant the "good news", that it was the Gospel that endured forever, thus turning the metaphysical into the phenomenal. Jesus was referencing the enduring nature and metaphysical essence of God not the salvation message. And therein lies the great deception of institutionalised religion that gave allowance to the growth of the false self and a belief in this world of illusion.

But for authentic religion therein lies the paradox, "that whoever would save his life must lose it". (Matthew 16:25). The finding of the true self is a continual negation, a perpetual loss of the phenomenal self. So long as the individual thinks of themselves as being separate from the underlying reality, as long as the individual continues to think of God as a personal God, and for some their own personal benefactor, they must remain in the outer courts of the temple and worship from afar. But when one has realised their existing oneness with the one imperishable reality, then there is no longer room for the personal god which they formerly worshipped and petitioned in time of need. They have stepped beyond the veil of separation, the sense realm alone, that has blocked true understanding and Divine Wisdom, and stepped into the inner sanctum of Infinite Intelligence, the Holy of Holies.

Greater understanding of the metaphysical aspects of our existence through scientific discovery has already entirely dematerialised our concepts of matter; and we now see clearly that we have two things to deal with. A root substance which science and quantum physics at present call the ether of space, and an active principle which we call life. We are now in fact face-to-face with the choice between the dual aspects of life and substance, or the monistic view that they are at root and in a last analysis one and the same.

Are we then compelled to make a choice between monism or dualism? No we are not compelled. In the end it is our choice. We choose an authentic spiritual life or settle for an unauthentic one and in keeping the inauthentic one be prepared to keep on fighting the same tired old psychological wars.

A human being we all understand is distinguished from the animal by its superior mentality. In the first instance the human being manifests an amazing capacity in the powers of mind or intellect; the power to formulate ideas, both abstract and concrete, the power to analyse, the power to synthesise, not nearly the phenomena of the objective world of nature, but also the subjective world of its own mind and emotions. A human formulates science and philosophy, and enquiry into the limitations of its own knowledge. And it is infinitely more self-conscious. But that is by no means all. A human being has discovered that it has feelings and emotions which are something much more than and essentially different from mental concepts. The emotions of love and hatred are not intellectual; neither is its sense of aesthetic values.

The whole colouring which a human being gives to their mental concepts as well as to their external perception, belong to a region of their nature which transcends mind. In short, the human being has a soul; or as it is sometimes termed a spiritual nature or a spiritual mind, or simply a spirit. But it is not the human being who evolves that nature; it is that nature which evolves the human being in so far as it is represented by a succession of individual forms.

What is spirit? Spirit is only another name for the one infinite, internal, creative force, and source of all that ever was, and of all that can be. It is the one life and the one substance. We distinguish arbitrarily between spirit and matter, but is there any distinction at the source? No. That which is transitory, that which does change, that which belongs to time, is simply the forms which appear and disappear in this metaphysical world as matter; forms which range from solar systems and the universe to electrons and atoms, all active in the physical world, and thoughts and desires in the non-physical.

How many of the original teachings of Jesus and even the Apostle Paul's, have been overwritten to make them appear to support an already formulated theology or alternately just simply removed, we do not know completely as yet, for we were not there in the early centuries of Christianity's birthing when the Catholic church bishops selected the writings to be included in the first Bible. But as scholarly research carried out since the archaeological discovery of documents such as the ancient Gnostic texts at Nag Hammadi and the Dead Sea Scrolls has shown, certainly there were many, and I am sure there are many more to be discovered in the future. For during another stage in the unfolding progressive revelation of God, Divine Intelligence I am sure will bring these more clearly into view.

The bringing to birth of the Christ in you is the realisation by the individual of their inherent spiritual nature, which is precisely the true purpose of authentic religion. The real person is a spiritual person in whom dwells all the fullness of the God bodily, the stature and the fullness of Christ. The true doctrine of immortality, of eternal life., is not a doctrine of survival, or even of salvation, but of the immortal nature of the spiritual ego in its own right and nature. It implies pre-existence as well as post existence, for spirit is the one eternal root and source of all.

This true doctrine was well understood in the early centuries of the Christian era, and it was only in the 6th century at the Second Council of Constantinople in 553 that the doctrine of reincarnation was made a heresy by the Catholic bishops.

What did that heretical judgement by the church regarding the doctrine of reincarnation say? It said? "Whosoever shall support the mythical doctrine of the pre-existence of the soul, and the consequent wonderful opinion of its return, let him be anathema". Anathema is a formal curse by the Pope accompanied by the official excommunication of the person from participating in any further Catholic religious ritual. It's a type of religious "go to your room and don't come out until you are prepared to behave."

Can any rational person, with anything beyond the most limited parochial outlook on the cosmic process, conceive that humanity as a whole has to pass through such a vast cycle of evolution, but that the individual only shares in that process for the one brief flicker, and then is gone, which is all that a single lifetime represents in the millions and millions of years taken to comprise the cycle. The concept that we are born, we live for a flicker in time, we die, we go to heaven or hell, the end. How could we be that unwise to possibly believe that teaching?

The world of today is what the individuals of the past have made it. The world of tomorrow will be what the individual of today is making it. That is denied by none. Is it to be supposed then that each generation as it springs up, consists of souls that come from nowhere, souls who have had no past, but have to reap what previous generations have sown, and will have no share in reaping what they themselves are now sowing? Shall the Divine Law, "What a man sows that shall he also reap", the Divine Law of Reciprocity, have no application here.

Nothing could be more irrational than to say that the individual begins when he is physically born with more or less already developed faculties, according to his fortunate or unfortunate parentage, and then voila, goes on forever and ever with no further share in the great evolutionary process. Nor is the matter improved by making a personal God responsible for every soul that is born. One a savage, another a philosopher, a third a child of the slums, and yet a fourth a pampered child of privilege.

What must be realised in the first instance is the distinction between the real immortal self and the temporary conventional I; between the self that must be lost in order that the true self may be found. That higher self is the Christ in you. All flesh, all that pertains to the lower personal self is as grass and the grass and the flower wither and fall but the self-abides forever. In the Genesis allegory, Adam is said to have fallen into a deep sleep, whereby the physical separation of the sexes was brought about to his still further fall or undoing and loss of his spiritual nature. And you could say that in this deep sleep the great majority of the human race exist to the present day. But as in Adam all die even so in Christ all shall be made alive again.

There is every evidence to show that there has always existed a real knowledge and understanding concerning the deeper aspects of the universe and of man's nature, a gnosis as it was called, which has always had its initiates, masters, adepts, and hierophant's. It was they who framed the allegories and symbols, who wrote the Ancient Scriptures of the world, who built the great pyramid, as they otherwise harnessed and made manifest this ancient wisdom. To suppose that all the pre-Christian or pre-Muslim nations were without any 'real' spiritual knowledge or truth, or had only a dim light to guide them, is one of the great deceits of institutionalised religion.

It might perhaps have been a believable deceit some one hundred or so years ago when Western societies knew little of Eastern spiritual belief, when practically nothing was known of eastern religions and philosophies. But in this modern Google age it cannot be a deceit held for one moment by anyone who has made any study or explored the information available on comparative religion and philosophy. Millenniums before the Christian era, millenniums before the birth of Islam, how many we do not know, the ancient mystics, seers, and initiates had already arrived at the conception of one eternal immutable principle which is the universe in its wholeness. And they had already arrived at the conception that the individuality of the individual was a mere appearance; that in reality there was nothing separate from the one life force.

My conclusion then, is simply this. The authentic religion of the future will be no new thing, it will be a clear understanding and appreciation of what has been taught by the mystics, and the seers, and the initiates in all ages and from all spiritual backgrounds, centring on the oneness of all the universe and all living things in it. Its fundamental principle has never been better realised or stated than in the ancient teachings of the Upanishad's and in the words of Jesus, where at every point of his life on earth and every part of his nature expressed in form, he focused on the oneness of humanity and his oneness with Divine Intelligence. At times even simply but profoundly when He said things like "I and my Father are one."

The more a person de-individualises themselves in belief, attitude, and deed, the more will that person's consciousness expand towards the universal. But conversely the more a person continues to individualise their existence, the more their consciousness will contract. Hence it is precisely a person's present sense of separateness, which is in fact manifested in inauthentic institutionalised religion the great illusion, the great heresy, the great fall. It is nothing but this individualism and self-seeking which is the cause of all the bitter strife and conflict in the world, including the obvious de-individualisation of each religion from the other and each offshoot of each subsidiary religion.

Authentic religion or authentic spirituality in its proper understanding is the return of an individual to a realisation of the existing alignment of their conscious existence with that of Divine Intelligence, and with that a Cosmic Awareness of their inherent spiritual powers is birthed.

"Through the long evolutionary history of the human race the self-conscious individual has gradually and for many through bitter experience, learnt to transcend their animal nature one of pure instinct, through the cultivation of the intellect. Some have then further transcended those higher powers of the rational human mind, ultimately bringing them to complete reliance on the highest of powers, the Mind of God and its powers of spirit".

This is the true evolutionary journey through consciousness, the completion of the goal of our soul to return back to the source from whence it first emerged. Let it not be thought then that any mere conformity to a particular religion or belief in any specific doctrine, is the end of the struggle, the attainment of the goal. Much less it cannot be thought that it is a mere question of being saved in the sense of going to heaven forever and ever, a term which evangelicals use very loosely, as in asking a church attendee the question, "are you saved?"

"The individual who has really attained the highest level of consciousness, who has reached the goal of the present evolutionary cycle of humanity, possesses a cosmic consciousness and cosmic powers the very possibility of which would be commonly denied by the great majority".

Nor would it be fitting that the world at large should realise the possibility of the possession of these powers merely by attending regularly their singular insulated place of worship, for until the "principle of Divine compassion" has been correspondingly developed, those powers may be used for selfish ends, with dire results for the individual and for humanity. We have seen many instances of this occurring in recent decades with the rise of the charismatic Pentecostal based mega-churches. Hence the possessor of these powers must remain unknown to the world in general, ongoing evidence that they have attained the right stage of spiritual maturity.

This was the attitude of Jesus, and when he laid hands on someone, and they were healed, he did not immediately go out and start to build a mega-church based on his own personal "gift of healing." He simply departed to another place where adoring crowds did not gather. The individual who has attained that level of consciousness not of their own will and design but purely for the helping of humanity out of their sensitivity to humanity's great pain is the individual who has truly attained Cosmic Consciousness.

The Apostle Paul, in trying to explain this to the Corinthian people said, "Love never comes to an end. There is the gift of speaking what God has revealed, (prophecy) but it will no longer be used. There is the gift of speaking another language, (speaking in tongues) but it will stop by itself. There is the gift of knowledge, (a word of wisdom) but it will be no longer be used. (God's Word translation). You could add all the other gifts to that, including the ministry gifts as they are known. For they were merely for a season, for a time, for a purpose, and for a reason, and all these gifts will pass. And all that will endure is the Word.

Many years ago I visited the Crystal Cathedral in Orange County Los Angeles to see this magnificent structure that housed the ministry of Dr. Robert Schuller, a non-denominational church with what was at the time a huge congregation. The Crystal Cathedral formed a backdrop for Schuller's television program Hour of Power, which first aired in 1970 and eventually went worldwide. When I entered the beautiful edifice, I did not think wow look what God has built to glorify Himself, I thought look what man has built to glorify the institution he was building. As I look back I realize that perhaps I was being a little judgemental because only Robert Schuller would have truly known his heart at the time he conceived the idea.

Perhaps for Dr. Schuller it was not his personal intention but that is what happened. His "successful interdenominational mega-church", one of the first, not aligned with any institutional church, after time through internal strife and turmoil fell apart and was eventually swallowed up by the institutionalised religion of Catholicism. Does that mean Robert Schuller did not achieve anything worthwhile. Not at all. Many lives were changed for the better during his ministry. But he had finished his work and then the ego of others took control of the edifice. Similarly you could say as when the Axial Sages had finished their work, institutionalised religion took up the mantle, seeing strife and rancour open their door.

How did that happen for Robert Schuller? Robert Schuller was an emblematic post war evangelical, and you could say Orange County showman. He was an ordained minister in the Reformed Church of America, a branch of the Dutch Reformed Church, and made a splash when he began preaching above the snack bar at the Orange County drive-in theatre near Disneyland. It wasn't just the setting, but also the content of his theology that drew adherence worldwide. He stripped the dour elements from Calvinism and became a reliable blue-chip in the prosperity Gospel, which experienced a boom in the 1980s until the scandal broke revealing that many television preachers loved prostitutes as much as they "loved Jesus."

But Schuller was not one of those. Even though Schuller ran into some tax issues, mostly not of his personal making, but perhaps more due to lack of oversight, and his church into trouble after him, he was above all a family man for whom there seemed little actual space between a cheerful gospel and a cheerful life, because for Schuller both went hand in hand. He loved Jesus, he loved family, and he loved life.

The Reverend Robert H Schuller, the Southern California tele-evangelist and author who beamed his upbeat messages on faith and redemption to millions around the world from his landmark Crystal Cathedral only to see his empire crumble in his later years, died in 2011. But before he died at 88 years the Roman Catholic Diocese of Orange County purchased the church for a "bag of silver" in the form of 60 million dollars. And that particular institutionalised organization had once again gained another edifice to glorify its own existence.

When a cathedral has changed denominational hands in the past, it's usually been through the work of the sword. From the Hagia Sophia in Turkey which saw institutionalised Islam challenge Christianity resulting in the former Greek Orthodox Cathedral becoming a. mosque, to England's Canterbury Cathedral, now the seat of the spiritual head of the Church of England.

The Canterbury Cathedral was originally built as a Catholic Cathedral and subsequently violently changed hands to the Church of England or the Anglican Church as it is now called, after the murder of the Archbishop Thomas Beckett by four nights of King Henry 11 of England, apparently on the orders of the King. Not forgetting Germany's Magdeburg Cathedral, which went from a Catholic Cathedral to the principal Evangelical Church in Central Germany.

This is inauthentic religion at work. Church shifts of ownership were often violent and murderous in times past, now they are amicable ego driven events. Nowadays they are simply transactional as were the dealings of the money lenders in the temple in the day of Jesus. The conversion of the former Crystal Cathedral from a mainstay of 20th century Protestant tele-evangelism to a Roman Catholic

Cathedral was not the result of a second counter reformation, but a relatively seamless commercial exchange, and one in which Robert Schuller its founder actively favoured as the Catholics were taking his place in the bankruptcy court.

How far the religion of the future can be institutional and yet avoid the fearful evils which have so far attached themselves to institutional religions, is a problem which can only be worked out gradually; but it is the clearest of the clear that there can be no possible intermediary between the individual and his own Divine self. Each individual must work out their own salvation or more appropriately I would say evolution of consciousness, in and though their own experience. No one can possibly do that for them. The deep quality of faith in one's own inner nature will if met in stillness supply the right motive, and the right will, and the right path forward to an ever increasing realisation. The only true religion is one lived in spirit and thus in truth, a life that is above all doctrines and creeds.

The authentic religion of the future may still be institutional in some manner, but it will have no resemblance to the present methods or claims of any priestly hierarchy. It may be instructional yes, but the instructors will be those who are of a knowing, that is beyond all time and space and far beyond all doctrines and creeds and the religious jurisprudence that accompanies them.

For some there will be no places of worship, for the worship will be in the heart. Places or edifices of worship belong to the primitive ideas of duty, the anthropomorphic conception of a personal God who requires acknowledgement of his sovereign power, who requires adoration, who requires subservience, honour, ritual, and a particular type of court etiquette. Divine Intelligence does not abide in temples of stone and rock but in the temple within. That is its true home.

The authentic religion of the future will be free from forms and formulas, and yet make use of these for precisely what they were meant to be used for. For providing evidence and understanding of one central truth, it being that we are above the innumerable forms of inauthentic religion in which humanity at various times has endeavoured to create, and that we no longer have need of them for spiritual sustenance. It is then we will see as the Apostle Paul expressed it, "that we all with an unveiled face, or rather you could call it an unveiled mind, rendering as in a mirror the glory of the Lord the spirit, will be transformed in this present life into the same image, the image of God in which we were created". It is then we will find ourselves at the end of the Light having become as one with Infinite Life.

CONCLUSION

There is nothing you cannot be, there is nothing you cannot do, there is nothing you cannot have, there is nothing you are not. You are the most magnificent, the most remarkable, the most creative and splendid being that the universe has ever created. But at times you forget who you really are and think a great deal less about yourself than the Creator of the Universe thinks of you and knows about you. And at times you do not completely understand who you could be and the unlimited potential that lies hidden in the depths of your being.

But Infinite Intelligence does know everything about us because we read in the scriptures, "before you were formed in the womb, I knew you, and approved of you". Infinite Intelligence is the only one who knows how well you have done, and how hard you have tried, and how great your potential to successfully navigate this temporal life is. Even when we disapprove of ourselves Infinite Intelligence still approves of us and accepts us.

All of us have in times past set the guidelines for the person who we have become in the present, and in the same way it is all of us who will set the guidelines for the person we have the potential to become in the future, not the person we think we deserve to become because of past errors in judgement. Your past is not a one way ticket to your future. We determine in what form our future will appear. Infinite Intelligence does not reward you in the present according to how well you have delivered in the past, that is institutionalised thinking. Infinite Intelligence only rewards you or blesses you on your achievements in the present moment.

You decided in the past even sometimes subconsciously who you desired to be, and you set your intention even sometimes subconsciously, and you set the guidelines to become that person, and you set the pace at which you would travel. No one else. And if you have not become the person you wanted to be no matter what your age, or who you are, or the circumstances that surround you, and the imagined obstacles that assail you, you can still be that person if your intent is right, and the ethical state of your intent is aligned with those of your Creator and the Universe, regardless of how many times in the past you have imagined you failed. Forget those things that have passed and press on. Remember:

"It doesn't matter where you leave from, it only matters where you land".

All you see in your world is the outcome of your idea about it. Do you want your life to truly take off? The universe does. If you agree with the universe then your life will ultimately take off for you, "when you choose to allow it". Make a choice now. Choose life don't continue to let life choose you. If you feel on reflection that you have procrastinated for far too long and it has become a protracted procrastination, then now is the time for you to promulgate and produce what you've been promised by Infinite Intelligence, what is going to be, and who you can be and how you are going to do it. Just decide and the universe will come to your aid to sustain you, guide you, and assist you in the journey.

Now is the time to take possession of the Keys of your New Kingdom. If you abide in Infinite Intelligence and Infinite Intelligence abides in you, you can ask for what you will in line with the Laws of the Kingdom and it shall be done for you. Continue no longer to abide in the disappointment of today and the regret of yesterday. Sure perhaps our personal world would not be in its present condition were we to have completely listened to our experience in the first instance, but we all make that mistake in the early baby stages of our evolutionary journey through consciousness.

The first small steps of a young child can be easily fraught with falls and sometimes even fractures. I know it was for me. As a small child I fell out of a huge backyard mango tree in my novice attempts to do a Sir Edmund Hilary and climb to the highest limb, a feat that my mother had emphatically told me on more than one occasion not to even think about attempting. But I still came back to the tree for another go, and it only needed one fall to the ground to teach me not to ignore wisdom. The result of our not listening to our experience is that we keep reliving it over and over again. But you cannot resist something to which you grant no reality. So treat the past as illusionary, and thus gone. Stop giving it present moment reality, stop giving it oxygen.

This is the principle of detachment at play. If you look at something, truly look at it, you can see right through it and right through any illusion it holds and thus haunts you with. But in the face of ultimate reality, the present moment, your puny illusion about the past has no power, it can no longer hold you in its weakening grip. Separate yourself from your own thoughts, your own opinions, and your own illusionary beliefs if they don't serve you and your best interests and separate yourself from the thoughts and opinions and illusionary beliefs that others may have of you if they don't edify and support you.

Voluntarily constantly monitor your every thought, word, and deed. Sure in the first instance it takes some self-discipline and at times you will falter, but you decide if what you want is worth it. Life is a continual roll of "the dice of choice". To roll the dice is to take a chance on your own capacity to make the correct and wise choice. Make a right roll with the dice of wisdom and you will automatically win. That how the unseen metaphysical aspect of the universe works. Make a wrong roll with the dice of folly and you will in some way lose, that is if you don't immediately accept it, embrace the fact that it happened, forgive yourself for allowing it, and then do it differently and with greater wisdom the next time. But if you don't do a certain something in the first place then you will never know.

If you do something and fail your mind will say, "well you missed your chance there", and thus, and here's the key, "if you allow it," you open the door of the Collective Unconscious to "regret" and unknowingly invite it in to enter the fray. And if we accept that, the "well I just missed my chance," rather than try again, if we are just content to wallow in self-regret, our life will become a series of regrettable lost chances. That is not the joyous way to live that Jesus spoke of, for Jesus desired that our joy might be complete. If you occasionally "miss your chance", breath, reflect, and try something else.

I want to remind you to continually dream, and dream really big. What dream or vision do you want to turn into reality? But if you aren't willing to try and then go all the way, don't even start. If you are fearful of what result will occur don't be. A wise man once said, "do the thing you fear, and the death of fear is certain". Just do it, start. Mark Twain said, "the secret of getting ahead is getting started". Joan Baez said, "action is the antidote to despair". Walt Disney said, "the way to get started is to quit talking and begin doing". Theodore Roosevelt said, "do what you can with what you have where you can".

Lao-Tzu said, "a journey of 1000 miles begins with a single step". Bruce Lee said, "knowing is not enough, we must apply, willing is not enough, we must do". Mahatma Gandhi said, "action expresses priorities", an old Chinese proverb says, "talk doesn't cook rice". Nike says, "just do it", the Buddha said, "there are two mistakes one can make along the road to truth, not going all the way, and not starting". Ralph Waldo Emerson, the American lecturer, poet, and essayist and a leading figure in transcendentalism said, "an ounce of action is worth a tonne of theory".

Remember fear is an energetic force similarly as is faith. Don't attach yourself to fear, rather detach yourself from it and attach yourself to faith in your own evolutionary journey through consciousness. Detachment is a Divine Principle or Law whose power is underpinned by Infinite Intelligence. In detachment lies the wisdom of uncertainty, in the wisdom of uncertainty lies the freedom from our past, which is the prison of past conditioning.

> *"In our willingness to step into that unknown, that uncertainty, we surrender ourselves to the creative mind that orchestrates the "Divine Dance of The Universe."*

You are a big creation machine, and you are turning on your manifesting capability liberally as fast as you can think, and because of this how we think and what we think should be our absolute priority. For as a person thinks in their heart, they become then in their deeds. We really do paint our world with our thoughts and our level of self-belief. But always remember we have been given a choice to choose between selfless belief and selfish belief, to choose a mortal life or an immortal life, to choose Life or Death.

You are a threefold being, a body, a mind, and soul wherein is housed the intelligence of the universe. And your life experience is threefold, physical, emotional, and metaphysical. The process of creation starts with a perception thought. How you perceive something determines how you react. How you react is always based on your level of consciousness. Do you align your reaction with Infinite Intelligence or purely past experience? And therein lies the key.

What you desire is not your first priority in exploring the secrets of manifesting, but your state of being or consciousness is. For how deeply you have penetrated the higher levels of consciousness, to the degree that you have progressed in your journey through consciousness, is the catalyst for how well you will succeed in manifesting. The principle will always work because it is a universal law that just is, but to the degree that you have progressed in your journey of consciousness is determined the eternality and worth of what you manifest.

That's why all these things like positive thinking and visualisation work to manifest "things" in your life, if you persist, because they are mostly applied to material things that can be impacted on and influenced by these vibrational principles embedded into the functional universe. So when motivational speakers such as Tony Robbins say things like "we can do, have, and be exactly what we wish", he is exactly right I know. I preached the same secular gospel when I was an instructor with the Dale Carnegie organization, it does work, and I saw the practical aspects of many people's lives change for the better. But it is not eternal change. It will eventually rust and decay if not underpinned with a growing level of consciousness.

And people will gravitate towards this type of enthusiastic encouragement given at motivational conferences. Why? Because they are unknowingly searching for a deeper level of consciousness. And because in the moment the speaker's words are heard and embed themselves in a person's thoughts it gives them an emotional energy, a vibrational charge, and they leave the meeting with a thought process of "yes I can do it".

But for many, having spent their hundreds or thousands of dollars to get to the course, the energetic vibrational charge they receive in the vibrational moment is not sustained. Why? Because it does not increase their level of consciousness or take them closer to the source of all things. It merely changes their immediate creative energetic vibrational wave to a higher level of manifestation. There is no "eternality" attached to the process, it is just a clever use of a universal law, one of the laws that Thomas Edison who I spoke of in Chapter 4 was referring to when he said, "I know this world is ruled by Infinite Intelligence. "Everything that surrounds us, everything that exists proves that there are Infinite laws behind it. There can be no denying this fact".

You see when I spoke of Divine Principles throughout this book, whilst I mainly centred on those which relate to a human being's

Conclusion

relationship with a fellow human, those laws that alter vibrational influences that bring "things" into existence in the material world were not in fact left out. They were included too. And Infinite Intelligence has left it up to us to choose what we decide to use these principles for. Some will choose material wealth and prosperity, things which lean towards the "spiritual death" principle, because all material things eventually decay and disappear as dust in the wind, and others will prioritise "relationship principles" that lean towards the "spiritual life principle" which never fades and never disappears.

Does that mean if I choose the "spiritual life" learnings I must live my life poor? Of course not. Jesus despised neither the rich nor the poor. He had friends in both circles. However he did emphasise that it is harder for a rich man to enter the Kingdom of God (to return to their Source) than a poor man; not impossible but harder. Why? Because material wealth becomes a person's psychological life insurance and can become their priority causing them to compromise, to neglect, or even sometimes abandon their focus on their journey through consciousness.

An over focus on material wealth causes a person to adopt a self-survivalist attitude which is a Divine neglecting attitude in itself. God no longer becomes the source of all things in their mind. I personally started off and lived life dominated with a self-survivalist attitude. Nowadays I delight in testing myself as to how much I can live without, rather than how much I need to accumulate to live with. And for me it brought a dramatic change in my level of consciousness and sense of peace. Stress comes through a lack of acceptance and a sense of gratitude for what we have, for what we have already been blessed with and a continual desire for something more. The finding of the true self is a continual negation, a perpetual loss of the phenomenal self.

Remember "like produces like". If our life preparedness has primarily been about everything temporal or carnal, and our eternal or cosmic existence has been neglected, then life will, to relieve this ongoing subconscious sense of boredom, bring about a continuous cycle of replacing those things that are temporal as they rust and decay, with more temporal things, and it will continue this way, new material things, new experiences, new relationships, an endless cycle of rust and decay and replacement, and then we physically die having never reached a state of consciousness higher than that of Simple Awareness, and the legacy we leave behind for humanity is simply one which too shall eventually rust and decay.

The type of response we make to life will be in accord with our mental and spiritual state of preparedness, and in our response lies our potential for some sort of growth of our consciousness which will enhance our lives. If our state of preparedness has been voided of Divine Wisdom, relying continually on Simple Awareness alone to deal with adverse circumstances, our level of consciousness will decrease, but if our life in a thinking and behavioural sense has had an ongoing underlying platform of Godly Wisdom sustaining it, and we choose Godly Wisdom in that moment, our state of consciousness will be enhanced, and we will evolve to a higher level of conscious awareness or presence, and with that a higher level of sustained circumstantial success.

Life is all about filling the psychological and practical vacuum in our existence with things eternal not things temporal, and if this is happening then life will automatically bring forth circumstances and results in accord with all things eternal, in accord with Divine Principle or Universal Divine Law.

I started off this book speaking in one of the earlier chapters Chapter 3 to be exact, using the life of Viktor Frankl the Holocaust survivor as an example of a person who truly discovered the "power of purpose" as an energetic force that helped him to survive midst the most tortuous, barbaric, and brutal conditions that he woke up to daily, and will finish this book with this thought.

Conclusion

Even amidst intense suffering, whether it be emotional, physical, or financial, a human being has the potential to use that suffering as a means of transcending to good outcomes. All human beings are subconsciously strongly motivated to live purposefully, and meaningfully, and a meaningful life is not birthed in existing circumstances but comes through responding authentically and humanely as a matter of habit, to not just life's challenges, but also to the world around us in general terms.

The universe evolves, circumstances evolve, situations arise, some good some not so good, joy arises, grief arises, sadness arises, chaos arises, peace arises, positivity arises, and negativity arises, and how we respond in all situations is pre-determined by the attitude and habits of response that we have pre-embraced through our life preceding the circumstances that are causing us difficulty in the present moment. Whether we have or have not psychologically programmed and through disciplined consistency, built purpose filled intent as a regular habit into our lives, determines our life outcomes.

We must remain acutely aware that problems will always arise for all individuals in the universe as humanity progressively evolves through the various stages of consciousness. As discussed in this book we must always remain aware that life is in fact a spiritual warfare for the soul of humanity, and during this war some will get washed away mentally and emotionally by the human or principality and power induced circumstances they are encountering; and yet others, such is the platform of psychological programming and disciplined habit that has been established in their life thus far, will "transcend their existing situation" and use those winds and waves of adversity that are buffeting their ship of life to propel their safe passage to future freedom and peace.

I have outlined in the following few pages some simple tools that I use in my own personal spiritual daily routine, some daily spiritual practices, which some readers may find helpful in their own process of evolving. Be blessed in your endeavours. Grace and Peace.

DAILY SPIRITUAL PRACTICES

Regarding spiritual practices I can only share what I have experienced personally that has brought a positive benefit to my own life. I share these insights with you because I have noticed in all the books I have read, that the majority of spiritual teachers are pretty close mouthed about the spiritual practices they have personally employed that have gotten them to this particular stage of their spiritual journey.

Jesus was not, for we see him giving a practical example of the manner in which his followers should pray. In the Book of Luke we read, "One day in a place where Jesus had just finished praying, one of His disciples requested, "Lord, teach us to pray, just as John taught his disciples". So Jesus told them, "When you pray, say", and then continued to give them what has become commonly known as the Lord's Prayer.

In my own spiritual journey over the decades I have tried much, but many times have grown weary with the effort that was required to continue a certain practice and discipline, midst the clutter and haste of life, usually ending up chastising myself for not being consistent. I finally came to realise after much trial and error, through quiet reflection on the words of Jesus that said, "My yoke is easy, and My burden is Light" that things might need to change.

In the ancient writings of the Proverbs discipline means to instruct, correct, chastise, and rebuke, but it must all be done in an attitude of self-love and self-acceptance, and it does not mean to punish yourself psychologically or beat yourself up as you progress, and I was beating myself up for my lack of consistency. For me that realisation caused me to make a firm decision to only continue with those disciplines and regular practices that whilst they may not necessarily come easy in the first instance, would through a measured amount of disciplined consistency and surrender eventually became habitual and with that life changing.

If you Google for information on how long it takes to create a habit you will get all sorts of answers as it is all relevant to the individual. The infamous "21 days" myth as espoused by many in the past spread after a book called Psycho-Cybernetics was published in 1960 and became widely popular. The book was written by a plastic surgeon who noticed that his patients seemed to take about 21 days to get used to their new faces and in his book he used the psychology of that to apply it to any new habit.

However that 21 day theory that had become widely accepted, was eventually disputed some years after, but not before many of those who had read the book became fixed on the idea that if one was doing it right change should be noticed within 21 days, and if change wasn't noticed then one must doing something wrong. I was one of those people. I too read the book in the late sixties and subsequently became fixated for many years on the 21 days target, which when on many occasions it was not met, say in something like meditation, I felt extremely disappointed in what I regarded as "my lack of discipline". But it was all a myth.

So how long does it take to create a habit? For most people for a habit to become fixed and automatic there must be certain conditions met. First it must be believable, meaning you must have faith in the expected outcome, and then it must be achievable within the truthful time constraints in your life. In other words be realistic that the time set aside for it does fit in with your other life responsibilities. And it must be measured and then monitored for time and place adjustment if necessary. However one size does not fit all. More recent research carried out at the University College of London has shown a huge variation in individual times among participants attempting to create a habit, anywhere from 18 days to 254 days.

There can also be different levels of individual resistance to creating a new spiritual habit, because remember this is a spiritual and psychological warfare, we are involved in. Some people having what might be termed fixed perhaps slightly unspiritual habits if taken to extremes, might find it takes longer to create a new spiritually based habit. Perhaps six glasses of wine before a meditation session might not be appropriate.

But in the end whether it is something like present moment awareness as Eckhart Tolle teaches or a mantra that the ancient masters taught, it all comes back to as I said, "believability and time based achievability" in the first place, and then good old practice. It is no different than if you were learning how to play a musical instrument.

The following life habits are those that have worked for me and become habitual within around 90 days of commencing, but even more habitual after 12 months, and time wise would be I believe relatively achievable for most people. If any reader finds them too time consuming perhaps it might be helpful to relook at what their own personal life priorities are. My own personal routine that I commit to doing without fail are as follows.

1. Upon rising I give personal thanks for the day, and immediately pray a prayer of gratitude and intent, which I have outlined for you further in the book. I then verbalise my intent for the day and surrender the day into the hands of Infinite Intelligence for Divine Wisdom, understanding and guidance. This takes about ten minutes.

2. Immediately after this I spend ten minutes reciting whilst listening to one particular mantra, in my case it is what is known as the Moola Mantra. I give details on the concepts surrounding the chanting or listening to a mantra in the following pages as well as the meaning of the Moola Mantra.

These two things are done without fail, and the whole process takes a maximum of around 30 minutes. What time you arise each day is up to you, but from personal experience in years past I know that late nights do not bode well with early starts. My early start is around 4.30 a.m. Nature arises around that time as soon as the early morning sun begins its own purposeful intent. However the time you arise is up to you.

I choose an early start and my reasoning for doing this is based on the ancient Hindu philosophy that speaks of the Amrit Vela or the ambrosial hours (from the Greek ambrotos meaning "immortal") just before dawn as being the best time to wake up and to practice things of the spirit in order to maximize the potential for spiritual awakening. This time of day is said to be the time when the veil of the ego is thinnest, offering fewer of the distractions that are present through the rest of the day. I have found this to be true.

For yogis Amrit Vela is commonly known as early morning meditation time. How early you may ask? To be precise for yogis it's 4 am. What is so appealing to yogis about this, what some people might describe as an unearthly hour? Well Amrit means nectar while Vela means time or moment. As one sits in meditation or in contemplation of God one is able to taste the nectar, the sweetness, of this Divine relationship and take sustenance to empower the self. For yogis it is a very special, silent, and personal time with Infinite Intelligence that is much more difficult to recreate once the world begins its busy, noisy, day. It is the only time to fully without interference "breath in the breath and power" of God.

During the rest of the day I go about doing what I must do whilst always seeking to apply the "7 Daily Habits to Cultivate" that I have listed in the following few pages. But if occasionally I miss the mark with something I do not condemn myself in any way, neither does Infinite Intelligence condemn us, for whilst the unregenerated human nature looks upon outward circumstance God looks only on the heart's intent. And as such when I can, I remind myself during the day that:

"Authentic religion or authentic spirituality is evidenced in a life lived as if you are sitting at the foot of the master, even if you can't see him, you know that he sees you".

Authentic religion is to be in a state of constant awareness of the non-duality of your nature, and the all-encompassing love that consciousness entails when we understand that God sees us even if we don't see God. It is like we are a servant before a loving king conscious of every step we take and every word we say and doing everything out of gratitude for being welcomed into the Kings Palace of kindness. When someone is living in this state of fusion with the Divine, they begin seeing all of creation including themselves as nothing but a united reflection of the creator.

7 DAILY HABITS TO CULTIVATE

1. **Always greet the new day with gratitude, with some sort of gratitude dialogue.**

The day should always be greeted with a "Good Morning God" attitude and not with a "Good God it's morning" attitude. Starting off the day with positive intent engages Universal Law and makes all our goals easier. Our thought process has to be aligned with God's thought process from the get-go, which is, "in everything give thanks for this is the will of God concerning you." (1 Thessalonians 5:18 and Colossians 3:17.)

I have attached my personal morning prayer of Gratitude and Intent that takes only 5 or 6 minutes to complete.

2. **At every opportunity engage with Infinite Intelligence talk to the Holy Spirit or Ruh al-Qudus in your mind.** Commit your day to the guiding Hand of the Spirit. Talk to the Spirit if you need to make an important decision. Seek guidance. If you practice it regularly enough it will eventually become an automatic response in any situation similar to a child who has an imaginary friend they continually converse with. It does not have to be some sort of disciplined prayer routine, just quiet, relaxed, silent, or audible conversation. Cast your cares upon the Holy Spirit because She cares for you. That's why She is called the Comforter.

3. Live life deliberately focused on everything that comes into your life.

If you are talking to someone, give him or her your full attention. If you are doing something, give the task your full attention. Fully engage with everything that comes before you. This will minimise the opportunity for you to get lost in trivial and wasted thought. Give the present moment your full attention. Live life deliberately and not just accidentally as unfortunately most people do.

4. Take some time, at least once a week, to get "lost in stillness."

What do I mean by that? Take time out from the inner and outer noise of the universe and spend time with the stillness of the universe. You may decide just sitting quietly breathing rhythmically or meditatively is what you need to do. Or take a walk at the beach and drink in the peace, or a walk in the park, or just a walk down the street, but not in this instance as a means of exercise, rather as a means of observing in a non-judgemental way the universe you live in, the goings on around you.

5. Take time occasionally to deliberately examine your thoughts, to observe your thoughts.

It does not have to be a regimented routine just do it when you think of it. You will be amazed at how many trivial and useless thoughts you entertain all the time. Just occasionally stop, step back and become 'the observer' of your current thought and it will surprise you how much you are living through your mind thinking about past events or future scenarios and expectations, usually with some regretful or anxious connotations. Then immediately say to yourself or out loud if you can, "my mind holds only what I think with God, a child of God can suffer nothing, I am that child." Actions like this are all part of the renewing of the mind process, which is the key component of the Atonement process.

6. Take a moment every day to deliberately forgive someone and to deliberately bless someone.

During the day at any particular time you think of it, take a moment to forgive deliberately and sincerely someone, anyone that comes to mind. At first you will find yourself choosing only those who you have minimum psychological discomfort with, then as you progress you may or should deliberately move on to the more difficult ones. It is a powerful spirituality influencer, an energetic force for not only your good but for the good of the beneficiary of your forgiveness. I spoke of this principle in Chapter 12.

Another powerful influencer on your state of consciousness is the "bestowing of a blessing." Just wish God's blessing on someone's life. If you pass a person in the street you don't have to say it out loud just say it to yourself, but if you pass a person in your car or are sitting at a stop sign and notice a person, you can bless them out loud.

7. Go for a brisk walk and take some deep breaths as you do.

Develop a habit of getting some sort of exercise daily. It has all kinds of health benefits mental and physical. Does not have to be strenuous. Does not have to be of the Arnold Schwarzenegger type. Just a brisk 30-minute walk will suffice. Remember life is all about finding balance in everything.

A PRAYER OF GRATITUDE AND INTENT

The following is my early morning wake up discipline that I have been carrying out every day without exception for around ten years or more to the point where I pretty much know it off by heart. It is a combined affirmation of gratitude and intent. Gratitude and Intent are both powerful vibrating energy waves that operate according to Divine Law and over time can have a powerful impact on your life.

Gratitude, the word itself, comes from the Latin root *gratus,* and *gratus* is also the root of related terms such as "Grace." It's Proto-Indo-European root *gwere* means "to praise, to celebrate, to be in contact with the Divine." In the renowned neuro-scientist, author and spiritual teacher Deepak Chopra's article titled "Sowing Seeds of Gratitude to Cultivate Wellbeing," the co-authors reference clinical studies that prove the positive effects of gratitude on the recovery of patients with many illnesses including symptomatic heart failure.

Science had been providing for many years now clinical proof supporting what many religions and spiritual traditions have been predicating for eons, that gratitude does you good. In his article Deepak also draws a powerful association between the physical and mental wellbeing that comes from an ongoing attitude of gratitude and the subsequent development of a higher level of spirituality.

Intention is the starting point of all our dreams and is a vibrating energetic force within itself that fulfils our needs. Everything that happens in life begins with an intention thought. The sages of India observed thousands of years ago that our life is shaped and impacted on by our desires which intention comes forth from. The classic Vedic text known as the Upanishads declares, "You are what your deepest desire is. As your desire is, so is your intention. As your intention is so is your will. As your will is so is your deed. As your deed is so is your destiny." Jesus said, "Desire first the Kingdom of God, and all the things you need shall be added to your life."

The morning prayer can be recited out loud or read slowly and silently to oneself, or you can do as I did if you have a computer, record it with pauses between each main point enabling you to play it and repeat that section out loud, play the next section and repeat it out loud etc.

It takes about six to ten minutes each morning, but you will find over time it will be the most valuable six minutes of your day that you will ever spend. Try to keep focused on each part of the prayer as the morning mind does tend to drift out of immediate focus into thoughts about the day ahead. The prayer covers many areas that we have discussed in this book including Holy Spirit engagement, our thought processes, the Mind of Christ, the intuitive mind and the rational mind, creativeness, forgetting the past, forgiveness, achieving balance, embracing stillness and having respect for our body our instinctively operating earthly vehicle.

I am grateful Infinite Intelligence for today. I am grateful today for who I am, I am grateful today for where I am, I am grateful today for everything I have, and I am grateful for what I am doing right now. I am grateful for the Holy Spirit who you sent. Holy Spirit I align my will with your will for my life and ask that you would today guide my thoughts, guide my will, guide my reason, guide my intent, and guide

A Prayer of Gratitude and Intent

my actions and behaviours that they be in accord with God's will for my life and the part I will play in God's will for humanity.

I am grateful Holy Spirit to open my eyes today, I am grateful for another day to live my life, for a new start. I am grateful to feel the breath in my lungs and the beating in my heart. I am grateful Holy Spirit for today, for the opportunities in the next twenty-four hours; I welcome the chance to do something amazing and creative with the day today.

I choose to make the most of today, I energise my thoughts, I focus my intention, I remind myself of how far I've come and believe that I will go the distance today to whatever goal or vision I have in mind. I remind myself of achievements accomplished successfully and channel my focus to today only and the present moment only that I might make the most of the next twenty-four hours and not be bothered as to what comes after this.

I am grateful Holy Spirit for this body and vow to treat it well today. To eat well, to nourish it well, hydrate it, exercise it, stretch it, move it and relax it. I am grateful for the Mind of Christ within me, for my intuitive mind and my rational mind and vow to use them both well, to focus on learning to applying knowledge gained, to reflect, and to hold myself accountable.

I place my rational mind in subservience to my Christ Mind. I commit to staying humble, I agree to talk and think well of others and myself and to channel my focus in conversation only to the positive. I commit to let go of wasteful thinking, to let go of dwelling on the past where there are no more lessons to be learned, to let go of fear and anxiety of the future and instead focus on what I can control, my own actions and my own thoughts, my own reactions and my intent.

I am grateful Holy Spirit for the people in my life, those who are supportive and those who I in some way have learned from. I take a moment to remember all the small and great things done for me; there is so much to be grateful for. Whether something simple like a door held open, a smile from a stranger, or the gift of time and attention from another.

I am grateful Holy Spirit for what I give myself, the time to reflect alone in stillness, to clarify my thoughts and to remind myself to press on. I am grateful for the courage I have, to do what feels right instead of following the crowd, balancing listening to others and my own rational mind and listening to my intuitive voice, the voice of the Holy Spirit within me.

I am grateful Holy Spirit for the basics, to breathe, to eat, to sleep and to move. I remind myself that not everyone has these basics; I remind myself that I am privileged to have them. Today is all I have, and I promise to use my time well. I am grateful for this day these twenty-four hours; I am grateful for the unlimited potential that lies inside of me. I promise to use my time well, to use my thoughts feelings and actions well, to be clear on my intent, to be flexible and adaptable, and to respond with good grace to life's unexpected events.

I commit to work towards being the best that I can be today, to realise my unlimited potential, to continue with my goals, to stay strong and ignore distractions, and to let others negativity just pass by. I refuse to feed or entertain my own doubts, I commit to being the best that I can be today, from thinking to clarifying intention, from clarifying intention to taking action, with the time energy and resources available. To be the best in heart, mind body and spirit for myself and for others, to give the best of myself as I focus and set intention, as I clarify my vision and next action steps, I am grateful dear Holy Spirit for today and I am ready for today. Thank you, thank you, thank you for today.

SIMPLE TIPS TO RISE ABOVE EGO MIND IDENTIFICATION

1. PAY ATTENTION...Listen to the voice in your head continuously.
2. PAY ATTENTION...To repetitive thought patterns.
3. PAY ATTENTION...To your current emotional state, your feelings.

It will surprise you how many trivial, destructive, or negative thoughts you filter through your mind impacting on your emotions.

AS YOU DO THIS

Recognize that there is a voice there and I am listening to it or recognize that there is an emotion present, and I am feeling it. Don't try and fight it just observe it, like a teacher in a classroom who gives an occasional glance in the direction of a misbehaving child whilst saying nothing.

DON'T

1. DON'T dwell on the thought or feeling.
2. DON'T analyse the thought or feeling to see where it's coming from.
3. DON'T judge the thought or feeling.

JUST OBSERVE IT

1. Watch the thought almost in a way letting it know you are watching it but not embracing it.
2. Observe and feel the emotional energy it produces inside of you. Identification with the mind gives it vibrational energy; observation of the mind withdraws that energy.
3. Try to avoid conversations with others that push for an opinion on or a judgement against some particular situation or person. These things are all manifestations of the ego mind.

"Remember thoughts and emotions feed each other. If we continually entertain a particular thought we give it energy, spiritual vibrational energy, power to create after its own kind."

If we reject that thought with words or thoughts like "my mind holds only what I think we God," or "I am as God created me, the son (or daughter) can suffer nothing, I am that son," (or daughter) then we will de-energise, deflate, and destroy the thought and it will eventually disappear totally. When the thought is gone the emotion goes with it, and the vibrational energy that is withdrawn from your mind will transform into peace filled presence. Life will psychically and emotionally feel a whole lot easier to navigate.

THE DAILY MANTRA

A mantra is a sacred utterance, a numinous sound, a syllable, word, or phonemes, or a group of words in Sanskrit, believed by practitioners to have religious or spiritual powers. A numinous sound is a Latin term used to describe a mysterious or awe-inspiring sound that arouses spiritual or religious emotion. It is a word meaning a deity or spirit presiding over a thing or space. It describes the power or presence or realisation of a divinity. A phoneme is a unit of sound that can distinguish one word from another in a particular language.

The word mantra means something that protects the mind. Mantras originated in the religion of Hinduism and Buddhism. In the mainstream Buddhist and Hindu practices, mantras were and are still considered as the most essential practice in attaining spiritual advancement and enlightenment. Every ritual practiced in the Hindu, or the Buddhist culture is based on mantras, as they are believed to bring positivity, strength, spirituality, and wealth too, if desired. How do they do that?

Mantras are sounds that create vibrations that evoke the subconscious mind and spiritual forces. As discussed earlier every word that we say, produces an energetic wave a vibrational wave that affects our physical and mental well-being and can influence those around us. These vibrations are also sent out to the universe. Some temples and churches have a positive energy based on the fact that these places have positive vibrational waves in a way lingering, simply because a lot of prayers and mantras have been and are still recited by certain spiritually conscious people who have attended there. You may have noticed this in visiting a Cathedral as I have, that there is only what could be described as a calming peace filled presence.

How do mantras impact you? Chanting mantras stimulates the endocrine system. The act of your tongue pressing against the palate at the top of the mouth stimulates the hypothalamus, thalamus, and pituitary glands. The pituitary gland is formed in the foetus from cells of the roof of the mouth that rise into the brain. This is why pressing the tongue against the roof of the mouth stimulates the gland.

When you recite a mantra, you hit the palate with your tongue. In the palate, there are 84 Meridian points: 64 in the hard palette and 20 in the soft palette. This vibration emanating from the hypothalamus directs the actions of the pituitary gland which governs the endocrine systems. It is also in charge of releasing chemicals and hormones throughout the body into the brain. This vibration releases chemical hormones that balance the body and have healing effects.

The vibrations from mantras have the power to rearrange your molecular structure. Each sound has a distinct vibration, and as a result, each mantra has a different effect. All sound affects your molecular structure. Furthermore all sounds with words attached such as a mantra impact your consciousness. Think about how certain music puts you in a particular mood. Or consider how you feel when there is a lot of noise or when someone is yelling. Mantras are designed to adjust your experience through the subtle vibrations they cause in your being. Each mantra is designed to have a distinct affect.

Everything you seek is within. When you feel that you are not experiencing something, it is because you are not tuned into its vibration. When you are vibrating something, you are tuned into it. For example, if you are vibrating love, you'll see it everywhere, if you are not, this vibration lacks. This is also how you are attracted to people and how you can experience that alignment with your karmic vibration.

Chanting a mantra tunes you into the experience of the particular mantra. This alignment allows you to experience this vibration by becoming this vibration. The more sensitive to the sound you are, the deeper you'll experience the effects, and also, the longer the time spent and the more focused you are on the mantra, the more impact it will have on your consciousness.

It is not only the mantra that has a strong impact on your being, but more so every vibration that is crucial. When you think negatively, you create a subtle vibration. The longer this vibration persists, the more it affects your being; the vibration of the thought then creates an emotional vibration, which generates a vibration in the physical body. This is where all the sensations come from in the body.

The same way the chanting of a mantra impacts on your being or consciousness, so do your thoughts, words, and actions. This is how habits in your life become patterns. You create vibrations and then, consciously, and unconsciously, you react to them. Repeating mantras can have help liberate you from these ingrained personality patterns. If you want to change your karma change your vibration.

As I previously said my morning without fail mantra is the Moola Mantra. But when I find time during the day, I will also chant either the Humee Hum Brahm Hum Mantra or the Ek Ong Kar mantra. I share some detail on the Moola Mantra below.

THE MOOLA MANTRA

The Moola or Sat Chit Ananda mantra is probably one of the most extensive, profoundly beautiful, and powerful descriptions of this energetic cosmic force that I describe as Infinite Intelligence or God throughout the book. Whenever you listen to the mantra or better still listen and chant the Moola Mantra, even without knowing the meaning of it, that in itself carries power. But when you know the meaning and chant with that feeling in your heart then the energy will flow much more powerfully.

The mantra is like calling a name, just like when you call a person, they come and make you feel their presence. So in the same manner when you listen to or chant this mantra, the Supreme energy manifests everywhere around you. It is also very important to know that the invocation with all humility, respect and with great necessity makes the Divine Presence stronger. The actual mantra is Om Sat-Chit-Ananda Parabrahma, Purushothama Paramatma, Sri Bhagavathi Sametha, Sri Bhagavathe Namaha. Hari Om Tat Sat.

The breakdown of the key words of the mantra and their meaning is as follows.

OM

OM has 100 different meanings. It is said, in the beginning was the Supreme word and the Word created everything. That word is OM. If you are meditating in silence deeply, you can hear the sound OM within. The whole of creation emerged from the sound OM. It is the primordial sound or the Universal sound by which the whole universe vibrates. OM also means inviting the higher energy. This divine sound has the power to create, sustain and destroy, giving life and movement to all that exist.

SAT

SAT means all penetrating existence that is formless, shapeless, omnipresent, attribute less, and quality less aspect of the Universe. It is the Unmanifest. It is experienced as emptiness of the Universe. We could say it is the body of the Universe that is static. Everything that has a form and that can be sensed, evolved out of this Unmanifest. It is so subtle that it is beyond all perceptions. It can only be seen when it has become gross and has taken form. We are in the Universe and the Universe is in us. We are the effect and Universe is the cause and the cause manifests itself as the effect.

CHIT

CHIT is the Pure Consciousness of the Universe that is infinite, omni-present manifesting power of the Universe. Out of this is evolved everything that we call Dynamic energy or force. It can manifest in any form or shape. It is the consciousness manifesting as motion, as gravitation, as magnetism etc. It is also manifesting as the actions of the body, as thought force. It is the Supreme Spirit.

ANANDA

ANANDA means bliss, love, and friendship nature of the Universe. When you experience either the Supreme Energy in this Creation (SAT) and become one with the Existence or experience the aspect of Pure Consciousness (CHIT), you enter into a state of Divine Bliss and eternal happiness (ANANDA). This is the primordial characteristic of the Universe, which is the greatest and most profound state of ecstasy that you can ever experience when you relate with your higher Consciousness.

PARABRAHMA

PARABRAHMA is the Supreme Being in his Absolute aspect; one who is beyond space and time. It is the essence of the Universe that is with form and without form. It is the Supreme creator.

PURUSHOTHAMA

PURUSHOTHAMA has different meanings. Purusha means soul and Uttamam means the Supreme spirit. It also means the supreme energy of force guiding us from the highest world.

Purusha also means Man, and PURUSHOTHAMA is the energy that incarnates as an Avatar to help and guide mankind and relate closely to the beloved Creation.

PARAMATMA

PARAMATMA means the supreme inner energy that is immanent in every creature and in all beings, living and non-living. It's the in dweller or the Antaryamin who resides formless or in any form desired. It's the force that can come to you whenever you want and wherever you want to guide and help you.

SRI BHAGAVATHI

SRI BHAGAVATHI is the Feminine aspect, which is characterized as the Supreme Intelligence in action, the Power (The Shakti). It is referred to the Mother Earth (Divine Mother) aspect of the creation.

SAMETHA

SAMETHA means together or in communion with.

SRI BHAGAVATHE

SRI BHAGAVTHE is the Masculine aspect of the Creation, which is unchangeable and permanent.

NAMAHA

NAMAHA is salutations or prostrations to the Universe that is OM and also has the qualities of SAT-CHIT-ANANDA, that is omnipresent, unchangeable, and changeable at the same time, the supreme spirit in a human form and formless, the in dweller that can guide and help in the feminine and masculine forms with the supreme intelligence.

Suggestion:

In learning a mantra the easiest way is to listen to it regularly in the first place to gain understanding of the pronunciation of each phrase, and then slowly begin voicing the words until eventually you will find it becomes automatic. Then in your mantra time just listen and chant at the same time. You can do it in a sitting position or lying down. Namaste.

Here is the You Tube link for the Moola Mantra just type into your browser of alternately go to You Tube and search Moola Mantra Jumakha.

https://youtu.be/T4CLazqxslc

Also, by
MICHAEL R MUNDY
Available at Amazon

Everything's Gonna Be Alright…The Holy Spirit Knows What She's Doin'
(Straight talk about God, Jesus, the Holy Spirit, Religion, Heaven and Hell)

Lila - The Shepherd and The Wolf
(A story of love, lust, lies, and loss of spiritual innocence)

The Love Connection
(An interfaith, psycho-spiritual journey into the workings of the Soul)

www.ingramcontent.com/pod-product-compliance
Lightning Source LLC
Chambersburg PA
CBHW071850290426
44110CB00013B/1091